ONE PA

"A TRUE STORY OF ABU ... ... V I O R Y"

MW00896095

By Debra Bell-Vanzant

Library of Congress

Copyright Office

Washington, D.C. 20559-6000

CreateSpace A DBA of on-Demand Publishing, LLC

7290 B Investment Dr.

Charleston, SC 29418

Disclaimer:

Some names have been change to protect the innocent and the author.

Acknowledgements

To our Heavenly Father:

My Lord Jesus, Glory be to God, and only You! The Holy Spirit took me back to all those difficult, dark, suppressed, hurt and painful places in my past life. I say to you openly with a sincere and forever humble heart, I thank you for your favor, protection, mercy and your grace.

If it had not been for you, I don't know where I would be. I could be sleeping in my grave, but you saw fit to save such an unworthy person as myself.

Lord, my prayer is that every person who reads my story will see Your love towards me, so they, too, will know they can be saved.

I acknowledge You as Lord Jesus, Son of the Living God, the Father with the Holy Spirit as One...My Lord, I thank you. I am Your servant seeking and trying to do Your will.

To my loving husband:

Sweetheart, I thank you for all your prayers, patience, understanding, compassion, caring support and unconditional LOVE. It was a rough road, but with God's grace and mercy, we made it through. We know now that with our LOVE stands strong. We also know that if we continue to seek after Him, He will continue to bless our marriage, our home and our family.

I believe in you and I believe in us. You were the blessing I needed and you made my dreams come true. This life we now share is a testament to God's favor for us. I love you, Poppie.

To my Pastor, Rev. Dr. Clinton L. Johnson, Sr.:

Pastor, all I can say is I thank God for you! We appreciate you! Ronald and I love you for all that you do. You are truly an anointed man of God.

You have inspired us through God's messages to continue to look forward by leaving the past—where it belongs—and to be the household that always blesses the Lord. Thank you, thank you, and thank you. God bless you!

To the Women's Resource Center in Racine, Wisconsin:

Oh, my Lord, how can I thank you all enough for what you've done for me in my time of desperate need! Coming to this shelter in 1991 kept me and my children alive and safe. Being there helped me to grow, to come to a reality about my own denial and to understanding what the word love does not means. I learned to honestly ask myself how much did I love my children and myself, as well as, how badly did I want to live.

I finally understood the true meaning of abuse. It took a number of times with me coming in and out of this shelter, like a revolving door, to get it. I realized that I was worth more than someone's punching bag, that I had self-worth and that I was somebody. I learned that I did have something called self-esteem, and how to pull it up from under beneath my feet.

You gave me the tools to take control of my life. I learn how not to give the power of my life to anyone but my Lord. You taught me that it really wasn't my fault for all the abuse that I had encountered over the eighteen years. I finally got it.

I learned that I was in a cycle, a family curse, and you taught me how to break it! I learned that this was not the life that I wanted to live. Thank you for igniting the courage within me to stand up and finally say 'NO'!

I will forever be grateful to you for being there for me and my children. You are and have been a blessing for so many and I needed to take the time to say God bless you all—God bless the Women's Resource Centers all over this world! Thank you, thank you!

To the one who came for me:

I must give a special acknowledgment to one particular person. She went above and beyond what was expected in her job, without even a thought, to save me and my children. She came to my home and rescued us when I needed help to get away. After the countless of times that I went in and out of the shelter, she knew that this was it; that I was tired of being sick and tired. Twenty-one years ago, she helped save my life.

Thank you, Colleen. You will forever have a place in my heart. I love you more.

To all my children:

I Love you all. Thank you for believing in your mother, despite all my shortcomings. I thank you for standing by me in so many difficult situations throughout your life with me. I am so very proud of each and every one of you.

Follow the instruction book, The Holy Word. Set your goals and follow through. Never go against the grain, and follow your gut. Remember, you can't fly like an Eagle if you're hanging with Pigeons. And, please stay out of harm's way.

Stay close with the Lord and put Him first in all that you do. Hold onto your Faith and Trust in Jesus, and everything will be alright. Stay with the Lord. I love you more!

To Sister Lue Ella Carter:

There are no words to adequately describe the love that I have for you. I truly thank the Lord for your courageous spirit! You put on your Suit of Armor and with no fear, you went BOLDLY into the lion's den and the burning flames to introduce me and my children to our Lord and Savior Jesus Christ. You are one of the true soldiers of the Lord. I will always love you, and never forget how you came for me. I love you, 'Ma'.

To the editor, Betti Clausell Chaney:

I would like to personally acknowledge someone who believed in me and saw the vision, the dream, the enthusiasm, the passion, and even the fear, in my wanting the world to know how the Lord brought me out of so many hopeless situations. I wanted the world to know that all the Glory must be given to our Lord and Savior, Jesus the Christ, and only unto Him.

How you embraced my spirit, worked diligently, and talked with me for countless hours! You stepped into the world that I lived, and I felt that you shared in the hurt, pain, sorrow and the laughter. How we rejoiced in the victory!

I had already gone through one publisher and four other editors. I was so desponded when you came along. That's when I knew that the Lord had placed you into my life.

You never tried to change my mind or to direct me in a different way of telling my story. I thank you for helping me to tell the "raw truth" of my Life.

Thank you for your patience and humble spirit. You are the EDITOR of the Year! May the Lord continue to bless you. Thank you, Sis Chaney. I love you more.

A Special Thank You...

This is a genuine, heartfelt 'thank you' I want to offer to some amazing individuals for their love, support and encouragement. These are the people behind the scene who cannot be forgotten.

From Las Vegas, Nevada; from Camden to Fordyce to Lea Ridge, Arkansas; to Atlanta, Riverdale and Jonesboro, Georgia; back to Chicago, Illinois; from Racine to Milwaukee, Wisconsin and all the way down south to Mobile, Alabama.

Thank you all for bringing out the strength in me that I didn't even know that I had. Just to name a few:

To my church family and friends who have helped me along the way, I thank you for the good and indifferent. Many of you helped to get me from one place or another, but even more you helped me to understand that I have to have faith and trust in the Lord in all that I do, and to lend and depend on Him.

To Aunt Dorothy:

You are the true meaning of a loving aunt. I never in my life had an aunt to love and care about me the way that you do with an unconditional, Godly type of Love. No matter what time day or night, I can count on you for that listening ear, and at times that crying shoulder to lean on. Thank you for being honesty with me and never sugarcoating anything.

Thank you for helping me to come to a better understanding of myself, as well as other people. I know now once I understand something or someone, I can deal with the situation and move on in my life. I no longer dwell on that I need to give to the Lord or have to scratch my head and shuffle my feet. Thank you for your Wisdom, Knowledge and Understanding and, most of all, your Prayers! I love you, Aunt Dorothy.

To Sister Barbara Johnson:

I truly feel that it was destiny for us to cross paths. Before you knew anything about my struggles, you became my friend. Although we come from two totally different backgrounds, you never looked down on me in any form or fashion.

Thank you for believing in me, pushing me to the limit and for all the things that you do behind the scene. Thank you for still being the same friend you were yesterday as you are today. What a wonderful gift it is to have a friend like you! Who would have ever thought that my special friend would be the First Lady of my church home? I thank God for a friend like you.

God Bless you, my dear friend...

To Sister Minnie Wiley:

People have said that you never know who the Lord will place in your life and be a blessing to you. I thank you for holding onto me and not letting me go when my son was killed. Thank you for every Sunday school lessons and phone calls when I was overwhelmed with grief, angry, and sorrow. You took your time and helped me to understand that I must reach out to the Lord and not blame or run away from Him.

Thank you, Holy Spirit, for that on-time blessing! You blessed me with an obedient and humble spirit by the name of Sister Minnie Wiley.

I love you, Sis. Wiley.

To Monica:

Thank you for being there for me and my children when we needed you the most. You cared enough to say enough is enough! I know now what it would feel like to have a sister because I have you. We will always be sisters in our hearts. I love you more!

To Veronica:

I never thought that I would ever meet someone that I could call my best friend again. When I met you, I came to realize that you have that loving, giving, witty, honesty, trustworthy and calm spirit that I needed in a friend.

You will forever be a close, spiritual friend to me. I can count true friends on one hand; you are definitely in that number. God bless you, my friend.

To all my loving grandchildren:

When God decided to give me grandchildren, he looked at all the other grandchildren in Heaven and He picked the best ones just for me. He blessed me with all of you! Nana loves you all with all my heart. Trust and believe in God, and be obedient to your parents and surely to God.

Stay in school and do well. Put God first in all that you do, and you, too, will be blessed. Nana will always love you more!

Reviews

"Riveting, fascinating...this book held me captive! This is a must-read, especially for the young and vulnerable. Bell-Vanzant brings her graphic story to amazing life in this revealing and tantalizing book. It is written in the genre of Donald Goines, but with a message of redemption and breakthrough, triumph over tragedy with God's grace and mercy present all the time. For me, this is what will make "One Pair of Panties" an instant Urban Classic. Five Stars!"

Mark S. Marsh, Founder

Blackfunnel.net Internet TV

Chicago, IL

"For every woman who has been abused and betrayed by someone who was supposed to love and care for her, this book will be a beacon of hope. It is a testament to the human spirit. Debra didn't just survive a level of brutality most of us can't even imagine; she reassembled the broken pieces of her life and learned to thrive. A belief in the future is often the hardest thing for survivors to reclaim. New dreams are hard to imagine when you have been living in hell. Yet Debra emerged on the other side with grace and dignity, and you can, too. It's not easy, and often not always pretty. But Debra's story shows that it is possible. I was blessed to be able to walk with her for a part of her journey but Debra, like all survivors, saved her own life."

Colleen Carpenter, Executive Director

Daystar (Shelter for Women)

Milwaukee, Wisconsin

"This book is an inspiration and a MUST READ to all who are experiencing or who have survived violence in the home!! Debra demonstrates the courage it takes women to leave these situations against almost impossible odds! She has become an educator and advocates in the Mobile community to let victims know they can leave the violence and live peacefully! Our Motto "Peace on Earth begins at Home" is exampled by Debra's story!

Melanie Day Bankhead, ACSW, LCSW, PIP

Shelter Supervisor, Penelope House Family Violence Center

Mobile, AL

"This story about Debra's life is truly 'in the raw.' When you love someone who is afraid to leave her abuser, you have to pray and ask God with faith to help her to help herself, especially since no one else cared or was allowed to. Women, girls...Listen up! YOU DON'T HAVE TO LIVE LIKE THIS. God sees everything and if you ask him for help, you must be ready to die if it means to help yourself. If you don't do it for yourself, always remember to do it for your children. You can't help how you were raised, but you must help how your children are raised and what you expose them to inside your house. Debra asked God to come and stay in her life. God made a way for her and the children to strive.

Keep God in your life. Remember, YOU DON'T HAVE TO LIVE THIS WAY. There are people who love you enough to help you if you only reach out and yell loudly for it. The police would have loved him. Most men who beat up women are scared to death of another man. Keep going on your journey of faith, love and respect for yourself always. I'm glad you are sharing your nightmare with others, Debra. This may help them run like hell to get out and take control of the life God intended for them to have. I love you always.

Your sister,

Linda hall, RN

Chicago, IL

"This book is based on a true story of the saddened and complicated life of a "Little Girl". Like most, some problems start at home, especially without a stable, ideal background such as a father, mother, children in an educated, influential home. Like most Black American homes, there was music, night life and children in the background entertaining themselves.

They saw the grown people who live there just come and go; "Hi and Bye" and very little time "With." There was no real Father figure although there were men present such as uncles and auntie's and mommy's boyfriends who did not really take an interest in the children. There was no real family orientation although everyone was family. However, there was a Grandmother who was the Matriarch.

This "Little Girl" needed so much more of the right things in life and therefore, got Lost in the Shuffle. But, unlike a lot of others, she persevered and survived the rough streets that we live in. Some people don't live to talk about it. This book should be read by all who have growing boys and girls in their families. I call it "A True Lesson Learned" and what better way to learn other than First Hand. God Blessed the "Little Girl."

Your sister,

Brenda Phillips, Administrative Secretary

Chicago, IL.

Love. Confusion. Pain. Bitterness. Survival. Victory. Love. These stages of life are typically for many of us. Debra's life was slammed on every turn with experiences many of us could never, never imagine—all because of poor choices and consequences. God knew she'd take the low road in certain situations, but He was there and never left her. She was a mere vessel so she can testify the Lord granted her favor all along the way. This book will change the lives of women everywhere who are caught up in abusive, loveless and desperate situations. I applaud and admire Debra Bell-Vanzant for the courage and determination to tell this raw truth. You will never forget this story of victory achieved through a faith as small as mustard seed!

Betti Clausell Chaney, Editor

Mobile, AL

In memory of...

To all my love ones that has already entered those Pearly Gates and walked on those Golden Streets and taken their seat with our Lord, I thank God for you being place in my life, for whatever the reason or season. I've lost so many of you who are still so dear to my heart. I thank God for the time that we did share.

Losing a father, mother, grandparents and mother-in-law was so hard, but the loss of a child is the most heart-wrenching experience. It leaves such emptiness in your heart and soul. But, oh, how good is God!

I feel so blessed that God handpicked all of you just for me, and if it wasn't for you I wouldn't be the person that I am today. I pray that I will see you all standing at the Pearly Gates on those Golden Streets in the present of the sweet Angels playing my song as our Lord and Savior stretches his arms out saying to me "Come on in...Well Done... My Child...Come on in..." To God be the glory!

Dedication

I don't know any other way to share my life with you other than to take you in the world that I was in, and give you the full graphic details of it all. For this reason, I dedicate this book to all of you who are in any one of the situations that has been described in this book. Whatever the problem may be, you CAN overcome!

Nothing will change in your life if you keep doing the same old thing and getting the same results! Only when you get sick and tired of being sick and tired, and change your people, places and things, will you get different results! Look to the Lord and He will help you!

No weapon that is formed against thee shall prosper.
Isaiah 54:17
I can do all things through Christ which strengtheneth me.
Philippians 4:13
Grace be with you, mercy, and peace, from God the Father, and
from the Lord Jesus Christ, the Son of the Father, in truth and love.
II John 1:3

Introduction

This is the story of how a family exposed a child to abuse, adultery, lies and deception behind the closed doors of their seemingly perfect middle-class existence. It explains why this little girl became rebellious and felt forced to live on the streets of Chicago at the age of fourteen—lost, lonely and looking for love in all the wrong places.

It also covers her introduction to a life of drugs, more abuse, dishonor, shame, loss of self-respect and total abandonment by her family at such a young age. It was a life that she never should have been exposed to.

It's a story that's intended as an eye-opener for young girls alerting them that there are wolves in sheep's clothing out there just waiting for them to run away from their parents and into the streets.

No longer a child, the woman described here has lived a life of trials and tribulations, but overcame her struggles and is now a survivor of an obvious hopeless situation for over eighteen years.

These words will hopefully serve as an inspiration for women currently trying to escape the cycle of abuse. By the grace and mercy of God, you will be able to make it through; not necessarily by duplicating the efforts of this woman, but by the path that the Heavenly Father has laid out for you.

I am Debra Bell-Vanzant and this is my story...

Section 1

This was not the life I was looking for…

When I left for the final time, all I had was one pair of panties. I remember it like it was yesterday. I was thirty-three years old, I was afraid and the mother of five children to care for. I didn't know how I was going to get away, but I knew I had to.

I had been thinking about that day for a long time and prayed to God to show me a way out. I had no idea that it was going to end with me feeling as though I was half-dead, but that is exactly what happened. The morning after, I finally decide to make my move. That was it!

We were living in Racine, Wisconsin in a one bedroom apartment on the corner of 6th Street, right off the alley. It was the nastiest dump I'd ever lived in or seen. This was the area where nothing mattered. Garbage and big tom rats filled the streets and people hung out like it was a sunny summer evening.

From corner to corner, the streets were filled with people that only lived to get high on crack cocaine and the drug dealers who sold drugs to the ones that were on fixed incomes.

Racine is a small town located 30 minutes outside of Milwaukee. We moved to Racine because my husband James relocated our family from Arkansas.

Living in Racine was pure hell for me. I spent most of my young adult life there and it was a life-changing experience for me and my children. It was in Racine that I learned the true, cruel meaning of the word abuse. The most important thing about living in Racine was that I discovered who my Savior really was.

1

If it wasn't for the hell I was in—being married to Lucifer himself—I might still be caught up in that destructive, dysfunctional lifestyle in a place called Racine, Wisconsin. Yet, it was home.

It was the beginning of fall, the night before I left. My children had just finished with their homework and were getting ready for bed.

That night, James had beaten me so badly that my eyes were swollen shut, my lips were busted and my mouth was filled with blood. I had deep gashes above both eyes that required stitches. I didn't dare go to the hospital. He would not have let me go, anyway. Besides, I had no way of getting there.

I kept screaming for him to stop, "No, James! Please, don't do this to me!" I continue to yell, but he hit me repeatedly in my face with his fist—all the while screaming at me, "Shut the fuck up before I kill you!"

Determined to keep me from leaving the house, he started ripping my clothes off. That's when he grabbed my back pocket, saying, "You got some money, bitch?! You been out fucking around?!" He tore the pocket off and the money I had wrapped in a napkin fell to the floor.

"So you're hiding money from me, bitch?!" he shouted. He discovered the fifty dollars inside the napkin.

This was money to feed the kids. At that point, I wondered if he would have backed off, if I had just given it to him before he started beating me. It was too late now.

I didn't think it could get any worse. He brutally raped me that night. I remember him standing over me shouting, "Oh, you wanna fuck? I knew you were a whore!" Then he punched me in my mouth and the blood went everywhere! He yelled, "You'll never be anything in life without me! Don't you know you belong to me, bitch?!"

Section 2

This is it! I'm going to die!

That's when he grabbed me by my throat and forced me down on my stomach. James had a huge stick that had thorns on it.

I begged, "Please! No, James! Please don't hurt me no more!" I thought he was planning to beat me with the stick; I never imagined it could get any worse until he rammed that stick up my ass, tearing the soft tissue as he forced it inside me! I thought this was going to be the death of me! I screamed like I had never screamed before, "Oh, my God! Jesus, please help me!"

"Is this what you want?" he yelled. "I'll teach you to give my pussy away to some other motherfucker!"

I can't begin to describe the pain! All I could feel was him repeatedly ramming that stick inside me, in and out, in and out! He jammed it inside me even harder as his hands got tighter around my throat!

He rolled me over and pinned me to the floor with his hand around my throat even tighter. Taking advantage of the opportunity while I gasped for air, he unzipped his pants and forced his penis in my mouth!

He growled, "I dare you to bite me, bitch. I'll kill you and you'll die with my dick in your mouth!" The look in his eyes was different; I'd never send him this angry before! He was in a fiery rage! The drugs had him out of his mind!

There was an evil grin on his face as he ripped the stick from my ass and forced it into my vagina! I'd never experienced anything so painful and degrading in all my life. I felt like I was literally being ripped apart on the inside, while James humped into my face so violently that I gagged as he crammed his penis into my throat!

3

He finally pulled it out, cum spewed all over my face and hair. In that instant, I vomited all over him as blood and shit gushed from between my legs! If the brutal attack was not bad enough, he stood up and began kicking me repeatedly in my face, my stomach—wherever his foot landed, all because I threw up on him.

I was sure that I was going to die that night. I could only pray that God would have mercy on me and spare my life so I could take care of my children. I could hear them crying and screaming, "I want my Mommie! Daddy, stop! Leave Mommie alone! Mommie, Mommie!"

Throughout this pitiful, senseless and cruel beating, James yelled back at the kids," If the next motherfucker screams, I'm gonna come in there and beat the hell out of y'all."

I asked the Lord that if he would see me through this nightmare, I would do everything in my power to get my children away from James before he killed me.

Section 3

My Secret Lover

In my mind, I thought maybe I deserved it. I thought I deserved it because I lied about being with his sister that night when I was actually with my secret lover. Little did I know that his wife had come to my home and told James that I was with her husband! She told him she would appreciate it if he kept his wife away from her husband.

No matter how bad my marriage was, I knew it was wrong to cheat on my husband, but the chemistry with my lover was nothing short of beautiful. We both were married which made it even more wrong. Neither one of us wanted it to end.

He really cared about me and my children and did everything he could to make me feel love. He would even give me money to buy food for the kids when there was nothing in the house to eat—something that James never did.

I was on welfare at the time and received my check once a month, but James would take it to buy drugs, methadone, heroin, cocaine, syrup, Tee's & Blues, valiums, weed and alcohol. It was up to me to feed the kids, so they looked to me, not their father, for food.

The beatings were hard on me, but our children suffered emotionally and mentally. They would usually huddle together in their bedroom whenever James jumped on me. I would hear them crying, but there was nothing they could do to save their mother or make their father stop.

They were scared and I was scared for them. James was a madman when he flew into a rage, so there was no telling what he would have done.

Section 4

What about my Children? Enough is enough!

James had never beaten me like this before; he actually beat me until the sun came up. I truly believe he had some type of adrenaline rush to kick my ass that night. I think he must have thought to himself, "How can I fuck her up? What else can I do to beat the shit out of her, to make her feel less than the person that she is?"

I bet he thought that if he beat me until I wished I was dead, then he would be certain that he had conquered me, and I would never leave him or give my body to another.

I'd never been so happy to see daylight in my life. He got so tired of kicking my ass that night he passed out.

All I wanted at that point was for my kids to go to school, to get out of that house so they would be safe. I got the kids up and ready for school. I whispered for them not to worry about Mommie and that I was gonna be alright. It was so hard to look into their sweet little faces while they stared back at my bruises. I could tell they had been crying so hard because their eyes were swollen.

It was clear that my eight-year-old twins, Tyrone and Jerome, were in shock. Jerome said, "You sound like Mommie, but you don't look like Mommie anymore," as he reached out to touch my disfigured face.

My daughters Tyra, Ericka and Patrice just stood there looking at me with fear in their eyes and tears streaming down their faces. Meanwhile, their father lay on the bed drugged out, drunk and exhausted.

Finally, Tyra said in a whispered voice, "Mommie, come to school with us. Don't stay here. Daddy is gonna kill you!" She then looked over at him stretched out on the dirty, blood stained, smelly mattress.

Then Tyrone mumbled, "I'm gonna kill him when I get big!"

Jerome added, "Yeah, I hate him. One day he will get his!"

"Stop talking like that. Your father is sick and he needs help," I said. "He really didn't mean to hurt Mommie. He loves us."

Patrice cried out, "Look at your face, Mommie!"

"I know, baby," trying to comfort them. "I'll be okay, come on now. Hurry up and get ready for school so you can eat the school breakfast. I know you all are hungry. You know that there is nothing here to eat and you do not want to be here when your father wakes up! Now hurry up and get ready. Your daddy is going to be okay. He won't fight Mommie no more. I'll be alright, don't you all worry."

I couldn't tell if I was trying to convince the kids or myself. "Be quiet, shhh! We don't want to wake up your father. Now hurry up."

"I'm not hungry, Mommie, I want to stay home with you," cried Ericka.

Section 5

Pray!

"Tyra, come help Mommie get your brothers and sisters together so y'all can get on the school bus. Hurry up now."

I didn't want to wake him up. I could barely see my children's faces that morning. My eyes were swollen shut and I was in so much pain. I hadn't even looked in the mirror to see how badly James had beaten me. I was actually afraid of what I would see. I knew it was really bad this time because of the look in my children's eyes said it all.

I gave the kids hugs and kisses when they were ready to leave for school. I always hugged and kissed them before school, but this time it was different. I really wasn't sure if this would be the last time that I'd see them since I had no idea what kind of mood James would be in when he woke up.

I wanted to believe in my heart that God was going to take care of me, but you never know what can happen when you're dealing with a drugged-out lunatic.

Tears streamed from my eyes and my heart felted so heavy as I watched my children head out the door and get on the school bus. I was relieved that they were going to be safe even if it was just for a few hours.

I wanted to leave right behind them, but I had nowhere to go, nowhere to hide. Even if I did have the nerve to leave, I knew James would find me. I was frightened. I prayed that God would help me to be free of James as I stared out the window and watched the school bus pull away. Then it dawned on me that I could have died last night, which could have been my last ass kicking.

I asked myself how much more was it gonna take for me to wake up and realize that he really doesn't love me. James does not love me as much as

I love him. He said that he loved me. He said that he would never hurt me. Oh, how I wanted to believe him.

I have been with him since I was fourteen years old and we now have five children together. Where can I go? Who can I turn to? I was alone in the house with him and if the least little thing set him off, he could do whatever he wanted to me and no one would know or even care. He could dump me in the alley with the rats. Remember, I live where anything goes.

I crept toward the bathroom, hoping the floor wouldn't squeak as I walked past the bed where James was sleeping. Even though he would have a hangover and half remember anything, I still couldn't run the risk of waking him up.

Once I made it to the bathroom, I looked in the mirror at the horrified twisted mask that was once my face! "Oh, my God! Oh, my God!" I cried.

My eyes were swollen shut and the open gashes were so wide that you could see the white meat! I could only peek through the open cracks of my eyes! There was so much dried blood and black and blue bruises that it looked like I had been beaten with a baseball bat! My face was so battered that it was hard to make out where my eyes, nose and my mouth were.

'Lord, help me!' were the only words that could come out of my mouth. 'Please help me, I am tired now.'

I turned on a slow trickle of water, praying that it wouldn't wake James. Then I grabbed one of the boy's dirty tee shirts from the floor and soaked it to clean my face. There was no hot water in the house, so I did the best that I could. I couldn't pay the heating bill because James had used all the money to buy drugs.

Section 6

This is some bullshit!

There was no soap in the bathroom for me to use. James kept the soap, so I had to ask him for it—he didn't trust me. He would make me wash-up in front of him so he could inspect me to make sure I wasn't screwing around. Sometimes he would make me lie down on the floor and he would put his finger inside of me. If it was tight, then I was allowed to finish cleaning myself, but if it wasn't tight as he thought it should be... Well, do I need to say more?

I never understood that. How in the hell did I have control over how tight my vagina was! This motherfucker was really crazy!

Those drugs have gotten him fucked up! I hid the bloody tee shirt behind the sink because I didn't want James to see it.

I carefully made my way back to the living room hoping not to wake him and sat on the three-legged couch. I had to put books under the corner of the couch where the leg was missing. During the previous week's fight, he slammed me into the couch causing the leg to break from the weight of my fall. I was finally able to breathe a sigh of relief as I sat there waiting for an answer from God, an answer that would provide a new life away from James.

I knew that if I really believed in God, he would help me—at least that is what I wanted to believe. I looked at it like this: Hell, I tried everything else! Let me try Jesus. 'God, let me trust in you, believing that you will bring me through and make a way for me and my children.'

Section 7

Behind those pretty curtains

As I sat there, I looked around and thought about our apartment. It smelled bad and it looked even worse. There were empty 40-ounce beer bottles, cocaine and weed residue, and even the bottle top that James used to

9

cook heroin left sitting on the table. I didn't dare clean up after James because he would get pissed if he came in looking for something only to find out that I had thrown it away. I would just wait until he decided to tell me to clean up.

I even thought about the pastel blue curtains hanging in the windows that I bought at Goodwill. My Nana always told me to hang nice curtains. That way, if you didn't have anything in your house, at least people wouldn't be able to tell you were poor from the outside. You never know what goes on behind those pretty curtains hanging in someone's window.

We didn't have much, really nothing at all—just the three-legged couch, one chair and a lamp without a shade that James kept in the living room. I felt bad for the kids whenever they had homework because they would have to finish it before the sun went down or they wouldn't have any light.

There was a 14-inch black and white television in the living room that the kids were only able to watch when James wasn't looking at it. There were two mattresses on the floor, one for the kids in the bedroom and one for James and me in the dining room.

The refrigerator was so old that it had the type of handle you had to pull down to open the door. And when you did pull the door open, it made such a loud noise that it was almost funny. I guess the noise was because the refrigerator was usually empty; there was hardly ever any food in it. I rarely got a chance to buy food because James would take most of the food stamps, leaving very little to last for the rest of the month.

It wasn't always like this. We had some good times. I could tell when James was in a good mood… He would often cook a full course meal while telling stories that we all enjoyed. He knew how to make homemade pizza and it was so good. James used to say that he was going to write a cookbook called 'A Po Man's Cookbook' because he could make a full meal for $10 dollars.

Section 8

What happened to my James?

Those were the good times. James had cute little nick name for all of us. We were only happy when he was satisfied. We would watch James' favorite black and white old movies with James Cagney, Humphrey Bogart and Clint Eastwood. He even liked John Wayne. Those were the good times.

I often slept ready rolled; you know, in the same clothes from the day before. I smelled really bad and hadn't washed since the day before this last beating. It felt like I still had James' cum inside me. I was so disgusted, shame and hurt by how bad he had beaten me that I didn't care if I used soap at all. Part of me wanted to just die and the other part willed me to live for my children.

James had started back using drugs so heavily that he didn't trust me at all. He became a paranoid, bipolar dope-fiend. I caught the flux. I wasn't able to wash my panties because James would check them to make sure there weren't any new stains that he hadn't seen. If I didn't pass inspection, he would beat me all over again, claiming that I had been with someone—you know, 'fucking around', as he called.

Section 9

One Pair of Panties

I had been wearing the same panties for over a week. My panties had brown and yellow crusted stains and smelled bad. They were just plain nasty. Hell, I couldn't stand the smell myself! Whenever I would go to the bathroom and sit down, the smell would come up and hit me in the face. Damn!

Whenever I left the house, I'd take my panties off and put them in my purse. Then I would put them back on just before I got home. Sometimes, I'd put tissue inside me in case I had a discharge. I laugh now thinking how I used to push tissue so far inside me that there could still be tissue lodged in there.

I had one pair of panties! One pair of panties! I hated James for that. I hated him for forcing me to live like that. I wondered how he could put me through this when he said he loved me and would never hurt me.

I continued to gaze out the window looking at nothing, but feeling everything. I was a fucked up physically, mentally and emotionally.

Section 10
Wake up! Stop dreaming!

I weighed only about 105 pounds and my brittle hair was constantly breaking off. I did my best to manage it by pressing it with a straightening comb, but that was torture. My head was always so tender from James pulling my hair out in clumps.

It was so hard to stop crying. I tried to be quiet because I didn't want to wake up James. I couldn't stop wondering how things had spiraled so far out of control. It was hard for me to understand why James had turned on me after eighteen years. I'd been with him since I was fourteen years old, and thought he was the love of my life—the one that I was going to spend the rest of my life with.

I thought about us growing old together, sharing the joy of our grandchildren when that time came. It was only a dream and deep down I still loved him. I just couldn't understand how he could treat me like he did. I wanted him to die! I have these thoughts constantly. I wouldn't dare say them out loud because he would surely kill me.

I nearly wet my pants when I heard James yell, "Debra! Debra! Where the hell are you?"

His voice was like a lion roaring in a jungle after catching its prey. I braced myself as I wiped my tears because I knew it was only a matter of seconds before he would be standing in the room with me.

Regardless, I wanted him to see my fear, to see how badly he had beaten me. Maybe he would realize how much he loves me and would never hurt me again. Then it dawned on me, I was crazy as his ass! Was this LOVE?

Section 11

Just a trifling ass!

James was wearing a pair of dirty boxers when he walked into the room. He looked bad and smelled even worse.

"Didn't you hear me calling you?" he asked. "What were you doing?"

"Nothing." I continued to stare out the window. I didn't want him to see me crying, but I was sure he could hear it in my voice.

James came over to the couch and sat next to me. For the first time in a long time, I got a really good look at him. He was so skinny that I could see his ribs and his face was sunken in. His feet stank and there was crusty white shit caked around the corners of his mouth. His breath smelled worse than my panties.

Section 12

Love is long gone!

I flinched when James leaned over and raised his hand to my face. His expression softened as he said, "I'm not going to hit you Debra. I love you."

"Just leave me alone, James. I don't feel like being bothered."

"What's wrong, baby?" he asked as if nothing had happened. When I didn't respond, he jumped up, pushed the side of my head, and stormed off shouting, "Fuck you, bitch! I don't need you. You need me! Ain't no motherfucker gonna want your ass with five kids! You better stay out of my way today or I'm gonna beat your ass again!"

I thought to myself, *'It's my fault. Why did I do that? I should have just turned around and looked at him like he told me to, maybe he wouldn't have gotten mad.'*

I continued to stare out the window hoping he wouldn't come up behind me and start beating me again. I heard James in the distance grumbling about how good he was to me, that I didn't appreciate him, and if I only did what he told me to, he wouldn't have to hit me. I caused him to treat me like this.

Section 13

Don't believe the lies! It's a trick!

After a while, he came back to the living room. Looking directly in my face, he said, "Baby, oh, my God! Damn, Debra! See what you made me do! I'm sorry! I didn't mean to hit you like that! Debra, I love you! Please forgive me! No one understands me like you do."

I was a little stunned when he began to cry as he pulled me close and laid his head on my chest.

"Debra, I'm sorry," he sobbed. "It's the drugs. I got a problem, baby. I'm sick. I need help. I love you, Debra. You're the only person in the world that gives a damn about me. I'd die without you."

We were both crying. I wrapped my arms around him and said, "Don't cry, it'll be alright. I know it's the drugs. I know you didn't mean it. I love you, too, James."

I was shocked when he asked, "If I check myself into the hospital to get help, will you stay by my side?"

I couldn't believe it when I replied, "Yes, James, you know I will. Don't worry, I'll never leave you."

I thought about how my children were looking at me before they left for school, how worried they were about me and how much they feared their father. Then I thought about what my face looked like and how James had raped me. At that very moment, I realized that I wanted out. I was shocked by James' confession, but I still realized I needed to get away.

Section 14

I got a plan—whatever it takes.

I had to leave for my life and for the life of my children. I knew if I could get the support of the Women Resource Center, the shelter for the abused and battered women, I would be free.

I called my sister-in-law Monica. She had also been in an abusive relationship, so I knew she would understand what I was going through. I told her I feared for my life and asked her to help me get away from her brother. I had barely survived James' beatings and told her the next time I might not be so lucky.

"Girl, you know you can call the shelter. I'll call them on my line," and she began to dial their number for me. "You see, I couldn't do it anymore. I got out! I can't help you until you get tired and help yourself and want out for good."

Colleen answered the shelter's hotline. After I told her what happened she asked, "How long has he been gone? How long do you think he'll be gone? How soon before you think you can get away?"

We began to plan my escape so I'd never have to go through the turmoil of beatings again. I told Colleen that we got to hurry because he went to store to get some beer and he would be back soon.

"Go head, Debra, talk to them. You can do this, girl, I know you can! Call me when you get away. I love you."

Section 15

Are you sure you're ready?

I was scared to death as I peeked out the window thinking he was going to drive up and hear me talking on the phone.

Monica continued, "Say whatever you got to say to get him to that clinic!"

"Once he gets help, he might be alright?"

"Girl, stop! Enough is a nuff! Please think about those kids, those brothers with the same faces! It's not worth! It ain't no love worth what he did to you! JAMES DON'T LOVE YOU, DEBRA! DAMN!"

Colleen said, "I am calling the rehab clinic which is a few blocks from where you are. I will inform them that you are a victim and that your life is in danger. Debra, listen to me. You can do this! I know that you can! You are going to live, you are going to get away! Do you hear me?! Are you listening to me?!

Steady peeking out the window, I answered, "I'll tell you when he drives up."

After she contacted the clinic on the other line, Colleen came back to me with, "The rehab facility has agreed to detain him so you can have time to escape. The contact person is Jack."

Time was running out we had a plan, but I had to wait until James got home.

The plan was that Colleen would come to the house to get me and the kids, but we had to wait until the kids got home from school. We needed to get my husband to agree to check himself in and get him there ASAP. They could detain him long enough for me to escape. Colleen promised that all I had to do was to get him to go and they would take care of the rest.

I agreed because I was a woman on a mission—freedom! This was my break. My prayers were finally about to be answered.

"Here he comes! Here he comes!" I said frantically when I saw him drive up and park. I hung the phone up and quickly dialed a wrong number in case he checked the last call dialed. I made sure that the cord was not moving as I placed the phone down.

He stood outside for a few minutes talking which gave me more time to run to the kitchen to cook a can of pork 'n beans. I had to cook them on a hot plate because we didn't have a stove in the house anymore. He sold it and promised he was going to get another one.

I had cleared the table and had thrown all of James' empty beer bottles away. By the time the pork 'n beans were heated, I was moving fast, but still in a lot of pain.

When James walked in, I was sweeping the floor with our homemade broom. "There are some pork 'n beans on the hot plate."

James sat down and once he popped the top on his beer, he started the song and dance again about how sorry he was and that he didn't mean to hurt me.

'Too little, too late' I thought. The plan was already in place. I told James that he would have my support while he went through the process of cleaning himself up, that I loved him because he was the father of our children. I was hoping that he believed my words. *I had a plan.*

James was sitting there smoking weed laced with cocaine. "You promise you won't leave me?"

I looked him straight in the eyes and responded, "I love you, James. No, I won't leave you."

With this deep frown, "Look me in my eyes and tell me that you don't love that motherfucker you been fucking with!"

"No, James, I love only you. I will always love you." *I had a plan.*

"Well, call the motherfucking rehab center up the street and ask them if I can come in today. I mean, right now before I change my goddamn mind!"

When I called the clinic, I instantly recognized the name of the person who answered. It was Jack, one of the people who was in on the plan. Going along with the setup, I explained that my husband wanted to check himself in to get help for his drug problem and asked how soon he would be able to do so. I was told he needed to come right now because patients were admitted on a first-come-first-serve basis only.

"Yeah, alright. Just let me finish my beer and my primo because ain't no way I'm going to a rehab clinic sober. Hang the motherfucking phone up. Tell them I'm on my way." Once he was finished, he reluctantly said, "Come on, let's do this!"

Pouring on the innocence, I said, "Okay, James. I love you, James." *I had a plan.*

I guess he was still looking for sympathy when he said he wanted to get help only because he loved me and didn't want to hurt me anymore.

I'm standing there thinking, *'Yeah, right, and you almost killed me!'*

There was an eerie silence in the car on the way to the drug rehab center. James just sat there staring out the window, smoking another joint laced with cocaine.

He kept asking, "Debra, are you gonna stay by my side while I go through this?"

"Yes." I guess I seemed a little too calm because he asked, "You're up to something! What is it?"

18

I sweetly replied, "Nothing James, I just want you to get better so we can be happy again." *I had a plan.*

"What, you're not happy with me?"

"No, that's not what I'm saying," as I tried to remain calm. "James, you just scared us last night. Look at my face. You were high so you didn't realize how much you were hurting me. I know you love me, James. That's why I want you to get better. I love you and the kids love you."

"Oh, okay." He believed my words. *I had a plan.*

I was a little uptight because I wasn't sure if he would jump out of the car, or even worse, push me out of the car and run me over. James was in the habit of going off without warning, so I knew he was capable of anything at that point.

Section 16

I can do this.

I was a bundle of nerves when we arrived at the rehab center. I was sweating and I was scared. A complete nervous wreck! I prayed that everything would go smoothly so I could leave him and live my life with my children.

Watching it all play out was like watching a horror movie. The monster was close to the trap, but he could sense something wasn't right.

I saw that James was uncomfortable. He had a problem with white people because he didn't trust them. These white people were too nice and everything seemed too perfect. He was reluctant at first, so I tried to act as normal as possible.

I forced a smiled to reassure James that everything would be fine. The big sunglasses hid my swollen and bruised face, and I had to act as if nothing had happen. I needed to really pour on the love to put him at ease. If not, he would have backed up. James always followed his gut and I didn't want him to change his mind.

The staff was aware of my plan and had done their part to help with my escape. All I had to do was go through with it. I was known to back out when it came to any kind of separation from James. I needed to play the role of the loving wife to reassure him that there was nothing to worry about. James was told that he was required to undergo an evaluation as part of the admissions process. He would be taken to a separate room, and I could join him after the evaluation. It was actually a tactic used by the staff to separate the husband from the victim in cases where they were helping a woman escape an abusive situation like mine.

I told James that I needed to go pick up the kids anyway and that I would be back. That was my way out! *I had a plan.*

When he asked if I was sure I was coming back, I gave him an empty smile and said, "Yes baby, I'll be back." *I had a plan.*

As I walked toward the door, the door that would be my gateway to freedom, my feet felt like they weighed a ton each. If I could just get through the door without him running after me, I would be free.

I suddenly heard James call out, "Debra! Debra!"

I panicked when I turned around and saw him headed in my direction! I wanted to run, but he was closer to me than I was to the door! I kept walking and in no time, James had caught up to me!

I flinched when he grabbed me by the arm. Instead of a harsh demand, he calmly asked, "Are you sure you're coming back?"

I wanted to cry. He looked so pitiful. It was a struggle to hide the panic in my voice. I offered him a sweet smile, "Of course, I'm coming back James. I love you." *I had a plan.*

I pulled the door to me to exit. He stood in front of me before I could step out. I couldn't believe it when he demanded "Give me a kiss, but kiss me like you mean it so I'll know you are coming back!"

Before I could object, James pulled me into his arms and kissed me forcefully. I was disgusted by the kiss, but I couldn't let him know. Yet, I found myself holding onto him as I realized I still loved him. I couldn't believe that the man I loved so much had turned into such a beast. But little did he know, that was going to be the last kiss we would ever have. *I had a plan.*

Tears were rolling down my face by the time the kiss ended. When he asked what was wrong, I replied, "I love you so much and I want you to get better."

"Debra, I love you, too.

"I know you do, James."

"I'd better go. I need to get home before the kids get off the bus or they won't be able to get in the house. I love you. I'll be back. Now, go on in and wait for me."

Section 17

Run like hell and don't look back!

The door clicked behind me and I was free! I got in the car and raced to get the kids, so I could leave my nightmare behind.

That was the man I had loved for over eighteen years! All I could think about was James somehow leaving the clinic and getting back to the house before I could get the kids and leave.

The closer I got to the house, the more paranoid I became. I still couldn't be sure that James hadn't escaped and wouldn't be waiting for me when I got home. I only had a little time to get home, get the kids and get out of there before James realized I wasn't coming back! I was terrified and all I wanted to do was run and never look back!

I was waiting anxiously at an intersection near our house when a car pulled up alongside me blowing the horn.

"Oh, my God!" I said in a panic. I was sure it was James. Then I heard someone yelling, "Debra, Debra!"

I turned to see James' cousin in the car next to me. "Where's James?" he asked. "I just left the house and he wasn't there."

I relaxed a little as I replied, "I just dropped him off. I'll tell him you're looking for him when I go back to pick him up."

When I turned the corner and could see the house, I was relieved that I'd made it home. As I pulled up in front of the house, I cut the car off before I put it in park. I was really scared!

As soon as I got inside, I called the shelter and told Colleen that I was home. "Please, come before he gets here!" I yelled.

I looked out the window and saw the kids getting off the school bus. I ran outside and yelled down the street for the kids to hurry up! "Come on!"

As the kids ran into the house, I told them to get their stuff. "We have to go!"

The kids got a few trash bags and grab as many of their clothes as they could. Like me, they didn't seem to care about the few items that we had. They wanted to get away just as much as I did.

The kids were tired of watching their mother being beaten and abused by their father who was supposed to love us unconditionally. It didn't help that he was constantly threatening to do the same to them if they tried to help me.

Tyra pulled me aside and asked, "Mommy, where's dad?"

"Your father's at the rehab clinic. We have to get out of here while we have a chance, before he come and catch us!"

I called Monica to tell her that I did it! I explained that James agreed to check himself into rehab and I was waiting for someone from the Women's Resource Center to come pick us up. I told her that I was leaving the key to James' car under the seat and that I really appreciated her help with everything.

I heard a horn blowing so I told Monica, "She's here! I gotta go! I'll call you as soon as I know we're safe! I love you, Monica."

It seemed like Colleen was at the house in five minutes after I hung up the phone. I called out to the kids, "Our ride is here! Let's go! Now! Let's go!"

I was still looking around praying that James wouldn't jump out of the bushes as we ran out of the house dragging the garbage bags of dirty, roach-infested clothes. I hustled the kids into her car and once I closed the door, I realized our life with James was history!

Everything was going to be different! We were finally leaving behind a dangerous and abusive life with James.

Once we got to the shelter and settled in, I thought about my life and wondered how I ever ended up like this. As I **lay** my weary broken spirit and bruised body down, I took a full reflection of my life.

Section 18

I remember back when.

Let me back up and start from the beginning and then maybe you'll see how this relationship came about. I'll go back to my early childhood to give you a little background on how my life got so far out of control.

I lived on the south side of Chicago on 69th in Cornell. Whenever I go back, I visit with my childhood friend Nesa who lives right across from the empty lot where my house once stood. I like to reminisce about the good times which were very few. I think about Nana and all that she taught me and how she loved me. I will only allow the bad times to remind me of how my life has changed and how far from this place I have grown.

I was born Debra Denise Dent to Charles and Marian Dent in Chicago, IL on April 4, 1958. I grew up living in the house with my grandparents, Nana and Papa, along with my mother Marian, my little brother Chuckie, my Auntie Janice and my Uncle Tom. I will never forget my Uncle Tom.

I was eight years old when my Aunt and Uncle came to live with us and this is when our lives began to change. Oh, yeah, don't let me forget our dog King who stayed in the basement all the time.

The house that we lived in was a two-story single family home with a basement. It was painted lime green with white trimming. There was a big front porch where my Nana had two dark green chairs flanking the front room window. There were beautiful soft orange drapes hanging in the window with pretty off white sheers. Nana swagged the drapes and made the window look so elegant to me.

My Nana took great pride in her front room, especially when people complimented her as they walked by.

Nana would say, "Debbie don't ever forget when you grow up and get your own place, always put pretty curtains at your windows—no matter if you have nothing in your house. That way, nobody will ever be able to tell what's on the inside of your house, even if you're poor."

There was a narrow gangway led back to the alley which ran alongside our backyard fence. Next to the gangway was this huge house where twins Brenda and Linda lived. They were like my big sisters.

Section 19
My Daddy & his side of the family

Sometimes on the weekend, my cousin Beverly would come over to play with me. She didn't come over often because my Auntie DD, my mother's sister, did not like the way Uncle Tom, their brother, talked to me. Auntie DD didn't want Beverly to be exposed to that.

One afternoon, I was sitting in my Nana's bedroom watching TV with my cousin Beverly. I was eight years old and I'll never forget it. As I got up to go to the bathroom, Beverly shouted, "Look, Debbie! Your daddy is on TV!"

I turned to look and saw my Daddy's picture, as the reporter continued, *"We have Breaking News. Charles Dent was shot and killed today. The suspect tried to flee after stealing a watch out of an apartment complex on 63rd in Rhodes. Officer Power states that he warned Dent with 'Police, Stop, or I'll shoot! The officer fired a fatal shot in the back. Dent apparently was a heroin addict trying to steal the watch to buy some drugs."*

25

One of the few things I remember about my dad was that he bought me a bike when I was seven years old. I vaguely remember him taking me somewhere one time or another.

I was told repeatedly as a child by Aunt Lilamae, my dad's sister, that my mother and father had a shotgun wedding. She told me that my grandfather promise to kill my dad if he didn't marry my mother because she was pregnant with me.

Aunt Lilamae always told me my mother acted like she was too good for my dad and there was nothing he could do to please her. She said because my mother treated my dad so badly, she felt like that was the main reason he used drugs. She claimed that's what messed up his mind. "Your mother didn't let CC visit with you whenever he wanted to."

I was told that my dad moved on with his life and remarried, but never got a divorce from my mother; he was a bigamist. Out of this fake marriage, he had two children—a girl and a boy. Can you believe that the little boy's name was the same as my brother's?

I asked my Aunt why my daddy would marry another woman when he was still married to my mother. She just laughed and answered, "Well, that's CC. He just did it. You didn't know your father. He was something else."

Whenever Aunt Lilamae shared these stories about my parents, it was apparent that she didn't like my mother.

"I don't have anything against your mother; she has never done anything to me. I just didn't like the way she treated my brother CC!"

Well, that's it. She didn't like my mother, I said to myself. I even thought about how I would feel if somebody hurt my brother Chuckie the way she say my Mommie hurt her brother. I think I would feel the same way.

When I visited Mama Angie, my dad's mother, I would tell her about the stories that Aunt Lilamae told me and I wanted to know if they were true.

Mama Angie always had a softer spin to the stories. For instance, the story about when my mother got pregnant with me, my grandfather Papa forced my father to marry her.

"Why my dad didn't want to marry my mother?"

"No, it wasn't that. They were both too young at the time, but because Marian was pregnant with you, her father made them get married and they called that a shotgun wedding. There was no actually shotgun at the wedding. I want you to know that your father loved you so very much. He would have done anything for you."

"Is it true that my daddy is a bigamist? He married somebody else and I have a half sister and brother? That's what Auntie Lilamae said."

"Yeah, now that is true. CC did marry another woman who had six children by three fathers. So that tells you something about her, now don't it? Yes, you do have a half sister and brother, but I doubt that you will ever meet them. You don't need to worry about what Aunt Lilamae is telling you. Your Aunt Lilamae ain't too short from the funny farm herself while she trying to tell you something about CC!" And we laughed until we cried.

Mama Angie told so many funny stories about my dad when he was younger. She had a way of saying things that would make me laugh, but she always told me the truth.

I believed my grandmother; why would she lie to me? I think maybe because I wanted to blame my mother for my father's death. I wanted to believe my daddy's side of the family.

As time went on, Mama Angie and I spent a lot of time together. I was so glad that my mother no longer objected to my visiting with her. My great-grandmother Mommie Sammie, Mama Angie's mother, tried to convince my mother to allow me to visit more often with Mama Angie. When my mother saw how happy it made me to be with my daddy's family, she gave in. I loved to play with Aunt Lilamae's four children, two boys and two girls. We would have a ball together.

My Mama Angie used to make hats and matching purses. Nana would take them to her job to sell. I was so happy whenever Mama Angie came by—she loved me so much. It seemed like whenever she saw me, I lit up her day. Her eyes were so bright and her smile said 'I love you, Debbie.'

Between my Nana, my Mama Angie and my great-grandmother Mommie Sammie, I had a tremendous circle of love that helped me to withstand living in the same house with my Uncle Tom.

 Mommie Sammie

Mommie Sammie lived in her own place for a while, but when her husband passed away, she moved in with Mama Angie.

When I was much younger, Mommie Sammie took me to church with her. Every time I would see Mommie Sammie, she was wearing something white. She was a missionary and traveled all the time. I don't remember my mother questioning me after being with Mommie Sammie, but with Mama Angie, she would drill me for days! My mother wanted to know if they were talking about her to me. My grandmother shared only the funny things about my dad—we never discussed my mother.

I would tell Mama Angie little things about how my uncle treated me, but I didn't want to say much because it would upset her and she would raise hell with my mother. I tried to keep it as quiet as possible, all the while wanting to tell it all. I didn't want to jeopardize anything that would prevent me from seeing Mama Angie.

I wanted to tell Mama Angie about my Mommie's new friend, but I knew Mommie would not want her business known. Three months or so after my father was killed, my Mommie had a boyfriend.

My Mommie had a friend that was really nice to me and I looked up to him like a father figure. If my daddy's family founded out, I was afraid that they wouldn't love me anymore, so I kept it from them.

Section 20

Lies and Deception

Years went by and nothing too much had change. I am still getting my ass kicked by my uncle. He is still beating up on my Auntie Janice, and my Auntie Eunice's husband is still beating up on her. You know, the everyday thing.

The same faces would come for about three to six months at a time. On the weekends, everybody came to Nana's house to drink, play cards and be merry. Just when you got used to a face, a different one would show up. Out with the old and in with the new.

My mother had a friend by the name Rob. He came into my life when I was eight years old, and three months after my daddy was killed. He was really nice to me. I learned to trust and love him; he treated me like a daughter and did things with me as a father. He always told me that even though he was not my real father, he loved me just the same.

He took me shopping for clothes and even to the park. Mommie would let him take me to get ice cream by myself in his car. He was so nice to me and he loved me.

Whenever Rob was going to pick me up, Mommie dressed me extra special. She reminded me to be good and not to beg him to buy a lot of things. I even went to church with his mother a few times. He said that I was his baby, his only little girl. He knew that my real daddy was dead, so he told me that he would be my daddy. Rob said that he would never leave me, and if I ever needed him, he would be there for me. Rob had been in my life for the past three years by now. He said he loved me.

I believed him until the day I saw his car parked at the corner, at the end of the block. He never parked there before.

I saw my mother talking to him as he was about to leave, so I ran up to him to give him a hug. Then I noticed a little girl about three years old in the back seat of his car.

I didn't know who she was until I asked. He said it was his daughter, and that he was sorry he would not be able to see me anymore because he had to spend all of his time with her. But, he said he loved me.

I was crushed. He was the closest thing that I had ever had to a father. He and my mother had been lying to me all along; they never told me that he had another child. He said he loved me.

"You not my daddy! No way, I hate you! I never want to see you again!"

I ran back in the house crying to my Nana. I couldn't understand why nobody wanted to be my daddy. I asked my Nana why he would say he wouldn't see me anymore. What did I do wrong?

My daddy left me and now Rob is leaving me. It's not me, it's my Mommie! She is running them away!

"He said he love me, Nana, what I do?" as I cried in her arms.

Section 21

My Nana made the pain go away.

Nana just held me close to her and told me that everything was going to be alright.

She lifted my chin so I could see her eyes, "Your Nana loves you, Debbie. You are my favorite grandchild and don't you ever forget it. I want you to remember that you will always be Nana's favorite grandchild until I die. Now that's our little secret. Okay? Who needs him? If he doesn't want to be with you, then that's more time for you to be with your Nana. Okay, now go wipe your eyes. You don't need him when you got your Nana, right?" She smiled at me with that gold crown sparkling.

"Yeah, you right. I love you, too Nana." She then gave me a real tight hug with a big kiss.

I felt so much better knowing that I was my Nana's favorite grandchild and that was our little secret. If it had not been for her, I don't know how I could have made it through this. I was so hurt. I still didn't understand, but if Nana says I'm her favorite, that's all that matters to me. I was so happy—I got the best Nana in the whole wide world!

Nana was disappointed about how my mother and Rob handled that whole situation with me. I heard her tell my mother that she needed to do something special with me to help get that off my mind. She told my mother how devastating it had been for me.

My Mommie replied that I will be alright, that I would get over him, and that I didn't need to be depending on any man for love or anything.

Sure enough, that summer my mother took me and my brother to Disney World and Bush Gardens. We had an awesome time. My mother tried hard to make the sadness go away, but I could tell I was looking at her in a different way now. It's hard to explain: It seemed like I was watching her every move, especially when different men approached her or gave a certain look.

Don't get me wrong, I loved my Mommie with all my heart, but it was something odd that I felt. Did I not trust my Mommie with men anymore? Was she going to bring home another Rob? Will the new one hurt me like he did? Anyway, going to Disney for a whole week really did make me feel better, at least for the time being. It brought us closer and gave us the time that we wanted to spend together away from home. It was like we had Mommie all to ourselves. I wish we could have stayed on vacation forever.

My Mommie was hugging and kissing me more than I could ever remember her doing before. I was so happy. I had my Mommie, my little brother with me, all to myself and that's all I ever wanted. Well, Nana is number one, but you know what I mean.

Mommie bought me a big Winnie-the-Pooh and a Mickey and Minnie Mouse stuffed animal. We had so much fun. We rode the Monorail and saw all the exotic birds at Bush Gardens.

Once we got back home, things got back to its normal routine. As the time passed, I guess Mommie was right—the pain of my missing Rob was soon gone. I thought about him from time to time, but I never saw him again. I always wondered how that could be when his mother lived just blocks from us.

Section 22

My Daddy's letter

I'm ten years old and curious about a lot of things. I remember this one day when I was in the bathroom. There was a closet there with stuff in it—old clothes and winter coats hanging up and this huge chest. I was always curious to know what was in the back of the closet behind all those clothes, and especially what was in that chest. Remember now, I was always told by my mother, "Don't go rambling in the closet because it is not anything in there for you."

Well, early one Saturday morning my mother had gone to the beauty shop, my brother was outside, my uncle was washing his car, and my Nana was busy doing stuff downstairs. I decided to snoop around in that big, old beat up, dark brown chest in the back of the closet.

There were all kinds of old stuff in it, but what caught my eye was a big envelope with 'C.C' written on the front with a bunch of letters inside of it. My dad's nickname was C.C. and I wanted to know what the letters had to say. I was so curious.

I had already locked the bathroom door, so I wouldn't get caught. I was really excited to see the letters even though I didn't know what was in them. Just the fact that they had my daddy's name on them was exciting to me. I was praying they were letters from my dad. Oh, my God, they were! I got a chance to see what his handwriting looked like and as I read them, I could almost hear his voice. I couldn't believe I was holding letters that my father once held in his hands.

As I continued to read, I ran across one letter that stood out from all the rest. After that, I truly believed in my heart that it was my mother's fault that he got killed. The letter read:

Marian, I love you so much; all I want is for you to give me one more chance to be with you and my children. I really miss you and the kids. They're growing up and they need their father in their lives. Marian, I need you in my life.

Please don't throw away the love that I have for you and the kids. Please don't close the door on us. You're my first love and I will always love you. I've been clean for a while and I was hoping you would let me come home so we could be a family again. Debbie and Chuckie need me in their lives, I miss them so much.

Please take me back. I'm so sorry for hurting you, for being a disappointment to you. My life means nothing if I can't have you and the kids. I would rather die than to live my life without you. Please give us a chance. I love you. C. C.

Tears rolled down my face as I read the letter. I couldn't believe my mother did that to my father and now he's dead! Dead because she didn't take him back. I kept telling myself that if my mother had taken my father back, we could have been a family. He would not have used those drugs like the news reporter said. But, most of all, he would not be dead!

I really do believe that after I read that letter, I began to have different feelings toward my mother and my actions showed it. I became very rebellious. I began to act out and took on this I-don't-care attitude. I never told my mother that I read that letter. I never told anyone in my family.

I hurried and put things back the way they were and got out of the closet. Just as I closed the door, I could hear someone coming up the stairs. I turned the water on quickly as if I was washing my hands. Actually, I was wiping the tears from my face.

Then I could hear my uncle's voice, "Who's in the bathroom?" He knocked on the door.

"I am, I coming out now," shutting the water off. I walked right passed him and began to run down the stairs.

I could hear his voice echoing, "Stop running down those damn stairs, Debbie!"

It was too late. I was already at the bottom of the stairs and on my way out the front door. I ran all the way to my friend house Rochelle house, but she was not home.

Then I went to Lottie's house, and I began to tell her what happen, as I cried my heart out.

"Maybe you should not have read the letter, then you wouldn't feel this way." Lottie made me mad.

"You just don't understand! If my mother had taken my father back, maybe he would still be alive and I would have a father! I see you later. I just want to be by myself right now."

I walked home thinking all kinds of stuff. Lottie lived on the Cregier Street that was just a few blocks from the house. I was so hurt by what I had read in that letter that I even went so far to think what if my mother really didn't want to have children. What if she didn't want me? Is that the reason why she doesn't hug and kiss me like Auntie DD does my cousin Beverly? I continued to cry as I walked home.

To soothe myself, I tried to think of all the good things like Nana doing all the cooking, pressing my hair and always showing me genuine love. Nana was the one who taught me what to do when I got my menstrual cycle. She made sure I knew how to wash clothes, keep the house clean and most of all, how to love.

I knew for sure that if I had received the kind of love from my mother that I did from my grandmother, I would be a happier child and things would have been a lot better. Nana was love and my true mother. Everything about me that was good came directly from her and I love my Nana for that.

Section 23

Why does he hate me so?

My Uncle Tom never seemed to like me. Even though I never knew what it was about me that he hated so much, he made it his business to show me verbally and physically how much he disliked me.

He would beat me for no reason. Mostly, because I wouldn't wash his nasty ass underwear by hand! The bad part was nobody in the house ever did anything to rescue me from his ungodly whippings or verbal abuse.

My uncle loved to call me his favorite names, bitch and whore. He didn't mind telling me that "You ain't never gonna amount to shit when you grow up, but turn out to be a little lying bitch." These were the kind of words my uncle would say to me. He had no problem letting me know that he hated my little ass. I never understood what I did to deserve that—I was just a child, a little girl. Sure, I had a smart mouth, but it was no different than any other kid my age.

He would embarrass me in front of my friends. My girlfriend had even told me that he made sexually overtures toward her with his old ass and we were still in grammar school! Can you believe that?

Nettie was healthy for her age and she was pretty with a dark smooth completion. She looked like she was eighteen years old and she could fight really well.

She said one time when my uncle beckoned for her to tell her something. Whatever he said to her and whatever she responded back in a real low whisper caused him to never to say much to her whenever she came by.

Matter of fact, he didn't like her anymore. Nettie told me that she didn't like my uncle, that he wasn't right. She knew that from the way he treated me. It was years later that she told me she told my uncle he reminded her of a man who would sneak into a little girl's bedroom.

Section 24

Did jealous begin here?

I noticed that when my cousin Beverly visited, she would get the utmost respect and compassion from dear Uncle Tom. You would think she was his daughter the way he was so loving and kind. I guess it was because her mother, my Auntie DD, was the type of woman you didn't want to cross, especially when it came to her daughter. You see, my Auntie DD carried a gun.

She made it her business to remind her brother, "You try that shit with my daughter if you want to and I will shoot your ass!"

I wasn't the only one that didn't understand why my mother would let my uncle treat me the way he did. DD didn't like it one bit that my mother chose to be a bystander in the whole situation.

Nobody loved me like Nana; nobody knew how. I could not wait to get old enough to move out of this house.

Section 25

My Papa

My brother and I were responsible for cutting and raking the yard, and once we were finished, Papa would give us ten dollars each. That was a lot of money back then!

Papa was a beautiful medium brown, wore a low haircut and had big brown eyes and a warm smile. In addition to his job at the steel mill, he owned a garage in South Chicago. Papa always wore dirty overalls and smelled like oil and grease from working on cars. Papa was never around a lot to know what was going on at home, but he treated me fair and with love.

Papa was really fat and he would get winded when he walked. He was too fat to cut grass in the hot sun, so he paid Chuckie and me to do the work.

Chuckie didn't like to cut the grass or rake leaves, so sometimes he would run off to hang out with his friends. I hated doing the yard work by myself, but Papa would reward me by giving me Chuckie's share of the money for working so hard.

After he gave me the money, I'd go to the store and buy candy. Chuckie would get mad because he didn't have any money. I'd give him a few dollars, anyway.

This would happen every other Saturday morning. Later, I'd go to the laundromat for my Nana and wash her rugs and silks. Nana called her panties, bras and slips her silks. She said that it was more ladylike to say silks instead of panties and stuff. She would give me ten dollars and I felt like I was a big girl even though I was only eleven years old.

Section 26

Me and my Nana

One sunny Saturday morning, Nana said, "Come on, Debbie, get dressed and walk on 71st in Jeffery with me."

Boy, I was happy because that's where all the stores were. I was sure my Nana was going to buy something for me. As I got ready, I remembered that Chuckie had already left the house to go outside and play, so it was just me and my Nana hanging out for the day. I didn't even care that it was about a nine-block walk. Just me and my Nana.

I always thought of Nana as a very sophisticated lady, for a grandmother. She was about five and half feet tall and used a black rinse that made her hair looked blue/black when the sun hit it. Nana wore glasses, but she only needed them to read.

Her complexion was a smooth caramel that she complimented with coral lipstick. She had a tooth on the right side with a gold crown that gleamed when she smiled. It's hard to explain, but there was no mistaking the love in her eyes when she looked at you.

Nana also has this contagious laugh; you can't help but laugh with her. She smoked Trenton cigarettes and as she blew out the smoke, and held the

38

cigarette just so, she would smile. You could see that gold crown and I thought it made her look so sophisticated and important.

When Nana hugged you, the hugs were so tight that your back would bend from the pressure of her pulling you close. Then she would kiss you on the cheek. Boy, I loved her hugs and kisses!

After the hugs and kisses, she would always say, "You know your Nana loves you!" I'd always reply, "I love you, too, Nana."

I guess I was taking too long to come downstairs when Nana yelled, "Debbie, are you daydreaming again? Come on, girl! Let's get a move on if you are still going with me. You know I want to get on 71st early!"

"Okay, I'm ready," running downstairs like somebody was chasing me. I didn't want my Nana to say she'd go by herself and for me to stay home.

"Well, come on. Don't forget the grocery cart. We are gonna to need that." We left the house and started our walk.

Nana looked down at me and told me I was growing up to be a very pretty girl and that she loved me very much.

"Debbie, it looks like you're developing breasts. It's time for you to get a training bra."

My eyes widened as I looked up with a big smile. "Yes, it's time!"

"Debbie, you're something else!"

I was excited about getting my first bra because all of my friends were already wearing theirs. I was eleven years old. I couldn't wait to tell my best friend Rochelle that I had finally gotten mine. I got so quiet that Nana thought something was wrong. I was thinking about how excited Rochelle would be to see my new bra!

My grin must have given me away because Nana laughed out loud and said, "Come on Debbie, let's stop at Woolworth's first."

I remember getting ribbons for my hair and Nana picked up a few items for herself. My hair was really long and pretty. I weighed about 95 pounds and was always so skinny.

Rochelle also had long, pretty hair. She and I were the same size and everybody always told us we looked like twins. I still love her like a sister.

Once we were finished in Woolworth's, Nana and I walked to three or four other stores shopping for odds and ends.

As we headed home, the last stop was the hardware store. Nana asked, "Debbie, didn't you say you wanted to get your ears pierced?" I eagerly responded, "Yes, Nana!"

They pierced ears in the back of the hardware store for ten dollars! You couldn't get the earrings right away, instead you went home with a string in your ears, like the way you thread a needle. That's how they did it. Who cares? Rochelle had gotten her ears pierced two weeks earlier and was already wearing earrings.

I was surprised that Nana allowed me to get my ears pierced after my mother told me no. My mother didn't like the way they pierced ears and said it wasn't safe.

It really didn't hurt that bad and I was glad about that. Once it was done, Nana bought a hammer and some nails before we headed home.

We stopped at a boutique that was owned by one of Nana's friends. She was a stylish woman with lots of pretty clothes and always wore a big wig and big eye glasses. She was plump, but not really overweight. All in all, she was a nice lady. Sometimes Nana would call that lady and order her silks and then send me to pick them up.

Nana always stopped by her shop to talk whenever we were out, which usually ended up in a very long conversation. I was ready to get home so I could go outside and play with Rochelle. I had to sit there while they talked forever.

Every now and then, Nana would look over and catch me swinging my legs impatiently back and forth.

She finally said, "Oh, that's what I came in here for. I need you to measure Debbie for a training bra."

"Yeah, I think it's time for her to get fitted. Look at her little boos coming out."

I was filled with so much excitement. I sat up straight up as I looked at Nana with a big grin on my face. Then, you could hear the bell ring that was hanging over the door…someone had just come into the store! What? I was ready to get my bra!

I was sitting in the back and I couldn't see who it was. I was surprised when I heard my mother's voice! What I didn't know was that Nana and my mother had planned to meet at the boutique so we could all share in the experience of getting my first bra.

Section 27

My First Training Bra

I jumped up and ran to her shouting, "Mommie, Nana is getting me a training bra! Can you believe it? I'm a big girl now! I'm getting a training bra! I was so happy!"

"Isn't Debbie silly?" as she laughed. My mother was very pretty with very keen features and the darkest, piercing eyes. She had a beautiful smile with pearly white, perfect teeth. It was later that I founded out that my mother had false teeth. You would never know it.

She had long black hair that came down to her shoulders. When she walked, her hair would bounce and blow with the wind. She was very petite and wore a size 3 or 5. Mommie shopped only at the high-end stores on Michigan Avenue, Water Street, the Water Towers and Sax Fifth Avenue in Chicago. Her make-up was always perfect, flawless.

She was the best-dressed lady in our community; no one could out dress her back then. Mommie was very smart and worked as an IT tech at the John Hancock Building. When the computers broke down, they would call her to fix them.

She had a good reputation and carried herself as a lady should. Walking down the street with my mother, I'd noticed men as well as women turn whenever she walked by. Her favorite perfume was Charles of the Ritz.

I remember it came in a silver bottle with burgundy stripes on the bottle and smelled so pretty. You could even smell it in her clothes when she picked them up from the cleaners. Every man and woman admired her thin body.

"Hey, Marian," the boutique lady said. "Lock the door behind you and pull the curtains so Debbie can take off her blouse." In no time, I was being fitted for my first bra.

"Hold your arms up and be still." She wrapped the measuring tape around me.

The boutique lady brought out white bras in different styles. They allowed me to pick out two, my mother and Nana each picked out two. I was so excited that I had six bras! Rochelle only had two. It was a day I will never forget.

As we walked home, my mother started talking to me about boys. Nana would chime in every once in a while and tell her, "I told Debbie that" or "Didn't your Nana tell you that already?"

There I was between the two of them listening to all that 'grown up' stuff. I really didn't understand why they wanted to talk to me about sex because I hadn't done anything like that before. I wasn't really paying attention. My mind was on everything else but what she was talking about.

As we got closer to home, my mother mentioned she had an appointment at the beauty shop on the corner of 71st in Cornell.

"Debbie, we'll get your hair done next week." I was so excited about my bras that it didn't matter too much about my hair.

"Don't forget to be in the house when the street lights come on."

Nana turned to me and said, "Debbie, were you listening to what your mother was saying?"

"Yes, Nana, I heard her." When we got home, I helped Nana take the bags inside.

"You can go outside, but don't forget what your mother said. Be back before the street lights come on."

"Ok, Nana."

Well, Chuckie was at home upstairs in our bedroom. We shared a bedroom—he had his side of the room and I had mind. Chuckie used to pee in the bed and he was so scared of the dark.

He asked, "What did you get from the store?" I told him what Nana had bought for me.

"What did y'all get for me?" I told him nothing.

"You should have stayed at home this morning and you would have gotten something. You always try to run out early in the morning so you won't have to do house work," I teased. Right then he hit me and ran down the stairs.

"Nana," I yelled, "Chuckie keep messing with me."

After Chuck left, I decided to run over to Rochelle's to show off my new bra and my pierced ears. Nana reminded me again about being back at home on time.

Rochelle lived right across the street from me on the corner in that three- story, six-unit apartment building. She lived on the third floor with her grandmother, mother and sister. I ran over to her house and rang the doorbell. Her mother answered over the intercom, "Who is it?"

"It's Debbie. Is Rochelle home?" She buzzed me in and I ran upstairs. Rochelle was standing at her door waiting for me.

Section 28

Me, my best friend and my new bra

I had this great, big smile on my face as I told Rochelle, "Let's go to the back so that I can show you. I got a new training bra!" I raised my blouse and we both screamed! You could hear her mother in the background, saying, "Alright girls, keep that noise down back there."

"Let's go in the bathroom so we can look in the mirror." When we got in the bathroom, I raised my blouse again and you could tell that my bra did not fit that good. I still had some growing to do. So, I got some tissue and began to stuff my bra.

"Does it look even or should I put more in the right side?"

"Nah, it looks straight to me."

"Can you go to the playground now?"

"Yeah, I can go. Ma, can I go outside with Debbie for a little while? We're just going to the playground."

"Yeah, but you know what time to be in front of this house."

Once we got outside, I suggested to Rochelle that we walk to 70th in Cornell, turn the corner and come up the alley.

"Why you want to walk that way? You just want that boy Piggie to see you?"

"Yeah, I do," as we both laughed.

In the alley, you would see some of the teenagers, like Brenda and Linda, with their friends and the bigger boys playing music, dancing, smoking weed and burning incense.

The playground was the place in the neighborhood where everybody hung out. We had the girls' playground that was right behind my backyard and the boys' playground at the end of the alley. Today was really nice outside so the playground was packed with kids playing basketball, hop-scotch, double-dutch jump rope, dodge ball, and playing on the swings.

Section 29

The boy on the next block

There was one boy in particular who lived in the house on the corner of 70th in Cornell whose nickname was Piggie. There was always a bunch of people, family and friends, hanging out at his house. His real name was Ronald, but everybody called him Piggie. He was light-skinned and thin, not skinny, and he had a big mouth. You know what I mean, he talked a lot, too much! He was one of the boys that played basketball all the time and he was really good.

Piggie was a little taller than I was and he had bucked teeth. Well, not so much bucked as they were slightly larger than the other teeth, like rabbit teeth. He was one of those boys that always made fun of the girls, especially if he wanted to talk to you and you didn't want to talk to him. He would make fun and call you names, and embarrass you when he was with his clique.

I would always tell him 'fuck you' when he talked that way to me. That just left the door open for him to say things like… 'Baby, that's all I want to do is fuck you. You messing around with that punk Patrick, when you need to get with a real nigga like me,' as he would grab himself down there.

Ughhhh, I hated when he did that to me. And all the other boys in his little group would laugh and tease me. But, when I saw him alone without his friends, he was really nice.

It was just hard to trust a boy like that because he talked too much. Still, there was something about him that I liked. I could never really show him because I was afraid of the things he would say, you know, spread rumors about me that were not true. I already had a bad reputation, and I ain't did nothing no more than play 'catch-a-girl, kiss-a-girl' like everybody else. Anyway, I was too busy trying to be with Patrick. At least, he showed me respect.

The boys were always calling me out of my name, saying that I was fast and a hoe. The girls probably said the same thing about me, but they wouldn't say it to my face because they knew I would fight. The name-calling began because some of the kids would come by my house and they would hear my uncle call me bitch, tramp and whore and say that's all I was going to be.

I didn't care. I just kept on going about my business just as long as nobody put their hands on me—at school, that is.

Section 30

Little brothers can piss you off!

"I thought you liked Patrick? Why did we have to walk past Piggie's house?"

"I do. Everybody knows I've liked Patrick since kindergarten. I just want to see if Piggie noticed that I got on a bra before we go to the playground. If anybody will notices, it will be him with his big mouth."

We laughed because we knew we were right. Rochelle and I were so close that we knew what each other was going to say next before we said it. We were like twins sisters.

Well, there was nobody out in front of that house, which was unusual, so we just turned around and walked back down my street 69th in Cornell, and cut through the gangway.

I was so nervous about having the tissue in my bra. Rochelle asked, "What if some of it falls out?" We both laughed and said I would act like I didn't know where it came from.

We made it to the swings just in time before some other kids came up. We took turns pumping each other, swinging real high and bailing out. Rochelle remembered the tissue and asked if it felt like it was coming out. We laughed again because it was still there.

Rochelle spotted Chuckie on the playground. "Hold my swing. I'm going to get Chuckie because he hit me earlier today. I'll be back," as I bailed out and ran towards him.

Before I got up on him, he saw me and took off running. He ran pass Patrick as I chased him and he yelled out, "Patrick, Debbie got a bra on!" Right in front of everybody! I was so embarrassed I could have hidden under a rock!

I ran even faster determined to catch my little brother. He slipped and fell and I grabbed him, hitting him in his back real hard. Chuckie began to cry like I was killing him, saying he was going to tell Mommie on me.

"You should not have hit me this morning. Now stop crying and get up, I didn't hit you that hard. And you ran past Patrick and yelled out that I had a bra on! What you do that for?"

"I'm sorry, Debbie, I was just playing. I didn't mean to make you mad. Come on." Chuckie then asked, "You got any money? I want to buy some candy."

"Are you going to tell on me?"

"No, I won't tell." He then smiled, hit me again and ran off to the store with the three dollars.

"I'm gonna get you, boy! You play too much!"

Section 31

It's all about Patrick.

"Come on, Rochelle, let's go on the other side of the playground!"

As we were walking, I heard Patrick call my name! I was in shock! I was glad that he was calling me, but I was so afraid that he was going to say something about this bra.

"Rochelle, how do it look?" as I turned so she could see.

"It looks okay."

"Wait for me, walk slow and keep up with me."

"Alright, go see what he wants."

Patrick and I walked towards each other. All I could think about was how fine he was and that he called me in front of everybody out here.

"Yes, Patrick, what you want?"

"Well, Debra, I was wondering if you would braid my hair tomorrow."

"Yeah, I'll braid it. Where am I going to braid it at?"

"At your house. Do you think your mother would let me come over?"

"Yeah, she doesn't care. What time?"

He looked at me with those light brown hazel eyes and asked, "Can I have your phone number and I will call you tonight and tell you what time?"

You could have bought me for a nickel! Patrick, asking me for my phone number! He wants me to braid his long sandy brown hair! I gave him my number right away.

"Can you remember it?"

"Yeah, I'll remember it," with this smile on his face.

"Okay then, I'll talk to you when you call me tonight." I turned to walk away from him, but he grabbed my hand and said real softly, "You don't have to wear that in your bra. I like you for who you are."

I turned around and ran toward the house with Rochelle behind me. I got in the gangway and began to pull that tissue out of my bra and throw it to the ground!

"What he say Debra? What did Patrick say to you?"

I told her everything real fast. "I have to go ask my mother can he come over and I got to ask if I can talk to him when he calls me." I was so nervous! My dream had just come true. I couldn't wait to get in the house and tell Nana what Patrick said to me.

I ran in the house, "Nana, Mommie, guess what?"

Nana asked, "What's wrong Debbie?"

"Nothing! Guess what? You know that boy I was telling you about, Patrick? Guess what he asked me? Can I braid his hair over here! And he asked me for my phone number, too!"

My eyes were so big and I had the biggest smile on my face. "Can you believe it, Nana? He wants to come over my house! What am I going to do?"

By that time, my mother came downstairs and asked what was going on. I told her what had happened.

"Well, I'll just have to see about all that. You are too young to be dating!" I could have cried when she said that.

I begged, "Mommie, please can he come over? I gave him the phone number and he said he was going to call me tonight. Can I please talk to him? He just wants me to braid his hair, that's all. Mommie, he is so cute! He is the most popular boy in the whole school! Please, can he come over?" as my voice began to tremble.

"Mama, what do you think about all of this?"

49

Nana looked at me and she saw the disappointment in my eyes. "Well, Marian, I don't see the harm in it. One of us will be home."

I looked at my mother and waited patiently as she picked up her glass of beer and began to drink it. I just stood there waiting to hear what she was going to say. She never uttered a word; she lit a cigarette and just kept looking at me.

"Can he come, Mommie?"

"I'm thinking about it. Have a seat." Can you believe it? She got up and went to the bathroom with the cigarette. We had a bathroom right off the kitchen, so I just sat there waiting for my mother to come out of the bathroom.

I looked up at Nana and she nodded her head like 'Yeah, he'll be able to come over and call.' I put my head down. I wanted to believe my Nana, but sometimes my mother goes against what Nana says. I really couldn't believe anything until my mother said it out of her own mouth.

It seemed like she took forever to come out of that bathroom. Finally, I heard the toilet flush, then the water running.

I knew she was washing her hands and was on the way out. When that door opened, I sat straight up in the chair. Still, she did not say anything, just giving me this look.

She sat down and asked, "Where did you meet him?"

"Mommie, he goes to Parkside. He is in one of my classes."

"Why haven't I heard about him before now?"

I looked at Nana and said, "I told Nana. She knows about him, Mommie. Can he?"

By that time, Nana said, "Marian, let that girl have that boy over. Damn, you act like she's going to be screwing him! Shit! Gone back outside, Debbie!"

Mommie said, "You make sure that when he comes over you keep your ass right here in the living room."

I smiled and went to give my mother a hug, but she waved her hand at me and said, "Go head now. Gone back outside!"

I gave Nana a hug instead, "Thank you, Nana." She hugged me back.

I ran out the kitchen and I heard my mother say, "Stop that dam running and come here." I just knew she was going to change her mind, but she asked had I seen Chuckie. I told her he was in the playground.

"Well, you better be in before the street lights come on, go and get your brother."

"Okay!"

I talked to Patrick that night and he came over for me to braid his hair. I had the finest boy in school over to my house sitting between my legs with my fingers going through his sandy brown hair. That was it! I knew then that he was the one for me; I just had to get him to see that I was a good girl and I would be the perfect one for him.

He would come over almost twice a week for me to do his hair or just to hang out with me. My mother began to trust him as well as like him and Nana adored him. He was even allowed to come upstairs in our bedroom to play, like pillow fights. Every now and then, we'd sneak a kiss or two.

Section 32

At my Nana's house?

We attended Parkside Elementary which was right behind my grandparent's house. My brother and I went there from kindergarten through eighth grade, so we knew everybody that went to the school.

My grandparents' house was always busy on the weekends. There was usually a card party at my Nana's house every weekend with plenty of beer and alcohol.

One of my mother's male friends would always show up along with my aunt's boyfriend and Uncle Tom's current girlfriend. This was a nonstop practice.

My family didn't consider themselves as functional weekend alcoholics; they just called it a family enjoying each other over the weekend for cocktails. Patrick would stop by sometimes. My whole family got a change to meet him and they all liked him. He was so respectful.

My Auntie Eunice would always bring the music. She would have a stack of 45s and albums to keep the party going, and she would always make tacos which meant a good time for me because I'd eat at least five or six of them with no problem. That was the best part of the weekend for me.

Everybody would tease me, "Look at Debbie eat all those tacos! She is something else!"

"Just greedy!" my mother would say.

My mother and my uncle couldn't go a weekend without playing a chess game. That's one good thing Uncle Tom taught me and my brother, the basics of playing chess.

He taught us the word *pseudo* which meant phony or not real; he drilled that into us. That came about after he fell in love with one of his lady friends only to find out that she was gay. She chose a woman over him. After that, I caught holy hell from my uncle, but my brother would usually run away from home so he would not get beaten.

Section 33

My brother had to go away.

My mother sent my brother to an Audy home. That was where they sent boys who were bad and always in trouble. My uncle told her to do that! My brother was around ten years old when that happened.

He didn't stay long; I think it was just a school semester. My brother was growing up with everybody telling him he was so bad. That was all you heard in that house was how bad Chuckie was and how he was going to grow up and go to jail. Our Auntie DD would always call Chuckie a 'bad ass little boy' and of course, Uncle Tom had to put his two cents in, too.

Uncle Tom was the only one who always told me that I was a lying bitch, whore, and a tramp. We also heard that my brother and I weren't going to be anything when we grow up.

I couldn't believe that my mother sent my little brother away. I vowed that one day I was going to get them back for treating my brother the way that they did.

Yeah, I know that my brother was breaking in the neighbors houses, and trying to steal cars, but I just thought that little boys do that kind of stuff, at the least the boys he was hanging with did that.

I think what made my mother send my brother off to that place was when Patrick's youngest brother bullied him all the time. He bullied everybody and no one liked him. I mean who likes a bully?

One day, Chuckie got tired of being bullied and ran home and got Papa's gun from up under his mattress. He brought it to school, on the playground with all the kids and told that boy to leave him along or he was going to shoot him!

I remember Rochelle running up to me saying, "Your brother got a gun! Debbie your brother got a real gun!"

"What?! Where is he?"

"In the girls' playground!" she screamed.

I ran as fast as I could to get to my brother. By the time I had got to him, he had run back to the house and put the gun back.

I asked him, "What's wrong with you? You crazy?! You could have killed yourself! You know better than that!" I grabbed him and gave him a hug saying, "I love you. Don't you ever put a gun in your hands again! Now, what happened?!"

My brother was scared and crying. He went on to tell me that this boy was bullying him all the time and he was not going to let anybody else do that to him ever again in life.

"Well, you know this is going to get back to Mommie and you are going to get in trouble. Uncle Tom, everybody is going to whoop you. Listen, it is going to be their word over ours. Never tell that you did that and I will never tell on you, okay? I don't want you to get in trouble. So, pinky swear!"

We put our pinky fingers together and made a promise. I promise from that day that I would never tell on my little brother no matter what the cost, even if it meant that I would get in trouble.

I hugged my brother and told him to lie down in the bed like his stomach was hurting, like he had been in the bed the whole afternoon. My mother didn't fall for it, and she sent him off. Uncle Tom keep saying, "You better send him off to that school or you gonna catch hell from him later! He gonna be in and out of jail just like CC!"

Section 34

Living in a fantasy world

I daydreamed about any place that I thought was good and far away from home. I wanted to be an airline stewardess. I saw these TV commercials with pretty ladies dressed in their crisp uniforms with beautiful hair and white teeth. They always looked so happy, so professional. They were on their way to faraway places that, in my mind, were beautiful, romantic and fun with no bad people to call you bad names. I would be able to fly away to wherever I wanted—Paris, Rome, Italy and even New York.

I also dreamed of having the perfect family. I wanted a loving husband like the fathers on television and a big house with a white picket fence. I envisioned six children who had everything they wanted. My family sat around the dining room table with lots of food and everybody was happy. My husband would be Patrick saying a prayer and we would go to church with everyone holding hands.

I grew up during a time when shows like Leave it to Beaver, Bewitched and The Brady Bunch, and The Andy Griffin show, Good Times, The Jefferson's and The Cosby Show were about loving families with obedient children and supportive fathers and mothers. I loved these shows, but even though I saw black people on TV, I thought you had to be rich or something.

I guess I had a big imagination for a little girl from the south side of Chicago.

Section 35

Was it enough?

My mother made sure that my brother and I wore the best. We went serious clothing shopping three times a year—summer, fall, and winter. She would buy ten to twelve outfits each along with shoes, socks, underwear and matching hair pieces. Whatever we needed she made sure that we had it.

I went to the hair salon every two weeks once I got a perm in my hair. My brother and I had it all. I had all the finest things in life all accept one thing, one very important thing. I did not have love and affection from my mother.

Sure, I knew that my mother loved me, just as any mother would love their child. But, what I did not have was that closeness that my cousin Beverly had with her mother, like the hugs and kisses and hearing my mother tell me how much she love me. I don't remember too many times that my mother said that she love me. I'd have to say first.

55

On the other hand, my grandmother Nana would tell me all the time how much she loved me, all the time and how I was her favorite grandchild. She would say nobody comes before me and her little Chuck-u-Luck, my brother. Nana promised that she would not let anybody hurt me.

You know how some kids need to be shown, as well as told how much you love them? That was me. I needed that because I was receiving nothing but hell from my uncle.

Section 36

Shopping with Mommie

One evening before I went to bed, my mother said she was going to take me shopping with her downtown to get my school clothes. She believed in dressing sharp and only wanted the best for me and my brother.

I remember that morning like it was yesterday. I went to bed early the night before so I would be good and rested for the trip downtown. I was up with the sun, took a bath and got dressed.

I really wanted to look pretty so I put on my best clothes. I felt like I should look worthy for the clothes that my mother was about to buy.

My mother yelled, "Debbie, come on, girl or I'm gonna leave you!"

I rushed and ate a bowl of cereal real fast, turning the bowl up and practically swallowing it.

We headed out to catch the bus then transferred to the Dan Ryan train to go downtown. I remember staring out the window wishing the train would go faster.

My mother loved to read and always had a book in her purse, so she pulled it out and started reading. I was really excited and kept asking question after question about our trip downtown as she tried to concentrate on the book.

She finally shot me a harsh look and said, "Girl, be still and stop asking so many questions!"

I tried my best to sit still but I was still very excited.

I bounced in my seat as the train pulled into the Michigan Avenue stop. My mom could tell I was excited and said, "Debra, you better act like you got some home training today or else!"

The cool air hit me in the face once we stepped off the train. People were rushing and pushing which scared me a little so I grabbed my mom's hand. I didn't want to get lost like the stories I'd heard about kids getting lost in the big city.

I couldn't believe it when we headed for Michigan Avenue where the rich folks shopped. It's called the Magnificent Mile and I felt magnificent!

Our first stop was Marshall Field's. At the time, it was the biggest and fanciest store on Michigan Avenue. My mouth fell open when we walked through the door and headed for the girl's department. I couldn't believe my eyes; there were so many beautiful clothes and I wanted them all!

I anxiously asked where we should start.

My mom noticed my excitement and casually bent down and whispered through gritted teeth, "Debbie, act like you got some sense; don't embarrass me in front of all these people."

I couldn't believe how cool my mom was as she shopped like we were rich. She picked out several beautiful dresses for me and some casual clothes too. When we left the store, we had so many bags that we could hardly carry them. We bumped into one of my friends with her mom and they only had one bag.

After we left Marshall Field's, we headed to Carson's. I couldn't believe we were going to do more shopping. My mother picked out all kinds of clothes for me.

Once we were through shopping, my mother asked if I was hungry. I told her yes, so we went to Ronnie's Steakhouse.

She ordered for me when we arrived at the restaurant. We had steak, baked potatoes, garlic bread and salad; it was probably the best meal I'd ever had.

My mom got a kick out of how much I was enjoying the food. She would laugh and I would eat. I remember her joking, "I don't know where you put all that food with your skinny butt."

I was in for another surprise after we ate; we took a taxi home which was something we hardly ever did. When we got home, I took my bags to my room and laid the beautiful clothes out on my bed. Then I matched each outfit with socks, shoes, hair ribbons, and even underwear. My Mommie even bought me three different book bags to match my outfits—I was so happy. I couldn't wait until school started so I could wear my new clothes.

On the first day of school in the sixth grade, I got dressed in one of my new outfits and headed to Parkside Elementary School. I ran into two of my girlfriends on the way and smiled as I waited to hear what they thought of my new outfit, knowing that I was looking so pretty. I had on a pink two-piece skort set, with a white blouse that had a round collar with ruffles around the edge of it that lay over the pink waist length jacket.

I had on pink bobby socks and my white canvas tennis shoes with pink shoe strings. My hair was in two ponytails with white and pink ribbons, white and pink hoop earrings. And, of course, I wore my black eye brow pencil with my lip gloss. I had my pink purse and my new book bag that matched my clothes. I always made a statement when I got dress.

"Debbie, you look so pretty," Cookie said.

Another one of my girlfriends Lottie added, "Yeah, you look really cute Debbie."

"Y'all look pretty, too."

Section 37

She took me under her wing.

I was a good student and made good grades, especially in my favorite subjects, Social Studies and Science. The only problem was I was 'too fast' for my age. I didn't grow up in church. My grandmother only took me for Easter or some other holiday that people who don't go to church regularly feel they have to.

Miss Betty, Patrick's mother, began taking me to church with her. She was like a second mother, nurturing me with motherly advice and spoiling me like the daughter she never had. She loved having me around.

Miss Betty had three sons, but I was madly in love with the one named Patrick, and she knew it. She treated me more like I was his sister rather than like his 'girlfriend'. I remember going to her house every two weeks to get my hair done. She even bought me a few pretty dresses to wear to church with her.

I didn't mind spending time at his mother's house because she spoiled me. Can you believe it, she told me she loved me and I'm not even her real daughter?

Section 38

The only thing on my mind

I was only thinking about seeing Patrick. Patrick was the love of my life. He was tall, slim, and bow-legged with the coolest walk. His complexion was high yellow with skin smooth as a baby's bottom. His hair was sandy brown and he had light hazel brown eyes. His voice was deep and sexy, and to me he was as fine as Smokey Robinson.

I wanted to marry him, to have his children – I didn't care how young I was. I just wanted him to love me back. He said that he had too much respect for me and he didn't want me to carry myself like that. What a way to let a girl down so nicely! Patrick was also one of the cleanest and neatest boys at school. Ms. Betty made sure of that.

Section 39

We will always be friends?

When we got to school, everyone was running around trying to find their classes. I hoped I would be in the same homeroom with Patrick so I could sit near him. That way he could see how pretty I was. It turned out that he wasn't in my homeroom, but the room next door.

As I headed to class, I noticed a new face in the hallway. This one girl was very beautiful and had a well-developed body for a six grader.

I saw Patrick talking to the new girl during lunch. Everybody called her Bobbie. Judging by the way he was looking at her and the way she was looking at him, I could tell he really liked her. I confronted him in the hallway at school about him talking to her and he got mad at me. I said some bad words and he slapped me in the face! That hurt my heart like I never thought anyone could. I looked at him in a total different way after that. I still loved him, but it wasn't the same anymore. He walked off and I sat there on the school steps crying. One of our classmates asked me what had happen. I told him and he was very upset.

Now, this was one of the boys that could beat up everybody in the whole school and nobody messed with him. He was built like a muscle man and he was the darkest boy in the school with a real cute smile. I heard that he found Patrick and slapped him back and told him to keep his hands off of me.

I thought this girl was going to be trouble for me, but Patrick showed me that it wasn't her, it was him. I went the other way and try to avoid him all that day at school and when school was out, I went straight home.

Lottie and Cookie came up to me saying, "Debra, Patrick is talking to that new girl. We saw him put his arms around her."

"Patrick and I don't go together anymore. We been broke up, didn't you know? I don't care about him talking to nobody." Deep down inside I did care.

Later that day after school, Patrick came over to my house to say that he was sorry and to officially break up with me. He was very nice and polite like that.

Ain't that bitch! He said that we will always be friends and that he would always love me in his own little way.

He told me that he liked Bobbie, and if I really loved him like I said, he didn't want me to make trouble for her or for him.

"Fine, I don't care if you go with her. Just keep your promise with me that we will always be friends."

"I promise, Debra," as he leaned down and kissed me on my cheek. "I will always have a special place in my heart for you, Debra, and don't forget that. Stop acting like you are fast and easy when you know that you are not. Remember, you have to be a young lady all the time."

"Yeah, yeah, I know. Tell that to your new girlfriend, not me," as I laughed.

"Okay, I love you, too, Patrick. I will always hold a special place in my heart for you, too."

I then reached up and grabbed him by his shoulders as I pulled him close to me and kissed him right smack on the lips.

"Now is that the fast you're talking about?" We began to laugh and he walked out the door.

"I hope she loves you as much as I do."

"I don't think nobody will ever love me the way you do, Debra. I love you. Bye."

As I watched him walk down the stairs, I went out on the porch just to see him turn the corner. I had always considered Patrick to be my boyfriend, but it really was never meant to be. I was too fast for him and that was not what he wanted in a girl. And, when he put his hands on me, that hurt was still there. We will always be close friends and nothing else. I will be here for him to death do us part and I hope that he feel the same way about me one day.

Section 40

My two friends

My Nana always thought it was so cute the way I was so crazy over him. She called it puppy love. Hell, I wish he had had puppy love for me, but he had his eyes on the new girl at school. That was hard to swallow because I really wanted him to be with me.

Time went on and he ended up having sex with Bobbie and she got pregnant, and guess what? She became one of my best friends.

It really worked out all the way around, being friends with Patrick and Bobbie. It was really nice—I got the best of that deal. She became a closer friend to me than Patrick, at the time. I wanted their relationship to work even though he left me for her.

Later, I founded out he really wasn't what I thought. He really dogged Bobbie. He did her so wrong. And it is sad to say, but one day he will pay for how he treated her. God don't like ugly, like Nana always says.

He's a boy and I believe that all boys are just like that; they want to do the oochy-coochy with you then talk about you, and leave you. I'm so glad that he and I decide to be just friends.

Section 41

Is this what I got to look forward to when I grow up?

As the time goes on, my uncle continues to call me names and my mother never really says anything to him about it.

Everyday my mother gets off work, she drank a 40 oz. bottle of Budweiser beer.

Still on the weekends, my Auntie Eunice comes over, makes Tacos, and brings her 45's.

Uncle Tom is still beating up on my Auntie Janice. Sometimes she leaves and goes down south to visit her family.

Uncle Tom still brings different women to my Nana's house and introduces his new girlfriend to everybody during the time that his wife isn't there. He even sees the twins Brenda and Linda's big sister Julia. He gives her money all the time and she knows he is married.

Section 42

Who's the joke on?

One Saturday, my Auntie DD was over to the house and Nana and Mommie were in the kitchen. I remember asking my Auntie DD, "Why Uncle Tom brings so many girlfriends to Nana's house? What if Auntie Janice founded out or came home and saw them?"

My mother pointed her finger at me and told me to mind my business and keep my mouth shut in a real stern voice.

"Debbie, you better not ever tell Janice who he brings over here, and if I find out you did, I will whoop your ass! Do you understand me? Anyway, they're just his drinking friends. Ladies that like to come over and have a drink with him," and she picked up her glass of beer and smoked her cigarette.

"Marian, leave Debbie along. She just asked a damn question. She ain't gonna say shit." Nana lit a cigarette and picked up her cocktail. I think she was drinking something called Scotch.

"Debbie knows better than that, Marian. Damn, give the girl some credit. Shit, Janice knows that Tom is cheating on her. She's the damn fool for being with his ass as much as he kicks her ass. She needs her ass kicked just for staying with him. Hell, she just might have some nigga down south that she is fucking that he don't know about." Then they all laughed. "Debbie, go check to see if Tom's car is out there. We talking about his black ass and then he walk in on us saying. Ain't that some shit!"

They laughed even harder, but as I went to go to the front room to look out the window, my Auntie DD said, "Let him come in here talking shit to me. I got something for his ass, as she put her gun on the kitchen table." And they laughed at that even more.

"Go ahead, Debbie, and check."

Nana laughed, "Put that away, DD. Damn, you always talking about shooting a motherfucker."

Section 43

I love my Auntie Janice.

My uncle was cheating on my Auntie Janice right here in the house where she lives and everybody knows it, everybody but her.

I wonder how she would feel if she founded out that he was fucking different women in the same bed that she was sleeping in. I wanted to tell her so bad, but I was too scared—not just for her, but for myself.

Maybe she already knew he was cheating like my Auntie DD said, "Janice ain't no damn fool to that shit. She knows her husband is a whore and fucking every bitch that will open their legs. That's why she leaves and comes back the way she do. She might not care what the hell he do because she's probably getting tired of him kicking her ass."

It must have been real bad for Auntie Janice, living in Nana's house. My Nana did not like her at all. Uncle Tom and everybody else knew it. That's why he was able to bring every loose, hot stray to my Nana's house. He was being so disrespectful to his mother, his wife and he made himself look real bad, yet he was still talking about me and calling me out of my name.

I felt like nobody cared about her, but me. I really love my Auntie Janice. One day Uncle Tom is going to pay for all the wrong he is doing to her, lowdown dirty bastard!

Section 44

Why me and not his wife?

One day, my uncle asked me to wash his underwear by hand in the bathroom sink. This was not the first time. I was used to washing his nasty ass drawers all the time. I didn't want to do anything he told me to do. Even though I did not like it, I did it because I did not want to get yelled at. Plus, he was going to give me five dollars.

My brother always teased me whenever he saw me washing Uncle Tom's nasty, skid-marked drawers. I then threaten to put the drawers in his face and make him smell them!

Once I finished and asked him for the five dollars, he yelled at me. "I know what I said I was going to do. Your ass is gonna have to wait until I get paid next week, I don't have no money."

I was so mad that I went and told my mother, in tears. She just told me if he said he's going to pay me, then I'd have to wait.

Much anger was building up inside me for all the things he would say and do to me. This was a perfect example of what I endured as a child.

I always said I hated my Uncle for making me wash his drawers. I'd ask myself all the time why he didn't wash his own drawers or make his wife do it, or why my mother didn't tell her brother that I can't do that?

Section 45

Being fast and curious got me the crabs!

I decide to get on the bus and go out in South Chicago just to look around in the stores. I loved to look around in Goldblatt's that was the biggest store out there. I had just turned thirteen years old a few weeks ago, but I would tell everybody I was fifteen years old.

I met this boy named Bee-Bee while I was out there and he walked to all the stores with me and showed me around. He kept telling me how pretty I was. He knew I was not from around there.

We went by one of his friends' house for a few minutes. It was in walking distance of the stores. Then he asked me to come to his house and I did. It was still daylight and I had a long way to go before the street lights came on. So, I decide to go with him because he seemed so nice.

As we walked to his house, I thought about this was the area where my mother meet my father. My mother grew up in South Chicago, on Buffalo Street around Commercial Street area.

When we got to his house, it wasn't a pleasant site. I didn't want to act like I was better than he was. Compared to his house, we were living in the upper class section. That didn't mean anything because before I knew it, I was up in this boy's house, lying on this nasty, smelly ass bed with my panties down, legs wide open.

"Okay, we can try it a little bit. Just don't hurt me."

My Nana had told me that if you go to lay down with someone and they smell, you better get up and say no because cause you might bring something home. And guess what? I didn't listen to that little voice that was telling me, 'Don't do it!'

I should have known because of how nasty they kept their house. Besides that, he had on dirty underwear, or… the color was grey!

Boy, I'll never forget that experience. It didn't last long. I made him get up when he was trying to put it in. I kept moving around because it hurt every time he tried. I didn't like the way that felt so I pushed him off of me.

"No! I want to stop, I got to go home. I'm not ready to do it yet." We heard somebody coming up the stairs as I pulled my panties up.

I don't know what happened, but by the time, I got home I was scratching and itching something fierce down there. I did not know what was wrong with me. I was scratching so bad the next day my mother asked what was wrong. I didn't know. I kept scratching really bad.

My mother asked, "Have you been doing anything?"

"No, I have not. I ain't did nothing."

"Go to the bathroom and take off your clothes. Get undress from the waist down."

I was so scared. I asked, "I'm going to get a whooping? I didn't do anything."

"Just go to the bathroom, Debbie, and do what I said, right the fuck now!"

I began to walk up stairs. I stopped in Nana's bedroom and told her what happen. I told her the truth and that I tried to have sex for the first time with a boy out in south Chicago.

"Debbie, when and why in the hell would you take your ass way out there to mess with them nasty ass boys out there?"

"I don't know. I'm sorry, Nana," as I began to cry.

"Well, Debbie, it's going to be alright. Don't worry. Now, go in the bathroom and do what your mother said. It will be alright."

When my mother came in the bathroom, sat on the toilet and told me to come to her so she could look down there, I was so embarrassed.

"Pull your panties down and let me look at you. It better not be what I think it is, or I am going to kick your ass." Well, whatever it was I didn't want it because I sure did not want my mother to whoop my butt.

My mother jumped up and pushed me back saying, "You went out there fucking around and caught the got damn crabs," and hit me up side my head.

I didn't know what a crab was. "Huh?"

They were little bugs biting me! That's why I was itching so bad! "Bugs! That is so nasty! I got bugs on me!"

"Yes, motherfucker, you got bugs on you!" as she hit me again up side my head. She then told me to go to my room and take off all my clothes and sit there until she got back.

"And I mean you better take every last thing off your ass! I'm gonna to beat your ass, you nasty little motherfucker!" Mommie was mad.

"Now I got to get up and go to Walgreens and get some Blue ointment because you wanna take your fast ass out and fuck some nasty ass nigga. I'm gonna beat your ass when I get back," she yelled as she went down the stairs.

While my mother was out going to get this blue ointment, my cousin Beverly came over and she came upstairs to my bedroom.

"What's wrong, Debbie? What you do?"

"I tried to do the oochy-coochy and got the crabs. Now my Mommie is going to whoop me real bad when she gets back," as I used the sheet covering my body to wipe the snoot and tears.

"You did IT?

"Yeah, I did."

"Wooooo, Debbieee, you gonna really get it. You in trouble."

"I know."

"What are crabs?" she asked, but before I could tell her, Nana yelled up the stairs that Beverly's mother was here to pick her up.

"Bye, Debbie. I'm sorry you gonna get it. I love you."

"Me, too. I love you, too."

By the time my mother got back, I had cried myself to sleep, only to be awaken with the extension cord striking my naked body!

"I told your fast ass to leave those damn boys along, didn't I?" My mother would raise her hand and go way back with that cord and then come down real hard on my body.

"Now, take your ass out there and do this shit again, and I will fuck you up. Do you understand me?" as she swung that cord over and over again.

"Yes, Mommie," I screamed. "I'm sorry! I won't do it no more!"

"Scream again! Say one more motherfucking word and I'll kick your ass! Shut your damn mouth. I ain't hurt your ass yet!" she yelled. "Now, stand up so I can put this shit on you, you nasty motherfucker."

I stood up and saw that I had welts all over my body. I was even bleeding in some spots. With this horrible itch and the ass whooping that I just got, you would think that I would not ever want to call myself having sex ever again in life!

I felt so dirty and worthless! I felt no one really loves me in this house but my Nana.

69

Section 46

You shouldn't throw rocks at a glass house.

I never did that again, but I was never going to live that down. My uncle called me so many names behind that, I felt just as low as he put me down. Finally, he got what he wanted – he broke my spirit. A low self-esteem began to set in. I considered myself the whore or the nasty ass bitch or the tramp that I have been called all my life.

I told my Nana how my mother and uncle made me feel. She always told me not to talk like that.

"You are very special to me. You are beautiful and you are not any of the things that they call you. I'm going to talk to them and see that they stop calling you out of your name like that. I don't like that at all. Now, Debbie, you're going have to stop having such a smart mouth with your mother. You have to show respect to her. Just be quiet when she says something to you. I know Tom can get on anybody nerves. Hell, he makes my asshole hurt sometimes." We laughed.

Nana continued, "He reminds me of his father. He won't be living here long. Him and his wife will be out of my house and I will be happy. He's bringing all that shit and confusion in my damn house. I'll be so glad when he get his own damn house, then he can beat his wife's ass and I don't have to hear or see none of that shit. I'm so sick in tired of Tom and his bullshit. Debbie, Nana keeps peace in the house and I don't say anything to him at all because I don't want to hear his damn mouth. So, just do your best to stay out of his way and stop talking back. Okay? Promise Nana that you are going to try harder."

"Nana, I promise I will." With that, she gave me a hug and a kiss.

"You remind me so much like your Auntie DD when she was coming up," as she held me in her arms so tight. "Everything is going to be alright, Debbie. Everything is going to be alright."

Section 47

Me and My Auntie DD

Uncle Tom was a mama's boy like my Auntie DD called him all the time. Auntie DD said he only got away with that bullshit because Marian allows him to do that to me. "But, let that motherfucker put his hands on my daughter like he do you and his Mama will be burying his ass."

Auntie DD said he whoops on Auntie Janice because she allows him to do that shit and that she needs to get her a damn .38 to carry in her purse.

"And the next time that punk motherfucker put his hands on Janice, she ought to shoot that nigga in his legs and cripple his ass. That would teach him to fuck with her ass." She picked up her Scotch cocktail, holding her baby finger out as she sipped.

My Auntie told me that a man once slapped her and before that nigga put his hands down she had cut up his hand. She said she would have killed his ass. I loved to listen to my Auntie DD tell old stories.

When she came to Nana's house, she got straight to the point and nobody messed with her. They didn't even talk crazy around her. Guess what the best thing about all of that was? She really loved me!

She loved me like she loved her own daughter, my cousin Beverly. Whenever Auntie DD came over, she always asked, "Where's my Debbie? Come here." She would hold out her arms for me. I would be so happy when she came over. She hugged and kissed me all the time.

My Auntie DD is so pretty. She doesn't take junk off anybody, and none of her brothers or sisters mess with her. They all knew that she was the one with zero tolerance of bullshit. Auntie DD is married to Uncle Fred and he is nice to me, too. He has never called me out of my name nor has he ever mistreated me. Uncle Fred and Auntie DD are my favorite uncle and auntie. They both like to gamble—playing poker and the horses. Auntie DD claimed they would win all the time.

One day, Auntie DD took me to Ted's store and the 5&10 Discount Store on Stoney Island. She bought me a pretty flowered sundress, two short sets and a pair of white sandals. She said that this was our little secret and that I didn't have to run back and tell my cousin Beverly about my new things.

"Okay. Thank you, Auntie."

I was so happy that she bought me something. It meant more to me than all the stuff that my Mommie had bought for me. Maybe it was because when she bought it, she gave me a big hug, told me how much she loved me and how pretty I was going to look in it. It was our little secret. She always told me how pretty I was and how I was going to be somebody when I grow up.

She would ask me what I wanted to be when I grew up, and tell me not to listen to what Uncle Tom was saying. I was going to be just the opposite of all of that, according Auntie DD.

I could hardly wait to get home to tell Nana. I didn't keep any secrets from Nana, just my Mommie. I guess Auntie DD didn't want my cousin to be jealous because of the things she bought for me.

Auntie DD even sent money to Africa for one of the poor kids who is really hungry, one of those kids that you see on TV all the time in the commercials. They sent her a picture of this little girl who Auntie adopted and supported.

Auntie DD would say, "Don't you be bad like Chuckie. And you tell me the next time my brother Tom put his hands on you. I'm gonna come over here and kick his ass." She would then embrace me with hugs and kisses.

"I will be back later. Tell Mama, and don't forget it's our little secret. I love you, Debbie. Be good."

"I love you, too, Auntie DD," closing her car door and running to the house to find my Nana who kept that secret and told my mother that she bought those things for me.

Section 48

My brother's last punishment

Nana said to me one Friday evening, "You know what I am worried about my little Chuck-a-luck and you. You both know better than to steal Papa's change out of his pocket. I see you learned your lesson after the last ass whooping you got, but I don't see why Chuckie would go back and do the same thing."

Nana called Chuckie 'Chuck-a-luck' because whenever Chuckie got in trouble, he would run as fast as he could to get to Nana and hide behind her duster, holding her tight, crying and saying, "Nana, don't let Mommie (Uncle Tom, or Papa) whoop me!"

This time it was Mommie. Chuckie was going to get a whipping because he took some of Papa's change out of his pocket while he was sleep, and we had just got a whipping last month for the same thing.

Papa had already whipped him; Uncle Tom had gotten a hold of him and when Mommie got home, he was going to get another whipping.

Well, Chuckie made it to Nana.

She said, "Marian, don't whoop him. He already got his ass whooped. Just put him on punishment! Y'all shouldn't be beating these kids the way that you do! Now, ain't nobody gonna touch him, dammit!" She put her arm

73

around him from behind, protecting him. "Just put him on punishment and leave my Chuck-a-luck along."

Chuckie had escaped another whipping, so he thought, and was put on punishment for a whole week. It was the first week of summer. Later that evening, he went upstairs and all we heard was Mommie whipping Chuckie's butt. He got a real bad whipping. He had whelps all over his body because Mommie made Chuckie take off all his clothes.

I felt sad for my brother. We used to compare how many whelps we had to see who got it the worst. Last time I got more, so it's Chuckie's turn now. My brother hated to get a whipping.

The next day, Saturday afternoon, was a beautiful, hot, sunny day. My Auntie Eunice was over. Nana, Mommie and I were sitting on the front porch. Nana had made some lemonade with real lemons and there was plenty of ice in the pitcher. I was sitting on the porch steps just listening to them tell old stories. Papa was at work at the garage that he owned in South Chicago. Uncle Tom had been gone all that morning and was not expected home for a couple of hours. Auntie Janice was sitting outside with us.

Every now and then I would go in the house and see what Chuckie was doing and he would ask me to bring him stuff from the kitchen.

When I got back down stairs, I asked if I could I go to the store to buy me some candy. Chuckie wanted some candy, too.

"Yeah, Debbie," my Mommie said.

When I got back and was on my way in the house, my mother said, "Debbie don't you give Chuckie none of that, he is on punishment."

I said okay, knowing that I was going to do just the opposite. After I sneaked Chuckie the candy, I went back down stairs.

I could hear them laughing on the front porch from Nana's bedroom window. I felt sad for my brother because he couldn't come outside, watch TV or nothing, and all his friends were outside and the playground was full.

Section 49

The last time my brother ran away

Soon the mood was about to change in the whole house. Papa and Uncle Tom had come home within five minutes of each other. Uncle Tom came up on the porch saying, "What y'all doing out here, just gossiping?" He laughed and went on in the house with all his bags.

Papa walked up the stairs and greeted everybody. He looked so tired. We all just sat there on the porch, still listening to Auntie Eunice tell these way-out stories of how they use to do things when they were young back in the day. I decided to go to the playground to play with Rochelle, Cookie or Lottie.

All I heard was my name being called by my Uncle and Papa, then calling Nana. Everybody jump up and went into the house.

Uncle Tom asked me, "Where is Chuckie?"

"He's upstairs in our room."

"You little lying bitch," he yelled as he slapped me across my face. "Marian, Chuckie then took Daddy's money from under the rug and left! That was Mama and Daddy's mortgage money for the house note!"

"I be Damn!" he continued yelling. "Let me get my hands on that little motherfucker. I am gonna kick his ass for real!"

I had no idea of what Uncle Tom was talking about. I just couldn't believe that he had just slapped me and that my Mommie only response was, "Don't hit her like that, Tom."

I told Nana, "I don't know what happened or where Chuckie is. I was sitting on the front porch with you all."

My mother said, "Debbie, you went in the house with Chuckie a couple of times! You know where he is at! Tell me what happen!

"I don't know, Mommie!

Next thing you know, Papa said, "I'm gonna whoop his ass and Marian, you gonna have to move and find you some place to stay! I cannot have no thieven ass kids in my house!"

I was crying because I did not know where Chuckie was.

What Chuckie did was snooped around in Nana bedroom and found a lot of money hid under the rug. Then he climbed out of Nana's window right over the front porch where we were sitting. He then walked around to the side of the roof and climbed over onto the apartment building next door, ran down the stairs, down the gang-way and got away. You could see that he had taken the screen out of the window and how he got away.

Section 50
Everybody is pissed off!

My Papa was furious and my uncle had grown death horns on his head. He was really going to hurt my little brother, if only he could get his hands on him. My Nana was crying and trying to calm Papa down, but he just yelled and told her to go on in the kitchen somewhere. He was really mad. I have never heard Papa raise his voice at Nana before.

My mother just walked away with Nana into the kitchen and Auntie Eunice kept saying over and over, "That's a damn shame, that's a damn shame. He shouldn't be allowed to come back in this house if he could do something like that! Marian, what is wrong with your kids? That's fucked up. A damn shame is what it is."

I wanted to say what a damn shame it is the way you let your husband kick your ass. Talking about my little brother!

Uncle Tom began screaming again, "Debbie knows where he is at! This little lying bitch know just where the fuck he is at, and she is going to take us to him!"

He grabbed me by my collar and I stumbled and fell, but it did not stop him. He dragged me out toward the door. I was screaming and crying for my Mommie, shouting to her, "I don't know where Chuckie is at, Mommie! I didn't even know that he was gone!"

Section 51

Mommie help me!

I cried and yelled, "Mommie, please help me! Uncle Tom is dragging me! Mommie, help! Help me!" She never came to make him stop. She was right there in the kitchen! My mother never came to save me!

"Nana! I want my Nana!"

"Shut the fuck up!" yelled Uncle Tom as he reached down and got a good grip of my clothes. He picked me up and slammed me against the wall in the front hallway.

His eyes were red and I had never seen him this angry before. My brother was in big trouble and I was getting all the ass whippings for it. I didn't even know what had happen.

Uncle Tom continued, "We are getting ready to go outside and I better not hear a word from you, or I will bring your little ass back into this house and beat the shit out of you!" He grabbed my blouse tighter and pressed his fist up to my throat. "Do you understand me?"

I just looked at him with tears of hatred and nodded my head.

He didn't want the neighbors to see how he was treating me. They had that perfect imagine of a family at 6909 South Cornell—all behind Nana's pretty curtains. You never knew what was really going on in our house.

He held on to me tight, knowing that I was going to flee once he let go. He opened the car door, slung me in the backseat and slammed the door. We were in Papa's car and he drove around to the next block which was East End. All the while, Papa kept saying, "I got to find him before he spends that money!"

Uncle Tom persisted, "This little motherfucker know where he is at and if I have to beat it out of her ass then that is what I am going to do!" He repeatedly slapped me on my head and in my face. I continued to cry and say that I did not know where my brother was.

Papa drove up to one of the apartment buildings and we got out of the car. They began to ring all the door bells—it didn't matter whose bell they were ringing, they just wanted in the building.

It was a whole block of apartment buildings on 69th East End on both sides of the streets and they were determined to go to each and every last one of them to find my brother.

Section 52

He pulled a loaded gun on me and she said nothing.

We had already been to three or four buildings by now and when we got in that fifth apartment building hallway, someone had buzzed the door and Papa went up the stairs. I was so scared. I didn't know if Chuckie was in this building or not. They knew that he had lots of friends.

As I wiped my eyes, I looked up at my uncle and this crazy motherfucker pulled a gun out of his pocket and put it to my head with the barrel thing cocked back! Told me that he would blow my motherfucking head off if I kept on fucking with his family and I better tell him where Chuckie is at!

He scared me so bad that I peed on myself! Pee just came out and ran down my legs, all in my shoes! I was too scared to scream. He told me that I better not say a word or even look at him the wrong way! Said my mother would be burying me if I kept fucking with him, his mother and father and his sister!

I couldn't stop crying. I just wanted to go back home and tell my Mommie what he just did to me. Even if I did know where my brother was, I was not going to tell on my brother. This bastard has lost his motherfucking mind!

'You just wait till I get home and tell my Mommie what he just did to me, her dear sweet brother.' These were the thoughts that ran across my mind as all of this was happening. I also prayed to God to please don't let my uncle kill me.

When Papa came down the stairs, Uncle Tom put the gun in his pocket and pushed me toward the door.

"Try it, if you want to." Try what? Running?

Papa went to a few other places, but Chuckie was nowhere to be founded.

We headed back to the house and I was so glad. Uncle Tom made me sit on my hands because I had peed on myself and he didn't want to get Papa's car seat wet. It was also easy for him to keep reaching to the backseat and hit me over and over again. I was just thirteen years old. I was still a kid, but a smart mouth little girl who was saying, "What the fuck!"

When we got to the house, I ran inside and straight to the kitchen, falling down on my knees holding my Mommie so close, crying, telling her what Uncle Tom had just done.

"He pulled a gun on me, Mommie, and held it to my head! He said that he was going to kill me, and you was going to have to bury me! Your brother hit me in my face, see!" I raised my head up so she could see the hand print on my face. Then I could hear him and Papa coming in the house.

"Mommie," I cried, "he pulled a gun on me!"

Just as I said that, Uncle Tom walked into the kitchen, "You lie on me one more motherfucking time and see what I do to you!" pointing his finger at me. I held my mother tighter with my face in her lap.

"Debbie," pushing me off of her, "be quiet and go upstairs. Stop exaggerating. He didn't do all of that. Just go upstairs." She picked up her glass of beer and began to drink it. "Did you tell them where Chuckie is at?"

"I don't know where Chuckie is at, Mommie!"

I ran upstairs crying, holding my face. Can you believe that shit? I really don't believe what just happen to me! This motherfucker just put a loaded gun up to my head and my Mommie didn't believe me! She believed her lying ass brother! What the fuck! Are they fucking each other or what? I am her daughter! How could she not believe me when I'm telling her the truth!

I know what I'm going to do… I'm going to call the police on this bastard! His ass is going to jail! I'll show him what a little bitch I am! I picked up the phone and dialed 911.

"Hello, District 5. What is your emergency? How can I help you?"

I told them my name. I was crying and said my uncle just put a loaded gun up to my head! He was going to kill me!"

"Stop crying, little girl. Where are you? Where is your uncle? Is he there with you now?"

"Yeah, he is! He is downstairs with my mother!"

"What is your address? I will send an officer over there right now, okay? You stay upstairs until the police get there, okay?"

I replied okay and hung up the phone.

It was only minutes and I heard the doorbell ring. Then I heard the walkie-talkies. It was the police—I was so glad. I could hear them talking, coming closer to the living room, close by the stairs.

I was listening to the officer. They had received a call from this address from a little girl stating that her uncle pulled a gun on her. You could hear my uncle say, "Why would Debbie do something like that?

My mother said, "My daughter is always making stuff up. We're sorry, officer, let me get her down here right now."

"Debbie," she yelled up the stairs. I walked slowly down the stairs, crying.

"Debbie, have you been playing on that damn phone again and called the police, and telling lies on your Uncle Tom, saying he pulled a gun on you? Why would you do that?"

I looked up at my Nana, and she slightly shook her head for me to say no. I just stood there with my head hung down and said, "I don't know," shrugging my shoulders.

My mother looked at the officer and said, "We are sorry that you were called, but as you see everything here is alright. We will make sure that she won't do that again."

The officer said that they had been getting a lot of prank calls from children who do not understand how serious it is for them not to do that.

"Oh, I guarantee you will not have any more calls like that coming from this address."

"Thank you, ma'am. Have a good day." And the police was gone just like that. Nothing was done about it. They never talked about that incident ever again, as if it never happened.

Section 53

He was boss hogging.

From that day forward, I vowed that I will get my uncle back for that bullshit. I planned that one day when I get big, I was going to get somebody to fuck him up, just kick his ass for all what he has done to me.

It was days that I didn't see my brother. I sent word out by his friends that I was looking for him and to meet me in the boys' playground on Saturday. When I finally saw my brother, he was with four of his friends and they all had on new Converse gym shoes.

There is this store on 67th in Stoney Island, Frank's 5&10 Discount store were you could get those gym shoes for $10.00.

"Chuckie!" I grabbed him and gave him a kiss. I told him how worried I was about him. "Are you okay? Yeah, I see that you are. You took Papa's money and I got in trouble for that, but I'm okay now."

"I'm not coming back home, Debbie. I can't take no more whoopings!"

"What? Where are you going to go?"

"I got somewhere to go."

"Ooooh, you bought everybody some new gym shoes with Papa's money. What you gonna give me since I got in trouble for you?"

"Here's $20.00. Now you gonna tell on me, tell that you saw me?"

"Nah, you don't have to ever worry about me ever telling on you. You are my little brother and I don't want you to get in trouble. Remember we pinky-sweared."

"Yeah, I do. Do it again." We put our pinky fingers out to do the pinky swear.

"I promise, Chuckie, I will never tell on you and you promise me that you are not going to get in trouble out here." We both agreed to our pinky-swear as brother and sister. From that point on, we had a bond that no one could come between.

"Tell me where you gonna be so when Nana cook, I can sneak you some food." He told me where he was going to be hiding.

"I got to go, he said."

"Be careful, Chuckie, and whatever you do, don't let Uncle Tom catch you." I went on to tell Chuckie quickly how he had put a gun to my head and all of that stuff.

"Give me a hug. I love you. Be careful. See you soon," I said. I hugged and kissed my little brother on his cheek. We went our separate ways, looking back at each other with tears in our eyes until we turned the corner.

The next time I heard from my brother was when my Mommie said Chuckie was in the jail for bad boys for trying to steal a car. He had to do 6 months and he was only eleven years old.

I was so sad that my brother was gone. He promised me that he was not gonna get in trouble.

My uncle told my mother, "That's good for him. Let his little ass sit in jail for a while. He'll be alright. It's gonna either break him or make him."

Well, if I know my brother, it surely was not going to break him- - whatever that meant! The house became so lonely without my little brother being there. I didn't have anybody to play with, anybody to tease. The months went by so slowly.

Section 54

The child my uncle denied

So, much stuff happened in just those few months that my brother was gone, things that I only want to touch on and share briefly, and others go into more detail.

My mother started drinking even more beer after Chuckie left. Sometimes when she ran out of beer, she would drink gin or vodka. My uncle was still beating up on his wife, cheating with different women at Nana's house, drinking on the weekends and kicking my ass.

Uncle Tom would drink Michelob beer or some wine. He would tell my mother that she should try this good wine, go into details of where the wine come from, what year it was bottled and all that kind of stuff.

I tried my best to stay out of his sight. I came home when the street lights came on, and not before, and go straight upstairs to Nana's room to watch TV. When I heard him coming up the stairs, I would go to my bedroom.

There was a short timeframe when he and Auntie Janice moved out, but ended up moving right back.

I came to realize that my uncle thought he knew everything and what he said was law, when half the time he didn't know shit. He just liked to run his damn mouth all the time.

My mother was smarter than he was because he used to always ask her what she thought about this or that, like he was getting her advice or some type of approval. Yet, she just didn't have enough sense to stop her brother from 'disciplining' her children. Why would she? That way she didn't have to be bothered with us.

I always wondered why Uncle Tom didn't have his own damn kids to beat on. He would tell my Mommie all of his secrets. I would hear him tell her that Auntie Janice couldn't have children.

I even heard them talking about one of his girlfriends telling him that he had a child. He said that he ran into that lady one day and she told him that she had had a baby girl and it was his.

He did not want Janice to find out. Man, he would curse up a storm, "That ain't none of my damn kid! That bitch is lying! What if Janice finds out, then there goes some more damn bullshit!" They were playing Chess at the time and my mother told him, "You need to go ahead and tell Janice. What the woman is asking is that you need to try to be a part of the little girl's life."

He would raise so much hell I thought that he was going to get into a fight with my mother. She would say calmly, while sipping on her glass of beer, "That's your damn business. Do as you please, but you need to do the right thing."

Oh. This means he cheated on Auntie Janice and the truth came out with a baby. I knew his ass was going to get caught. This happened long time ago based on what they were discussing.

He said he didn't want to have anything to do with the child. My mother tried to make him see that he should be a part of that child's life.

My mother and Nana would talk about him whenever he was not at home, so I got a chance to hear all that stuff. I'd be washing the dishes and taking it all in.

"Hurry up, Debbie, and get through washing those damn dishes and stop being so nosey. You better not go back and say a word about what me and your Nana is talking about."

"I'm not."

Hell, I just wanted to hear them say something about him spending more time with his daughter, then maybe he'd stop whipping my ass and whip on his own kid. I just didn't want him kicking my ass all the time.

It's been on my mind for a while now that we, my brother and I, are not his children. What gives him the right to put his hands on us the way that he does? My mother gives him the right! One day I'm going to get him back. My mother was so concerned about his out-of-wedlock child and not even worried about her own children right here with her. Why is that? My brother and I should be more important than what my mother is focus on.

Section 55

In my Nana's bed!

I came home from school for lunch and I didn't know that my mother was home. I ran upstairs and when I got to the top of the stairs, there I saw this naked man lying in my Nana's bed—and it's not my Papa!

I looked with my mouth wide opened! I turned to go in the bathroom because I heard the water running. There my mother was standing there butt naked, washing up! I was so hurt! I screamed at her, "That's why my Daddy and Rob didn't want you!"

I don't know if I was more hurt for the fact that I had just caught my mother naked with some man that I had never seen, or because she had somebody in my Nana's bed! I ran down the stairs before she had a chance to say anything to me.

I ran out of the house and across the street to my friend Nesa's house. I was crying and telling her what had just happen. Nesa went to Parkside with me. She was considered one of the big girls at school because she was so much more mature than Rochelle and me.

It was only just a few years before this that I was sneaking downstairs to get some grapes, knowing that I was not supposed to because they were for

Papa's lunch. If caught, I was in big trouble. When I got half way to the bottom of the stairs, there were naked people all over the floor, including my mother and one of my aunts. They were on top of men kissing and stuff—right there on my Nana's floor!

It made me so mad that my mother would bring different men to my Nana's house, and that my uncle was with all the different women. You would have thought they were running a race.

Between my mother, uncle and even my aunts, they were turning my Nana's house into a weekend-of-pleasure house like you see on TV, you know what they called it.

My Nana would go upstairs around 6:30-7:00 and not come back down for the night. Papa worked nights, so the house was open on the weekends. Maybe because my mother was so pretty that all the men wanted to be around her. They were her drinking friends like Uncle Tom's lady friends were his drinking friends, I guess.

Section 56

Be careful of the men you bring around your daughters!

A few weeks later, my mother had a friend who rode a motorcycle to come by. His name was also Rob. He was light-skinned with a beard and he always wore black leather clothes. It was something about him that was creepy to me. His eyes weren't right or something.

All I know is that every time he would hug my mother, he would look at me and wink his eye. I did not like him at all. I told my mother that he was creepy.

"Why would you say that? He has never said anything to you but 'hello'? Now, has he said anything other than that to you?"

"No, he hasn't."

"Why would you say something like that? Stay in a child's place, Debbie, and keep your mouth shut."

"Okay." Dag! All I said was he looks creepy to me.

A month or two later, one night I came down stairs to ask my mother something and he was in the kitchen drinking with her. He was drinking some liquor called Canadian Mist and my Mommie was drinking her Budweiser beer.

When I walked in the kitchen, he said, "There's my pretty girl," and grabbed me by my waist pulling me closer to him, hugging me and kissing me on my forehead.

I look at my Mommie like I do not like him. Then he pulled out his wallet and said, "Here, let me give you a little something. How are your grades in school? Don't you want a little something for getting good grades?"

"Fine," I said in a low voice.

"You can talk louder than that," and picked up her glass of beer and began to drink.

I eased away from him and stood by my mother so that I could ask her something.

She stood up and said, "Sit down for a minute, Debbie, and wait until I go to the bathroom."

I sat down in the seat she was sitting in, waiting for her to come out of the bathroom. Her friend pulled out a twenty-dollar bill and put it on the table. He looked at me with those creepy eyes, putting his hand on top of mine, leaned across the table and whispered, "When you get big, I'm going to have you."

I jumped up, pulling my hand back and screamed, "No you not!"

When my Mommie came out of the bathroom, I told her what he said to me. My mother turned to him and said, "I know you just didn't do that?"

"Marian, how could you ask me something like that? You know how I am!" He stood up like he was offended by what she had just asked him.

"You see, I just gave Debbie $20.00, trying to be nice to her! That's all! Debbie's is just a kid. She's like my daughter. Please!" He picked up his glass and drank all that was in it. Picked up his bottle and put it in his pocket as if he was going to leave.

My mother turned and looked at me, "Debbie, when are you going to stop lying all the time? He was only trying to be nice to you. Now, go upstairs."

She put her glass of beer on top of $20.00 bill. "You won't be needing this."

I walked away thinking why won't my Mommie ever believe anything I tell her when I'm telling her the truth? I hope his ass have an accident on that damn motorcycle! Drunk, lowdown, dirty bastard!

All I wanted to ask her was could I go to the sock hop at the social center at school tomorrow night.

It was around six months later that I heard my mother in the kitchen on the phone as she was drinking her beer. Rob was killed on Lake Shore Drive. He was drunk while on his motorcycle.

Section 57

Too hot to trot!

I was now in high school now. I met an older boy named Mack and he was a dream come true. It was Mack who going to make me forget all about Patrick and that BS at home. I met him at a pep rally and I was instantly in love with him. I had the hots for him. I walked up to this boy and introduced myself. I told him how sexy and fine I thought he was. Then I ran off with some of my other girlfriends.

89

Two of my best girlfriends were on the pom pom squad and one was a cheerleader. I never made it on anything like that. I tried, but I just didn't cut it. I guess I was too busy looking for the love in all the wrong places.

One morning at school, Mack asked, "Hey, Debra, that's your name right?"

"Yeah," I replied with this curious smile on my face looking into his big beautiful brown eyes.

"Would you like to come over to my house? I live just across the street from the school. I mean, if you are not afraid of coming by yourself, that is?

"I see you with your two girlfriends all the time and just thought that we can get to know each other a little better if we spent time by ourselves."

We attended South Shore High School on 75th in Constance. The remarks I made to Mack at the pep rally must have gotten his attention.

"Sure. When do you want me to stop by? But, wait a minute! Why you want me to come by myself? Ain't nothing gonna happen. You think you're slick," as I laughed.

"Nah, baby, you can bring your friends if you want. I just thought that you wanted to get close with me, to get to know me a little better." He then grabbed my hand spinning me around, pulling me closer to him with his arms wrapped around my waist and looking into my eyes. "I promise you, after the first time, you're not gonna want them to come with you anymore."

"Whatever!" I then pushed him off of me. "When do you want me to come over?"

The next day I told Cookie and Lottie about that boy that I was talking to yesterday. "Did you see him?"

"Yeah, Debra, but he is a junior and you are just a freshman! You know he is too big for you to be messing around with."

"He wants me to come over to his house and it's just right across from the school. Please, you guys come go over there with me so that at least you will know where I am at, okay?" Cookie and Lottie agreed to go with me.

I saw Mack second period, between classes, hanging out under the dome with some other senior guys. I went up to him and asked, "Can I talk to you for a minute?"

"Sure, baby, come over here so we can have a little privacy." He leaned up against the wall and pulled me in front of him holding me by my waist. "What can I do for you, Ms. Debra, with your pretty self, looking at me smiling?"

I told him my girlfriends agreed to stop by your house with me. So the question was when did he want us to stop by?

"You can come over during your lunch period today if you want. I just want to get you over there and spend some time with you. I want to show you something that you never seen before."

"Oh yeah, and what is that?" He put his hands so gently on the side of my face and kissed me in a way that I had never been kissed before. I heard the school bell ring and stopped the kiss.

"I'll see you there." I walked away looking at him like I had just fallen in love.

"Hey, Debra, there's a lot more where that came from. You'll see." I smiled and ran back into the school.

My girlfriends and I finished our lunch and decided to go to Mack's house. I remember he told me he lived right across the street and it was in the Manor subdivision.

When we got to the door and rang the doorbell, he opened the door with a smile. "Come in."

When we walked into the front room and he told Cookie and Lottie to have a seat. He grabbed my hand and led me into the kitchen. "I want to ask you something." I looked back at my girlfriends with this huge smile.

When we got in the kitchen, he said, "Debra, I want you to be my girl as he picked me up and kissed me. He was holding me ever so tight as I put my arms around him and just followed his kiss. I really didn't know how to kiss, but I did whatever he was doing to me.

He eased me down on top of the kitchen table and stepped between my legs. "What do you say? Do you want to be my girl?"

I looked at him and said, "Yeah I do, but do you know how old I am?"

He said it didn't matter to him. All he knew was that he wanted me to be his girl.

"Mack, I'll be your girl."

That's when I could hear Cookie and Lottie calling out, "Debra, it's time to go! We got to go! We gonna be late getting back to school."

"Mack, I'll see you tomorrow," as I went to walk away from him. "Here I come," I yelled back to my friends.

"Debra, wait!" He placed my hand on his penis so that I could feel how big and hard he was.

"Stop!" pulling my hand back. "What's wrong with you!"

"Baby, this is what you do to me."

Section 58

Seek and you will find.

"I will see you tomorrow, Mack."

"Come over here during your lunch period and come by yourself, okay?"

"Okay, Mack. I'll be back." I gave him a quick peck on the lips as I ran out the door to catch up with my girlfriends headed back to school. I told them what had happen. I was in unbelief. Cookie warned, "You are going to get in trouble if you mess around with that boy. He is too old for you." Lottie said that he seemed to be sneaky and too slick for me.

"Yeah, that he may be, but he is fine as hell. You got to give it to him."

"He is that," Cookie said.

"Plus, how can you'll call him sneaky or slick and you don't even know him? Anyway, I'm going over to his house tomorrow."

When school was out, I had to walk home for about eight to ten blocks, so all I thought about was this boy. I could not wait until morning came! You couldn't tell me anything! I was just coming out of grammar school, starting my freshman year and one of the finest boys, a junior at that, wants me to be his girlfriend. Really! I thought that it no longer mattered that Patrick did not want me—and that Piggie talk too damn much—because now somebody else does want me.

That made me feel so good that somebody wanted me, even though at home I was being told that I was nothing and that I was ugly and so skinny, in addition to being a whore and a bitch.

I did not know how to tell Nana what was going on with me. I didn't want her to be disappointed in me. I had already made it up in my mind that if he wanted to have sex with me in the morning. I was going to do it.

I looked at it like this: It is going to be the first time I have sex. The other time didn't count because that boy was so nasty and he didn't put it in. I got scared and pushed him off me.

That was some time ago and now that I have met Mack and he is different. He is not nasty and his house is so clean, just the way my Nana keeps her house. I am kinda of scared, but when lunch period comes at school tomorrow, I am going to ask him a lot of questions. I'm not just going to pull my panties down—no way! Not after that ass whooping my mother gave me!

Anyway, by the time I got home, Nana was on her way home from work, so I made sure that the kitchen was clean. All I could think about was this boy Mack.

I went upstairs in my room and got my outfit out and laid it on my bed. This is what I was going to wear for school in the morning. I made sure that I laid out brand new, matching panties and bra. Just in case my clothes come off, my Nana said you must always have on clean underwear and socks in case of an accident or an emergency.

I heard the front door and it was my Nana. I ran downstairs to help her with her bags; she always had bags to bring in when she came home from work.

As I helped Nana, she stopped and watched me for a while. "What's going on with you, Debbie?"

"What? I'm okay."

"You sure you don't want to talk to me about anything?"

"No, I'm okay. Why you ask me that, Nana?"

"Because I know you, Debbie, that's why."

"Well, Nana, it is something that I wanted to say," as I grabbed the kitchen chair and sat down with this grin on my face.

Then I heard the front door open again. It was my mother.

"I'll talk to you later, Nana." I got up from the table and looked into her eyes to let her know I did not want my mother to hear our conversation.

"Okay, we'll talk later."

"Thank you, Nana." She reached to give me a hug and a kiss.

"I love you, Debbie. Be careful."

I eased up the stairs quickly, taking two steps at a time. I didn't want my mother to hear me running. I went in Nana's room and got down on the floor and turned on the television. Bewitched, one of my favorite shows, was on.

Mommie came upstairs to go to her room to put her purse and stuff away. I got up and went into her room.

"Hey, Mommie. You look pretty today. You have a hard day?"

"Hey, Debbie, what you been doing today?

"I ain't been doing nothing. Just watching TV in Nana's room. That's all."

"Oh, okay, just making sure you stay out of trouble. Anything happen at school today that I should know about?"

"No, nothing happened today." I asked Mommie could I give her a kiss and I went back into Nana's room. She didn't like to be bothered too much when she first got home. She always had to unwind, drink her 40 oz. and talk to Nana for a while before Uncle Tom got in from work.

I was kinda nervous when my mother asked me if anything happen at school today. How did she know? My mother always told me that she knew all, that anything I ever did would always come back to her, and that she had eyes in the back of her head.

Well, I knew that she would never know what I did or what I was going to do. I'll make sure of that, I thought as I watched television. I could hardly wait to see Mack the next day. That was the longest night ever, but when daylight came, it was time to go to school.

Section 59

He caressed my body first.

I went to some of my classes that morning. As I stood at my locker, Mack came up from behind me and said, "Come on and go with me."

"Wait, I got a class that I got to go to," still letting him pull me by the hand.

When Mack saw that I was really holding back, he stopped and came up to me and looked into my eyes, "Debra, I couldn't stop thinking about you all night long."

"Me, too. I couldn't stop thinking about you, either."

"Come on and go to my place with me. My mother and father is not there. We will have the house to ourselves for the whole morning." He went on saying how much he wants to show me that he cares about me.

I gave in and said, "Okay, come on, let's go."

He held my hand all the way to his house. Every now and then, he would stop and began to kiss me right in public, holding me so tight and very close to him.

He said he wanted the whole world to know how much he loved me. As we got closer to his house, those tingly feelings were all over the place. I was feeling it from the bottom of my feet to the tip of my fingers.

When we finally got to his house, he stopped at the door and asked, "Are you sure you want me as much as I want you?" He then picked me up and started kissing me on my stomach.

"Yes, I do. Put me down," I laughed. "But, I need to tell you something."

He put his finger to my mouth and said, "Shhh, it's okay. I already know. Come on, let me take you in the house. He carried me inside. As he eased me down, he placed his hands on my face.

"Debra, I love you," he said repeatedly, kissing me all over my face. "Let me show you now."

"Wait, Mack, wait a minute." I sat down on the foot of the bed and I told him to listen. "I got something to tell you."

He got down on his knees right between my legs and said, "What is it, baby? What you want to tell me?"

I looked at him with tears in my eyes, "I really never did it before. I mean, I'm scared. I want to, but it might hurt me real bad."

"Don't worry, I promise I won't hurt you. I'll never hurt you." His voice was so gentle and soft.

He took my hand and began to kiss me, "Just lie down and don't do anything."

I got in the middle of the bed and I laid there as he told me. He eased on top of me, kissing me on my legs, my thighs, stomach—all the way up until he reached my mouth. I could feel the hardness of his penis rubbing against my vagina as he grinded on top of me. It was a feeling that I really never felt before.

I liked the way he was making me feel. I moved with him and held him so tight only because he was holding me tight. I didn't know what to do, so I just flowed with his motions.

He got up and took off his shirt and pants, and stood there holding his hand out for me to stand up with him. I could see his penis bulging out of his underwear; I had never seen a penis before—not really, not in person and not up close to me, not like this.

That first encounter that I had with that nasty boy, it was dark in that room, so I never saw him at all. Mack began to kiss me as he unbuttoned my blouse and unfasten my bra. He then began to kiss me on my breast, then back up to my mouth. He began to unfasten my shorts and pulled them down. I stood there in my underwear with my hands on his shoulders.

"Let me look at you," as he stepped back a step or two. I stood there looking as though I was shamed and he saw that in my eyes as I dropped my head.

Mack walked up to me, "You got the most beautiful body that I have ever seen. You are my baby. Look at you. You look so good to me and I want you so bad." We kissed some more. By, that time I was wondering what all he was doing and why didn't he just get back in the bed with me and for us to do it.

He said, "This is your first time. I want you to always remember this day. So, come on let me help you take your bra off." He reached behind me and unfastened my bra. His hands went down the sides of my body so gently, down into my panties as they fell to the floor.

At that point I thought I was ready. There I was standing naked in his mother's bedroom! He took off his underwear. *Oh, my God! I had never seen a penis so big, hard or long like that before! Hell, I had never seen a penis!*

I almost went into a panic thinking all of that was not going to fit inside of me. It looked like it was going to hurt. Still, I wanted to try it with him. He said that he wouldn't hurt me.

"Come on, Debra, let's take a shower together."

What? I ain't never done nothing like this before? Do girls supposed to take showers with boys? I was curious to try this with him.

"I can't get in the shower with you. I'll get my hair wet and I just got it done." He laughed and gave me a shower cap.

"If your hair gets messed up, I'll perm it back for you, or pay to get it fixed. Whatever you want, Debra. Baby, you can do whatever you want with me. I just want to be the first to do it with you so that you will know how beautiful this is going be and should be."

He was so gentle with me. He washed my body with his hands—touching and rubbing every part of my body. He never took his eyes off of me, telling me how beautiful I was and how he wanted to make me feel good.

He smiled and placed the soap in my hand for me to wash his body. "I want to feel your hands rub me down," as he moved my hand over his soapy body. *The steam in that shower was so hot!*

I washed his body while he looked me in my eyes. When I got down to his penis, I went all around it, not sure of what to do. He placed his hand on mine and slowly moved my hand down on his penis. We were staring at each other the whole while.

"I want you to rub me, feel how hard I am for you. This is how bad I want you. This is how you turn me on."

I smiled and caressed his penis as he showed me. He let go of my hand and put his soapy body next to mine and we kissed even more—down on my neck, down to my breast, my stomach and down on my vagina. He kissed me on my vagina! The feelings that went through my body were unexplainable.

He rinsed off our bodies and we stepped out of the shower. He wrapped a towel around me and led me back to the bed.

He grabbed a sheet out of the linen closet, spreading it over the bed. "Come, lay down, baby. I want to rub your body down with oil."

Section 60

The very first time

"Are you making this stuff up as you go, or have you done this before?"

"Nah, baby, this is all new to me, too. Just like it's the first for you, it's the first for me and I'm glad that it's with you. Now lay back and relax. I want you to feel the love that I am trying to give you."

He began to rub my feet and kiss my toes and my ankles! What in the world is he doing to me, as these feelings were rising up inside of me! I was feeling tingles that I never felt before!

He kissed the inner side of my thighs, and before you knew it, we were making love. I didn't know that sharing your body with someone could ever be like this. *He was gentle, patient and so passionate with me that I felt no pain.*

He held me so tight and he whispered in my ear the whole while we were making love, "I love you, Debra. Easy baby, take your time. I love you. Do this, turn this way."

He guided me sweetly through the whole experience. We had baby oil all over our bodies, slipping and sliding on each other for about two hours straight, none stop.

Mack was doing things to me and showing me how to please him in ways I had never imagined. Something that I would have called nasty, he turned it into something so good and beautiful. When I was unsure and didn't know what to do, he took his time and showed me just what and how to do it. He was wonderful. There was so much passion between the both of us that the sweat on are bodies became like oil on top of water.

Oh! I am in love, in love with Mack. Truly my Nana was right about Patrick was just a puppy love. But this, right here, is LOVE.

We took another shower when we were done sharing ourselves with each other. It was time for me to go home. School had let out about 20 minutes ago.

"How did you feel? Are you pleased? Did I hurt you at all?"

"Yes, I feel real good. I never knew being with someone could feel so good. Let me say that in a different way: Being with you made me feel so loved, and no, you did not hurt me, not at all." I kissed him, saying, "I love you, Mack, I love you."

He helped me to get dress, all the time telling me how much he loved me.

Section 61

I'm in it for the long haul.

"Are you going to come back tomorrow? I want you to."

100

"Yes, I will be here," thinking to myself *you know I will be back.* "I will come during my lunch break, that's okay?"

"How about you come just before school in the morning and during your lunch break?" He kissed me with this big smile on his face. "I don't want to let you go. Did you feel how we are meant for each other?"

"Yeah, I did, Mack. I did feel that."

"Come on, baby, I know you got to go." We kissed each other and I headed to the door. "Wait a minute. I want to walk you home and meet your family. I want them to know how much you mean to me."

"Umm, wait. Let's wait before you meet with my family. I got a different kind of family and I want to make sure that it is the right time for you to meet with them, but you can walk me home, at least to the corner of my block. Do you understand? I mean, is that okay with you?"

I didn't want Mack to meet my uncle and hear him call me names. I would be so embarrassed.

Mack walked me to my house. He even stopped at the corner liked I asked him. I showed him where I lived and he said in due time he would meet my family. He kissed me right there on the corner. I pushed back and said, "No, what if somebody sees us?"

"I don't care, do you? I know what I want and I want you."

Looking around, I replied, "I want you, too, but if my mother catches me kisses you on the corner, or if some nosey neighbor or my mean ass uncle sees us, I'm gonna get my butt kicked."

"Oh no, baby, I can't have anybody putting their hands on you! Are you telling me that's what's going on at your house?" Just as he hugged me, my uncle pulled up in front of the house. There I was in plain view.

"Mack, there he is! That's my uncle. He just pulled up in that brown and black Camaro. I am going to get in so much trouble." He saw the fear in my eyes.

"Come on," as he began to walk toward my house holding my hand. I was in shock! I just followed his lead and walked with him.

We walked up on the porch and Mack sat down on the chair. I knew it was over for me, that my uncle was going to curse me out right in front of Mack. But, when my uncle came up to the house, Mack stood up and said, "My name is Mack and I am Debra's friend. Are you her father? He held his hand out to shake.

"No, I'm her uncle, and what did you say your name was?"

"Mack, my name is Mack Nelson, and it is a pleasure to meet you, sir. I look forward in meeting her whole family soon."

With this grin on his face, Uncle Tom said, "Oh, yeah, a gentleman. Okay." He went in the house.

I couldn't believe what had just happen! I looked at Mack and said, "You are good! You are real good! Thank you. Now, go ahead. I'll see you in the morning."

"In the morning, before school." He quickly gave me a kiss and smiled, "Yeah, I'll see you before school starts.

Mack walked on and I just stood there watching him walk away. He is so fine. He stands about 5'9" and weighs about 160. He is slim, but has a firm body with wide shoulders and strong arms. Those very arms picked me up and held me so tight. His complexion is light-skinned and has very keen figures—with just the right size lips. His eyes, oooooh, those eyes! Big as buttons, dark brown with long eyelashes! He even had dimples. He worn a perm in his hair that he kept up himself. Every strand of his hair was in the right place.

Section 62

Get a life and stay out of mine!

The door opened. "Debbie, come in the damn house! Come here!" yelled Uncle Tom. "Who is that slick ass nigga you got coming over here? Where did you meet that little punk?"

"What?"

"Don't what me, dammit! You heard me! Don't you be bringing no off-the-street, motherfucking niggas over here! Do you hear me?" He was screaming and pointing his finger in my face.

By that time, the front door opened and it was Nana coming in the house. Tom turned around and went back into the kitchen.

I went upstairs to the room to watch TV. I do not know why he wants to call Mack out of his name like that and he doesn't even know him. Mack was really being nice to him. I will be so glad when I get big enough to get out of this house!

"Debbie, Debbie," Nana called for me.

"Yes, Nana, here I come," running down the stairs.

"Stop that motherfucking running before I whoop your ass," said Uncle Tom.

Before I knew it, I said, "Dag, I can't do nothing right in this house!" He jumped up and Nana said, "Wait one damn minute! What the hell is going on? Leave her alone, Tom! I called her down here to do something for me! Wipe your eyes, Debbie. He ain't gonna lay one hand on you. I just got home from work and I am tried. Don't feel like this bullshit!"

Uncle Tom got up from the table. "Okay, Mama," and he walked out of the kitchen.

"What's wrong with him, Debbie? What did you do?"

"I didn't do nothing." I told her about what happened with Mack.

"Well, I need to meet him, so have him to come tomorrow when I get off work. Ain't this some shit? Now I need you to help me put this food up and peel these potatoes for dinner."

"Okay, Nana."

Shortly after that, Uncle Tom came into the kitchen and told Nana that he would be back he had an errand to make.

I sat there quietly, peeling the potatoes after I had put the groceries up for Nana. I was thinking about what Mack and I did today, and it brought nothing but joy to my heart.

Nana went upstairs to change her clothes. I stopped and called Mack, hoping that he would have made it home by now, but he hadn't. His mother answered the phone.

"Hello, my name is Debra. How are you? May I speak to Mack, please?"

Section 63

I'm smelling myself and you can't tell me nothing!

"Well, this is Mrs. Nelson, Mack's mother and he isn't in at the time. Would you like to leave your number?"

"No, ma'am. Will you tell him that I called? Thank you."

"Well, Miss Debra, you have such a sweet voice. When am I going to get the opportunity to meet you?"

I smiled and said, "I will ask Mack to bring me by so that I can meet with you. Thank you."

"Okay, I look forward to meeting you. Goodbye."

Wow! I just talked to his mother, and she wants to meet me. My Nana wants to meet him. This is great! I sat there and continue to peel the potatoes like Nana told me. I smiled and began to picture us in the shower and didn't hear Nana come in the kitchen.

"What are you daydreaming about now, Debbie?"

"Oh, huh, nothing. I'm not daydreaming about nothing."

She sat down, looking at me. "Oh, yeah? Look at me for one minute, Debbie."

I raised my head to look Nana in her eyes. She said, "Hum huh, tell me a little more about this boy named Mack. Does he go to school with you?" I couldn't keep the smile off my face when I spoke of him, and my eyes were gleaming like I was in a daze.

Nana asked, "Debbie have you been with this boy? Don't lie to me because I already know that you have."

"How you know, Nana?"

"Oh, so you have been with him. Lord, help her."

"You gonna tell Mommie on me?"

"No, Debbie I just need for you to be honest with me.

"Okay, Nana, I will."

"Before you say anything else, I want to meet him, okay?"

"Okay, he'll be over tomorrow? What about Uncle Tom?"

"Don't worry about him. He won't be here. He got an appointment after work and so does your mother."

I got up and gave her a hug and a kiss. "Okay, Nana, I love you."

The rest of that day went really well—no more name calling. I did what Nana wanted and went upstairs to watch television. I couldn't wait to see him in the morning. I went to the bathroom. Just as I sat down, the phone rang and Nana yelled up the stairs for me, "Telephone!"

"I'm coming out the bathroom. Here I come. Is it him?" She didn't answer, so I hurriedly washed my hands and ran down stairs. I knew it was him because I heard her say, "I look forward to meeting you."

Nana smile and handed me the phone. I asked her could I take the call up in her bedroom. I ran upstairs and yelled back when I had picked it up.

"Hello, this Debra."

"Hey, baby, this is Mack. My mother told me you called. Is everything alright?"

Section 64

We are a family.

"Everything is fine. Guess what? My grandmother wants to meet you tomorrow. Is that okay with you?"

"Hey, baby, I told you that I wanted to meet your family. What we will do is when I see you in the morning and during your lunch break—," reminding me of our plans with a little laugh. After school, you come over here. My mother should be home early and you will get to meet her. Then I will walk you home to meet your grandmother. How do that sound?"

"That sounds good, just like you sound good over the phone. I sound good to you, Mack?"

"Yep, you do. You gonna show me how good I sound when you see me in the morning?"

"Yeah, I am."

"So, I will see you then, okay? What are you gonna do now, Debra?"

"Oh, just watch some television and get myself ready to see you in the morning."

"Okay, then I will talk to you later. I love you, Debra."

"I love you, too, Mack. Goodbye."

I'll be so glad when the morning comes. I want to be with him again, I thought as I lay on the floor watching television.

A few hours had past and my mother was home. I must have dozed off. She peeked into my room and asked, "Debbie, are you sleep?"

"Huh? No, I'm not sleep. Hey, Mommie," and I got up to go into her room.

"What in the hell happen to your head?" I looked at her then touch my hair and said I took a shower after gym and I got it wet.

"Well, you gonna have to wear your head like that for the next two weeks until you go back to the shop. That is money wasted, down the drain! If you cannot take your shower at school without getting your hair wet then I will no longer be getting your hair done. Do you hear me talking to you?"

"Yeah, I hear you." I walked back into Nana's room. Once my mother changed her clothes, she went back downstairs. I went back to my room and lay across the bed. I was so tired.

The next morning finally came. I went over to Mack's house early like we said, around 7:45a.m. We were so happy to see each other! We began doing the oochy-coochy again like it was the very first time.

When we finished, we went to school. On my lunch break, we went back to his house and started all over again. I did meet his mother and he met my Nana. That turned out really great on both ends. I was so pleased that his mother liked me and that my Nana liked him.

So life was grand for me at that time. Mack and I went on like this for about six weeks straight. It was so much fun being with him. We loved sharing ourselves with each other. We went through his whole house—every bedroom, living room, dining room, kitchen, back room, every floor. We were even in the garage.

Section 65

A true spirit of joy and happiness

In the sixth week or so, I noticed that I was getting tired all the time. I wanted to sleep and began craving certain types of food, mostly fruit. More importantly, I had missed my period. I had been going home after school and lying down, staying out of my Uncle Tom's way.

I told Mack that I had missed my period and that I was afraid I might be pregnant. He was so happy! I mean, he jumped for joy! I was not so sure. I was afraid of what my mother was going to say.

"Debra, do you think you are?" asked Mack.

"I'm not sure, Mack."

"Well, I hope that you are! Yes! We are going to have a baby!" He picked me up and swirled around like a crazy man.

"Mack, are you sure you want to have a baby with me?"

"Yes, if you do! What? You don't want to have a baby?"

"Yes, I want to have a baby. I got to make sure that I am pregnant first. Okay, come here and sit down so we can talk."

As he held me by the hand, "Debra, there is a Family Plan Parenthood Clinic right around the corner on 75th in Jeffery and we can go there in the morning. It's free and they will not tell your mother. I will go with you. Now, how does that sound to you?"

"Well, Mack, if you go with me, then, yeah, I'll go." Later that day, Mack was walking me home and we saw Cookie, Rochelle and Lottie. They all complained, "We don't see you no more since you started hanging out with Mack!"

Mack laughed. "This is my baby. Who else she gonna be with? She's not looking for a man. She got one," as he put his arms around my waist, and we walked off.

Mack and I talked all the way to my house about what if I was pregnant. He said that his mother would be so happy. That we would not want for anything for the baby.

"What time are we going to go to that clinic in the morning?" I asked.

"We are going to be the first ones there. They open at 7:45. Do you think you can get up and be here by then? Do you want me to meet you?"

"Yeah, that's what I'll do. I'll meet you on your way to my house. Just walk straight down Jeffery and you'll see me. Mack, do you want a girl or a boy?"

"I want for you to be okay and a healthy baby. It does not matter to me, girl or boy. I have to make sure you eat right and everything. You know this right?"

He looked at me with those big, pretty brown eyes. I didn't know how he was going to react if I was pregnant. I'm only thirteen years old and he's a week from being seventeen.

"Oh, you gonna take care of me?" I asked.

"Yeah, if you are pregnant. Yes, I will take very good care of you." He stopped. "Don't you doubt for one minute that I will not be here for you. We are in this together. You did not get this way by yourself, so you will not be by yourself. Okay?" He kissed me.

"Okay, Mack."

We got to my house and I thanked him for walking me home. "I love you. See you tomorrow."

"Hey, Debra, you know I love you even more." Mack looked at me with a serious face and said, "I don't need you to worry about anything. Don't tell nobody until we are sure and I will be with you when you tell your mother. I will tell her. We will be together." Then he kissed me again.

"Okay, Mack, I won't tell."

I went in the house. I was so nervous. I wanted to tell my Nana, but I was afraid. Nana was in the kitchen cooking. I sat down at the table and we began to talk.

"What's going on with you, Debbie?"

"Nothing, Nana."

"You been by Mack's house today?"

"Yeah, I went by there."

"How's he doing?"

"Oh, Mack is doing fine, he walked me home."

"I see you really like each other. That's good, Debbie. You know, I really like Mack. He's a good boy."

"Nana, I really like him, too." All of a sudden, it felt like I had to throw up. I ran to the bathroom and began to vomit.

"Debbie, you okay?"

"I don't know, Nana. I mean, yeah, I'm okay."

"Yeah, you are pregnant. That's what's wrong with you."

I rinsed out my mouth out and went back to the kitchen. I laid my head down on table. "How you know, Nana?"

"Debbie, your Nana has had eight children. Remember when Nana told you she had those twins and they died?"

"I remember you telling me that."

"Well, I know you more than you know yourself. When are you going to tell your mother?"

Section 66

We're having a baby.

"Me and Mack are going to the Family Plan Parenthood clinic in the morning to take the pregnancy test. Then I'll know. Mack said that he was going to be with me to tell Mommie. What you think she's going to say if I am pregnant?"

"Well, Debbie we will cross that bridge when we get there. Don't worry. Everything is going to be alright," as she came over to me with a hug and a kiss.

110

We heard the front door open. "Hurry up and go upstairs, Debbie. Lie down and rest yourself. I'll tell your mother you're coming down with a bug. Go to your room, hurry up now."

I ran upstairs and went straight to my room like Nana told me. I felt so sick! I wanted to call Mack to tell him how I was feeling.

I just lay there, thinking about what if I am pregnant, what I am going to do. I was kinda scared, but like Mack said, we will be together and he would not leave me. I put my hands over my stomach, "I'll have a baby of my very own and I will love this baby. I will not call my baby out of its name and I will hug and kiss my baby all the time. I could even get a job cleaning somebody house since I'm too young to work at McDonald's."

My mother would be home soon. I didn't know if that was her or not that came in the house. Then that's when I heard my mother's voice coming up the stairs, "Okay, Mama," talking to Nana.

I just lay there, afraid to say anything. I didn't know if she was going to know I was pregnant like Nana did. Mommie came in my bedroom. "Mama said you didn't feel good, that you were coming down with the bug. How you feel? Let me see if you got fever." She felt forehead.

"Nah, you not with fever. Just lay down, you'll be okay. You probably got something from school. I heard that the bug was going around."

"Probably so. Okay, Mommie, I'll just lay here."

"Yeah, you do that. You will be alright. I will be up here to see about you later on."

I turned over and pulled the blanket over me. I just wanted to go to sleep. Soon after Mommie went downstairs, Nana came to my room and asked me how did I feel and did I want anything.

"Can I have a peanut butter and jelly sandwich and some orange juice, Nana?"

"Yeah, just continue to stay in your room and I will bring it to you." When Nana came back with my sandwich, she whispered, "When you and that boy go to that place in the morning and find out, I want the both of you to be here by six o'clock. I will be back from the hair dressers by then. I want to make sure I am here when you tell your mother." She placed her hand on my forehead, "Lord keep her."

She continued, "Okay, Debbie, we'll be here by the time you get home. Now, you eat that and get some rest. Nana loves you and everything is going to be alright, you hear me?" She leaned over giving me a kiss and a hug.

I ate my sandwich and went to sleep. Throughout the night, I got up a couple of times to use the bathroom. I think I was just nervous about going to that place in the morning.

Well, today is the day, as I woke up. Today I will see if I'm pregnant.

I woke up feeling happy. I realized that I wanted to have Mack's baby. I wanted to be pregnant. I got myself cleaned up and hurried and got dress to leave the house. Whenever I got up for school, there would not be anybody home. Everybody would have left for work already.

I started walking toward 71st in Jeffery and when I got on 71st street, Mack was coming up the street already. He was coming to my house to get me. I smiled and ran to him. "I thought you said you were going to meet me? You didn't say you were coming to my house. You walked all the way here."

"Hey, baby, I didn't want you walking by yourself, thinking all kinds of crazy stuff, so I just got up a little earlier and decided to meet you here," and he put his arms around me, giving me a kiss. "Good morning, baby, how you feel?"

"I feel fine, how about you? Did you get any sleep last night?"

"Well, to be honest, I didn't. I know that you are pregnant and I want them to tell us, so I'll know what I have to do."

We walked and talked. I told him how I felt yesterday after he had walked me home. "Why didn't you call me? I would have come right back, you know that."

"Yeah, but remember, you said don't tell nobody."

"Oh, yeah, I did. I told my mother that you might be pregnant. She is waiting to hear the outcome of what the clinic is going to say."

"You told your mother? What she say? She is happy?"

He kissed me. "Well, here we are. Let's go in and find out if we are going to have a baby."

Yes, ma'am. You are pregnant. You are about five weeks along." Mack jumped up screaming, "Yes! Yes! We are going to have a baby!" He grabbed me, "I love you, Debra! I love you! We are going to have a baby!" as he kissed my stomach.

"Wow! A baby is inside of me," I said out loud. A real baby! I am holding life inside of me as I felt my stomach. "Wow, Mack. I love you, too! We are going to have a baby!"

The lady who gave me the test laughed at Mack's reactions to the news, "We know who is happy!" He kissed me over and over again, telling me how happy he was and how happy his mother was going to be. I just listened at him, smiling, but wondering on the inside how my mother was going to take this news.

They gave me prenatal vitamins and told me about a doctor and all that stuff, and what I had to do. Mack was right there listening at everything she was telling me. "Yes, yes," he keep on saying as the lady was talking.

Section 67

We all welcomed the baby.

We went to Mack's house for the rest of the day. "Come on, Debra let's lay across the bed. You got up early, so you need to rest." He lay next to me

113

and called his mother to tell her the news. He put me on the phone with her, "I am so happy that you are going to have my grandchild! I will make sure that you have everything that you need for the baby!"

She asked if I had told my mother yet. "No, ma'am. I have not. We are going to do that today." Mack talked to his mother saying we are going to need everything for the baby.

"I don't want Debra to want for anything while she is carrying my child." He answered Okay! Right! and Yes! to whatever his mother was saying.

When he got off the phone, we talked about a lot of stuff. He said that we were going to get an apartment together. His dad was a policeman and they had property. We would be able to live in one of the apartments.

"I didn't know that your dad was a policeman."

"Yeah, remember I told you that?"

"Oh, yeah, you did. So, he got an apartment building and we can live in one together?"

"No, I have property in my name. It's my building, and, yes, we can live in it together, only if you want to."

"Mack, I am thirteen and I won't be fourteen for another seven months. My mother is not going to let me move in with you."

"Well, when you have the baby, we will talk about it then. Don't worry about that now. We have lots of time to talk about that." He began rubbing my body, telling me how beautiful I was and how much I turned him on. We began to make love, and every time we do, it feels like it's our first time. The passion between us is unbelievable, so genuine and magical.

We both took a nap, and soon it was time to go home and face the music. I knew I was not going to get a response like Mack did from his mother. I just didn't know what to expect. It was 6:15p.m, so Nana should be home now.

On the way to my house, Mack told me. "No matter what, Debra, I want you to know that I love you and our baby. You don't have to worry about anything, okay? You believe in me, don't you?"

"Yes, Mack, I do believe in you."

When we went into the kitchen, Nana, my mother and Uncle Tom was sitting at the table. Mack held my hand the whole time.

"Hey, Mack!" Nana greeted. She knew from the look on my face. "Come on in and have a seat. What are you and Debbie up to?" She turned to Uncle Tom and told him that she needed something from the store and she wanted him to go and get it.

My mother said, "Have a seat, Mack." She then went to the bathroom.

Uncle Tom said, "Mama, I was just gonna drink me a beer. Get Debbie to go. She just got here."

"Tom, I need for you to go. Debbie needs to talk to her mother. Now, here." as she reached in her duster pocket, gave him some money and sent him on.

Section 68

Guess what, Mommie?

My mother came out of the bathroom. Tom had left the kitchen.

"Debbie, what do you have to talk to me about?" She continued to drink her beer.

"Well, Mommie, I, ah, ah," I stammered and stuttered. "I wanted to tell you—…."

Then Mack jumped in, *"Mrs. Dent, I came over here with Debra to tell you that Debra is pregnant and I am the father, and that I am going to take care of our baby. I've already told my mother and she is willing to do*

115

whatever is needed to make sure Debra do not want for anything. We went to Family Plan Parenthood today and got the results and prenatal vitamins. They told us that Debra is five weeks pregnant with my child."

My mother didn't say a word as she continued to drink her beer and refill her glass. Finally, she responded, "Oh, yeah? Well, isn't that something? Debbie is pregnant! Did you hear that, Mama?"

"I heard, but I think that is so nice of Mack to come with Debbie to tell you this. That shows a lot of responsibility on his part and his mother said she would do all she could to help her. I think that is good."

My mother looked at me, "Debbie, what do you have to say for yourself now that you went and got yourself pregnant?"

"Well, Mommie, I'm sorry about this, but, Mack loves me and I love him. We are happy that we are going to have a baby."

"Oh, are you now? What you say?" She lifted her glass of beer to finish it off and went to the refrigerator for another 40oz. It was a Friday, so she had more than one bottle of beer in the fridge.

She told Mack, "Thank you for coming over here with Debbie to tell me that you got her pregnant and how much you all love each other. Now I need to talk to my daughter, so I will show you out and Debbie will get back with you later."

"Bye, Mack, I'll talk to you later. I love you."

"Okay, Debra, call me when you can. Thank you, Mrs. Dent, and thank you, Nana for allowing me to come and be honest with you about my intentions for Debra and our child."

That was that. Mack was gone. I was sitting there waiting on my mother to come back to the kitchen.

"Nana, what you think Mommie is going to say?"

"I don't know, Debbie, we have to wait and see."

Section 69

Getting ready for the new baby

Mommie came back into the kitchen and she just sat there looking at me. Didn't say a word.

"Mommie, I'm going to have a baby and Mrs. Nelson said that I didn't have to worry about anything. She was going to help me with the baby."

She continued to drink her beer. "Oh, yeah? Is that what his mother said? Debbie, you think you did something! Go upstairs with your fast ass! Just go upstairs, get out of my face right now! I will deal with this, you just wait and see!"

I went upstairs like she told me. I gave Mack time to get home and called him to say thanks for being there with me and I how much I love him. I told him that I would try and come over to his house tomorrow afternoon.

"Debra, I love you. What did your mother say?"

"I think she's mad, and she told me to go upstairs, so that's what I did. I mean, I'm pregnant now and it ain't nothing that she can do about it now, right?"

"Nah, it ain't nothing she can do. Love you." We hung up.

A whole week had gone by and my mother had not spoken about me being pregnant. The only person was talking to me was Nana and sometimes Auntie Janice who would make a comment or two. It was all good, at least that's what I thought.

Mack and his mother had gone out and bought everything that I needed for the baby. She made one of the bedrooms into a nursery. I had never seen such a pretty room for a baby. It looked like something you would see in a magazine. She had the room painted and had it completed with everything— Pampers, changing table, a rocker and even stuff animals.

I had told Nana and Auntie Janice what his mother had done. My mother never said anything about it, no more than, "Debbie I do not want to talk about it. I got something for you. Just wait and see."

I never knew what she meant until that second week. My mother said, "Come on, Debbie, get dress and come go with me."

"Where we going, Mommie?"

"Never, mind that. Just come on with me. Uncle Tom and Auntie Janice was coming with us." I should have known that something was wrong because I never went anywhere with them altogether.

I got dress and went downstairs to see Nana, but she was in the bathroom.

"Bye, Nana. I be back. I'm going with Mommie somewhere."

Before Nana got a change to say something to my mother, she continued to rush me. "Come on, Debbie, hurry up! We got to go!"

I got in the backseat of the car with my mother. Everybody was so quiet. I didn't want to say anything because I didn't know if my mother was mad at me, and I didn't want my uncle to start talking crazy to me. So, I just sat in the back looking out the window. We turned into a doctor's office parking lot. It was my mother's doctor.

"What's wrong, Mommie? Why are we at the doctor's? You sick?

"No, Debbie I am not, but the doctor wants to see you regarding this baby you are carrying."

I thought to myself that my Mommie does care. She got me a doctor so I don't have to go the Family Plan Clinic.

We all went into the office and sat down. They call my name and we went to the back of the doctor's office. Auntie Janice went back there with us.

The nurse came in and asked how far long was I and my mother told her that I was about six or seven weeks now. The nurse told her that they needed to do another pregnancy test. My mother said that would be fine.

"Debbie, take this. Go in the bathroom and pee in this cup. The doctor wants to see really how far you are in this pregnancy."

While I was in the bathroom, I heard them talking in the room, but I couldn't make out for sure what they were saying. I came out and gave the cup to my mother who handed it to the nurse.

My mother stepped out of the room and when she returned, the nurse was with her. The nurse told me that the doctor had to examine me and for me to take off my clothes from the waist down. I covered myself with this sheet she gave me.

Section 70

I am your mother! You do what I tell you!

"Why I have to be examined, Mommie? Is something wrong with the baby?" I began to tear up. My mother only responded, "Get undress, Debbie, and lay down on that table."

When the doctor came in the room, my mother stopped him at the door and began to whisper something to him. I was really scared. I thought that they saw something in my pee or something I didn't know.

The doctor said to my mother, "You are going to have to tell her." He walked over to me and asked, "Your name is Debra?"

"Yes. Is something wrong with my baby?"

"Just lay back and relax. I need to see how far along you are."

"What you gonna do? Is my baby okay?" He put on gloves and told me to put my legs up on these things.

"Just be quiet, Debbie," my mother said. "Do what the doctor is telling you to do."

I started to cry. "I want to call Mack, Mommie! Can I call Mack? Please? He will come here and be with me. He is gonna want to know if something is wrong with the baby."

"Now, be still," the doctor said. "I am going to put two of my fingers inside of you and press down on the lower part of your stomach a little bit. It won't hurt."

"Mommie, I don't want to do this! I want Mack here with me!"

Then the doctor put his fingers inside of me and began to press down on my stomach. After he finished examining me, he tossed the gloves and told my mother he'd be back in five minutes.

My mother then told me that I was there to have an abortion! She was not going to be a grandmother and that I was too young to have any children! She said that she was my mother and I was going to do what she say do whether I like it or not! And that was it!

I began to scream and cry, "I don't want no abortion, Mommie! I want my baby! Mack wants his baby, Mommie! Please don't make me do this, Mommie! Can I please call Mack?! Can I call Mack, Mommie, please?!"

She gave me the phone and I dialed his phone number. His mother answered the phone. I began to cry even harder asking for Mack, telling her what my mother was making me do. Mack was not at home and his mother just cried and begged, *"Debra, please don't kill my grandbaby! Don't do it, Debra!"*

"I'm not, I want my baby. My Mommie is making me do this!" My mother grabbed the phone from me, "I am Debra's mother and she is only thirteen years old, too young to be having any damn children! I am not going to be a grandmother! Goodbye!" and hung up the phone.

I cried and pleaded with my Mommie over and over again, but she did not hear anything I was saying to her. Even Auntie Janice said, "Marian, why don't you let Debbie have the baby?"

"This is my daughter and she is not having nobody's baby at thirteen years old! Now, lay down, Debbie, and close your damn mouth before I kick your ass right here in this doctor's office! You thought you did something slick," as she slapped me across the face. "I told you I was going to get your fast ass, didn't I? Now shut your goddamn mouth and when that doctor come in here, you better not say a word! Do you understand me?" she yelled, pointing her finger at me. Auntie Janice left the room.

Section 71

What could I have done?

The doctor came back in the room and asked my mother was everything alright.

"Yes, everything is just fine. We can go on as planned."

I lay there crying, not knowing what to do. I was so afraid. I wished Mack were here to help me! I don't know what to do or say! My Mommie is going to kill our baby! What is Mack going to say? He's not going to love me anymore!

My mother just stood there waiting on the doctor to come back in the room.

"Mommie, I'm scared! Please, Mommie, don't kill my baby! Mommie, please!"

"Shut up, Debbie! Don't let me have to tell you again! You got one more time to open your damn mouth! One more time!"

The doctor walked back in the room. "Now, this will not hurt at all. I need to give you a shot and we can proceed." The doctor stood between my legs and said again, "This won't hurt at all and we'll be done in five minutes."

You could hear a noise like a vacuum cleaner and I could feel something moving inside of my body in my stomach. "We're almost done. Yep, we are just about done."

The tears streamed down my face as I lay there—helpless, crying and dying on the inside. How could I have let my mother do this to me, and why did my mother do this to me?

"Mack!" I cried so deeply for Mack.

The nurse had this container. The doctor had this machine. Next thing you know, it was over and they were giving me something called a D&C. I was no longer pregnant! I let my mother kill my baby! I thought what kind of person am I?!

When we got back home, I went straight to my room and cried. Lying in my bed, I cried for Mack. How was I going to tell him that our baby was dead, that I let my mother kill our baby! I just wanted to die.

All that day and the next, I stayed in my room. I was in so much pain and bleeding a lot. I had never seen that much blood. I thought that I was dying. I told Nana what my mother had done to me. I told her that I would never forgive her for that.

"She killed my baby, Nana," I cried. "My Mommie killed my baby!"

"I know, Debbie, I know," as she sat on the side of by bed and held me in her arms.

"Nana, please, Nana, tell me why my Mommie did that to me! What am I gonna tell Mack? Mommie killed my baby!" I cried over and over again, "Mommie killed my baby!"

Nana wiped her eyes, "Everything is going to be alright, honey. Nana promise it will be alright. Lord, help my Debbie. Now, lay down, honey, Nana precious baby. Lie down and rest yourself." She got up and walked out of the room. I cried all day and on into the night, with no understanding of why this had just happen to me.

Later that night, around 11:00, I had got up to go to the bathroom. Nana came in the bathroom to check on me. "Debbie, how you feel, honey?"

"Nana, I keep bleeding a lot. There's blood all on my bed and dark black blood clots are coming out of me! See!" as I lean forward so she could look in the toilet.

Nana looked in the toilet and said, "My Lord!" She began to pray for me as she placed her hand on my forehead and stomach. She then gave me the supersized Kotex pads to use.

She took me back to the room. "Debbie, lay down and take this sheet. Place it over your bed and in the morning I will give you clean linen. Debbie, call on the Lord. He will hear your cry." I was in so much pain.

"Nana, did Mack call me?"

"Yeah, Debbie, I talked to him."

"Does he know what happened?

"Yeah, I told him."

I began to cry again—as I walked through my mother's room to get to mind, not wanting to wake her out of her drunken sleep.

Section 72

I'm so sorry!

Early the next morning, Mack came to my house. I didn't go to school because I was bleeding so badly. When I finally got downstairs to answer the door, he was turning around to walk away. I called out his name. He ran to me and held me so tight, crying that he was so sorry. He felt like it was his fault.

He said we should have not told my mother, and then maybe I would still be carrying our child. I cried holding him as I told him that I was sorry that I let my mother kill our baby. We went back and forth for a while. He was so glad that I was doing okay and wanted to know how I was feeling. I told him that I was in a lot of pain and that I was afraid because blood clots were coming out of me. Mack assured me that I was going to be okay. He said that I was strong and was a fighter, for me not to give up. The next time you get pregnant, we will not tell your mother. He laughed and kissed me at the same time.

"What? Wait a minute, Mack! You already talking about having another baby and I'm hurting like this? Yeah, right!"

"Come on, Debra, it is nothing that we can do about it. What has happened is under the bridge. We have to move on and let it go. I need for you to stop crying and so will I. We have to. Okay, baby? Maybe your mother thinks she is too young to be a grandmother, and she does not want to take care of any babies. Or, she may feel we are too young. But, listen, this is between you and I. Now we know what we want and we want to have a child together, right?"

"Yeah, Mack, I want your child."

"We have all the support that we need to take care of a child. Don't you agree? Look at our nursery that we have already and we can set up a college fund for our child. And when you turn of age, we can get married. You know I have an uncle who is a preacher. I can see if my mother can get him to marry us and nobody will ever know until the time is right. And I want you to know you can always move in with me and my family."

"Mack, I love you. You will do all of that for me?"

"Yes, Debra, I will because I love you. Now, get better so that we can start our family," as he patted me on the butt.

"Stop, I'm still in pain," laughing and crying at the same time. We both began to laugh together.

"I want to give you time to heal, so I will come by and check on you when your family is not here in the mornings. Then I will come back when they are home, you know just to show your mother that she has not ran me off. So, pull yourself together for me, for us."

"Okay, Mack, I will."

"You go back in the house and get some rest. I will be back later to see you. Remember, I love you always."

"Okay, bye, Mack." We kissed and I shut the door.

A few days went by and Mack did what he said he was going to do; he came to see me in the mornings, but when he came in the evenings, the only one that received him was my Nana. My mother said that I didn't need to be around him, that he wasn't gonna do nothing but pump babies inside of me.

My uncle was still a jerk. Whenever Mack came by, my uncle would stop him at the door. He even told him that there was no need for him to ever come over here again and that my mother did not want me to have anything to do with him. He went so far as to demand that he not come by! What an asshole!

That didn't do anything but make me want to hurry and get well. Mack would still come see me in the mornings and because I wasn't getting any better. He thought something was wrong. One morning, we went to the Family Plan Clinic and told them what happened. They examined me and said that I had an infection due to the abortion. It wasn't too serious, but they gave me some antibiotics to clear it up.

Two weeks later, I was feeling back to my old self. My mother never mentioned the abortion in the house; nobody ever spoke on it—like it never happened. My mother told me to never speak of this outside of our home. They did not want the neighbors to find out. I didn't care anymore. I knew what my family thought about me outside of my Nana, my brother and my daddy's side of the family.

Well, life went on. I moved on like it never happened, but deep down in my heart, I will never forget what was done to me.

I had gone back to school and back to Mack's house. We shared our bodies with each other even more so. I started to not care about school too much—all I wanted was to spend time away from home, with Mack.

Section 73

Does a mother always know what's best for her daughter?

I went to my classes and I did my work, but my mind was elsewhere. It wasn't six months later that I was pregnant again. This time, we were not going to tell my mother. I waited until I was three months along before I told Nana, but she already knew because of the food I was craving. My Nana said she would help me hide the pregnancy from my mother, and maybe by the time she found out, it would be too late to abort the baby.

Nana would fix me certain foods and buy different fruits for me. I did my best in hiding it from my mother: My mother would come in the bathroom, at any given time, to check to see if I was on my period. I would put a Kotex on my panties and pour ketchup and water on it so when she asked me if I was on my period, I would tell her yes and she could see the "evidence." She knew when I should be on my period, so during that time I would wear a watery, ketchup-filled Kotex! I never knew when she would come in on me. I even told her that I was out of sanitary napkins when actually I was very pregnant—trying to save my baby.

Mack made sure that I had whatever I needed at his mother house. He bought me some tee-shirts that were a size too big. We didn't want it to be too obvious. My Nana bought me a few pretty blouses, the ones that tied in the

126

back and were loose fitting in the front. That was the new style, so my mother never knew. I was determined to have my baby and not let my mother know.

I knew what she was going to do if she found out. She'd already shown me that. I stayed out of my mother's way. When she came home, I was gone and when I came in when the streets lights came on, I went straight to Nana's room. Before my mother came upstairs, I'd go to my room and pretend I was asleep.

My mother didn't care, nor did she know where I was or what I was doing, whenever I was outside as long as I came in the house before the street lights came on.

Then one day, I heard my Uncle Tom coming up the stairs. I tried to hurry and go into the bathroom and close the door before he got up to the top of the stairs. I was not able to make it! As he stood at the bathroom door with his foot half way in, he asked me to wash his underwear for him and threw them in the face bowl where I was washing my hands.

There were maybe about 4-6 pairs of underwear with shit stains! When he asked me, I answered, "Why don't you ask your wife to wash your draws?! No, I don't feel like it!"

Before I knew it, he hit me so hard that I fell down on the side of the tub and hit my stomach really hard! He continued to hit me, screaming, "Who the fuck do you think you are talking to! You gonna wash them drawers whether you like it or not!"

He then grabbed a pair of those nasty drawers and put it in my face! "Oh, you gonna wash them, motherfucker!"

I yelled, "Nana! Nana! Tom is hitting me! Nana, help!"

"Close your motherfucking mouth! You smart mouth little bitch!" while still hitting me.

I could hear my Nana running up the stairs, "Leave her alone! Stop! Tom, Stop! Stop hitting, Debbie! She's with child! She's with child! Don't hit her no damn more!"

Nana got in front of him holding her arms out to protect me from his blows. By this time, I was over in the tub balled up trying to cover my stomach. I was hysterical! I told my Nana that he knocked me over in the tub and I fell on the side of my stomach.

"I didn't hit her! She slipped and fell! Lying little bitch! Mama, I asked her nicely to wash my underwear and she had to start talking smart at the mouth!"

I began to bleed like I was on my period, not bad, but it was a lot of blood. Well, it was too late. It was out and my mother would know it now! Uncle Tom walked out of the bathroom, "Wait to Marian hears about this! Just wait!"

Nana helped me up out of the tub and she began to pray for my baby, that it would be okay. Nana told me wash my face, lie down on the bed and get some rest. I needed to be still for a while. I felt cramps in my stomach for a little while, but soon it stopped and I fell to sleep.

Shortly afterwards, I woke up to my mother standing over me. "You think you've done something slick! You are not gonna get away with this, not if I have anything to do with it!"

My mother was so angry with me. She went on to say that she hadn't finish paying for the first abortion yet and how could I do this to her.

What I didn't understand was, what was I doing to her? I was going to have a baby, not her. I knew that it was too late to have an abortion. Nana said she heard my mother talking to a doctor and he said that it was too dangerous to try to give me an abortion since I was six months pregnant.

128

So, I didn't have anything to worry about. I was kinda glad that it was out because I was tired of hiding it from my mother and wearing those nasty ketchup Kotex sanitary napkins every month!

Section 74

It's bad when your grandmother can't help you.

A week later, after I hit my stomach on the tub from my uncle hitting me, my mother had my Auntie DD come over to the house with her friend that used to be a nurse.

I had no idea what was about to take place. My mother told me to come into Nana's bedroom. Auntie DD and her friend were sitting on Papa's bed looking at me.

"Hey, Auntie DD." I looked at them real curious and wondered what they wanted with me. Nana was right behind me as I entered the room.

When my mother said, "Debbie, get up on that bed and lie down," Nana began to plead with her.

"Marian, please let Debbie have the baby! Please don't do this to her."

"What you talking about, Nana? What are they going to do to me?!" I screamed and began to cry for my Nana.

My mother turned around and slapped me in my mouth and screamed at me, "Lie down on the motherfucking bed, right damn now!" She hit me again, but this time in my eye.

My mother turned to Nana and said, "This is my child, not yours! You do not have anything to do with this! So, please leave, and close the door behind you!" All I could hear was Nana praying, "Lord, help her. Protect my Debbie!" My mother slammed the door.

They were about to try and do a home abortion on me! They were going to try and kill my baby that was inside of me! I had no one to protect

129

me! They made me lay down and then they put this thing inside me. That lady was trying to get my baby! Oh, God, I prayed, please protect my baby!

I cried and cried, but it did no good at all! My mother was determined to make me lose my baby. She slapped me in the face again, "Shut your damn mouth! I can't hear myself talk with all that damn noise!"

This lady was putting this thing inside of me with my mother and Auntie holding my legs open.

"I just had to pay for an abortion and you go out there and get your fast ass pregnant again! Hell, I ain't finished paying for that one! I'm not going to be a grandmother! Now, hold your goddamn legs open!"

After a while, they realize that it was nothing that they could do and I was able to get up. I just knew that my baby was going to die, but it didn't. As I walked out the door, my mother said, "Don't think this is over, dammit!"

Section 75

My mother lied to me.

A few weeks went by and I was able to still feel my baby move inside me. Everything was going just fine—I was going to have my baby! I didn't want to tell Mack what they did to me since no harm was done to the baby. I thought everything was going to be alright.

My brother had come home from jail—the school for bad boys—so I was glad to have him with me. My Nana had cooked a big breakfast on this Sunday morning and called us down to eat. By the time I got downstairs, everybody was already at the table—Chuckie, my mother and grandmother, and, of course, Uncle Tom. As I picked up my glass of milk and began to drink it, my brother yelled out, "Stop, Debbie, they put something in your milk!" Sure enough, there were pills that had not completely dissolved at the bottom of my glass.

The "prenatal vitamins" that my mother was giving me every day were Humphrey 11 and Quinine pills! These pills were to make me lose my baby! I do not know how long she had been putting these pills in my food and drink! I do know that I have been taking them every day for the past two weeks!

My mother told me that she was sorry and that it was okay if I have my baby. That's why she went out and got 'prenatal vitamins' for me to make sure that my baby was going to be healthy. I believed my mother.

I really thought that my baby was going to be deformed or something because she had been putting a double potion of the pills in my food and drink. I was so hurt. I ran to the upstairs bathroom to try to make myself throw up, but I couldn't. I thought about all the times I ate a meal with my mother, and how she had asked me several times did I want some of her pop which had already been poured into a glass.

As I was going into my room, I notice on my mother's dresser that there were two bottles of pills—the same pills that she had been giving me! On the bottles it read that the quantities were 45 pills in each, but there were only 10 pills left in each bottle.

Later that night, I took the rest of the pills that were in each bottle! A total of twenty pills! I figured that if my mother did not love and want my baby, she did not love or want me!

That was the first time I tried to commit suicide. I wanted to die if I couldn't have my baby! I was thirteen years old.

Section 76

I feel like a murderer.

After I took the pills, I went into my Nana's bedroom and gently woke her up, letting her know of what I had done. Nana looked at me and put her hands on my head and prayed, "Forgive her, Heavenly Father, Lord, for she

131

know not of what she do." She then reached down and said, "Debbie, you go lie down, now. You'll be okay. Everything will be okay." She opened out her arms to me and gave me a big hug and kissed me on my forehead.

"Nana loves you. I promise everything is going to be alright."

That night, I went to sleep only to be awaken in the middle of the night with slight cramps in my stomach. I went to the bathroom and just sat there. Then I felt something come out of me! I yelled for my Nana, "Come see, Nana, something just came out of me!" I could hear Nana running.

"What's wrong, Debbie?"

"I don't know! Something just came out of me!"

"Lean forward and let me see!"

By that time, my mother had come into the bathroom.

Nana screamed, "Oh my God! She had the baby! Debbie had the baby!"

My mother said, "That's good."

"Grab a towel! Marian, get a towel!" My mother got a peach colored towel—I'll never forget the color—and handed it to my Nana who told me to stand up a little so that she could get the baby. As I stood, the baby touched my leg and I jumped.

"Don't you jump or be scared, Debbie! This is your baby! Your own flesh and blood!" Nana got the towel and wrapped my baby up in it. Told me to hold the baby close to me and not to drop it. I had to walk wide-legged to the bedroom because the baby was still attached to me.

When I got in my mother's room and sat on the side of the bed, with that peach towel covering my baby, I asked Nana if could I open the towel up and see my baby. Nana and my mother were trying to get dressed. "Sure, honey, you can open the towel and look at your baby!" When I opened the towel and looked down at my baby, it was the prettiest thing that I had ever seen in my life.

"A baby, my baby!" It was a baby boy! It had all of his toes and fingers! It just needed another layer of skin and it didn't have any hair! It was a big baby, too! I asked could I call my cousin Beverly and tell her that I had a baby. I couldn't believe that I had a baby! It hadn't hit me yet that the baby was still born, dead.

My mother said, "This is not a game, Debbie, dammit! What the hell do you want to call her for?"

"Let her call Beverly, Marian. Let her call her if that is what she wants to do! Go ahead, Debbie!"

I was so happy to tell my cousin that I had a baby boy. I described how the baby looked as I held him close to my body like Nana told me to. Beverly was asking me all kind of questions, "Where you have it at? Did it hurt? Is he crying?"

That's when it dawn on me or snapped into my mind that my baby is dead! Dead because of my mother, dead because my mother would have never known if my uncle had not knocked me in the tub! Dead from all those pills my mother gave me!

I was a murderer. I killed my baby. I will have to live with for the rest of my life. It was time to get off the phone and go to the hospital so they could cut the umbilical cord.

I asked the doctors could I keep my baby in a jar, you know, like you see on TV. The doctor yelled at me and said, "Little girl, you really don't know what is going on, do you? This is not a game. This is a human being!

"Yeah, I know it was a human life until you and my mother killed my baby!" I snatched the peach colored towel that my baby was wrapped in. "You killed my baby!" I cried. "You killed my baby!"

Again I had to have a D&C just like before. I was in pain. I didn't care anymore; life was not worth living.

Once I told Mack what happen to the baby, things change with us. It really wasn't there any more, his love for me. For me it was, but not for him. His mother didn't care for me too much after that and he lost all trust in me. I know they blamed me for the baby's death—I blamed myself. I blamed my uncle because if he had not made me fall in the tub, we could have hidden my baby from my mother.

I tried to stick around, but it seemed like Mack was pushing me away. After, the loss of two pregnancies, things between Mack and I became distant. He began to treat me differently. Whenever I went to his house, he would be in the nursery room and he cried a lot. We still made love, but it was not the same.

He had a friend named Wesley. He had just graduated from high school and was getting ready to go to college. He had come to my house a couple of times with Mack and played cards with my mother and Nana.

Section 77

No does means no!

One day, Wesley was visiting with Mack. When I came over, we all sat in the living room and watched TV. Mack asked me to come in the bedroom with him. He had something that he wanted to talk to me about. He reached for my hand.

Wesley laughed, "Don't ya'll be in there doing nothing."

I replied, "We ain't getting ready to do nothing."

Once I said that, Mack released my hand and I just walked into the room as he closed the door. Mack jumped on me and began to kiss me.

"Come on, Debra, I got to have you!"

"Wait, Mack, you got somebody in the living room! We can't do nothing with somebody in the house!"

"Why not?" and he unzipped his pants. He then reached under my skirt to pull down my underwear.

I really didn't feel up to it, only because his friend was in the house. There was never anyone at home before, so this was new to me.

"Wait, Mack, slow down! You're going too fast for me! Wait! Stop!" I pushed him off of me. He was being really rough with me.

"Oh, you can say stop to me, but you couldn't say stop to your mother! You let her kill my baby!!"

He was mad at me and I had never seen him like this before.

"Wait. Mack, please don't say that to me. I wanted our baby."

"Yeah, well, I can't tell! Where are they?! Where's the baby, Debra?!" He yelled with tears in his eyes. I began to cry.

"That is all you're going to do is cry, because you are not going to do nothing but let people do whatever they want to you! Just take advantage over you! You are not strong like I thought you were! Fuck you, Debra, I am done with you! You're just another bitch to me!" and walked out the room.

I sat there. My heart was broken. I could not believe he just called me a bitch. He said that I didn't mean anything to him. He was all I had! Nobody else loved me but him.

"Mack, please wait!" I ran to the front door as he was leaving out. He said something to Wesley, but I did not hear it. Mack turned to me and said, "I love you just as much as you saved my babies life! Make sure that you are gone when I get back and don't come back, bitch!" He was pointing his finger in my face!

This was so hard for me to believe. I backed up, and put my hands over my mouth and fell to the floor, crying so very hard. I couldn't believe what he just said to me.

Wesley came over there to me to help me off the floor.

"Oh, Debra, don't cry. You know how Mack is when he get upset."

"No! I do not! This is the first time he ever talked to me like that."

As Wesley helped me to the couch, he was holding me around my waist.

"Debra, don't cry. You know Mack loves you. Don't take it to heart. Don't cry. He'll be back." He was rubbing my back. He then lifted up my chin as the tears flowed down my face and leaned down to kiss me.

I yelled, "Hey, wait a minute! What are you doing? Don't do that!"

Wesley grabbed my face. "Oh, yeah, baby, I've been looking at you for a while!" He pulled me closer. I began to fight him back. He slapped me in my face and pulled on my hair.

"You can make this easy or you can make this hard! It's your choice! You see, Mack don't want you and he said that I could have you!"

"Leave me alone! No! I want to go home!" I cried.

"Not before you give me some of that good pussy Mack says you got!" He wrestled me to the floor. I was yelling for Mack! I didn't want to believe what he was saying to me!

I was pulling Wesley hair and his beard! "Stop! No! Please don't do this to me! Leave me alone!" as I kicked and yelled. Wesley did not want to hear me as he forced his big, fat, nasty 200-pound body weight on me!

I could not believe I was being raped by Mack's friend Wesley! How could this be? What did I do wrong? I felt so bad.

He hurried up and did his business, and let me go. As I ran out the door, Mack was coming in. I ran straight to his arms crying, "Mack, Wesley just raped me! He raped me, Mack!"

I was thinking that Mack was going to come to my defense, but instead he looked at me and said, "Oh! So you telling me you just had sex with my best friend! Is that what you are saying to me, Debra?!"

"No! Mack! Listen!" I cried. "He raped me! You know I love you and I don't want his fat ass! He raped me!"

Section 78
It's my fault! I killed our baby?

Wesley looked at Mack and said. "Man, after you left she got all up on me crying, talking about how much she loves you and she started kissing on me and shit. So, one thing led to another. You know how we roll! I don't care about a bitch! Hey man, this just goes to show you what type of bitch you got!"

Mack looked at me. "I thought I told you not to be here when I got back! And don't come back!" as he pushed me out the door and slammed it behind me.

I was humiliated, embarrassed and I felt just as low as the names my Uncle Tom calls me!!

I just wanted to get home to my Nana! I ran and cried all the way home. I ran in the kitchen and told Nana what had happen to me. She could not believe that Mack had treated me that way.

Nana still held me in her arms and told me that everything was going to be alright, for me not to cry any more. She got me a towel so that I could wipe my face. There were a few bruises and red marks on my face.

"Sit down and call over there! I want to talk to this boy! The same one, the same boy that came over here and played cards with us!"

"Yes, Nana, that's him!" I wiped the tears from my face.

Nana was so mad. She got on the phone and asked for him. "Wesley, Debbie just told me what happened and if you do not be over here at this house within an hour, I am going to call the police on you and have you locked up!" Do you hear me?!" She hung up the phone.

My mother was just walking in and heard the last of the conversation.

"Mama, who you talking to like that? And what is wrong with you, Debbie?" I began to cry again.

"Wipe your face and shut up! I can't understand what you are trying to say to me!"

"I'm not trying to say anything to you! I just said Wesley raped me!"

My mother slapped me across the face and said, "Who the hell you think you talking to in that tone of voice?"

"Nobody!"

Nana said, "I be damn Marian! Listen at Debbie! That goddamn boy just raped Debbie! Come here, Debbie! Sit down and tell your mother what happened!"

I began to tell them both what had happened, about Mack attitude's, saying stuff about the baby and blaming me for killing our baby.

"It was no damn baby! It had not even formed into a baby yet!" replied my mother.

I thought to myself she must be talking about the first baby she made me abort because the second baby was real! *I held a big 6lb, 13oz. baby boy between my legs! She makes me sick! It's all her fault!*

Section 79

He raped me and she invited him to the house!

"Now, stop crying, Debbie."

138

"Mack called me out of my name and when I told him what happened, he didn't want to believe me!!"

The doorbell rang. "Get my beer out of the refrigerator, Debbie, so I can get ready to hear this bullshit!" I couldn't understand why my mother would want to hear what he had to say! And, was going to make me sit in front of him after what he did to me!

My Nana answered the door. I heard his voice. It was him. I was scared and began to cry, moving closer to my Mommie.

"He raped me! I'm not lying, Mommie! He raped me!"

"Sit down, Debbie and be quiet, so I can hear what's going on."

Wesley walked into the kitchen. My mother said, "Have a seat and tell me what the hell is it Debbie talking about!"

Nana had walked over by me and sat down next to me and put her arms around me, "Shhh, Debbie, let your mother hear what he did to you." She pulled me closer and held me tight.

Wesley sat down and began to talk. My mother asked him if he wanted a glass of beer! "Debbie, get him a glass."

Nana said, "No! The hell she's not getting no damn glass for him! Marian listen at yourself! You haven't even heard what this damn boy said and you are offering him a glass of beer?!

"Mama, I got this! I know what I am doing! Let me handle this!"

Can you believe that shit, a glass of motherfucking beer! What the hell does she think this is, a social event?! This SOB just raped me and now he is sitting down at the table with my mother drinking a glass of beer! And this motherfucker said yes! He began to talk after he takes a swallow of his beer.

"Well, Mrs. Dent, we all were over to Mack's house. Debbie and Mack went into the bedroom for a while. He said they were going in there to have sex."

I blurted out, "No! He didn't! He did not say that!"

Nana said. "Shhh, Debbie, let him finish. Let your mother take care of this!" She continued to hold me tight.

He went on, "They were in the room for a long time when Mack came out yelling. It was over between them and Debbie ran out the house crying. And that was it. I have no idea what Debbie is saying. I guess she is just upset because Mack broke off with her," and he picked up his beer and began to drink it with this fucked up look on his face like he was telling the truth.

My mother said, "Debbie, that's probably what happened. Now tell the truth, Debbie, isn't that the way it happened?"

"No! Mommie he raped me!" I buried my face into Nana's chest and cried, "Why my Mommie don't believe me, Nana?!"

Section 80

My Nana said everything was gonna be alright.

"He did rape me, Nana!"

"I know he did, Debbie, come on. Marian, you are going to have to believe your daughter sometime! Who else can she turn to if she can't turn to you as her mother?" She grabbed a small plastic bag.

"You!" She picked up her glass of beer and began to drink more and poured more beer into his a glass. I walked by him and he winked his eye at me!

Nana went upstairs with me and kept saying, "It will be alright. Everything will be alright! Go to your room and get a change of clothes and underwear. Come in here and take a nice hot shower, okay? Go ahead. Nana is going to get the water ready for you."

"Okay, Nana."

"It's going to be alright, Debbie. Nana promise it's going to be alright. Lord knows it is." You could hear the tremble in her voice.

"Here, let Nana help you take these clothes off." She put everything in that plastic bag. "Now, wash yourself real good. I mean, wash real good, Debbie."

"Okay, Nana, I will." Nana tied up the bag.

"I will be in my room. Go get your pillow and blanket and come in the room with Nana, Debbie."

"Yeah, Nana, I will."

Nana left the bathroom and I cleaned myself like she said. I got scared thinking what if he comes upstairs and get me. I shut the water off, got out and put my clothes on. When I opened the bathroom door, there my Uncle Tom was standing right there! I screamed and covered my face. He said, "What the fuck wrong with you? Mama, I didn't do nothing to her and she screaming like that!" Nana ran to me putting her arms around me.

"Debbie, it's okay. What do you want, Tom? Don't come up here fucking with Debbie cause I ain't in the mood for no shit! Not right now! Ain't nobody fucking with Debbie!"

"Mama, I just came up here to ask you if you have a couple of dollars until I get paid. $20.00 is all I need."

"Debbie, get your pillow and blanket. Lay down right here and let me get some damn money. Damn! All this bullshit going on!" She reached in her purse and handed him some money.

"What, Mama, what's going on?"

"Nothing! Just gone! Nothing at all!

After Uncle Tom left her room, Nana said, "Are you okay, Debbie?"

"Yeah, Nana, I'm okay. Can I come over there by your bed and be close to you?"

"Yeah, come on over here and lay down right between mine and Papa's beds."

Nana had twin beds in her room. She and Papa did not sleep together. Papa was too fat and snored a lot. I have never seen my Papa and Nana in the same bed. After Nana took something for her headache, I lay there and watched a movie with her.

Nana told me that she was sorry about what had happened to me. She said that I should always watch myself and to not put all my trust in boys. Nana said not to mind what Mack is saying, he's just hurt because of the baby. I was going to have to move on.

Section 81

Stop looking for love.

"Debbie, if Mack don't want to be with you, then you go on. You hear me?"

"Yeah, Nana, I hear you, but it hurts. I love him."

"Well, I know that you do, but there are going to be plenty more Macks in your life until you meet the one that is going to love you for you. God is going to place that special one in your life. You just have to stop looking for him."

"If I don't look for him, how is he gonna find me?"

Nana laughed and gave me a hug. "You'll see when you get older Debbie. You have a long way to go. It will happen unexpected and he's gonna take good care of you. You'll see."

She laid across her bed and I laid close to her bed knowing that I was safe because I was with my Nana. We watched the television and soon fell asleep.

I don't know how long that boy stayed down stairs with my Mommie. We heard them laughing and talking together just before we fell asleep.

I never saw those clothes again, not even the shoes. Nana got rid of them and we never spoke about that day ever again, as though it never happen. I never saw Mack again either.

Section 82

A normal life

Months passed and our everyday life has gone back to 'normal,' you know, the normal stuff... Auntie Eunice getting beat-up and spit on by her husband—black eyes, busted lips, black and blue bruises. Nothing any different than what my Uncle Tom was doing to my Auntie Janice. It would not be the normal if this didn't happen—all the time.

Mommie was still drinking her Budweiser beer with her select male friends stopping by to visit her. My Uncle Tom's lady friends would stop by on the weekends, acting like they were friends of his sister's in case Auntie Janice would be home. They would still stay, you know, just to have a drink with him. Auntie Janice, well, she never knew that those so-called friends were sleeping in her bed when she was not at home.

Section 83

What is wrong with me?

My mother and uncle played chess all the time while they share their most intimate thoughts and secrets—like their love affairs—and talked about everybody else.

Nana is still working hard, coming home to cook and clean, trying to rescue me and my brother from getting our ass whipped.

Papa is working hard at the steel mill at nights, not knowing what's going on in his house. Everybody makes sure Papa doesn't find out what's going on. On the weekends, he's working at his shop out in South Chicago. So, he was never home.

My little brother Chuckie is going in and out of the bad boy schools which are like little jails.

And me, well, I went back to school and started hanging out with my old friends, but nothing was the same.

I'm fourteen years old now. At eight years old, I saw my father's picture on TV after the news reporter said he was shot and killed for trying to steal a watch. I already tried to have sex for the first time at the age of twelve and got the crabs, and got the shit beat out of me. I've had a loaded gun put to my fucking head, peed on myself, been humiliated by my uncle and my mother did nothing about.

I was forced to have an abortion, and miscarried at six month a 6lb. 13oz. baby boy that I had at home in the fucking toilet at the age of thirteen, and if that wasn't enough… I tried to commit suicide and that didn't even work! Then I got dumped by my boyfriend and I was raped by his best friend and my mother didn't believe me. She even invited the rapist for an evening of beer drinking after it happen! He raped me!

Where do I go from here?

Section 84

My play sisters' father even cared for me.

I kept a low profile. I didn't talk much to anyone and I became very depressed. Whatever anybody had to talk to me about, I had already done what they were thinking about doing. They were talking about school dances, football games, and parties, and I'm talking about sex, babies and abortions, and the crap that was going on behind my Nana's pretty curtains.

I had no one to really turn to, so I just kept to myself. Don't get me wrong; I was fine with that, too. It was okay.

I started going over to Brenda and Linda's house knowing that I could always get love from them. They really loved me. I don't have a real sister, just my brother.

They treated me like I was their little sister. Whenever she saw me, Linda would say, "You better get home before the street lights come on" and "I got my eye on you."

Brenda always said, "Debbie, you got to watch these boys out here, girl. All they want is to get in your pants... and then they gonna leave and talk about you, so you be careful out here. If you ever need me, I'm right here."

Right before the street lights came on, Linda would tell me, "Now, give us a kiss and go home. You know you can't be hanging out with us. We love you, little sister."

They always told any and everybody that I was their little sister, making sure that if I was doing something I had no business doing or somewhere I should not be, it would get back to them. And that was something that I didn't want.

I remember somebody told them that I was on the other side of Stoney. Linda yelled, "Debbie, come here! What is this I hear you being on the other side of Stoney?" Before I was able to get a word out, Brenda chimed in, "You know you don't have no business on that side of Stoney. They are too fast for you and it ain't nothing but trouble over there for you."

They would stop doing whatever it was they were doing just to make sure that I was okay. I remember their Dad used to sit on their front porch and you never saw him without a suit on. Sometimes he would even take me to the store and buy me candy, or stop the ice cream truck for me and buy whatever I wanted. He knew that I didn't have a father.

Whatever happened to my baby and Barbie dolls, my doll houses and my easy-bake oven? I did have one, you know. I can hardly remember any of those times sitting down playing with them. I really don't remember having a little girl's life. I did play jump robe, hop-scotch and even jacks. But, none of those things interested me now. I guess, I wanted to grow up too fast—just to get away from the bullshit that I had to face at home. So now, what is it left for me to do? I asked myself this questions so many times.

Section 85

Where do I fit in? Who am I?

I was still going to the laundromat for my Nana every other Saturday to wash her rugs and her silks.

I really need for you to see the picture of this side of Stoney Island verses the other side that I was living on. On the opposite side of Stoney Island from where I lived was Ted's Laundromat. All the taverns, Stoney Island liquor store and the fast food restaurants were on this side of Stoney Island strip.

On the corner of 69th Place in Stoney, there was Ted's Covenant Neighborhood Store. As you turned right at that corner, at the end of the block, right off an alley was the laundromat. The store and laundromat was owned by the same person.

Once you crossed that alley, on both sides of the streets there were houses and apartment buildings. Some were boarded up and barely any grass to call a lawn in front of any of the buildings. There was nothing but dirt and a patch of grass here and there. Paper, restaurant bags and chicken bones everywhere. Stray dogs were trying to eat what they could find from the leftover bags. Empty beer and wine bottles had been thrown upside the lifeless trees and sometimes you would even see drug needles lying around in the alley.

Never, ever did I come to wash clothes and not see lots of people hanging outside. It was wild all the time. People were in groups laughing, talking loud and drinking beer, liquor, wine and smoking cigarettes and weed right in the open. My Nana said that a lady should never smoke outside on the streets.

I remember one incident where I saw this woman yelling at somebody from the third floor, got mad and threw an empty beer bottle at them. It busted on the ground with glass shattering everywhere. I heard another woman yell back up at the person that threw the bottle saying, "Hey, bitch, don't make me come up there and beat your ass! Yeah! Bitch! My baby down here! I'll fuck you up if you hit my baby, while you wasting motherfucking beer!"

Then she said, "Bitch, bring me one of those forties down here," as she gave somebody high five. "Hell! I ain't got no money and I need a damn beer this morning!"

At the same time, she was trying to calm and feed her crying baby a bottle saying, "Shut the fuck up, boy, and take this damn bottle! Shit!" Then others would laugh, and they would go on about their business as if nothing had happened.

I just had never seen anything like that before in my life, but I was on the other side of Stoney Island. It always seemed like I was walking into another dimension or something.

Well, one early Saturday morning, I had to go to the laundromat. Nana got everything ready for me to go. She would get the bleach and pour it in a mayonnaise jar, and put the soap power in one of Papa's paper bags that she used for his lunch.

Then she would put both of them in a plastic bag, tied it up. She wanted to make sure no bleach got on her rugs or silks. "Are you watching me, Debbie, do this? You're going need to know how to separate and wash your clothes. Pay attention," she would say.

"I remember how to do it. You showed me already."

"Hush, Debbie and just listen." She'd sit at the kitchen table and pulled out a coin purse full of quarters from her house duster pocket for the Big Boy washer and dryer.

I'd get the grocery cart and she'd put that plastic bag down at the bottom of the cart. Then, she would fold her oversize and large throw rugs—about six—inside out and place them in the cart.

I asked Nana once, "Why you fold the rugs inside out?" She answered, "I do that so when you're walking to and from the laundromat. I don't want nosey-ass people seeing what kind of rugs I got! You know the neighbor across the street, Mrs. Truth, who sits in her window all damn day, just watching everybody? She knows everything that goes on with her nosey ass!" She began to laugh at herself and I was laughing right along with her.

"So, you make sure that when you come from the laundromat that you turn my rugs inside out! Her ass been then told the whole neighborhood what I got in my house."

"Okay, Nana, I'll fold them inside out."

"Debbie, listen. I need for you to do a couple of extra things for Nana. Do you think you can do it?"

"Yeah, Nana. What else you want me to do?" She put this plastic bag of underwear that she called her silks tied up on top of the rugs.

"Now, here's my silks. Remember you don't dry these and you wash them on the gentle silk cycle. Don't forget."

"Okay, I won't."

"Let me get this out the way for you so we don't get messed up," as she counted out the quarters that it would take to wash her stuff.

148

"This is for you—a few extra quarters so you can go to Ted's and buy you some chips and a pop while you wait in there with my clothes. Now, don't you go off and leave my shit, Debbie, cause those niggas over cross Stoney ain't got no good rugs and shit like this. They will steal your stuff out of the washer. You know that, right?"

"Yeah, Nana, I do."

"It's just a couple of things that I need for you to do on the way there, and then I'll let you go so you can get back here."

Nana placed some dry cleaning clothes across the cart, "On your way there, stop at Pete's Cleaners and put this in for me. Let Pete know I will pick it up on Wednesday. Then take this package to the boutique up there and give this to my friend. You know where I'm talking about, where you got your training bras from." She gave me this envelope.

"Yeah, Nana, I know."

"Put that up, put it in your pocket because it's money in there. And here, put this in your other hand. This is for you." Nana gave me $20.00. I smiled.

"Thank you, Nana. Okay, I'm ready."

"Now, you go there and come on back and Nana will see if you can make us a banana split when you get back, okay? Give Nana a kiss and stop being so sad. It's gonna be alright. God is taking care of you."

"Okay, Nana, I love you."

I did what Nana ask me to do. When I got to the laundromat, I put everything in the washer. I even ran and got me some chips and a pop from Ted's store.

Section 86

My friend no one knows.

While I was sitting there, with my mind just wondering as it always did, I noticed this girl in there washing her clothes. She's not from around here because I've never seen her in this laundromat before and I had been coming here for a long time. She came up to me and said, "Hello, my name is Hattie. What's your name? I see you come here often and you are always by yourself."

Now, I hesitated with a frown looking at this short, real dark-skinned girl saying something to me. She had this big smile on her face like she was trying to befriend me. I was wondering, why she was trying to talk with me? I had been through the ringer with everything at home, but she didn't know that.

"Yeah, my name is Debra." *I looked her up and down like what the hell you want cause you don't want none!*

Hattie said, as she backed away, "Hold up! I didn't mean any harm I just moved in the neighborhood and I don't know anybody and was just trying to make friends with you! That's all!"

"No wait, Hattie. I'm sorry. I didn't mean to look at you like that. I just been through a lot of shit in my life already and I don't have anyone to talk to. I mean, a friend that is. I come here across Stoney and every two weeks to wash my grandmother's rugs and stuff. I don't really hang around anybody, so I just come by myself. I really don't have any friends, either."

"Oh, yeah? Well, I just moved in about two blocks from here. Come here, let me show you." We stood in front of the laundromat. "See that big apartment building on the left corner? That's where I live, on the first floor. Would you like to come over to my place sometime? Actually, I got to go home now and drop off these clothes and get my cigarettes I left at home.

Would you like to walk with me? I'll come back up here with you and we can talk until you get done." She smiled at me.

I am very reluctant because my Nana said for me to never leave her rugs and silks at the laundromat because somebody might take them.

"Hattie, I would love to go with you, but I don't want nothing to happen to my grandmother's stuff. She'll never forgive me if I let somebody take her stuff while I am gone."

"Okay, that's fine. I'll go get my cigarettes and I be back."

"See you when you get back." As she walked away, I began to think that if she is on this side of Stoney Island, nobody knows me over here and maybe she could be my new friend.

Being on that side of Stoney was so different than the side that I lived on. The streets were always full of people walking, standing on porches, laughing, smoking reefers, talking loud and cursing.

Now on the other side where I lived, when the street lights come on, you didn't see a lot of people hanging out on the porches, drinking alcohol or smoking anything.

At night, mainly the bigger kids would be in the playground or in the back of the alley, never out in front of their homes.

The only house where a few people would congregate was in front of Brenda and Linda's house, but not often. It was so quiet over there—you didn't see paper, cigarettes butts, beer and wine bottles and stuff all on the ground, and everybody had grass and some flowers in their yard.

"Hey, Deb, I'm back." There was Hattie standing in the door of the laundromat, smiling.

"Hey to you, too. You got back fast."

"I told you that I live right there."

"Well, I'm finish washing my grandmother's stuff, so how about I walk with you and you can show me your apartment? Then I will take this home and come back over here. How do that sound to you?"

"Great, Debbie! That sounds good. Here, let me help you with this." She picked up the extra bleach in the jar and the soap power in the paper bag.

"Wait, Hattie. I can put that down at the bottom of this grocery cart, and put the rugs and stuff on top of it." That's how my Nana told me to do it and that's what I did.

Hattie and I walked to her apartment and I went inside. Wow! It was big. She didn't have any furniture yet, but the rooms were very big. The front room had windows that went around the whole front of the room and the dining room was big. It had three huge bedrooms and the kitchen was big enough to put two tables in it.

"You must really be happy to be living here on your own. Who lives here with you?"

"Oh, it's just me and my little boy, but he's with my mother all the time. So, it's just me."

I began to ask her how old do you have to be to get an apartment and all kinda stuff. She didn't mind telling me.

"Hattie, come on and walk with me to my house, so I can come back over for a while."

"Well, I'll walk you to the corner, then that way you can go home, and just in case you have to do something else for your grandmother, I won't be holding you up. Okay?"

"Okay, let's go so I can get back over here with you." At that point, I saw a little brightness somewhere, a little hope that things will be alright and God will take care of me as my Nana told me so many times.

I have found somewhere to go, to hide out, where nobody would ever find me. I didn't have to hear anyone talk about me or put me down or make me feel ashamed of myself. This is going to be good for me, I thought.

I began visiting Hattie every day. I would wake up early in the morning and go hang out at her apartment with her all day until it was time for me to go home. You know, when the street lights came on.

Hattie would even cook and show me how to make a few dishes that my Nana hadn't shown me. I was doing something different than the norm and it felt pretty good. Hattie and I became really close in just a few weeks.

Hattie asked me one day how old was I and I told her fourteen, but I usually tell people who ask seventeen. She couldn't believe that I was only fourteen years old. She thought that I was sixteen or seventeen. Hattie said she had some concerns about my age and being with her. She just didn't want to get in no trouble because I was so young.

"Nah, I'm just fourteen. Don't worry. You not gonna get in trouble with me at your house because nobody knows where I'm at."

I had been coming over her house now for about two weeks. After I told her my age, I then told her all the crazy shit that I had been going through. She said it was so hard to believe that I had been through that stuff at my age. She even told me that I was more than welcome to come and stay at her crib with her if things just got so bad that I couldn't stay there anymore. That was good to hear her tell me that. She's a friend for me at the right time, I thought.

Section 87

Is this infatuation or love?

Two weeks have passed and it's time for me to go back to the laundromat for Nana. I told Nana about my new friend Hattie. I didn't really tell the truth about where she lived.

I got the cart with the rugs and Nana's silks to do her washing. Once I finished at the laundromat, I decided to go to Ted's store on the corner to get me some chips and a pop.

I'll never forget I had on a pair of green shorts and a green multi-colored halter top, my hair was in two ponytails with green yarn tied in a bow with my green and white bobby socks with black shoes. Oh, don't let me forget—I was wearing some new lip gloss that my friend Hattie had given me two days before.

This time was different, even though the surroundings were the same. The people were outside still talking loud, cursing, drinking and smoking reefer and all that stuff, and it was a beautiful sunny day.

I turned the corner to go into Ted's. I was looking down getting change out of my small black shoulder purse. This guy came around the corner so fast that he bumped right into me and almost knocked me down. He was walking that fast. I shouted, "Dag, dude! Watch where you going!"

He grabbed me by the arm to catch me so I wouldn't fall. He apologized in the sexiest, softest, slightly deep voice, "Oh, I'm so sorry. Please excuse me, young lady." He held onto me so I could get my balance.

When I raised my head up and looked him in his eyes. Ohhh, those big brown eyes! I couldn't hardly get the words out to say, "I'm, I'm okay."

He looked at me with this smile on his face, almost like he was flattered because of the expression on my face. I just stood there, probably with my mouth hanging wide open—like the little girl that I was—looking at him from head to toe! He was FINE! Baby, when I say FINE, I mean FINE!

He stood there looking at me with this half smile. On the upper left side of his face, he had a slightly darker brown birth mark. His skin complexion was like a creamy caramel color. Skin was so smooth with heavy dark eyebrows and very long eye lashes. He had the prettiest straight white teeth that I had ever seen on a boy.

He was dressed in all brown. He had on dark brown snake-skin shoes, a pair of brown double-pleaded slacks, with a thin dark brown turtle-neck and a dark chocolate wide-brim hat with that little feather on the side.

"Are you okay?"

"Oh yeah, I'm fine, huh, thank you," as I smiled right back at him. He stood there with such a swagger, with one foot out in front of the other. He was so cool and had so much confidence about himself.

"Hmmm…What's your name? I haven't seen you around here before. Where do you live, with your pretty self?"

"Err, huh, my name is, huh, Debra. I live across Stoney," and pointed in the direction of where I lived. This boy, this big boy turned and kissed me right on the mouth! Then he walked away.

"I'll see you around. I'm gonna be looking for you."

He was walking so fast that by the time I did turn to look for him, he had already made it down to the laundromat. I was standing there in shock!

He almost disappeared in the crowd of people as he sped along gracefully with a slight lean and a dip in his walk.

That's a bad dude there! Who was that guy? I couldn't wait to get home so that I could tell my Nana about what happened.

I told her that it felt like I had just seen the finest boy ever. I mean, Patrick is gloriously fine; Piggie is mysteriously good-looking and Mack is pretty boy fine. But this one here, he is FINE. "Nana, he is FINE, FINE!!" I screamed.

Nana just looked at me and laughed, and said with a serious face, "Debbie, now you know what you just went through."

"Yeah, Nana, I know. I'm not going to get pregnant or nothing. He's a big boy. I mean he would never be interested in nobody like me."

"What I tell you about saying 'nobody'? You are somebody."

"Anyway, that's what happened, Nana. I just wanted to tell you. Can I go back outside for a little while?"

Section 88

Something told you not to go back.

I wanted to go back across Stoney, over to Hattie's house, but I didn't want that guy to think that if he saw me that I was looking for him. Man, I got to get back over there so Hattie can tell me what to do. Maybe she's seen him before.

I thought as I headed toward Hattie's apartment that I should have slapped him or something when he kissed me. You know, had some type of respect for myself than to have a stranger kiss me like that. I think I made myself look real easy.

Who knows better than me what being easy will get you—nothing but a hard penis, a sexually transmitted disease, an unwanted pregnancy, humiliation, disgrace and shame! Let's not leave out being disrespected with pointed fingers laughing at you! Let's throw in depression with suicidal thoughts!! Great! I looked like a damn fool!

Oh, well, that's all I'm good for, at least that's what I've been told! Hey, maybe he did that because he knew that he could, and he was flattered by the way I was looking at him? That's all. No big deal. What the hell! In the back of my mind, that little voice said, 'Yes, I must see him again.'

Section 89

Was it destined to happen?

I went back over to Hattie's apartment and told her what had happen and describe that young man to her. She said that she had not seen anybody like that over there. Weeks went by and Hattie and I got to know each other really well.

I found myself going to see her almost every day. I had forgotten about that boy who had kissed me, until one day Hattie and I was walking down the street. There were a lot of people outside on the porch at the house that sat next to the alley.

We decided to walk across the street and not pass through all those people. As we began to cross the street, we heard somebody yell out from that crowd, "Hey you, come here!" We both turned around to see who the person was talking to, but we were the only ones crossing the street.

Then we heard that voice again yell out, "Hey you, come here!" I just knew whoever that was, they was not talking to me because I didn't know nobody over there. We both turned and looked at each other and kept on walking. Then that voice yelled one more time, "Yeah! I'm talking to you with the skinny legs." And there he was!

It was him! He had on an olive green walking suit with dark green snake skin shoes. (My mother always said you can tell a lot about a man based on the type of shoes that he wears, whatever that meant. He did wear some good shoes.) He wore a wide brim straw hat that had an olive green band around it, with a feather on the side. He was running toward me with this big smile on his face.

He was screaming out loud "Here's my baby!" with his arms reaching for me. He picked me up in the middle of the street saying, "There she is! Here's my baby!" I was in shock! I couldn't believe what he had just done in front of everybody! All eyes was on me! Oh my God, this boy is crazy, I thought to myself, but it felt so good that he recognized me and he didn't forget how I looked!

By this time, I was up in the air with him holding me, saying that I was his baby and that I was just what he had been looking for.

"Stop, put me down!"

"Debra, you know I wasn't gonna forget you. You know that right?" he asked kneeling down so that he could look me in my eyes.

"Yeah, well, nah, I didn't know."

"What?! You didn't know that you were my baby? I told you when I last saw you that I was gonna be looking for you, and now that I got you, I'm not gonna let you get away. You belong to me."

He really took me by surprise! Hattie was standing there looking at me and I would have thought that he would look at her since she was much older and she had a pretty shaped body—much better than mine.

When he put me down, he kissed me again right on the mouth, and I didn't say a word. So, there goes that self-control and self-respect that I was going to have for myself right out the window! We walked toward Hattie and he introduced himself.

"My name is James, James Jr."

"This is my friend Hattie."

"Where are you two beautiful ladies on your way to?"

"We're going over to Hattie's place."

"Hmmm, do you mind, Miss Lady, if I tag along with you all? I would like to get to know my baby just a little more."

He slung his arm around my neck and had me walking even closer to him. Gee, he walks so fast. I got to keep up with him, otherwise he could choke me.

"Sure. Why not?" Hattie replied.

We could hear the guys on the porch making little remarks like, "Go head on, Jr.! You got one there! Yeah, he got a good one! How old is she?"

So, there I was walking with this big boy. He looks like a man. I don't know what to call him at this point. I don't even know how old he is.

I just know that he is older than Patrick, Piggie and Mack, and he apparently likes me, and that was good enough. Once we got to Hattie's apartment, he came on in and we sat down on the pillows that she had on the floor.

<h2 style="text-align:center">Section 90</h2>

<h3 style="text-align:center">You think the grass is greener.</h3>

Hattie asked him if he wanted a beer and he told her, "Sure." He asked if I wanted one.

"I don't drink. The only thing I do is smoke cigarettes sometimes. That's it."

"You mean to tell me you don't drink? What about weed? Do you smoke weed?"

"No! I do not, not at all. I don't do any of that stuff."

"Come here, girl and give me a kiss, just for being a good girl. And I'm gonna make sure you stay that way. You don't need to drink or any of that other shit."

"Yeah, now you want to talk to me like I'm a baby."

"No, that's not it. You are a good girl. I knew that from the moment I laid eyes on you. You are just what I've been looking for—pure and innocent."

"Oh, really? Well, I guess you found her and that's me," as I leaned over to give him a kiss. He leaned away and he told me that he didn't want me to catch his cold, so he turned his head for me to kiss him on his cheek. I thought to myself that he kissed me on the mouth when he saw me, so what's different? Well, it was only a peck, not tongue kissing.

James began to ask me a lot of questions. I got a chance to tell him all about me and where and who I was living with. I didn't bother going into details about the abortion and stuff. I think that would be too early for him to know and he might think bad of me if he knew I had had an abortion and miscarried a baby just last year. I began to ask him some questions as well.

He says he's nineteen years old. His father and one of his sisters live down south in Arkansas. His mother lives off of 51st in King Drive. He also has seven other sisters and two brothers that live down on the low end, as he called it.

"What's the low end?"

"You know, down on 35th, 47th and 51st off King Drive."

"I've never been down there before."

"Oh, you will. I plan on taking you down there soon." James told me that his older brother lives not too far from where we were. He's not married, but he has twin girls. They were born when he was younger, but he doesn't get a chance to see them at all.

"Wow, you have a big family. Are you all very close? I only have one brother. He's younger than I am and we are very close. He is all I have."

"Well, Debra, I want you to think about it as if I am all you have. I will protect you and nobody will ever hurt you again," referring to my uncle. "Debra, I would like to ask you something?"

"Okay, what is it?"

"How do you feel about having children? Have you ever given that any thought? I mean, you know when the time is right."

"Well, James I have thought about it and I would love to have a baby. You know, when the time is right and with the right one." I looked at him and dropped my head.

"What you do that for?"

160

"What?"

"You know, dropping your head like that?"

"Oh, nothing, it's nothing."

"Okay, listen, Debra, very carefully. Let me tell you something. No, look at me when I'm talking to you." He placed his hand on my chin and lifted my head. "I am going to be honest with you about everything that I do, and I want you to do the same with me, how about that?"

"Okay, I will."

That afternoon went great. Hattie came in and out of the front room, giving us time to talk. She came in again and asked, "Do you have a friend that I might be able to hook up with?"

James replied, "Hell yeah, baby girl! You know I got somebody just for you! Matter of fact, I am going to have to run, but I will see you later. Debra, how long are you going to be over here?"

"Well, I have a curfew. I have to be in the house by the time the street lights come on."

He looked at me and smile, "That's right baby. I need for you to get back on the other side of Stoney, and it's not time for you to be over here like that yet."

Section 91

Always go with your gut...

Hattie started laughing, "I know that's right! These niggas will eat her up over here and do her a job. Ain't nobody gonna do nothing to me!"

"That's right, baby. If anybody ask or say anything to you, you let them know that you are my girl, James' girl! James Jr.! You tell them that and they will know not to fuck with you! Because none of these motherfuckers on this side of town want to fuck with me, or make me mad."

161

He really got mad. He was yelling and spit was flying everywhere. He does care about me; he got upset just at the thought of someone bothering me.

I looked at him like, 'okay!' I couldn't understand why he was getting that upset. He could tell by the expression on my face that I was a little puzzled about his reaction to what Hattie said. James grabbed my hand as he walked to the door and said that I will learn that whether he was on the scene or not, just his name among niggas will respect you, if they know that I belong to him.

He leaned down and kissed me on my cheek and said, "Don't be too much longer over here. I don't want to see you over here after dark. Remember night time don't have no eyes and bad things happen to young girls out here by themselves without protection. Hey, Hattie! The next time I see you, baby, I will have my right hand man with me, just for you!"

"Okay James, I'll be looking forward to meeting him."

James was down those stairs and out that door before we got a chance to say anything else. I yelled down at him, "When I'm gonna see you again?

"Don't worry, baby, I will find you!" The door slammed and he was gone.

I was so happy that I felt like I was going to bust on the inside! I was giggling and turned to Hattie, "What you think about him?"

"Well, Debra he is too fast for you. It's something about him I can't put my finger on, but when I do figure it out, I will let you know. Now, he said he's gonna make sure he keep you a good girl and he is not going to let nobody hurt you. Other than that, I think that he is really cool." She gave me high five, laughing. "I just hope he don't bring no ugly dude over here for me to meet!"

"Listen, Hattie, it is getting late and I want to get home before my mother comes home, plus James said he didn't want me over here after dark!"

162

We thought that was somewhat funny! "I want to talk with my Nana about him and all what happen today."

"Dag, you tell your grandmother everything that you do?"

"Yeah, she is a cool grandmother. She loves me and I love her more."

"I wish I had somebody to talk to like that, you know, somebody I can trust."

"Yeah, I trust my Nana and she said that I was her favorite grandchild. I can talk to her about anything and she will keep a secret. Maybe if you want I can tell my Nana that you don't have anybody to talk to, maybe you can talk to her. She is really smart and she is not going to tell you nothing wrong."

"Thanks, Debra, but that's okay. I'll be alright."

"Okay, see you later. I be over tomorrow."

"Yeah, ahmm, wait. I got too take my son over to my mother's house and I got some errands to run... I'll catch up with you..."

"Okay then, bye-bye."

I passed that house where all those guys was still drinking and talking loud. I was so nervous as I walked on the other side of the street, trying not to look over there at them. I walked pretty fast. I couldn't tell whether or not James was over there. I just wanted to cross Stoney without anyone saying anything to me.

Section 92

Be anxious for nothing.

I was thinking about the different things that James had said to me. I wondered what my mother is going say to him when he calls me. He said that I was his girl and I didn't have to worry about anything. I was puzzled about all of this. I wanted to believe him, but I also didn't want to be hurt again either. When I got into the house I went upstairs to my room.

"Hi, Mommie. Hi, Nana." I kept walking.

"What's wrong with you, Debbie?"

"Nothing, Mommie. Nothing is wrong."

"Something is wrong with her," Nana said.

"Come here, Debbie!"

I turned around, "Yes, Mommie?"

"Where have you been? Come in here and talk to me. Sit down. What's going on with you? And for once in your life, tell the truth."

"Come on, Debbie, tell your Nana what's bothering you."

I sat down and began to tell them both what was going on. I told them how we met, how he reacted when he saw me. "He picked me up right in the middle of the street in front of all those people and kissed me on my cheek." I told how he walked me to the corner of the house and I showed him where I lived.

"He asked for my phone number and I gave it to him, but I don't really know what you are going to say to him when he calls, I mean, if he calls me. I think he likes me, too. Well, at least by his actions he does. I just need help to know how to go on a real date if he asks me. What if he asked me to go on a date or something? I mean he is a big boy and it's something about him that I like." I told them how well dressed he was and all of that.

"Hold on a minute, when are you going to bring him by here so that I can meet him? Have you been with him, Debbie?"

"No, Mommie! I have not had sex with him! I just meet him!"

"Hey, watch who you are talking to with that smart ass mouth of yours!"

"No, Mommie. I'm sorry. I have not had sex with this boy."

"Nana, he has a cold and he won't even really kiss me because he don't want me to catch his cold. He is nice to me."

"Well, I want to meet this James. I'll see for myself how nice he is and whether or not you can see him. Cause I'm not going to go through this shit with you over again, Debbie! Do you understand me?"

"Yes, I do, Mommie. I understand."

I turned to walk away. Nana said, "Debbie, I would love to meet this boy. I'm pretty sure he is nice to you. Don't get your hopes up. Just wait and see what happens."

"Okay, Nana. Okay, Mommie. Thank you."

A couple of weeks went by before I saw James again. I was going over to Hattie's house almost every day, but he was nowhere to be found. I wouldn't dare ask anyone about him. Sooner or later he will show up. I remember him telling me that he had business on the low end.

One day, I was walking to Hattie's house and someone walked up behind me.

"I know that you are young, but do you think your mother would let me take you out on a date?" It was him. It was James.

"Keep walking. Don't turn around. Just listen to me. It will be another couple with us. I want to take you some place special. Do you think your mother is going to let you go?"

"What? Like a double date?"

"Yeah, baby, just like a double date."

"I don't see why she wouldn't. I already asked her if could I go with you and she said that you have to come over to the house so she can meet you. So when are you gonna come? Are we going out to eat, to the movies, what?"

He just kissed me on my neck and said, "You'll see. I promise you it will be something that you never done before and you will like it. How about

Friday night? I'll tell you what, I will be at your house to pick you up around 7 p.m."

"Thanks, James. You know this is going to really be my first real date."

"Oh, yeah? That's good to know, as he smiled at me. "You are as sweet as apple pie. You like apple pie, too?"

"My Nana makes the best apple pie you have ever tasted before in your life. Maybe I can get her to make you one." I could feel this big smile on my face as we talked.

James was staring at me as we walked, saying, "Thank you, God, for blessing me with her. She is so sweet. I can train her."

"What you mean train me," as I leaned back looking at him curiously.

"I'm gonna show you how a man really wants his girl to be, that's what I mean. You want to make me happy, don't you?"

"Yeah, I do."

"Because all I want is for you to be happy and I know that I am the one to do it, if you just give me a chance. Trust me, Debra. Everything's going to be alright."

When he said that, I thought about my Nana. That is what she says to me all the time, so he must be the one for me.

My Nana told me to stop looking for somebody and I did. Look how we met each other. It must be that we are meant to be together. I trust you James.

Section 93

Do you really know who your daughter is dating?

That Friday came and my mother's girlfriend Candy was over. They helped me get dressed for my first date. I wore that blue/white top that Nana had bought me when I was pregnant with white pants. I fixed my hair like a

166

big girl and Candy had some lip gloss that she let me wear and put in my purse.

"Now, Debbie, don't be fast doing shit you ain't got no business doing!"

"I'm not, Mommie. How do I look?"

"You look just fine. Here, put some of my cologne." My mother sprayed a little on me. Oh, you just don't know how that felt for my mother to spray some of her expensive cologne on me! It smelled so good. It was Charles of the Ritz.

The doorbell rang and I looked at the time. "It's him and I'm not ready!"

"Oh, you alright. I'll get the door."

"Here I come, Mommie. Let me answer the door and let him in to meet you." I ran passed her.

"Okay, bring him into the kitchen so that we can get a good look at him."

I opened the door and there he stood with this long black cashmere coat on with a multi gray color chinchilla wide collar, a gray beaver hat, a gray walking suit with dark gray snake skin shoes, with this big smile on his face. He asked if I was ready to go out with him.

"Yeah, I'm ready, but you got to come and meet my mother. Come on in."

"Debra, you look so pretty."

"Wow, you look fantastic! You look like a grown man. You really look nice!" He chuckled a little and leaned over and whispered in my ear, "I am a grown man. John and Carmen are out in the car waiting on us."

"Okay, I'm ready. Follow me so I can introduce you to my mother. She's in the kitchen."

I was so nervous. I didn't know what my mother was going to say, but I knew by the way he was dressed, my mother was going to like him. She always said she admired a well-dressed man, and, baby, he was well-dressed!

"Mommie, this is James. James, this is my mother and her girlfriend, and this is my Nana, my grandmother."

"Hello, it's nice to meet all of you," as he reached out to shake everyone's hand. "If I had of known that I was going to be in the company of such fine ladies as yourselves, I would have made arrangements for you all to join us this evening." He was so charming!

"It's a pleasure in meeting all of you and I see where Debra gets her beauty from. She looks just like you," as he held my mother's hand and asked her name.

"Marian is my name and this is my mother Mrs. Norman and my friend Candy."

"Yes, I see that the real beauty started here," as he shook Nana's hand.

Section 94

Listen to the wise.

Nana just laughed and gave him a hug. "He smell good, look good and he knows how to talk a lot of shit. Yeah, he knows how to talk quick. He's one of those cool slick ass niggas. You got watch him. You better go head." They all laughed out loud.

"Listen at Mama. Don't pay her no attention." They continued to laugh at Nana.

"Well, on that note, Miss Marian, I do have another couple out in the car waiting on us. We're going downtown to one of the restaurants on Rush or Water Street. What time would you like for me to have her home?" Still talking, James turned to walk toward the front door.

"On Rush Street, are you? Well, she needs to be home by 12:30, no later than 1:00.

James stood at the front door. "Yes, I will make sure that she is back on time."

"Debra, are you ready?"

"Yeah, I am."

"I'll meet you in the car, okay?"

"Here I come," as I turned and smiled at my Mommie, saying bye.

My mother's girlfriend said, "Damn, he's fine! Girl, if I was just a few years younger...!"

My mother hit her on her arm and said, "Candy, stop!" as they both laughed. I stood in the doorway giving everybody a hug and kiss before I left. James was standing at the car, holding the door open for me. You could hear my Mommie saying, "Make sure you take care of my daughter."

He replied, "I'm gonna take real good care of her. Not to worry. I'll protect her like I own her. She will be back on time." He gave a little chuckle.

Section 95

Being exposed at a young age

I was so happy. This was my first real date. We got in the back seat. His friend John and his girlfriend Carmen was in front. James would always speak of them, but this was my first time meeting them. John had a Jeri curl and wore a brown suit with a tie. Carmen wore a big long black wig and had on a lot of make-up. And from what I saw from the back seat, she had on a real low cut halter top with no bra. She had real big, huge boobs.

They were very polite to me. I was really glad that I had finally met somebody that James knew. I felt real special and a part of something or someone that he cared about.

169

Carmen turned around to look at me chewing some gum with real red lipstick on her oversized lips. She asking me had I ever worked a job before, or was this my first time?

I said, "No, I don't have a job yet, but when I get a little older, I will be able to find one."

James immediately jumped in, "John, check your girl." Before you knew it, John was yelling at Carmen telling her to turn around and mind her own damn business. That she just better make sure she do what she got to do and don't worry about what I'm doing.

I leaned over and whispered to James, "I don't have a job yet. I have to be sixteen before McDonalds or Burger King will hire me."

He looked at me and smiled, "Don't worry, baby. I'm gonna teach you what to do. You'll be okay."

"Teach me what, to do about what? You know somebody who work at McDonald's or Burger King?

They all laughed. "Don't worry. It will be alright. Just sit back and relax and enjoy the ride," as he kissed me on my forehead.

Section 96

Growing up too fast

I thought about this being my first time ever being in a car with a boy after the street lights were on, and my Mommie said I didn't have to be in the house until 12:30 tonight or 1:00 in the morning.

Man, this is fun! They were talking among themselves and I was just looking out the window at all the pretty lights on the tall buildings as we drove on Lake Shore Drive. I never had seen Chicago at nighttime; well, only when Mommie would take me and my brother to see the Buckingham Fountain at night. And that was so long ago.

There it was, the Buckingham Fountain! "Look, James! Look! The Buckingham Fountain! Ain't it pretty? Wow!" We drove pass it and they continued to laugh even louder.

"What? You all don't like the Buckingham Fountain? I like it. It's pretty at night time."

I felt a little embarrass because it was nothing to them. I was acting like a little girl. I guess James could tell by the expression on my face that I was embarrassed.

"I'm going to take you there one day next week and we will just walk downtown so you can see the pretty lights. Would you like that?"

"Yeah, I would. You really would bring me here?"

"Baby, I will do anything for you."

Section 97

Your daughter is easy prey and you don't even know it!

"Hey, man, you got any more syrup left?" John asked James.

"Hold on, man." James was reaching in his pocket pulling out this brown bottle and took a few swallows before he passed it up front to John. I asked him what was that and he told me that it was cough syrup.

"What? You have a cold?"

"Something like that. I thought I told you that before that you have to listen and remember what I tell you. You will learn that I do not like to repeat myself."

"Okay, I didn't know you had a bad cold that you had to take medicine for it. If you have a cold, my Nana said that you're not supposed to drink after nobody because you can get their germs and even catch their cold. So, since John has a cold, too, he should get his own bottle. Otherwise, both of you are gonna stay sick." Dag, you would have thought that I said a joke or something. They all started laughing at me again.

"What is so funny? That is true what my Nana said. You will never get rid of your cold."

John said, "Man, where did you luck up on her?

"Man, you heard her. Give me my bottle back. You need to get your own." And they continued to laugh. "Man, she is sweet, yeah. I know that's why I'm gonna keep her real close to me and you better not even look this way." He put that bottle back into his pocket.

John pulled over on this side street and there were so many people walking the streets. It must have been some type of party or something. I had never seen anything like this before. There were a lot of ladies trying to get a ride because they were waving at the cars like they were cabs or something. I see why they were trying to get a ride. "Look, James," pointing at this lady, "she is real cold. She hardly have any clothes on."

James looked at me and said, "Baby you are the sweetest thing that ever happen to me," kissing me on my forehead, and rubbing the side of my face. "I think I'm falling in love with you already."

"I know you are," John chuckled, turning around asking me do I have any sisters. "Huh! She ain't got no sisters. She's all mine," as he hugged me.

John told Carmen as she was getting out the car, "You know what I told you—no longer than five minutes each and if it is a minute more, that's an extra twenty. "

"Yeah, I know, John. I'm doing this," as she shut the door behind her. John looked at James and said, "What's up is-am, zi-s-am fa-is-um …"

They were talking in a way that I hear my mother say all the time. It's called pig latin. I couldn't understand a word that they were saying. I just thought that it was none of my business since they were talking like that.

"Well, man, in a few years I will have it just the way I want it to be. Watch, this is gonna be a keeper for life."

John laughed, as he got out the car walking toward one of the ladies who was standing on the corner.

James reached in his pocket and took another swallow of that syrup and said, "Now, Debra, when I drink this syrup, it sometimes make me feel like nodding off, so I want you to just watch me to make sure don't nobody come up on me without you letting me first, " as he locked the door. "Is that too hard for you to do?"

"No, that's not too hard. I will let you know if somebody walks up to the car."

I just looked out the window at the different women walking and standing on the corner holding their small jacket close trying to keep the cold wind from blowing on them. Some were leaning over in different cars that had pulled up, talking to the driver. Sometimes they would get in the car and drive off and sometimes they would just walk away. I thought to myself they shouldn't be so choosey about who gives them a ride. It's kinda cold outside.

I was looking all around from the front, side and back—making sure that no one comes to the car without me letting James know. He was sleepy; that medicine had him leaning his head down. When I turned to the back window and as I gazed out, there was this one lady that was standing on the corner of this alley. She turned and looked at me with these dark piercing eyes.

She had on a wig just like Carmen's and a lot of make-up. She wore these real tall red high heel shoes with black fish-net stockings and white hot pants and a red bra for a top—all covered with rabbit fur jacket. She reached in her red purse and pulled out a cigarette and lit it. As she blew the smoke out of her mouth, she noticed that I was looking at her and she began to shake her head at me saying no.

Section 98

Do you talk to your daughter about the good and the bad?

I quickly turned around and began looking out the front window. I had no idea why she was shaking her head at me. Hell, I wasn't the one standing on the corner of an alley with hardly any clothes on, trying to get a ride.

There was this one man out there yelling at one of the ladies about something. Then I saw him hit her in the face and knock her down! Oh, my God, she's bleeding! I was trying to figure out what was really going on. It was a bar there and people where coming out of the bar and some of the men would even stop to talk to one or two of the ladies.

There's Carmen. What is she doing getting in the car with somebody else? I didn't see John; he had gone into the bar.

"James! James! Carmen just got in the car with somebody and John is in the bar! That man over there in that loud, long, ugly orange coat and that purple suit just hit that lady and now she's bleeding! The lady that is standing behind us with those red shoes on was shaking her head at me saying no! "I'm scared. I don't like it here. How long you think John and Carmen is gonna be and where did she go? Why would she get in a car with somebody when we are sitting right here waiting on her?"

"Slow down. It's okay, baby. Everything is gonna be alright," as he looked at me with those big pretty brown eyes, giving me assurance that it was okay. He knew I was ready to go.

"Now, you said who was shaking their head at you?" as he turned to look.

"That lady right there and you said that John was in the bar?"

"Yeah."

"Well, sit right here. I'll be back. It's time to go anyways. I got some business that I need to take care of and it's almost that time for me to get you back home. We're going to stop and get you something to eat. Are you hungry?"

"Yeah, I am."

"Okay, wait in the car. I won't go too far and lock the door behind me. And don't open the car door for nobody, but me. Do you understand me?"

"Yeah I do," nodding my head as I watched James walked toward the bar down the street.

Something was wrong; it just didn't feel right. Even though everything was exciting to seeing all of this stuff, I was still scared. I hope James don't think I'm a little girl and won't ask me to go anywhere else with him. I think I screwed up by waking him up because he really doesn't feel well. If he has to keep taking that cough syrup medicine and sharing it with his friend, he's not going to get well.

Oh, there's Carmen. She's back. I guess this is a part of Chicago that all the ladies try and see who can wear the least amount of clothes cause this just don't make any sense at all.

I can't wait until I tell my Nana how these people were looking. I have never seen anything like this before. I just don't understand what was going on and why.

She knocked on the window, "Debra, open the door." I leaned forward and opened the door for Carmen. And good, here's James, and John's coming out of the bar.

"Where did they go?" Carmen asked as she got in the car.

"Here they come now. Where did you go Carmen when you got in that car?"

By the time she got ready to answer me, James had gotten to the door.

"Hey, let's go over to Ronnie's Steak House and eat a little something. It's time for me to get this girl home. "

"Yeah, man, you know you better be on time with that," John replied.

Section 99

You're nothing but bait, easy pickings!

"I been there before. My mother took me one time."

"Yeah, that's good, baby, but we are pressed for time and we are gonna have to take a rain check on that. Hey John, I really got a taste for some livers and gizzards at Harold's Chicken."

"Ugh, I don't eat that, but I do like the breast of the chicken. That's the only part of the chicken I like." I couldn't imagine eating livers and gizzards.

"Harold's chicken it is then."

John turned to Carmen and asked her how she did. "Well, I got about 4-5."

"Good, just hold onto that."

James put his arm around me and leaned in to whisper in my ear, "I thought I told you not to open the door for nobody, but me?"

Just as I went to respond, he looked at me with this real strange look and said, "Don't let it happen again." He kissed me on my forehead and patted my arm as he held me real tight to him.

"Don't worry, baby, you will learn that what I say, I mean. Remember, I love you."

I laid my head on his shoulder and looked up at him. "Okay, I love you, too." John yelled out, "Bingo!" And he and James began to talk in pig latin again.

The drive back was really nice. "Debra, you know I have been looking for someone like you all my life and now that I have you, I'm not going to let you go. You belong to me, baby. Don't you want to belong to me for me to take good care of you, protect you and love you?"

"Yeah, that's what I want. Are you sure you want me, James?"

"Baby, you just don't know how much you belong to me."

I felt so good on the inside I finally got somebody to love me for who I am. I've forgotten about ever being with Patrick. We made a bond with each other that we will be friends. Mack hurt me too bad the way he the dumped me. Well, I hurt him by letting my mother kill our baby. And Piggie… He's just another boy that I was attracted to, but never gave it a chance because he talks too much and he spread rumors about me. Or, should I say he hung around all the boys that called me out of my name, laughed and pointed fingers at me.

We stopped and had something to eat and then he took me home. That was a very interesting night and it was just between us because James made me promise not to tell what I saw or where we were.

"Okay, Debra, I'll see you tomorrow. I want you to go over to Hattie's tomorrow and I will meet you there. Then I will show you where John and Carmen live. It's just around the corner from Hattie's house."

"Okay, I see you tomorrow. It was nice meeting you, John and Carmen. I had fun. See you guys tomorrow."

When I walked in the house, my mother was waiting for me in the kitchen with her girlfriend Candy. I told my mother what a nice time that we had. I told her we went out to eat at Ronnie's Steak House and just walked around downtown for a while.

"He is really nice. We held hands and talked. He said that he wants to take me to the movies tomorrow. Can I go?"

"We will see."

"Okay, Mommie, good night." And I headed upstairs.

"Debbie, I don't see why you can't go to the movies. It will be alright."

"Oh, thank you!" as I gave her a big hug and a kiss.

I went upstairs and straight to bed. I was tired even though we didn't do anything but sit in the car and look at all those ladies.

Section 100

For every action there's a reaction. This is true...

Being rebellious will get you in trouble.

I was seeing James on a regular basis now—well, whenever he came on that side of town. He had some type of job on the low end. I was still going over to Hattie's house, and every now and then, James would come around and take me over to John and Carmen's apartment.

One day, Beverly came over to the house and I told her about James and that I was going on the other side of Stoney. "Come on, Beverly, and go over here with me so you can meet him and Hattie. She's my friend and she got her own apartment."

"Okay, I'll go with you this time, but you better not get me in any trouble."

"I'm not gonna get you in no trouble. You'll get yourself in trouble. Come on with your scary self!" as we laughed together and ran across Stoney Island.

"Debbie, are you sure about coming over here? It looks dangerous!"

"These people not thinking about us, girl. Come on! You're gonna like them. And, I want you to see where I be at all the time. I've been coming over here now for about six months or better and nothing never happen to me. Everybody knows that I am James' girl, so I don't have to worry about anything over here. He is a big boy for real and people do what he says over here and everybody knows him."

Hattie was glad to meet my cousin. She was wondering when she was going to meet her since I spoke of Beverly all the time. Hattie said, "You must really love your cousin and you guys must be real close because that's all you talk about in your family, besides your Nana."

"Yeah, me and my cousin are close."

"So, how did you meet my cousin Debbie?" Hattie shared how we met, and we laughed and joked around.

Hattie had gone to the bathroom and Beverly asked, "Debbie, you sure she is nineteen? She looks older than that, and why she don't have no furniture in her apartment?"

"She just moved here and she is nineteen. What, you don't like her or something?"

"I didn't say that."

At that moment, you could hear voices and footsteps walking up the hallway. Someone knocked on the door several times real hard.

"Hattie, somebody's knocking at your door," I yelled out. "I'm gonna answer it."

"Okay, go ahead."

James wasn't there when we got there, but it was soon after he appeared with his friend Denzel.

"Who is it?" I yelled.

"James! Baby, open the door." James and Denzel came in.

"Hey, what's up? What the hell going on up in here? Who is this lovely lady?"

"This, James, is my cousin Beverly, the one I've been telling you about."

"What you been saying about me, Debbie?" as she laughed.

"Denzel, this is my cousin Beverly." When they made eye contact with each other, it was like love at first sight! They were looking at each other like they were in a daze.

"Look like you see something you like! Hell, yeah, he see something he like! Your cousin is fine as hell!" We began to laugh and give each other high five.

By the time Hattie came out the bathroom, they were drinking beer and smoking a joint.

"Let's get the party going!" shouted James.

We had so much fun that day! From then on, Beverly would visit me more often just so she could see Denzel. We still had to be home by the time the street lights came on, but one night, Beverly and I spent the night out with them at Hattie's.

We woke up the next morning to someone knocking on the door, screaming. "I know you are in there! Debbie! Beverly! Open this damn door!" It was my mother and Auntie DD! Oh my God, we are in trouble!

"Hattie, don't tell them we are here!" We ran toward the back, out the back door and hid. James had already left about 2:00 or 3:00 that morning, so he was long gone. Denzel, Hattie, Beverly and I were the only ones in the house.

Our hearts was beating so fast and we were so scared. We could hear their voices.

Auntie DD said, "You let me catch you having my daughter up in this nasty ass house and I will have your ass locked up!" My mother asked, "Where is she?" We could hear Hattie tell them, "They are not here."

"Beverly! Beverly! You hear me calling you, don't you run from me. Mommie is worried about you. Baby, come home." Then we heard my mother say, "Debbie if you don't come home, don't you bother to come back because this is the first and the last time I will come looking for you!"

Then you heard them leaving. Beverly and I were hiding under the stairs out in the basement.

180

"Debbie, I got to go! Come on! My Mommie is crying for me! She's worried about me!"

"Well, my Mommie's not! She could care less! You heard what she said! I'm not going! I'm running away from home!"

"Debbie, why you gonna do that! You really gonna get it!"

"Yeah, I know, Beverly. That's why I'm not going home cause Uncle Tom is gonna whoop me and my Mommie, too! I can't do it no more! I'm tired of him kicking my ass! You go! Go, catch up with your Mommie! Just don't tell on me and where I'm at, okay? Pinky swear?"

"Okay, Debbie, be careful! I love you!"

"I love you, too." We gave each other a hug. She ran from the back and around the corner to catch up with her Mommie.

So you see, my life started out with the wrong attitude. Even though I knew better, I was destined for trouble. For whatever reason, I didn't listen to that voice I heard saying 'Go Home!'

I wanted a baby and I needed to be loved. I rebelled against my mother and there was nothing she could do about it. Most of all, I wanted to get away from my uncle and his abuse. I believe that if he hadn't come to live with us, our lives would have been totally different.

That day was crazy! I drank my first wine cooler and I was smoking cigarettes. Denzel had left. I knew he was gonna tell James what happened. I didn't care.

"Hattie, you said that I could stay here with you. So, can I stay?"

"Yeah, Debra, you know that you can. You can stay as long as you want to."

Section 101

I want to go home.

After a few days, I still had not gone home. I was funky and I needed to change my clothes. I was missing my Mommie and I didn't want Nana to worry about me. Yet, I didn't want to hear my Uncle Tom's mouth calling me out of my name and my mother not saying anything to him—in almost agreement. James has not been by, so I don't think he really knows that I am here and that I didn't go home. Otherwise, he would be here. He said that he would take care of me.

"Hattie, I don't know what to do. I'm afraid and I want to be with James, but I miss my Nana."

"Debra, listen. Go home. Call your mother and just see what she is going to say to you. James is doing things that you don't even know about and you are really too young to be with him. He's not good for you, Debra. Go home."

There's always a moment in life that you look back on and know that you should have listened!

"Yeah, maybe you're right, right about me calling my mother. I will do that, but I'm not going to stop seeing James."

I did call my Mommie on the fourth night, crying, telling her I want to come home, but I was scared.

"Will you let me come back home? I'm sorry, Mommie. I won't run away no more. Can I come home?"

"Where you at, Debbie?"

"Down the street."

"Is that Debbie, Marian?" It was Nana's voice I heard.

182

"Will you tell Nana that I love her," as the tears streamed from my eyes. "Mommie, I'm sorry. I promise I won't do it again. I'm cold and I'm scared and I don't have nowhere to go. Can I come home?"

"Stop all that damn crying! You weren't crying for these pass three days! Were you?! Thought your fast ass was gonna be alright!"

"Marian, stop talking to her like that!"

"Debbie, let me tell you something. You got ten minutes to get your ass to this house! Not eleven! Ten! Ten fucking minutes! And if you are not here in ten minutes, you may as well stay out there another night since you want to take your fast ass out in the motherfucking streets!"

"Okay, Mommie, here I come!" I was right there on the corner of 69th in Stoney at the pay phone near the Burger King. I ran home so fast, I was there in less than five minutes! I was glad that I could come home.

James found out what had happened and called me. "Debra, I got to see you. I want your mother to know that I had nothing to do with that and I can't lose you. You are the love of my life. Don't you miss me, baby?"

My life seemed to be much better, I thought. I was happy to be home, but that only lasted for a short period of time. My uncle began calling me names all over again, like he was just waiting for things to die down.

It has been a month or so that I have been on punishment, but that didn't stop me from seeing James. I would go over to John's house to see if he was there. I went back to school and still something was missing in my life. I was so far behind that it was too hard for me to catch up. There was so much humiliation: I was being made fun of because I had been pregnant and had had an abortion. People were still calling me out of my name and looking down on me. I didn't have any one to really talk to. No one really knew or understood how I was truly feeling on the inside.

James was there for me. I would honestly tell him all these things that were going on with me—how mean and hateful my uncle was, about all he did was beat up on me and my auntie, and about the different women in the house with him when my auntie was not there. Hell, sometimes the other lady would be right there, but my auntie would think she was one of my mother's friends.

I told James everything that was going on in the house because he listened and asked questions. He was concerned and cared about me, and he told me that he would always protect me—something that's been missing at home for as long as I can remember. But, Nana loves me and she always tell me that everything is gonna be alright.

Section 102

Is this a wolf in sheep clothing?

James decided that he was going to come over to the house to visit with me. The night that he showed up at the door was when things really began to change.

My mother had one of her male friends over to the house and they were in the kitchen. James and I were sitting in the den, right off from the kitchen. My mother's friend told my mother that he had seen James down on 35th street pool hall and that he was a very dangerous person. On top of that, he told my mother that James was a heroin addict, that he shot heroin in his arm.

James was listening to him as he sat there with his dark sunglasses on, looking and watching everything that was going on, and talking to me at the same time.

My mother said, "James, come in here for a minute. Let me ask you something."

"Yes ma'am." as he stood up and walked toward the kitchen.

"James, take your glasses off in the house. It's hard for me to talk to you without me seeing your eyes."

My mother's friend said, "Yep, that's him. I knew I recognize your face. I've seen you down on 35th in Giles, down at the pool hall. I know you."

"Hey, man, you don't know nothing about me cause if you did, you would know not to talk to me that way! I'm sorry, Miss Marian. No disrespect, but, yes, I do go down to the pool hall to shoot pool. There's nothing wrong with that. So, what's your point, man, in telling these people this?"

"Is that all you shoot is pool?" my mother asked.

"Hell, no!" yelled my mother's friend. "That ain't all he shoot! This nigga is on heroin and you don't know who is messing with your daughter!"

"Is that true James? Let me see your arm."

"What! Ain't none of you motherfuckers got no right to talk to me like this! My name is James! Pointing his finger at my mother's friend, he declared, "You, little nigga, I will see you again!" He turned to walk away.

"Mommie, what you do that for? James!" I ran behind him to the door. "What's wrong? Why were you cursing in front of my mother like that?"

"You saw what they just did to me!"

"Debbie, come here and let that nigga go! He ain't shit and if you run after him, you ain't gonna be shit."

"Listen Debra," as he grabbed me by my arms, I love you! I told you that I would die if I didn't have you in my life! I told you that I would take care of you and you don't have to put up with this bullshit! I see now what you were saying!" He leaned down and kissed me. "I love you," as his voice cracked. "You know where I am at," and he walked out the door.

"Debbie! Debbie! Close that motherfucking door and bring your fast ass in here right now!"

185

What the fuck just happen! I don't believe this as I walked into the kitchen and sat down wiping the tears from my face. I sat there just listening to this man talk about James and how he was such a bad person. For him to say that James was on heroin was really bad. I was told that was what my daddy used, and because my mother wouldn't take him back, he died.

Is this what they want me to do—leave James so that he will die, too? I'm not going to do it!

"Debbie! Do you hear me talking to you?!"

"Yes, Mommie, I hear you."

"Leave that boy along and I don't want you back over there no more! Do you understand me?"

"Yeah, I do."

"Now go to bed!"

How could my life go so wrong now? I don't understand! I laid there in bed and cried. My life was over now. I will never find anybody to love me.

Section 103

Getting even comes with a price. Was I wrong?

My brother was still coming in and out of the house. Chuckie had done something and was going to get a whipping that day when we got home from school.

I came home and all of my mother's and uncle's clothes were on the couch with other items in the house. Papa said that Chuckie and his friends ran out of the house when he got home from work.

Uncle Tom came in the house cursing and calling my brother all kinds of motherfuckers and how he was going to beat the living shit out of him when he get his hands on him! Papa said that Chuckie was not allowed to come back to this house again, that my Mommie had to move and get out of his house. "They took my shot gun and took Nana's wedding rings."

My uncle turned and looked at me, "You are next! I've been waiting to get my hands on your little sneaky ass! I wouldn't put it pass you if you had something to do with it!" He slapped me up side my head and I fell to the floor.

Once Papa and my uncle left the house, I rose up and said this is it! I am sick and tired of this motherfucker hitting on me! Something came over me and all I saw was a way out, a way to get out of this house and away from my uncle and with his degrading, womanizing, self-centered, egotistic, pseudo black ass!

I got some garbage bags and filled them up with all of my uncle's stuff. I mean all of it! From his nasty ass drawers to his shoes—everything of his!!

Motherfucker, this is for me and my brother! All of these things were running through my head as I frantically threw his stuff into the garbage bags! I was so afraid of getting caught and too afraid to cry! I kept running to the window looking out for the car. I got four large garbage bags filled up, dragged them across the street and rang Nesa's doorbell.

Nesa look out the window and I yelled up, "Open the door! Come help me! Hurry up!" The door buzzed and I was in, dragging the bags in the hallway and Nesa ran down to help with the other bags.

"What's this, Debra? What you do?"

"I don't know, Nesa! I came home and all of my mother's and Uncle Tom's clothes and stuff was all over the couch in the den! Papa said that Chuckie and his friends had broken into the house! Tom slapped me in my face! Now they say Chuckie can't come back and Uncle Tom is going to whoop my ass when he got back! So, I just took all of his stuff!"

"Oh, shit! You took all his shit?"

"Yep!"

"So, what are you going to do now?"

"Well, I told you about James. You met him, right? He said that he would take care of me and that I could stay with him."

"Debra, are you sure?"

"Hell, I can't go back now!" We were dumping everything on the floor.

All of a sudden, you heard my Uncle's voice, "Debbie, you motherfucker, you black bitch ass motherfucker! Don't you bring your ass back to this house or I'll kill you! Motherfuck! You little bitch!"

Nesa and I were peeking out the window and we could see him just standing on the front porch yelling to the top of his lungs.

"Now, you see why I can't ever go back home?"

"Yeah, I do. That's messed up, Debra, how your uncle treats you!"

"Well, let him go out and spend money and buy him some new clothes! Who's the motherfucker now!" We just laughed at him.

I gathered up all that stuff. "Nesa, you got any Christmas boxes and gift wrapping paper?"

"Yeah, I think we do. What you gonna do?"

Section 104

You get what you ask for.

"I'm going to wrap this stuff up, put it in some boxes and give them to James as gifts."

"Are you sure you want to do that?" Hell, what he gonna give you?"

"Nesa, I'm going to be staying with him and I don't have a job yet, so this is what I'm giving to him."

My gut told me I was headed for trouble, but I ignored it and had no idea I was running into the arms of a wolf dressed in sheep clothing.

"How are you going to get this over there?"

"Well, there is still a grocery cart in the alley, so I'll get it and push the stuff over there. I got to hurry up cause my mother will be getting off work soon and I don't want her to see me crossing Stoney."

"Okay, come on. I'll help you down the back. Let me get the key to unlock the gate." Nesa got the key and I got all the bags together at the back door.

"Well, Nesa, I don't know when I'm gonna see you again, but I will keep in touch to let you know that I'm okay. Tell Nettie what happened."

"Be careful, Debra. I see you later."

I was so afraid of getting caught that I ran down and up the back alleys, trying to stay out of sight. I hope James like all of this stuff. I know he will.

Once I get across Stoney, I'll be okay. They won't come over here looking for me. Their standards are too high to be around the people over here.

I made it! Now, I just have to get to John and Carmen's house which is a few blocks away.

When I got there, Carmen answered the door. "James and John had just left to go to the store. They'll be back in a minute. Come on in. What is all of this you got?"

"I got some things for James. I hope he will like them."

"Oh, I'm sure he will. Did he know that you were coming over here?"

"No, he don't know. It's going to be a surprise."

"Are you sure you want to do this?"

"Yeah, I told you what happened. I don't know what else to do. What you think, he is not going to want me here?"

"No, that ain't it." Just as Carmen replied, James and John walked in.

"Hey, baby, what you doing over here? What's all this stuff? Is this yours?"

"Nope, it's yours." I told him what had happened. "Can I stay with you? I just ran away from home."

"You did what? What is this?" He opened the bags and the wrapped boxes.

"Hell! This is my kind of girl!"

"Man, you can't be no luckier than that," John laughed.

"Did anybody follow you?"

"No, I came down the back alleys and nobody is going to come on this side of Stoney to look for me. Nobody cares about what happens to me, especially after I did this."

"Yeah, I see your point. Hey, man, come in the room and let me holler at you for a minute. You just sit tight until I come back."

"Okay, I will." He and John went into the bedroom.

By the time James came out of the room, he looked really upset. He had a frown on his face like he was mad or something.

"Are you okay?"

"Yeah, I'm fine. Why you ask me that?"

"Because you got a frown on your face like you mad about something."

"Hey, don't worry about me, I'm good. I took some medicine and that's how it have me sometimes."

Months have gone by and I am still living with John and Carmen. James didn't have a house of his own. He never stayed in one place long enough. He would be gone for weeks at a time. He told me to stay there and I'll be alright. He told me that he will be back to get me; he had business to take care of. He had to go to work so he could take care of us. He promised me that we were going to get our own apartment.

Section 105

But, he gave me a place to sleep...

There was an empty apartment in the building across from the laundromat where I used to wash my Nana rugs and silks. This is same building that I once saw the lady throw a bottle out the window!

One day, James took me to that building. "This is our new apartment." I was so happy. I couldn't believe that I had my own place—just me and James.

"How much did this cost? How much do you have to pay for us to live here?"

"Listen, baby, you will learn that whatever it is, I have to go out and get it. Don't you worry about how much anything cost. I'm gonna take good care of you."

We stayed there for about two months. I was lying on the floor one morning when the door opened and this man asked, "What are you doing in here?"

"I live here with my boyfriend!"

"You do? How did you get this apartment?

"I don't know. My boyfriend brought me here and he said that this was our new apartment. He told me to stay here until he got back."

"Little girl, are you a runaway?"

"No, I'm not!"

"Well, let me tell you one damn thing! If you don't get your shit and get the fuck out of my building, I'm calling the police! Your boyfriend broke into this apartment, and has no right to be here. Now, get your little ass out of here before I call the police on you!"

I gathered up my little stuff and put them in a little bag and ran out of the building as fast as I could. I had no idea where I was going. James had not been around in two days and I was really hungry, and it was getting a little chilly outside. I had gotten a few things from the Goodwill store along with the few outfits that I had brought from home.

My brother should be back home by now. I worry about and miss him so much.

Section 106

Lonely and scared

I went into Stoney Liquor and asked my mother's friend that worked there if I could have two dollars to get something to eat. He told me that I should go home because the streets were no place for me. He asked me did I know that my mother had moved and my brother had gone back to the juvenile home for trying to steal a car.

"No, I didn't know that! Where did my mother move to?" He wrote my mother's address down and reached in his pocket and gave me $5.00. "She is worried about you. Go home, Debbie."

"Okay, I will... thank you." I called my Nana hoping she would answer the phone, but Tom answered and I hung up.

It was late and I had nowhere to go, so I walked east on 79th in Colfax to the apartment building where my mother now lived. It took me over an hour to get there and when I finally arrived, it was really late and I didn't want to wake my mother. I was also afraid of what she might say.

I looked on the doorbells and she was on the third floor, apartment #301. As this man was leaving out of the building, I snuck in and went on up to the third floor and sat on the steps right at her door. When she opens the door, she would see me lying there. It was about 11:00 o'clock and I was very tired.

I knew she had to go to work. I must have been really tired because I never heard my mother come out of her apartment and step right over me. She went to work and left me lying right there.

It was now about 7:30 a.m. when I heard some kids were running in the hallway on their way to school. I looked at my watch and knew for sure that she was gone. I knocked on the door, but there was no answer. I knew she had to be downtown by 8:00 a.m., so she had to leave at 6:00 o'clock this morning. I had just missed her.

Section 107
Why did she step over me?!

Well, what do I do now? I left the building, wiping the tears from my eyes thinking about she had stepped right over me like I was nobody. She really doesn't love me anymore.

I walked back on the Southside on 69th in Stoney. I thought about everything that had happened to me. *Where did I go wrong?* I felt like my mother, as well as my uncle, was glad my brother and I were out of the picture. They had no one to yell at and Mommie didn't have to worry about spending any more money on us.

The more I thought about it, the angrier I got. This really wasn't my fault, it was theirs! I didn't do anything wrong! My uncle got what was coming to him for all the shit he put my brother and me through. Chuckie kept running away from home and leaving me to get all the ass whippings!

By the time I got on the Southside, I was tired and hungry. I went to Hattie's apartment and sat over there for a while.

"Debra, I was worried about you! Where have you been?" I told her all what was going on with me and started to cry.

"Don't cry Debra, it will be alright. Don't cry," as she held me in her arms. "You are still a baby and need to be home with your mother."

"She don't want me anymore! She stepped over me and left me there lying on the steps!"

"I know, Debra, I know. Don't cry. Have you seen James? He comes over here with Denzel, so that's why I couldn't understand why you stop coming over here."

"He told me not to come over here no more because your house was open and I would get in trouble over here!"

"Oh, he did?"

"Yeah, but don't tell him that I told you that."

"Okay, I won't."

Section 108
I can't believe he did that!

I heard footsteps running up the stairs.

"Open the door, Hattie! It's me! Open up the door!" It was James and Denzel running in the house and closing the door real fast behind them!

"We got them motherfuckers! We got they ass!" James dumped a brown shopping bag full of food stamp booklets on the floor!

He was sweating and talking fast. He removed this .45 pistol that he had in the pants and laid it on the bed.

"Hey, baby, what you doing over here? I been looking for you. I'll get with you in a minute. I have to handle some business first."

He pulled out this thing that was an ink removal. He and Denzel sat there and took off all the ink that was on the food stamps. James was talking and said that he had just robbed the grocery store by the railroad tracks right off Jeffery!

"Them motherfuckers was slipping and I got they ass! I gotta sell these motherfuckers soon as I get this ink off of them! This nigga up here at this other store gonna buy all this shit! How much we got here? Hey, count this shit and tell me how much this is," as he began to throw some more food stamp books on the bed. "Get a motherfucking pen and paper and write this shit down!"

I thought that he was talking to Hattie until he turned around and looked at me and yelled, "Get the fuck up and do what I told you to do! Don't fuck with me when it comes down to my business!"

"Okay." He scared me! I'd never seen him like this before!

"Where is a pen and some paper, Hattie?" She was already getting it for me. "Here, Debra."

I counted the food stamps and Hattie put them back into the bag as James and Denzel frantically rubbed the ink off the food stamps.

He had me real scared. The only guns I had ever seen were the one that my uncle put to my head, and my Papa's shotgun that he used when he went hunting. I watched him rubbed the ink; he moved so fast and was talking the whole time.

"How much is it now?"

"I was still adding them up, but it's $2,310.00 so far."

"Man, this motherfucking shit is gonna go for half!"

"Fuck that! You know what I mean?"

"Man, when we get in this motherfucker, you let me do the talking cause I ain't taking no less than half! And if that motherfucker don't do right, I'm gonna hit his ass next!"

"Yeah, man, I hear you."

"These motherfuckers don't know who they fucking with when it comes down to my money!"

I didn't know what to think… He just said that he robbed a store! He is going to get in a lot of trouble if they catch him. He's got a gun! I didn't know he would do something like that.

"Hey!" he yelled. "Are you still counting?"

"Yeah, I am. You got $4,000 and something."

"That's good enough!" He grabbed everything and threw two $65.00 books on the bed. "Y'all go get something to eat in this motherfucker and we'll be back. Man, come on that's two gee's this motherfucker getting ready to give me!

Section 109

He just loves me, that's all.

James and Denzel walked out of the door and I looked at Hattie. "That was scary!"

"Yeah, it was and I really don't appreciate him bringing that shit up in my house! What if my little boy was here?"

"Why didn't you tell him that when he was here?"

"Girl, I ain't trying to get in no mess with them niggas. I know what I'm gonna do and that is move away from here! Come on, girl, let's walk up to Ted's and pick up something, some hog head cheese and crackers. "I know they like that."

"What's hog head cheese?"

"You ain't never had none of that before?"

"Nope." She laughed at me. "Well, what do you want?"

"I just want some baloney with cheese and crackers. That'll be fine. I'm so hungry! I want a pop, too. And some junk food, like chips and stuff."

"Get whatever you want. That's yo man and he said get what you want!"

"Yeah, that's right, he did! Didn't he? I began to grab some stuff off the shelves.

Hattie had the food stamps. She picked up some stuff, too. By the time we got back, it wasn't too long before they had to come back!

196

"Alright, baby, tell me what's up with you. Come in here and sit down and talk to me."

"Well, some man came in the apartment and said that you broke into it. He said we were not supposed to be there. If I didn't leave then, he was going to call the police on me. So, I got out real fast and haven't been back."

"Who that motherfucker think he talking to? He don't know me like that! He can't talk to you like that! I will kill his motherfucking ass!" He was yelling, sweating and spit was flying out of his mouth! Reminded me of the last time he did that.

"It's okay James. I'm alright. You don't have to worry about me. I'm okay."

Then just like that, he sat down and was talking real nice, in a very calm voice. I said to myself, he gets very mad if he thinks that somebody has hurt me in any way. He really does love and care about me.

"Hey, grab your shit and let's go!"

"Where are we going?"

"Don't ask no question, just come on."

"Okay, here I come." I grabbed all my snacks and some of that hog head cheese stuff that Hattie said James liked. He was walking so fast toward the door.

"Hey, man, I'm outta here. I'll holler at you later."

"Bye, Hattie. "I'm going with James," closing the door behind me. We were going down the stairs and James said, "Don't you ever let me hear you give no explanation to nobody about where you are going! You don't say nothing, but bye! You got that?"

"Yeah, I do."

"I see I have to train you because you don't know these things and a motherfucker will get over on you real easy! So you have to do what I tell you, when I tell you! Do you understand me?

"Yeah, I do."

"Okay then, come here. I ran to catch up with him because he was walking so fast. He threw his arm around my neck and began to walk even faster. I had to keep up. It felt like he was choking and dragging me along by the neck.

Section 110

He is really sick. I think he has a fever.

We didn't go too far. We went to John and Carmen's house, a few blocks from Hattie's house. James knocked on the door and Carmen answered.

"Come on in, James. Hey, Debra."

"Hey, Carmen how are you doing?"

"Fine, girl. Getting ready to go in here and lay down for a while. Feel like I'm coming down with a cold."

"Hey, baby, how you doing?"

"Fine, John. I'm doing alright."

"Hey, man, come on in here. I got something for you." He stood there with this frown on his face and he was scratching his arm and legs. That wasn't anything different for John. He did that all the time. I think he has real dry skin. I told him one time before that my Nana got some real good lotion that she bought for Papa's feet so he won't be scratching and it worked for him. He should really get some and try it.

"Remember what I told you before about you watching my back? Well, that is every time you are with me, you understand? Good girl, good girl. You just sit here and wait for me. I'll be out in a minute." It turned into an hour or more. James and John went in the bedroom to talk. You could hear them laughing.

But, when James finally came out of the room, he was rolling his shirt sleeve down and he had this frown on his face like he was in pain. I jumped up and ran to him, helping him to the couch.

"You okay? Sit down, you look tired. Do you need to take some more medicine? You look like you got the chills!"

"No, baby, I'm alright. Just remember what I said." He sat down on that couch and was really sleepy. He didn't look like he was feeling well at all. He was sweating, too. He'd sit straight up, but then his whole body would lean forward. I thought that he was going to fall off the couch. Just when he'd lean too far, he would bring his body back up again. There's even a little slob coming from his mouth. No wonder he wants me to watch over him. Somebody could beat him up or something seeing how sick he is. This went on for about an hour or two. I was getting hungry.

Section 111

Something I'm so familiar with...

I reached in my bag and began to eat some of my snacks, watching a small black/white TV that was on the table. All of a sudden, I heard Carmen screaming and yelling. "Okay, John! Okay, John!"

He was calling her out of her name. "Bitch, you gonna go out there and get my money! What you mean you sick?!" Bam! Bam! John was apparently knocking Carmen up against the wall and door. All we could hear was her yelling in fear, "Stop, John! Okay, I'm going!"

"Get your motherfucking ass up and get the fuck out of here and get my money!"

James just sat there like he didn't even hear them. "James, go help Carmen! John is fighting her!"

"Debra, mind your own business! That shit ain't got a damn thing to do with you, now do it? Then sit back and watch the damn TV. It's okay, I promise you. They go through this all the time. They are always arguing with each other. This ain't the first and it won't be the last. You just stay out of that, you hear me? I'm trying to teach you something. Stay the fuck out of other people's business! They will turn on you every the time! Okay, next thing you'll know."

Here comes Carmen and John out the room and they both look like they were mad. They did say, "Bye, we'll be back."

So I guess James is right. I'll just look at it like Uncle Tom and Auntie Janice. They always fight and they still together. My Auntie Eunice and her husband fight all the time, too.

The only thing that I couldn't understand was what money was he talking about? She must have loaned somebody his money and didn't go get it when she said she was. John is so mean! I began to look at him in a different way now because Carmen said she wasn't feeling well. He could have let her wait to go get the money in the morning. But, like James said, it's none of my business.

When they got back, things were back to normal. They were laughing with one another, just like my Uncle Tom and Auntie Janice would do. Even Auntie Eunice and her husband always made up with each other.

Wrong message, Debra.

Section 112

The policeman is in the room.

I stayed at the house with Carmen and John. James would go to work and come back in a couple of days. One morning, while James was gone and Carmen went to her mother's house, a lot of people were coming to the

200

apartment. They were in the bedroom. John said that they were gambling. I asked him could I come in and watch them.

He hesitated. "If you do that, I would have to answer to James. But, it would be good if you tried it one time."

"I know how to play gin rummy, petty-pat and spades for .25 a play. I got a couple of dollars!" I stood there with this big smile. John looked at me and shook his head.

"James don't know how lucky he is to have someone as sweet as you. Nah, baby, you sit right here at the window and you come knock on the door when somebody come to the door. Don't you answer it, you just come get me, okay?"

"Okay, I'll do that."

"Later, I will give you some money so you can go get you some cigarettes, a pop, candy or something. Here, take a few cigarettes out of my pack."

I sat there on the couch looking out the window. They must have had a big game going on because it was already about six people in the room—men and women. He was selling some of James' reefers also.

Then a policeman came to the door! I went and got John and told him that it was a policeman at the door!

"Okay, baby, I'll get it." John always had that frown on his face like he was mad, but he wasn't. That was the medicine that he was taking that made him look like that, well, that's what Carmen told me.

I was a little nervous because the policeman was at the door, but John opened the door and the policeman went in the room with everybody else! You could smell reefer all in the house and the policeman didn't do anything. He spoke to me and as he walked in the room, I heard him say to John, "I see you got a new one."

John told him, "Nah, man. That belong to James."

Every time someone came out the room they, too, had a frown on their face or they were scratching, "Man, that was some good shit! Thanks, man. I'll be back."

John was collecting money from all of these people at the bedroom door before they entered in the room. Even the policeman gave him money, and he told the police that the next one is on him.

When I saw different ones come out of the room, I thought to myself that John must have a lot of medicine he is selling, along with James reefers. But, it must be giving them a bad reaction because they are all scratching some part of their body. Man, I could make a killing in here if I was to buy up a whole bunch of that lotion that Nana bought for Papa!

I laughed as I thought about how much help I would need. They had ugly frowns on their faces when they came out the room, especially the policeman. He was bent over trying to scratch his back and talking real slow. That was so funny to me.

Section 113

You never know who is watching you.

I was hoping to see James walk up, but he never came. It was close to noontime and the guy that I had met some time ago came to the door. I ran to the door and opened it. "What are you doing here?" I asked. Then he asked me the same question. I was happy to see him and he was really cute!

John came out the room. He must have heard us talking.

"How much you want man?" He told him thirty cent. John was looking at me and I was just smiling because I hadn't seen this guy in a long time. He went to the high school where my mother used to teach. John gave him some reefer.

"You must know him from somewhere?"

202

"Yeah, I do. He knows my mother," as I grabbed his hand with a smile on my face.

"Oh, he do?"

"Yeah. That's okay, I'm gonna talk to him for a minute before he go."

"You are?"

"Yeah."

He went back in the room. My friend began to ask me all kinds of questions. He was telling me that I didn't need to be here. It was bad for me and that I should go back home and that he would take me home.

"What are you talking about? I'm fine here! My mother don't want me home with her! She stepped over me a few months ago when I fell asleep in her hallway. She stepped right over me and went to work as if I was nobody."

"I'm going to tell your mother where you are."

"You better not!" I heard the bedroom door squeak a little. I told him that I was there with James, James Jr.! "You know him, right? You better go now and I will never forgive you if you tell my mother where I am at. She doesn't care about me."

He leaned down and gave me a kiss. I hugged and kissed him back. "Bye. You take care of yourself!" And I shut the door.

Section 114

It was all my fault.

It was maybe thirty minutes after that, James came over. I was so happy to see him. He came in and gave me a kiss, "What's up? What's going on up in here?"

I would love to just hear him talk. He spoke with so much authority. I never heard anybody talk like that before. I told him about what was going on, about everybody coming out the bedroom with frowns on their faces, and about the policeman that was trying to scratch his back! "That was so funny!", I laughed out loud.

"You didn't go in the room, did you?"

"No. John said that I couldn't gamble, that I had to watch the door."

"Good girl, good girl," as he patted me on my head. "Pass me that beer."

He began to roll up a joint. "Is John in the room?"

"Yeah, he in there." John came out the room, "Come on, man, come on in here and let me put something in your ear right quick."

I thought about it and I hoped he don't say nothing about that boy coming over here. I wonder did he see me kiss him.

"No the fuck that bitch didn't!" I was scared! He told on me! James came running out that room toward me and began slapping me all in my face! He hit me in my eye! I was yelling and screaming for help, but there was no one to help me! John stayed in the room and never came out! He acted like he didn't hear what was going on!

"Don't you ever in your motherfucking life kiss another motherfucker! And then you turn around and kissed me as if you didn't do shit! You don't know who you are fucking with! You belong to me, you little motherfucker!"

He grabbed me by my collar and picked me up off the couch! He was yelling and spitting all in my face as he screamed at me!

"I'm sorry! I'm sorry! I won't do it no more," as I tried to protect my face.

Section 115

I know he loves me.

He was crazy, and it was all my fault. I was wrong. I shouldn't have done that then he wouldn't be mad at me. I know he cares about me because he would get so mad if he thought somebody was going to hurt me.

He threw me down on the couch and told me to shut the fuck up before he gives me something to scream about! I sat there and wiped my face. I didn't want him to be mad at me anymore. James went back in the room with John and when he came out, he, too, was scratching all over his body.

James sat down and looked at me. I just held my head down, not wanting to look at him.

"Look at me, Debra! Now you tell me what the hell happened and who was the nigga that came over here! And you better not lie to me!" I told him the truth about what happened.

"I don't like him. I love you, James. I was telling him to get away from here cause he said he was going to tell my mother where I was at. I told him that my mother didn't care about me."

"I'll take care of him! I know that little nigga and he ain't shit!"

James said that he was sorry and he didn't mean to hit me like that, but he just lost it. Just the thought of somebody else could have me, made him mad! He really cares about me and I should not have done that. I was wrong.

Few days later, James and I had walked to the store and I saw that boy that came over to the house. He had a black eye! He hurried and left the store when we came in there. He didn't even pay for his stuff!

"Yeah, punk ass nigga, get the fuck on fore I kick your ass again!"

Section 116

Nowhere to go...

That evening James left for about three weeks or more. I was on my own, with no money, food and no place to go. It was getting cold outside and I didn't have a coat. I went to the pay phone to call Nana, in hopes she would answer and she did! When I heard her voice, tears ran from my eyes. I was so happy to hear her voice and I wanted my Nana to hold me in her arms and tell me that everything would be alright. I tried to hold back the tears. She could hear and feel the hurt in my voice. I told Nana that I was hungry and I really didn't have nowhere to go.

"Debbie, you know that your Nana loves you, but your Papa says that you and Chuckie can't come back to the house anymore."

"I know, Nana. I just wanted to hear your voice. That's all."

"Where are you at, Debbie?"

"I'm right here by Burger King."

"Come over here so Nana can slip you a plate of food before your Uncle Tom gets here. Okay, hurry up and Nana gonna fix you a real nice plate."

"Okay, Nana. I love you."

"Nana loves you, too, and don't you ever forget it! Now, hurry up and get over here and be careful! Watch out for your uncle because if he catches you, he's gonna hurt you! Okay?"

"Okay, Nana, here I come."

I hung that phone up and ran across Stoney watching every car that went by, praying that I didn't see my uncle. I went up to the door and rang the bell. Nana came to the door in her duster and handed me a hot plate of food.

"Oh, my poor Debbie!" She gave me a hug and kiss. "Nana miss you so much, honey! Ohhh, you're cold! Look at you! Wait a minute, let Nana go get you something." She ran back into the house as I stood there waiting on the front porch.

"Here put this on. Now, this is one of Nana's good sweaters. It's a heavy cashmere! I paid good money for this and it will keep you warm. Here, take this trench coat. I know it will keep you good and warm. It's a London Fog!" She then placed some folded money in my hand.

"Now, you hurry up so Tom don't see you! Your mother's phone number is in one of those pockets. You call her tomorrow. Give me a chance to talk to her for you. Nana is praying for you and everything is going to be alright, you hear me?" She gave me this great big kiss and hug!

"Thank you, Nana! I love you." I looked up with tearful eyes, "Nana, will you pray for me that everything will be alright?"

She just placed her hand on the top of my head and prayed, "Lord, I cover Debbie with the blood of Jesus! Everything will be alright!"

"I love you, Nana."

"I know you do and Nana will always love you more. Remember, you will always be my favorite granddaughter." She watched me run away from the house with tears rolling down her cheeks.

Section 117

My Nana will always love me.

I ran around the corner on East End. I saw a car coming up the street and I didn't want to take any chances of that being my uncle and his seeing me. I shot down the alley right behind the house, came up in the gangway and sat down on the stairs. I got up in the corner and began to eat my food. I was so hungry. I couldn't remember the last time I had a home cooked meal.

Nana had made some dressing, greens, corn bread, macaroni & cheese, baked chicken, potato salad and sweet potatoes! And, she put a huge piece of apple pie in here for me, and two cans of pop. Tears rolled down my face as I ate Nana's food.

I wanted to save some for later, but I was too hungry and ate it all. I looked in the pocket and saw my mother's phone number. I placed it in my pants pocket with the fifty-dollar bill Nana had given me. Nana's sweater felt so good and it was dust dark and the street lights had been on for just a little while. I just wanted to be close to my Nana, where I felt safe. I didn't want to leave at that point. I had nowhere to go, so I just sat there wishing that I could be with my Nana.

I was really scared because cats always came in this gangway and I'm real afraid of cats. I think maybe because my mother told so many scary stories about cats. She was afraid of them, too. I just don't like them! I would run every time I saw one coming on the same side of the street I was on!

But, this night, I just sat there on those back steps right next door in the gangway from my Nana's house. I daydreamed of how it would be if it was just me and my Nana. I placed her coat over me and smelled her perfume. I closed my eyes and fell asleep. When I woke up, it was the next morning. I had slept outside in the gangway and I wasn't even cold because Nana had given me her sweater and coat. My Nana was praying for me.

Section 118
Dealing with rejection

That money that Nana gave me helped out. I stretched it a long way. I even went over to Hattie's and ask her did she have something that I could wear so I could wash my clothes that I had on. I wanted to be clean so that the next time Nana saw me, I wouldn't look so bad.

I slept in the gangway for three days so that I would be close to Nana. I felt safe even though I was outside. I called Nana again to see if she had talked with my mother yet and to see if she was going to let me come home.

"Debbie, I talked to your mother, but she needs time and she's not ready yet to talk with you. Your mother is going to call me when she's ready, and I will let you know. Okay, honey?"

I gave a sigh of disappointment, "Thank you, Nana. I'll talk to you later. I love you."

"I love you, too, Debbie. You be careful out there."

I stayed out on the streets for months after that. I didn't call Nana too much more because I knew that it was nothing she could really do to help me.

She had done all that she could do. Now that I know that my mother really don't want to be bother with me, I'm just out here.

I was really hurt because I didn't do anything to her! I only took her brother's stuff, but surely she can see why. I know she's mad because she had to move out of Papa and Nana's house. She had to get her own place and now has to pay bills! Whatever! I can make it out here by myself! I cried as I wondered where I could go next and where was I going to sleep that night. My stomach began to growl.

I'm fine! I don't need anybody! These were the thoughts running across my mind. During these months that I was out on the street, I went back and forth to Hattie's and John and Carmen's apartments. James was there off and on, and so much was going on that I really didn't understand.

James kept telling me that he loves me and that we were going to be a family—you know, children and all. But, he keeps disappearing and leaving me out here by myself with nowhere to go. I was still feeling bad because I made him get so angry at me when I kissed that boy. I didn't want him to get mad at me anymore, so I pretty much did whatever he told me so he wouldn't slap me around again.

Section 119
You are in denial and don't even know it.

Carmen kept getting beat up by John and I couldn't understand why she wouldn't just do whatever he said so he won't hurt her all the time. I thought about my Auntie Janice and Auntie Eunice a lot. I'm not going to be like that. *I'm just going do what he says because I know he loves me and he really don't want to hit me. I just have to stop pissing him off.*

One day, Carmen asked me to walk with her over to her mother's house which was on the other side of Stoney where Nana lived.

"Sure, I didn't know that you lived over here."

"Yeah, my mother do. I don't like it over here."

"Why?"

"It's too slow and boring."

"Carmen, can I ask you something?"

"Yeah, Debra, what is it?"

"Do you know why John and James keep drinking out of the same cough syrup bottle, and what medicines are they using that keep them so sick all the time and it makes them scratch a lot? You know that's why they stay sick so much is because they are sharing the same bottle. My Nana said..."

"Stop, Debra! You can't be serious!" She busted out, laughing...

"What? Serious about what? Yes! You will never get over a cold if you keep sharing and drinking after someone that is sick, too! My Nana told me this and she do not lie!"

"No, no, Debra, you just don't get it! They are not sick like you think. John and James are getting high. You know how they smoke and get high off reefers, right? Well, they are using all these different drugs to get high off of. The reason that they are scratching all the time is that's how heroin affects people's body when they use that stuff."

"Heroin?"

"Heroin! I know you heard of that!"

"I was told that is what my father used before he got killed."

"Well, then, you know! And the syrup has them nodding along with that. When you be saying he's tried and sleepy, I just look at you. I know you've seen me look at you crazy!"

"Yeah, but I thought you didn't really like me for some reason."

"No, I like you. I hate that you got with James because he is going to ruin your life like John has messed up my life!"

Run, Debra, Run...

"No, James not going to mess up my life!"

"Yeah, he is! You just don't see it right now because you think you're in love."

"I do love him and he loves me. Wait, when he uses heroin, what do he do? I mean is it a pill or what? I really don't get it, so don't make fun of me."

"I'm not, but you can't be going back telling James what I tell you. Then I will get it from John."

"I promise. I won't tell. Pinky swear?" I stuck out my little finger.

Carmen laughed at me again and pushed my hand down. "Girl, you are so green. Don't nobody do that shit! Pinky swear! That's why that nigga ain't gonna ever know how much money I really get from those tricks. I be putting me a stash up, so when I leave that motherfucker, I will have bank!"

Section 120
You know the truth. Now what?

"Come on, we are getting close to my mother's house."

"I got to walk on the inside because that's the house I use to live in."

"Oh yeah, you got a real nice house."

"I had a real nice house," as we began to laugh together. "Can't take my black ass back over there."

Even though I was laughing, it was still hurting on the inside. I still blame my uncle for running me away and my mother for allowing him to treat me the way that he did.

"Debra, John has been shooting heroin in his arm for many years, and James been doing the same thing. They share needles with each other all the time. Those pills, tee's and blues, methadone, syrup, valiums, relents, weed, and hash—that stuff is for them to get high off of, not because they are sick. Wake up! You too green out here in these streets! People are going to walk all over you!"

211

"No they not, cause James not going to let them."

"Okay," she laughed, "you'll see."

Section 121

But, he needs me.

Living on that side of Stoney with James was really hard for me. Each day was a different adventure: I had to fend for myself, or wait for someone to come in and out of the house and eat their scraps. Don't get me wrong, I did love the fact that I was with James for whenever he was around. Anything would better than living back with my uncle. It's different, I guess, when a family kicks you to the curb than when someone in the streets to do the same.

It's been over a year now and I'm still living on the streets and I have endured so much. I can't leave James because he's using that heroin stuff and he said he would die if I ever left him. I don't want that to happen, not like my mother did my father. I tell James all the time that he doesn't have to ever worry about me leaving him. I don't want him to die.

Section 122

He just wants the best for me.

I know that he will stop getting high soon because surely that's not what he wants to do for the rest of his life. He tells me that he will soon stop. I think about this all the time, but months have passed and nothing is changed. I know that it will soon. But, for now, things are getting worse. I seem to be making James mad at me all the time because he is slapping, hitting and yelling at me a whole lot more.

He tells me that he is sorry for slapping me and hurting my feelings. I tell him how sorry I am for making him mad at me. He says that if I just do what he tells me, then I won't get in trouble. He needs to train me on how to be a good wife and mother because I don't know how. I'm still young yet, he says.

212

James said that one day he's going to marry me and he wants me to have his baby. I really want to have a baby because then I won't make him mad. I'll be taking care of our child and doing the right thing.

I know it's my fault, and I won't do it anymore. Maybe my mother and uncle were right... I talk too much and need to be quiet sometimes. Then maybe, just maybe, he won't slap me around so much.

I don't want to keep making the same mistakes that my Auntie Janice and Auntie Eunice did because they got beat up, for real, all the time.

I'm not gonna be like them.

Section 123

My big sisters don't know the truth.

I was so hungry and I didn't know anyone that would feed me. James was gone to work, at least that's what told me. I thought about my big sisters, twins Brenda and Linda. I walked to their home hoping that they would be there. It's way after dark, so I don't have to worry about seeing my uncle, even though I'm going one building down from Nana's house.

I prayed they were home as I walked onto the porch. Brenda answered the door. "Debbie! Come in here, girl! Where have you been?" as she hugged me with relief. "What have you been doing?"

I looked pretty bad by now. All my long pretty hair had come out. It was so short that you couldn't even braid it. I looked like a boy about the head. I didn't have any pretty clothes anymore, and I had been too ashamed to

213

face the twins, but at this point, I had to put that shame aside because I was truly hungry.

"Brenda, I was just coming over to see if you would…if you could…that's okay. I'm doing fine. I just stop by to see you and to see how you are doing. Where's Linda?"

"She's not here. Debbie, I heard what you did over there at your grandmother's house. Why did you and that boy James Jr. break in there like that, and take their belongings? You know that was wrong! Are you on that stuff with him? You know you can tell me the truth!"

"What? No, Brenda I am not on no stuff! What stuff is you talking about?"

"Don't be playing dumb, Debbie. I heard that James Jr. was using that heroin shit. He ain't got you doing that shit, do he?"

"Nah, Brenda, hold on. Sit down and let me tell you what's going on with me and what happened."

"Yeah, you know you gonna have to tell me something. Where is James Jr. now?"

"I don't know."

"Come on in here. I was just going to fix me a sandwich. You want one?"

"Yeah, I'll have one with you."

"Okay, start talking. I'm listening and this better be good cause you know Julia still go over there. She still dates your uncle. I know what's going on because he tells her everything."

"Yeah, I bet he do, but he ain't telling her the truth! Brenda, just listen to me, please! I promise you I will not lie to you. Listen!"

I told her all about the first baby and then the second one. I broke everything down to her about how Mommie let Uncle Tom whip me and Chuckie.

"You know your brother has been kind of bad ever since he was younger."

"Listen, Brenda. They tried to do a home abortion on me in the house! They put pills in my food; I tried to kill myself and my Uncle Tom pulled a loaded gun on me and put it to my head! And when I told Mommie, she didn't do nothing about it! A whole lot of stuff been going on over there, you just don't know. I bet he didn't tell Julia all of that!

"And on top of all that, this lady name Jennie, Auntie Eunice's friend, comes over all the time. You know which one. The brown skinned lady that's real hippy with that blonde red in her hair. She's sleeping with Uncle Tom and Auntie Janice doesn't even know it! Auntie Janice thinks she is a friend of the family, but everybody else knows that she's sleeping with him. Nana knows, too."

"Yeah, he's low down cause he's still mess around with my sister Julia. You know that."

"I know. I'm just tired of all the lies. He got to kick me and my brother's ass all the time. He ain't shit and doing Auntie Janice like a dog. Brenda, listen. I'm not on no heroin or none of that other stuff James is using! He has never tried to get me to use anything, I swear!"

"You better not get on that shit or I'm gonna be through with you!"

"I'm not!" I told her about the day I came home from school and all their stuff was on the couch. "I took Uncle Tom's stuff. It was me. James didn't have anything to do with that."

215

I told her where and who I was living with and how bad it was for me. "I tried to get in touch with my Mommie, but Nana said she wasn't ready to talk to me yet."

"Well, no, not after what you did. I know your mother she is sharp, the sharpest thing around here. She knows how to dress; I got to give her that. She had all these different men over there around you and I didn't like that part. But, she is one bad lady and everybody gives her respect. She makes sure of that. Her business is never in the streets. I be seeing her sometimes slipping in late at night. You know Linda knows and sees everything, and she be telling me she sees your mother out."

"Brenda, I don't care about all of that! I just wanted you to know the truth! I'm just trying to tell you the truth, that's all."

"Well, I see where you would get upset for what your uncle did. Your mother should not have allowed him to put his hands on you and your brother. I bet he'll have to wash his own nasty drawers out now that he got to go buy some more!" We both laughed.

"So, what you need, girl?"

"I don't have any food and I'm hungry."

"Finish eating that and here, make you another sandwich. Do you have a place to cook food?"

"Yeah, I can take it over there and cook."

She grabbed stuff out of the cabinet and freezer to fill a brown paper bag for me. "This food is for you and not everybody else! You better be glad Linda wasn't here! You know she'd get on you."

"I haven't done anything wrong! I'll be okay, though. When Linda be back? Will you please tell her the truth for me? I don't want her thinking crazy and all that other mess. Let her know that I ain't on no kind of stuff—heroin or anything else for that matter."

216

"Oh, you know, girl, I can't wait until she get in so I can tell her!"

"I'm getting ready to go. Thank you, Brenda for everything. I love you."

"I love you, too, Debbie. You be careful out there."

"I will. Come by here anytime if you need us. You're our little sister and we love you!"

"I love you both. Kiss Linda for me. Bye-bye!"

Section 124

Doing my share and holding my own

Man, I felt so good! I hadn't felt this good in a long time! I couldn't wait to get to Carmen's house to see what my big sister had put in the bag for me. It sure was heavy. I had a full stomach after two sandwiches and some Kool-Aid. I was able to tell her the truth about what really happen and I got some cigarettes with the five dollars.

Boy, this is going to be a good night. I hope I don't say nothing to piss James off! Then I'll be in the mix, as they say. I was walking fast to get on the other side of Stoney. I know I saw her put some pork chops or something in here out of the freezer and a box of macaroni & cheese. Boy, they will always be my big sisters. That's good looking out.

By the time I got there, Carmen was asleep and neither James nor John were there. I cook and was so proud to do it. The house smelled good by the time the guys got in.

James said, "My baby know how to cook."

"Yep, my Nana taught me how."

"Where did you get the money to buy the food?"

"I went over to Brenda's house, the twins, and she gave me a bag of stuff."

John went into the room with Carmen and came right out he whispered to James. I didn't pay any attention. I just wanted to eat and to show him that I knew how to cook, you know since we are going to be getting married one day.

James came over to me. He stood behind me and grabbed me around my throat, pushing me over and down on the couch! "You're sure that's where you got that from!"

"Yeah, what's wrong?"

"Carmen said you had left out and you were gone for four to five hours. How long where you gone?"

"I was over there all this time!"

"This better not be nothing from the store, otherwise you got to some explaining to do!" James went in the refrigerator and began inspecting the food that my sister had given to me. Once he saw that it had come from someone's home and not the store, he said, "Oh, baby, I just had to make sure you ain't trying to get out there on me."

"Get out where? What are you talking about?"

"Go head, baby, do your thing. I'm ready to eat!" He hit me on my ass as I walked back into the kitchen. I was really scared. I know I didn't say or do anything wrong that time.

As I prepared the food, I knew Carmen went back and told on me! Why would she do that? I didn't tell on her when she said she was keeping money at her mother's house so when she leaves his black ass, she'll have bank! What if I told that on her!

I hope this is not the way he is all the time. I know he will change because he said he loved me. I got to hang in there with him.

Another year, I had gotten used to being away from home. It really wasn't that bad, at least that is what I made myself believe. I felt so sorry for

218

James with him being sick, well, with him getting high. That must have been pretty bad for him wanting not to do it, but needing help to quit.

I was so determined that I was going to help him, help him to change his life. I was not going to leave him the way my mother left my father and then he dies. I do believe my worst fear all along was his dying.

James would tell me all the time that he needed me and if I ever left him, that's what was going to happen. I told him what happened to my dad, so he knew that he needed me to be with him, or was it that I needed to be with him? Who else was going to watch out for him, but me?

Section 125

He introduced me to his mother Madear.

James took me to meet his family one time. I was so happy because Nana told me one time that when a boy takes you to meet his mother, he really cares about you.

His mom lived on the low end, right off 51st in King Drive. I'll never forget when I walked into her house. She was sitting in a zebra print chair in the front room, watching TV while looking out the window to see who was coming up the stairs to her home.

She was real short, maybe about 5'3", and a little stocky. Her complexion was real high yellow, with a small black mold right above her lip toward the left side. (You know like the actress Marilyn Monroe!) She has the prettiest grade of cold black hair that all she needed to do was put water on it for the waves to set in.

She had shapely legs and you could tell that when she was younger, she was a bad broad! She was shaped like a 'brick house' like people would say. She wore a pair of blue cut off pants to her knees, with a pink/multi-colored shell top.

When I walked in the door, he introduced me to her. "Madear, this is Debra. Gone and sit down. I'll be back," as he walked toward the back of the house.

The first thing that came out of her mouth was "Where in the hell are you going with this little girl?"

"Hello, how are you?" I reach my hand out to shake hers. My name is Debra and I'm James' girlfriend."

"Oh! Sit your ass down somewhere. You ain't nothing but a grammar school girl coming through a high school door!" She drank some beer, crossed her leg and shook her bare foot.

In almost a whisper, "If you knew what I know, you'll take your motherfucking ass back home to your Mammie! Where you live anyways?!"

"Over, on 69th in Cornell, on the other side of Stoney."

"You don't have to tell me where that's at! I already know about over there! Lived over there on that end for over ten years!" She called for James.

"James, you going to jail! This ain't nothing but a baby! How long you been away from home? What you do, run away? Being a fast ass! You done run your ass into the hands of a crazy motherfucker, is what you did!"

She was laughing, saying, "But that's my boy and I love the dirty ground that he walks on, wrong or right! Will raise all kind of hell and high waters, knock down brick walls for my boy! See, I can talk about that motherfucker, but nobody else can talk about him cause they will have to answer to me," pointing her finger at me.

I tried to say something, but she threw up her hand, "I don't want to hear it! I have heard all the stories and lies that a motherfucker could try and sell me! Yo Mammie better not try and have the police coming over here looking for you, fucking with my boy! Cause I'll tell that tramp this is a free world and country! My son ain't breaking your arm? You with him on your

220

free will, right?" She leaned toward me, still whispering, "James ain't got you here against your will, do he?"

"No, he doesn't!"

"Then that tramp oughtta know how to have control of her daughter. Yea, I called her a tramp!"

She continued, "Them tricks of mine, them bitches! I'll stand on their motherfucking neck! They can't bip or bop without me knowing where they at! Yo Mammie know you with my boy? You better tell that trick that I don't play when it come to my boy! She better know how to keep her daughter in check cause I don't wanna hear that shit! I'm the baddest bitch that there is! They don't come no badder than me! I cover the Southside of Chicago, all the way down to the low end. I got peoples everywhere! If I want to find you, all I got to do is drop a dime and your ass is grass!"

Section 126

Don't mess with Madear!

"I done did five years in the state penitentiary and I don't mind going back for my boy, or any of those tricks of mine! See, I love my kids!" She drank more beer and shook her foot even harder.

I just sat there listening at her, wondering what was taking James so long to come from the back of the house. I was a little afraid at first. Hell, I didn't know if she was going to jump up and beat me up, or what!

When she spoke, she spoke with authority! It was just something about the way she said things that made me want to listen and learn more from her.

This was his family, and the old saying is true—'the apple don't fall too far from the tree'—cause all her kids talked like their mother. They knew a whole lot more than I did, and I wanted to learn what they knew. They were living a different type of lifestyle that I had not been accustomed to living at home with my mother and Nana.

221

One thing that was different was when his mother cursed or said anything, it was nothing like what I have heard from Uncle Tom nor Auntie DD. She was more real and down to earth. She wasn't pretending and hiding behind those pretty curtains. And she did have pretty curtains, too.

Eventually, I really liked being around his mother. I had never heard a grown lady talk like that. She talked more shit than my Auntie DD and she didn't need a gun to back it up.

We left shortly after that, but he was now taking me to his mother's house more often. I was glad to be around her because she was an older person and I felt safe around her. I think she is warming up to me. I got a chance to tell her what had been going on with me. I even told her about my pregnancies at such a young age.

She listened to me and she understood what I was going through. Madear told me that as long as I was at her house, I didn't have to worry about nobody bothering me. I felt like she was going to be my safe haven like Nana was to Chuckie.

There were always so many people in the house. James has a very large family—seven sisters and two brothers—and some of his sisters had children. And they would all be at Madear's house!

Madear ran her house with an iron rod; she watched everything that was coming and going. Nothing too much got pass her. She would confront you and let you know, "You got to get up pretty earlier to outfox the fox, and I am the fox! I used to whoop bitches' ass coming and going, for breakfast, lunch and dinner! It didn't matter to me, so don't fuck with me cause I'll whoop your ass, too!"

She sat in that chair in the front room by the window, and believe me, nothing got pass her. She didn't allow anybody—with the exception of a few older children when they came to visit—to answer the front door.

I remember one time someone had knocked on the door and I jumped up to go answer it. I should have taken note that nobody else moved but me.

Section 127

Only the strong survives out here in this world!

"Sit your ass down," as she shoved me back down on the couch! "I'm the only one that pays bills in this motherfucker!" She turned and asked, "Do you pay bills here?"

"No, I do not."

"Well then, you don't answer no doors around here! Let's get that straight right now. It's only one hen in this house and that's me. That's why I don't fuck with no bitches! You let them motherfuckers in your house and they don't know how to sit their asses down!"

She opened the door and it was a Jehovah witness. Madear told him, "Not today! I believe in God and I thank you, but you came at a bad time, baby! Catch me tomorrow. I'll talk to you then!" She slammed and locked the door!

Madear always had advice and quotes for every situation. Madear told me that if I stick with her, she would make me tough because I was too weak to be out here in this world.

"If you ain't gonna carry your ass back home and your Mammie ain't gonna take you back, you better make the best of it and learn how to survive out here. Wipe them crocodile tears off your face! That shit don't work with me! I told you that I know all tricks and trades, I wrote the book! Let me tell you, don't nobody like no weak ass women out here! Only the strong survive! You got to be strong out here, you remember that! If you don't remember nothing else...only the strong survive!"

"Can I use the bathroom?"

"Yeah, it's back there, first door on your left."

"Thank you."

"Hell, don't thank me cause you got to piss," drinking her beer. "Gone baby, I'm just messing with you. But, I got to treat you this way cause you ain't nothing but a little girl out here in these here streets, and you don't know nothing. I can tell you now the rate you going you ain't gonna make it!"

When I got in the bathroom, my stomach was so nervous that I had to dodo. When I got done, can you believe there was no tissue in the bathroom?! Oh my God! What am I going to do now?

I yelled through the door, "Could somebody get me some tissue! Hey, can I get some tissue?" Somebody yelled back at me, "Some what?"

"Toilet paper! I need some toilet paper!"

"You got some right in front of you!" I looked and looked and I didn't see any!

"You see the telephone book? Well, that's it! Tear it out and rub it together! That's your tissue!" They started laughing, saying, "Why she talk so proper?" 'Can ah have some tissue...?' They continue to laugh at me.

I could hear Madear say, "Hold on, I'll bring you some. It's in my bedroom! I don't leave my shit out for these tricks. Here, open the door." She passed me a roll of tissue. "Don't leave it in there neither. Bring it right back to me like I gave it to you!"

"Thank you, Madear." I could hear her footsteps walk away. She walked real hard and could be heard from one end of the house to the other.

I sat there and thought, 'Why in earth would anybody use a phone book to wipe their ass?' That was the craziest shit that I had ever heard of in my life.

At my Nana's house, she always keeps four to six packs of tissue in the house. She would stock up on that kind of stuff. Well, I'm not at my Nana's house now, so I have to roll with the punches! I heard Madear say that to somebody and thought that was funny.

Actually, being around Madear was exciting. It was never a dull moment at her house. It surely didn't bother me with all the cursing and stuff because I was brought up by the best of them—my uncle and his fowl ass mouth.

He took me to his mother's house a lot. I think he did it because he wanted me to be safe, you know, with him working on the low end and all. I became very attached to Madear and she really did like me. She made me grow up. I didn't know anything compared to her kids.

You know it just hurts more when your own family members kick you to the curb and dog you out more than the people on the street. So, what I got to lose? I'm out here now.

One day James left his mother's house and said he'd be right back, but didn't show up for another two days. I was getting ready to leave because Madear made it clear that she does not take care of grown motherfuckers and since I was out in the street, I was considered grown. I have to feed myself because she got enough kids and grandchildren to take care of.

"I'm not hungry," just as my stomach growled.

"Sit down and eat this breakfast and drink some coffee. You drink coffee?"

"Yeah, I do." I really didn't, but she offered and I was hungry. She was being so nice to me.

"You tell me what are you planning on doing with your life cause you're not gonna be laying up here in my house with James! I don't play that shit! You are not married to him! Now you gonna be out here homeless! That's what you are! And if you not gonna take your ass back home and them stupid motherfuckers not gonna take you in, then you need your own place. I'm going to see about helping you get a place."

Section 128

He said when the time is right, he wants to travel to Arkansas.

James and I had been sleeping over different people's houses. We would go from his dropping me off at his mother's, at hotels and back to John's apartment. He told me that he had to take care of me. I had nowhere to go and would still be alone in the streets, but I was happy because I was with James. James made sure that wherever he had me, I was safe. He tells me all the time how much he loves me and how I was heaven sent to him.

James talks about going to Arkansas all the time. "Baby, my father lives down there, my other side of the family. I got acres of land. Living here in Chicago ain't shit! Wait till you go to Arkansas with me! Baby, I want to take you around the world with me! Once you get down there, it's so peaceful and quiet. No noise, niggas walking the streets, none of that! No gun shots, not unless somebody killing a deer!"

"What you talking about, in the woods?"

"No, baby. One day I'm gonna get a chance to show you when the time is right. The time got to be right, and I see it coming. Do you? And when I say it's time, you gonna be ready to go with me and leave everything behind! You going with me?"

"Yeah, I don't have anything to leave behind. Tell me more."

"The trees are so pretty when the fall comes in and it don't get cold down there. That is the place where you need to be because you are really a country girl." He laughed.

"No, I'm not! Why you say that? And what is a country girl like since you said that I was one?"

226

"Listen, baby, don't get offended, no harm intended. I just see that you are more laid back," as he grabbed me and swung me around, giving me a kiss. He hadn't done that in a long time.

James and I talked all the time of how it would be when we had our first baby. It has been months since James has not gotten angry at me, so I have been a good girl. Tonight, we were over one of his other friend's house. It was so peaceful there. We just laid there in that back room as he told me stories of how it would be when we got to Arkansas.

All I could think about was how happy I was going to be. I already decided I wanted six children. I could see all of us sitting at a pretty dining room table with James on one end and me on the other, and all of the children sitting around the table eating dinner. I went to sleep in his arms that night.

Section 129

I had a dream.

I woke up that morning from a very bad dream only to find out that James had left in the middle of the night and had not gotten back. I was crying, sweating, afraid and my heart was racing because I had a dream that Nana was crying. She was lying on the kitchen floor crying. I don't know why, but I saw her crying. I needed to get to a pay phone to make sure she was alright. I hadn't talk to Nana in almost two months. I felt so bad for not calling her. I know she's worried about me, but with my meeting James family kept me pretty occupied.

I reached in my pocket and I had fifty cents, enough for me to make a call. When I sat up on the bed I saw that James had left me $5.00. That was good because I could go downtown to Burger King or McDonald's and apply for a job. I couldn't work at the one on Stoney Island because everybody would see me. I had already slept ready-roll, so I just had to wash my face and stuff.

When I got to the pay phone, I prayed that Nana would answer the phone and again she did!

"Nana, this Debbie! Are you okay? I had a bad dream that you were crying! Are you okay?"

"No, Debbie, your Nana is not okay."

"What's wrong with you, Nana?"

"It's your Papa…he died last week. He had a heart attack and when I came home from work, he was lying on the kitchen floor. The funeral is today at 11:00 o'clock up there at Doty Nash on 87th street." Her voice was trembling.

You could hear in the back ground, "Who is that, Mama? Give me the phone. I'll tell whoever it is what they need to know."

It was my Uncle Tom! "Hello, hello…" Before I hung up the phone, I heard him ask, "Who was that Mama?" I don't believe Nana told him that it was me.

My heart went out to my Nana. I cried right there at the pay phone. My Papa was gone! I was looking a mess, but I didn't care. I had to get to the funeral home. It was almost time and I had a good ways to walk to get there.

I had on some old blue jeans, a navy pea coat, some brown bucks, an old blouse and no hat. It was chilly outside, but I don't believe I even felt the cold. I just wanted to get to my Nana and see her face, to put my arms around her and let her know how much I miss her. This could be the time that I would see my Mommie, as well.

Section 130

Beverly stopped and gave me a ride.

"Debbie, Debbie!" somebody was yelling my name. "Get in the car. Hurry up, run!"

It was my cousin Beverly with my cousin Tiffany from New York! They were in one of the family funeral cars. "Come on," as she waved her hand for me to come. I ran to catch up with them. She had told the driver to wait for me and I jumped in the car. She was so happy to see me and I was even happier to see her!

We embraced each other, and my cousin Tiffany, too.

"Debbie, where you been?"

"Nowhere. Just out in the street!"

"You look like you been out in the street," Tiffany said.

"Yeah, I know, but I'll be okay. I'm getting ready to move down south with James."

"Debbie, are you okay? Come to my Mommie's house! You know she'll let you stay with her!"

"I'm okay. Yeah, well, we're here." The car pulled over and everybody got out. Nana had already gone inside and sat down. I couldn't go up there and say anything to her because Uncle Tom was sitting right next to her and my mother.

I see Auntie DD, Auntie Eunice—my whole family was there, so many people. I felt so ashamed because I was dirty and smelly. I didn't want them to see me like that. I know they will talk about me. I didn't want to cause any trouble at Papa's funeral.

After everything was over, I got a glimpse of Nana as she walked down the aisle and out the door. I cried so hard, I cried for my Nana. I was so sad she no longer had Papa. What was she going to do? My brother Chuckie was still locked up at 14 years old.

My mother was coming down the aisle and I attempted to walk toward her. She looked over at me with such a disgusting look. She turned, shook her head and kept on walking out the funeral home door. *She never uttered a single word to me.*

Beverly said, "Come on, Debbie, ride with us back to the house. Maybe you can get something to eat. You hungry?" I looked at her and nodded my head as she put her arms around me crying.

At that point, I didn't know if she was still crying because Papa was dead or if she was feeling sorry for me. She had never seen me look so bad. Hell, I never looked so bad! I didn't really care about what I was looking like; I just wanted to see Nana.

I wanted to tell her that everything was going to be alright like she had told me so many times before. I wanted to say 'I love you Nana' and 'I'm so sorry for you' that Papa is gone.

The car pulled up to the house. I could see them helping Nana into the house. Everybody had gone in the house, so I asked Beverly when she goes in, will she ask Nana to come to the door, please. "Okay, Debbie I will." I stood there on the front porch waiting.

Auntie Eunice walked on the porch and I went to reach out and hug her. She stepped back and raised her hand. "Anybody that would steal from my mother, I don't want to have anything to do with them! I wash my hands of you!" and went into the house.

Auntie DD came to the door. "Debbie, your Nana is not able to come to the door right now. You understand, don't you?"

"I do." She looked at me and said, "Debbie! Debbie! Debbie!" She hugged me so tightly with tears rolling down her face. "I love you. You know that, don't you?"

"I do, Auntie DD, I know that you love me. Will you please see if my Mommie will come to the door so I can say something to her, please?"

"Wait here, let me go get her."

Some lady was trying to get inside, "Excuse me, excuse me, is the repast in here?"

"It is." I stepped aside so that she could pass. People were there to show their respect. And there I was standing there like a nobody, feeling like I was not even a part of the family. I was sixteen years old.

Auntie DD came back to the door only to tell me that my mother was not going to come out and that they wanted me to get off the porch and leave the house. She said she was so sorry.

"Who said that Auntie DD? Who said for me to leave? It wasn't Nana, was it?" My body jerked with hurt and the tears and snot flowed!

"No! You know it wasn't Mama!"

"So, my mother is not coming to the door to see me?"

"No, Debbie, she's not. Give your Auntie a kiss, baby. It will be alright, just give it some time. They will come around."

"Auntie DD, what is Auntie Eunice talking about somebody stealing from her mother? I have never stolen anything from Nana!" I was now angry.

"Don't worry about it, Debbie."

"Well, can I get something to eat? Will they let me have a plate?" Auntie DD placed her hand on mine, and said, "They don't want you here, Debbie. I know it's not right."

"Okay, then. I love you, Auntie DD." I ran off the porch in tears. I never looked back, nor did I ever step a foot back into the house that stood at 6909 South Cornell, the place I once called my home.

Section 131

All alone and nowhere to run!

I was still sleeping wherever I could. James was still not around. He was either down on the low end or working somewhere. He had different lady

231

friends that were working for him in his business who gave him money. So, sometimes he had to be gone for a while.

Whenever he left like that, he always came back with money for the both of us. I didn't want to go to Madear's house looking for him because I didn't want him to get mad at me and start that hitting and slapping shit. I would call and he was never there. I didn't have much money to keep calling.

He will find me like he always did at one of the houses where we often crashed. This time, no one was home and I really didn't have a place to go. Hattie had moved on me and I didn't know where she went. John and Carmen weren't really at home much, or if they were, they didn't open the door for me.

I think Carmen got mad because I told James what she said about leaving John and how she was going to have bank when she left. I only did that because she tried to get me in trouble when I got food from my big sister Brenda.

I visited with Nettie one time or two. She gave me something to eat. Nesa wasn't around much. I think she was staying with her dad, I don't know. All my old friends were no longer around. I couldn't show myself around them looking like this no way.

When night came, it was even colder. I often slept in the gangway, right next to Nana. It made me feel so much safer—cold, but safe. One day I walked by the house to sit on the stairs in the gangway. I had nowhere to go, but I was hoping to see or hear Nana come out the house.

I heard someone talking outside and it was my Uncle Tom with that nosey lady who sits in her window and watches everything. She was telling him that she been seeing me come in the gangway at night and leaving in the mornings.

"What, over here, in this gangway? Call the police next time you see her over here! I jumped up and ran as fast as I could, praying that he didn't see me. I needed to make it to the other end, hit the alley and I would be okay.

I ran and ran, with nowhere to go. I cried and my mind raced thinking about everything and how my mother didn't even come out and say something to me. I couldn't even get a plate of food.

Section 132

She's a liar.

Auntie Eunice does not know what the hell she's talking about! I didn't take anything from Nana! I took all of Uncle Tom's clothes and stuff! That was it! Nothing else! Fucking bastard! I thought she loved me! I didn't do nothing to her! She just decide she's gonna wash her hands of me! Then, so be it! Fuck her, too!

I cried because of the hurt and pain, knowing that I didn't do what she said. I couldn't understand why she said that to me! I use to babysit for her ass on top of all that! That's why her husband kicks her ass because she is a liar! A fucking liar! One day, I pray that she will be exposed for the liar she is! Lying bitch! Lying on me about my Nana!

Section 133

Have you ever eaten out of a garbage can?

I wanted to tell James about the pain that I was feeling so he could hold me in his arms and tell me that everything was going to be alright. I wanted to hear him tell me stories about how beautiful it was in Arkansas. I just wanted to get away.

Beep! Beep! A bus was blowing the horn at me! I ran into the street and didn't pay attention to the cars coming. I jumped on the bus and had no idea where I was going. I needed time to think. I ended up walking around downtown. I need a job! I'm sixteen-and-a-half now—I can work. I have to show my mother that I can make it out here by myself.

I filled out application after application. I stopped in a store and bought some candy. I tried to put another one in my pocket, but I think the lady saw me. I took it out and paid for that one. I only had five dollars.

I was so hungry. There was this white man in a suit and carrying a briefcase. He looked like he was on his lunch break or something. I don't know, but he was eating a sandwich and then he threw it in the garbage for whatever reason. It didn't matter to me. I immediately reached in the garbage and got the sandwich. I brushed it off, kissed it up to God and ate it.

That was the best sandwich I had had in a mighty long time! It was a corn beef sandwich on rye bread with those little black things on the bread! It had layers and layers of corn beef meat, melted mozzarella cheese, sauerkraut, spicy mustard, with a pickle wrapped in the paper! I must have stood right there, at the garbage can, eating as if I was the only one around. People walked by looking at me enjoying that sandwich!

I thought to myself that white man sure did do me some justice because I was hungry as hell! I wiped the juice from my chin. I didn't feel ashamed, and if I did, it was too late—I ate that bad boy up! I even skipped a few times thinking about how good that sandwich was!

Section 134

A policeman who cared.

I didn't know that I was being followed. "Hey, hey, little girl!" I turned to see who was trying to get my attention. It was a black policeman! He reached for my arm! What I do? I didn't do anything wrong!

"Hold on just a minute!" He tightened his grip. I tried to pull my arm away from him. "Stop! Right now! Stop pulling away from me! I'm not going to hurt you! Listen to me!"

"Okay, I am! But, what I do? I didn't do nothing! Am I in trouble? I bought that candy in the store and I put that other one back! See!" as I pulled out my holey pockets with dust, dirt and cigarette tobacco came falling out. "See, I don't have anything! Tears streamed down my face; I was so scared!

"I have been watching you, and I have not seen you around here before. This is my beat. What are you doing down here?"

"I came down here to fill out applications for a job at Burger King and McDonalds so that I can get an apartment and buy some new clothes."

"How old are you?"

"Sixteen-in-a-half. What? I can't walk downtown by myself?"

"No! Now I'm going to ask you a question and I want you to tell me the truth, or you will be in trouble. I will have to take you down to the station."

"For what? What do you want?"

"Listen, little girl, I am trying to help you. Are you a runaway? Well, let me put it like this, what is your mother's phone number?"

"Why you got to call my mother?" I reached in my pants pocket to see if I still had that piece of paper that Nana gave me with her number on it. "I don't see why you gotta call her! She don't care about where I'm at!"

"'Come over here." He pulled me aside so that he could talk to my mother on the phone.

"Yes, this is Officer Smith. I work the beat downtown here and do you have a daughter by the name of… What's your name again?"

"Debra, my name is Debra."

"Well, ma'am, I've been watching your daughter for over an hour and she ate a sandwich someone threw away in the garbage can. Hum, huh, yes ma'am. She looks like a real sweet girl and I don't want her to go down to juvenile because you will have to come and pick her up. Yes, I understand.

235

Yes. Yes. Okay. Now just in case you don't know this, let me tell you. You are held liable for her until she reaches the age of eighteen and the courts can come after you, or I can bring her home to you. Whatever happens after that is on you and your daughter. She is in my custody right now, so what do you want me to do? Okay... Your address is what? Let me just jot this down. Thank you, ma'am. I'll be bringing your daughter home to you shortly. Goodbye."

"I told you that my mother don't want me home with her!"

"Whatever the case may be, you will be home tonight with your mother, whether she likes it or not. Come on." He held onto my jacket. "Don't you try nothing because you will regret it!"

"What she say to you?"

"You will talk to her when you get home, so just sit back and be quiet!" He slammed the police car door. "I am so sick and tired of these young girls out here in these streets and the parents not trying to help or find their children! Where is your father?"

"He's dead."

"Single parent, that figures! Parents just don't understand if they are having trouble with their child they should get help for them! Don't give up on them! They'll end up strung out on drugs, prostituting or dead in an alley."

Section 135

She doesn't really want me here.

When we got to my mother's building, he rang the doorbell and we walked to the third floor. I thought about when I laid on these same steps, not too long ago, and my Mommie stepped over me and left me there. I am afraid of what she was going to say or do when she sees me, but I will be so happy to see her. I want to put my arms around my Mommie and tell her how much I love her. I don't see why she's not talking to me. I didn't take anything

236

from her! I took all of her brother's stuff! Surely, she's got to see why I did it. We're talking about the same brother who whipped my ass all the time! She said nothing and did nothing to him!

If it wasn't for him knocking me in the tub when I was pregnant, she would have never known about my baby until it was too late! So, no, she doesn't love me anymore. She just doing this because of what this policeman told her. Otherwise, she probably wouldn't let me in.

The policeman knocked on the door and she opened it. She gave me a look, then looked at the policeman. She unlocked the gate that was on the door."

"Come on in. Have a seat."

"No, thank you. I just wanted to make sure that your daughter was safe back at home with you. Now, Debra, talk to your mother. Ma'am, if you want, I could give you a phone number that you and your daughter to get some type of counseling."

"No, thank you. I will be fine. Thank you for dropping her off. Goodbye."

She shut the door. I just stood there looking at my Mommie. I was so happy to see her face and I even missed her sarcastic remarks.

"Hi, Mommie. I miss you," walking towards her to give her a hug.

"I love you, too, Debbie. You need to go in there, take off all those nasty ass clothes and wash them. Take a bath. You stink! You can do all of that in the morning. For right now, make a pallet on the floor! Do not put your funky ass on my couch!"

"Okay, Mommie." She headed to her bedroom. "Oh! Let me tell you one thing... James is not to come to my house! I don't want that no good trifling nigga nowhere near my house or your ass will be right back out there with him! Do you understand me? Now, cut the light off and carry your ass to sleep! You not going to give me no gray hairs! I'm too young for this bullshit! You thought you were slick having the policeman call me just so your ass could get up in here."

"But, I didn't!"

"GO TO SLEEP! I don't want to hear it! I got to go to work in the morning."

Section 136
Still afraid at my mother's house…

I got the covers, laid down on the floor and went to sleep. I was glad to be home with my Mommie. I wasn't cold anymore and even if she doesn't want me here, maybe as time go by, she will love me again. It's just me and my Mommie. Soon Chuckie will be home and then it will be just us as a family—without my uncle. That night was a good night for me. I didn't have to worry or be scared that a cat was going to come through the gangway, or some real big boys walking through there.

I remember one night it was really late. Three or four boys were in the gangway with some girl and they were smoking reefers. Then they started messing with her. She began to scream! They all raped her!

I was sitting under the stairs, covered up with my coat and I didn't move or say a word. I know how she felt because I was raped before. That was real scary, but I couldn't say anything because they would come after me.

Even though I was at my Mommie's house, I still found myself off in the corner behind the couch, pressed upside the wall. That made me feel safe. I fell asleep thinking about the crazy stuff that I had seen and been through while I was away from my mother. It has been two years already. That's a long time.

I wondered what James was doing. I'll call him in the morning to let him know that I am okay and he doesn't have to worry about me anymore. I wanted to let him know that I was back home with my mother, and soon she will be glad that I was there.

Section 137

Locked in and I can't get out...

Morning had come. "Debbie, where are you?"

"I'm right here, Mommie. I got up from behind the couch.

"What the hell are you doing behind my damn couch?"

"I was...."

"Get from behind there and don't get back there no more." I folded up the covers.

"I am going to work. You'll keep your ass in this house! And, I want you to clean yourself up and don't leave. I don't have to worry about that because I am going to put the gate on the door so you can't get out!"

"Thank you, Mommie."

"Don't thank me! You not in yet! We'll talk when I get home."

"I love you, Mommie."

"Yeah, you got a poor piss ass way of showing it!" as she shut the door and locked the gate. While my Mommie was at work, I cleaned up, cooked dinner and I even change her front room around for her. I hope she like it.

I called Madear. "Hello, Debra, where have you been? James been acting a damn fool cause he couldn't find you!"

"Nowhere."

"Well, don't you be out in them damn streets when you know that you can come over here! Don't be no damn fool!" She laughed and said, "You know I wouldn't talk to you like this if I didn't love you."

"Yeah, I know. I love you, too, Madear. Is James at home?"

"Yeah, matter of fact he just walked in."

"Is that Debra?" he asked.

"Yeah, talk to this baby girl. She sound like she's unhappy," as she handed the phone to James.

"Where have you been, baby? Where are you at right now? I'm coming to get you!"

"No, you can't come. I'm at my mother's house."

"Oh, you are?" His voice changed a little bit. "I thought I lost you. I've been looking all over for you. Debra, don't ever do that again," as his voice sounded like he was getting ready to cry.

"Yeah, well, I didn't know where you were at, so I was sleeping outside in the gangway by my Nana house."

"You did tell me that shit before and what did I tell you about that?! You could of gotten hurt real bad. Ah, baby you know I love you. What am I going to do without you?

"Well, my mother said that you can't come over—she don't even want me to tell you where she lives. I can't come outside cause she got the lock on the gate!"

"I don't want to come over to her motherfucking house, I just want you! Listen, Debra, who's been taking care of you since you been out here in these motherfucking streets? It's been me and Madear! Your own mother has not been there for you! Now she got my baby locked up like a dog! What you gonna do if a fire break out in the building?! How you gonna get out of there?! She didn't think about that, did she?"

"Nah, she didn't."

"Well, then! Shit! I know what I'm talking about! Madear been asking about you. I know you want to see her before we go. Matter of fact, she said that she miss you hanging around. I miss you, too. Baby, I need you. You know how I get when you are not with me."

240

"Yeah, I know, but maybe this way you don't have to worry about me. I can try and stay here with my mother, I don't know…"

"Baby, I'm not rushing you or anything, but I might be going to Arkansas soon. I don't know whether or not if you gonna be able to go with me cause when I decide that I'm ready to go, I am not gonna be coming out there to get you. I'm just going to leave. You are too far away from me. You know, all this time you been gone away from me, I have not been getting high."

"You haven't?"

"Hell no! I had been looking for you! You are more important to me than that shit! I can stop any time I want to! I don't need that shit! I just use the hell out of it," as he laughed. "Just think about it, Debra, who loves you more? You be the judge of everything. I put everything up front with you, and I don't hide or lie to you, right?

"Right." *Debra, think!*

Section 138

He said I belong to him. He really does love me.

"Well, everybody in your family has lied, hurt and let you down! None of them motherfuckers care and love you the way that I do! Be fair, you know this is true! I have invested two years of my life with you, and I'm not going to lose you! You belong to me, Debra! Just give us a chance baby! Come go with me to Arkansas and live the life that you deserve!

"I want to give you the happiness that you been looking for, and that's with me, baby! Remember when we first met and you always said it was meant to be? Well, you were right! It is meant for us to be together! Don't let your mother or no one else come between us!"

We talked like this for one week, back and forth, while my mother was at work. James told me not to tell my mother that we were talking, otherwise, he knew she would cut the phone off just to keep us apart. He really knew what was best for me. He was right about everything.

Look at what happen to me during Papa's funeral and when Uncle Tom pulled that gun on me—nobody did nothing about it! They even ran my brother away from home and put him in a juvenile home. When Mommie stepped over me... All this stuff was coming up in my head as James was talking back and forth to me.

He was right, that was all I could say. I think what got me was when he reminded me of what happen when I was pregnant.

"Debra, I want us to have a baby. I want to marry you, be my wife and the mother of my children. I love you and only you. Please come with me. I feel like I will die without you!" He was crying.

"When are you leaving, James? Don't cry! You not going to die! Don't say that!"

"I don't know, maybe tomorrow, this week, we'll see. I will leave no later than Friday, that's for sure."

"But, what if I tell you that I want to go with you?"

"Then we are going to have to make plans now because I still have to get the rest of the money together for us to leave."

"Where we gonna stay when we get down there?"

"I got a sister, cousins—it's plenty of places that we can stay down there. Don't you worry about that. I will take care of that part. I love you, Debra! You belong to me! I'm not letting you go!"

"I love you, too, James, and I want to go with you, too. Don't leave me! I don't want to stay here! I know my mother don't want me here!"

"Okay, baby, I'm gonna come up with a plan. We will leave before this week is out, okay?"

242

"Okay." I cried thinking that James was going to leave me here. "How I'm gonna get out my mother's house? She got the gate on the door locked with a big padlock!"

"Don't worry, I'll take care of that. Just let me think about it. You call me in the morning when she leaves and I will tell you what the plan is going to be. Okay baby?"

"Okay, James. Talk to you in the morning."

Section 139

I'm sorry, Mommie.

It's Friday and James said that we were going to leave today. I couldn't sleep last night waiting for this day to come. When my mother got up to get ready for work, I was already up and dress.

"Where do you think you are going, Debbie?"

"Nowhere, I just got up early. That's all."

"Tell me, whose number is this?" as she handed me this piece of paper with a phone number on it. It was James' number.

"I called the phone company to see what numbers have been dialing out of here while I was at work. I called this number and asked for James and they told me that he wasn't at home! What did I tell you about calling him? You just not going to listen, are you?! I got something for you when I get home today! I am sick of your sneaky ass and you're bullshit! Don't get on my phone today! I know what I'll do!" and she snatched the phone cord out of the wall and put it in her purse.

My mother walked toward the door to leave. "I love you Mommie," knowing that she would not see me again because I was leaving for Arkansas with James, at least that what he said.

"Debbie, you need to start loving yourself and decide on what you're going to do with your life cause you not gonna lay up on me and do nothing! We will talk when I get home."

When she left, I didn't know how I was going to talk to James, or tell him to come over here. I sat there watching the TV. I heard someone blowing a car horn. I ran to the window hoping that it was James…and it was!

He got out of the car when he saw me stick my head out of the window. I was on the third floor.

"Hey, bay!"

"Hey, James! I couldn't call you cause my mother took the phone cord! She know I been calling you!"

"Oh, yeah? Where she at now?"

"At work."

"Are you sure?"

"Yeah, she been gone. She got a business meeting or something today, I don't know, but she at work."

Section 140

He said we needed the money.

"You ready to go!"

"Yeah, but how?"

"Just buzz me in!"

I was so happy to see James and he was really happy to see me. I ran to the bathroom to make sure that I was looking okay and got a piece of peppermint to put in my mouth. When I opened the door, he was standing there—fine as ever, but looking just a little bit anxious. He reached his hand through the gate and pulled me to him so he could kiss me.

"Oh, baby, I miss you so much! What is this shit! She got you locked up in here! He looked around. "Do you know if any of these neighbors are home? Do you think that somebody could hear or see us?"

"Well, it's this old lady that stay across the hall. I don't know if she will come to the door!"

"Do she live by herself?"

"Yeah, she do."

"Well, I'm not worried about her then. Baby, I miss you so much! Listen, we ain't got a lot of time to waste! We got to get you out of here, okay?"

He picked up this big metal thing on the side of the wall. "What is that?"

"It's a lock cutter!"

"What? It can't cut this big lock!"

"Yes, it can and it will. You trust me, don't you? Well, I got this! Now, you know when you do this, your mother is not going to let you come back to her house! You can't come back here! Baby, you ready to go with me to Arkansas so we can get married and have a family?"

"Yes," as I smiled at him. I'm ready! Cut it so we can hurry up and go!"

James was trying to cut the lock and that old lady cracked her door. Before you knew it, James ran over there and grabbed her door knob before she was able to close the door back! He whispered something to her and she shut the door! I don't know what he said to her, but she never opened the door again.

"What did you say?" as I looked at him in fear.

"Don't worry about it, she's okay."

"Are you sure?"

"Trust me, she okay"! He must have tried three times, and the fourth try, the lock broke! He grabbed me, kissed me and held me tight.

"My baby! Now, listen, Debra. We need to take some of your mother's stuff! We don't have all the money to get to Arkansas!"

"What! Take some of her stuff! She is going to kill me! I can't do that! What stuff are you talking about?"

"Just little shit, you know, shit she can easily replace! Come on, let's see what she got," as he pushed me back into the house. "Yeah, I see a whole lot of shit! Get a garbage bag! Grab the toaster, microwave! I'll get the TV and the VCR! All this shit got to go!"

I was really scared now. My Mommie is going to be so mad at me and I will never be able to come back to her house again.

I was moving kinda of slow and James yelled, "Hurry up! It's too late now to be having second thoughts! You already cut the lock off, so you got to go! Or do you want her to put you in a juvenile home like she did your little brother? She don't give a damn about you! All that shit you said happen to you! Now tell me, how do she care? I'm the only one that cares about you, and you know this! Hurry up! We got to get on the next bus leaving!"

I began to put stuff in the garbage bags, thinking he's right. It's too late now, and my mother will send me off to a home somewhere. I can't go to Nana's, and if I don't leave with James now, I will be on the streets with nowhere to go.

"What about this?" as I picked up the toaster oven that she had on the counter.

"Yeah! Put all that shit in there! We got to go! Come on, hurry up!"

He had a Jitney down stairs waiting on him. It was somebody that he knew because Jitney Cab didn't come that far out. They only ran on King Drive. As we loaded the stuff in the cab, I thought to myself that he must

246

really love me. He got a Jitney to come all the way out here to get me. We are really going to be a family and one day I'm going to have a baby of my very own to love and my Mommie won't be nowhere around to make me get rid of it.

I know my Mommie is going to be hurt, mad and might not have anything else to do with me, but when she sees that I am happy and have a job, with my own house and a baby, I think she will be proud and really love me then. She won't have to worry about me or have to lock me in the house anymore. She can live her life without me like she is doing without Chuckie being at home. These were the thoughts running through my head.

When James put the last bag in the Jitney and we drove off, I turned and looked at that apartment building, knowing that I will never step a foot back in it again. This kinda felt like when I ran off the porch after Papa's funeral. I never went back.

So, after making such life-altering decisions at such a young age, the majority of my teenage life and on into my adult life, has spun out of control. And the sad thing about it is that I didn't even see it coming and it was right in front of my face!

Section 141

Jitney ride to the low end

James told the driver to take us down on the low end to 47th street right off King Drive.

"Don't worry about the money, man! Look at all this shit I got!"

"Yeah, man you got a lot!"

"I'm gonna hook you up as soon as we get down there and I get rid of this. Me and my baby gonna leave this motherfucker! We going down south!"

"Oh? What part?"

"I got people down in Memphis."

They went on talking and all I could do is think about how my Mommie would feel when she came home from work. I began to have doubts about what I had done, but it was too late and there was nothing that I could do about it.

James went from place to place and everything in the car began to disappear. There were so many people walking, talking, standing on the corner—yelling, screaming and even fighting. It reminded me of that place we went to on our first 'date', but it's worse because it's broad daylight!

As I sat in the cab and waited for James to sell an item, there was this lady walking across the street with a fishnet dress on, real high heels shoes, a long blonde wig on and lots of make-up. She had nothing on under that dress! I mean nothing! You could see her big behind, her pubic hairs and her huge breasts.

Cars were stopping and one man even hit the back of another car, trying to see her. She was really walking and waving the cars down that was driving by, saying she got it! I was trying to look to see what she had, but I didn't see anything in her hand but a purse!

You could hear this man that was standing on the curb yelling and pointing his finger at the lady, "That's the best pussy on 47th Street! Ain't none no better! Come on and get it! It's good!" Some man stopped and gave him money! "Better than Kentucky Fried Chicken, finger licking good!"

"Got one for you! Get in, don't worry! She be back! Give her five minutes and she'll be right with you! Park right over there," as he collected more money from a different man!

What the hell? There were some ladies with long dresses on the other side of the street, waving the Bible, yelling, "Repent! Repent! While you have a chance! You gonna burn in hell! Fire and brimstones! Repent!"

I was so scared and I didn't know what to think! Then, I thought it was funny for some reason.

James came back to the car and got something else; each time he got in or out the car, I would ask, "How much you get for that? What you gonna sell that for? What kinda place is this? Where are we?"

We were parked in front of a pawn shop. James was taking the TV into the store. He leaned down in the car with this odd expression and a weird tone of voice.

"Don't worry about it, baby! I got this! You belong to me now and I'm gonna take real good care of you! So, just sit back and shut the fuckup and let me take care of this business, something that you don't know nothing about! Do you understand me?"

"Yeah, I do. I just asked a question."

"Close your motherfucking mouth!" And he slammed the door!

Once he said that and the way he looked at me, I was shaken because I didn't want him to be mad at me and start slapping or hitting on me. This is supposed to be a good day. We are supposed to be leaving for Arkansas to be a family, to get married and even have children. That's what he said.

He asked me did I trust him and I do, so I better be quiet and let him do this because I don't know how to sell and I know nobody to sell it to!

We got to the last stop and everything was gone. James had a lot of money in his hands and began to count it. He gave the driver $35.00 and put the rest in his pocket. He put his hands on my leg, "See, baby, everything is going to be alright! You'll see! We are on our way to get the hell up outta here!"

249

Section 142

The Shooting Gallery

"Hey, man, I got one more stop and that's on 35th in Giles. You know the spot."

"What, the one on the corner?"

"No, the shooting gallery!"

"Yeah, man, I do. I got you. You gonna get me one?"

"Yeah, if you wait for me, then drop me and my baby off at the Greyhound bus station. Alright? Hey, I just want to take off one, so it won't be long. You know the drill."

"Alright, you okay, I'll wait for you." We pulled up at this old two-story brick building. "Come on, baby, go in here with me. Man, I be back."

"If you want, you can leave your girl in the car so she don't have to go in there with you."

"Who in the fuck do you think you talking to motherfucker? Come on, baby!" He grabbed my hand and pulled me out the car.

"No, no, it ain't like that man! Please, man. I didn't mean it like that, you still gonna get me one. I can't go in there!"

"You motherfucking right, nigga! I know it ain't like that! Now wait yo punk ass right here fore I take my bread back! Punk ass nigga!" and he slammed the door. He was walking and talking fast!

"Come on, baby! Now, listen! When we go up in here, I need for you to stand where I tell you to and don't move! You got it?"

"I got it."

"Don't be staring at motherfuckers, just mind your business and keep your mouth shut! Don't be asking no motherfucking questions and keep your eyes on me!"

Knock-knock! "Yeah!" Somebody yelled from the other side of the door.

"It's Jr.!"

"Who?"

"Jr., motherfucker! Open this bitch up!"

"Hey, it's okay! That's this nigga Jr.!

"Oh, my God! I could not believe my eyes when we went in! I was seeing stuff that I never in my life dreamed of! There was a room full of sick people!

"Wait right here, baby, and don't move! Smoke you a cigarette and by the time you are finish with it, I will be ready to go!

It was a huge, huge room with one couch and several chairs scattered throughout. There weren't any curtains at the windows and the shades were torn, ripped and barely hanging at the window. The room was filled with a heavy cloud of smoke.

The odor was very, very bad! I can't even describe it… I never smelled that before! The people were standing there with needles in their arms, legs, neck and one lady was sticking a needle in a man's penis! They had belts, scarves, and rubber ties tied around their arms, legs or whatever! Something is seriously wrong with these people! I wanted to get out of there fast, but I had to wait for James and act like I wasn't afraid!

I thought that they all had some type of disease and I was going to catch it by being in the same room. Some of them had so many open sores! Oh, my God! That lady just took that needle out of that man's penis and just stuck it in her leg! What the fuck is wrong with them? Please, James, hurry up!

James did not have to worry about me moving—I stood right there! I smoked my cigarette real fast and did not stare, but watched everybody! What the hell is this place?

"Hey, baby, you okay in there?"

"Yeah, I'm fine. Just waiting on you." He was in the dining room with his back to me, so I really couldn't see what he was doing. I hope not this shit cause that meant he got what they got—and I don't want it! Please, Jesus, don't let me catch what they got! Just as I finished my cigarette, James was walking toward me.

This man walked up to me real fast and said, "Let me get one of those cigarettes, baby," reaching toward my purse with these open bloody sores on his hands.

"Motherfucker, if you don't get your ass away from her, I will blow your motherfucking brains out!" James pulled this gun from behind his jacket!

"Okay, man!" and he threw his hands up and stepped back! Everybody else just stood there with needles still in them. "If he kills him, I got those shoes! I can get five for them and that watch, too."

My body must have frozen! I was in shock! I couldn't believe James had pulled out a gun and pointed it at that man! He will protect me no matter what! James really does love me.

James said to me, "Backup out the door and don't turn your back on these sick motherfuckers! He continued to point the gun at them, pushing me backwards toward the door! Keep your eyes on them! You watchin'?!"

"Yeah, I'm watchin', James!"

Section 143

What is your phobia?

That was crazy! I know better than to ask questions. I never asked any questions. But, why did he go to that place? I was ready to get on that bus so we could leave for Arkansas!

We ended up spending the night at his friend's house. I had never met them before. I wanted to call my mother and tell her that I was sorry and I wanted to come home. I told James how I was feeling. James looked at me with contempt, "Bitch, you belong to me now! You will never leave me!"

Just as quickly as he said that, he gave me a kiss and told me he didn't mean it. He said he was under a lot of stress. He knew that my mother had the police looking for him.

"My mother don't have the police looking for you!"

"Oh yeah? Let's go! Go in that room and get my jacket!" It was dark, so I turned to feel for the light switch.

Once I turned it on, I saw his coat on the bed. I walked over to his coat, picked it up and there was this big black cat under his coat! A huge Siamese cat was walking toward me! I screamed and turned to run to the door! James locked the door! I was terrified! I stood there very still as I watch the cat jump off the bed and come towards me!

I closed my eyes as the tears rolled down my face and my body began to shake. I heard James on the other side of the door, yelling, "Are you still going to leave me, Debra?! I won't let you out if you don't tell me you're going to stay! So, what's it's going to be?" and he laughed! I was too afraid to say anything! I was shaking even harder!

I could feel the cat walk through my legs, but I wasn't sure if it was gone! I fell to the floor, covered my eyes, with my knees up to my face. I can't remember how long I stay in this room—that is, how long he kept me locked in this room!

James finally opened the door! I was terrified to open my eyes and my body would not stop shaking. I was sweating profusely, crying and screaming! I thought he had a cat in his hands! I guess I scared James so bad he called the paramedics.

When they got there, I could hear them, but I could not stop shaking, nor could I say anything to them. I heard, "It looks like she's having a seizure. Did she hit her head?" They asked James, "What happened to her? What's her name? What brought on this seizure?"

James replied, "She just saw them damn cats over there and starting shaking and acting like this! Hell, ain't nothing wrong with her." I started shaking even harder; I had no control over my body.

One of the EMTs knelt on the floor and he began to talk to me, "Debra, it's alright. You're safe now." He placed his hand on my back. "Come on now, talk to us. Tell us what happened to you."

I opened my eyes just a little to see who was talking to me, making sure that it really was someone here to save me from those cats! But, when I did, all I could see was that black cat sitting over in the corner looking at me! I threw my arms around the man, gasping for air, yelling, screaming, "Get the cats! Please get the cats!"

"Somebody get those cats and put them up," demanded the EMTs.

"Y'all shit! They ain't none of my motherfucking cats! What's the problem? What's going on?! yelled James.

I could hear the EMTs tell James, "Get those cats out of here! Lock them up! Calm down! Calm down, you're okay now."

I saw the frown on James' as he walked towards me. I screamed, "He got a cat! He got a cat!"

"Debra, do you want to go to the hospital? I embedded my head into his chest and my body was curled up like a baby, holding on to him for dear life. I nodded to let him know yes!

The EMT said, "We are taking her to the hospital to make sure I was okay." I would not let go of that man. My heart was racing and my clothes were wet from sweating. I looked up to the sky as they rolled me to the back of the ambulance, not really understanding what had just happen to me. I just knew I was free of those cats. I could breathe again.

Just before they put me in the ambulance, I heard James say, "Let me kiss my wife before you drive off. I'll meet you there. Where are you taking her?"

He leaned over me and I flinched! When he got closer, he whispered in my ear, "If you tell what happened to anybody, the next time I will throw those motherfucking cats on you, bitch!"

Then he smiled and said, "Y'all take her on. Baby, I love you. I'm on my way to the hospital. Baby, don't worry, I'll protect you. I'll be there." I began to cry.

The EMT who rode in the ambulance with me put in an IV. He looked at me and asked, "What did he say to you? What really happened at that house?" I just shook my head and turned the other way.

Once the doctor saw me in the hospital, I found out I have a phobia of cats. He said it's so bad that I could have had a heart attack and died, and that I need to take this very serious.

"You be careful from now on being around cats. You should seek help regarding this immediately." He said as a doctor of 35 years, he had never seen such a strong phobia about cats.

Section 144

It wasn't his fault. He said he didn't know.

I stayed in the hospital two nights. I also founded out that I was pregnant. The doctor informed me that I needed to stay away from cats during my pregnancy or I could miscarry.

I was released with nowhere to go. James never did come to the hospital. I had to catch the bus. Luckily, I had bus fare. I had no other choice, but to go to his mother's house. I wanted to tell him the good news, that I was carrying our baby.

James was there. He apologized and said he had no idea that I was that afraid of cats. It was supposed to be a joke and that he just did not want me talking about leaving him again.

"I need you, Debra! You are all I have! Just like you want us to have a baby, that's how much I want and need you in my life. Well, when James put it that way, I understand a little more of how much he really loves and wants me.

Really? Debra!

Section 145

Living with Mom

"Debra, we will be leaving in the morning. I was waiting on you to come back. If I didn't love you, I would have left you here."

"Wait, James. Listen, I'm pregnant. We are going to have a baby!"

"Are you sure, Debra? Did they tell you this at the hospital?"

"Yes!"

"That's my baby! He gave me hugs and kisses, telling me how much more he loved me.

We left the following morning—a one-way ticket to Camden, Arkansas!

256

We stayed away from Chicago for almost two years. It was as pretty as James said! The trees were so tall, full, pretty, and green, and there were so many of them! The air even smelled cleaner! The streets were a little hilly, but that was fine by me—I'd made up my mind this is where I want to live, Down South!

We stayed with his sister who had this big pretty white house with a porch that went from one side to the other end of the house. There were four white tall back chairs on the front porch. Her house sat on the corner, on top of a hill. There were pretty flowers and plants all over the yard. It was beautiful. Everybody called his sister Mom.

I got a job working in a club and I enjoyed living there. Every now and then, James would get mad and slap me a few times, but other than that, he was really good to me.

He brought me down here and his family was so nice to me. Mom didn't really know me, yet she was more kind to me than my own family had been, with the exception of my Nana.

Mom went fishing a lot and that was dinner. She loved to fish. I ate a lot of sandwiches and potatoes; I didn't care for fish too much, maybe because I would see her clean the fish that she caught! Mom even caught a big frog and then gutted it! They ate frog legs! That was so gross to me, but James loved it!

Section 146

Don't need much to be happy.

So much stuff happened so fast while we were living down south. We even moved to the country with his Aunt Eliz who lived right off the highway in a small town named Lin Ridge, Arkansas.

Aunt Eliz was real dark- skinned, around five feet tall, and she wore an oversized dress with an apron.

She has big, pretty button eyes and her hair was black with mingling grey. She also chewed stuff and always had a spit can close by, with a rag to wipe away the spit juice on her mouth.

The house across from Aunt Eliz set just a little further back into the woods. They used an outhouse because they did not have a bathroom in the house. When night fell, you couldn't see the house. There was only one light that shined through the trees.

Have you ever driven down the highway and passed a house with people sitting on their porch and waving at the passing cars? Well, that was Lin Ridge.

Section 147

Only the early bird gets the worm…

Well, that's how it was here. Aunt Eliz even got her water from a real well. I learned so much from living in the country. On Sundays after church, I would help her cook the chicken and fish dinners that she sold to the 'men and the women of leisure,' as she call them, at the Jute Joint where they gambled, drank and dance.

James would be there every weekend. I wanted to go, but Aunt Eliz told me that it was not a good place for me, just a bunch of young and old men fooling around and doing stuff they ain't got no business doing. Then she spat into the can that sat a few feet from her.

"You don't know too much about cooking, do ya?"

"My Nana taught me a lot. I know how to cook."

"Well, I need you to go in there and clean those six chickens, seasoned them and lay 'em out to be floured and fried." Six! I don't know how to clean and cook six chickens.

She looked at me and laughed, "Your grandmother lives in the city, up there in Chicago. Well, you down here in the South and you need to know how to cook as we do down here." She spat in that can again.

"Will you teach me how to cook like you down here?"

"Long as you willing to learn, I'll teach you whatever you need to know. I don't know about my cooking, it ain't all that, but to tell you the truth, it ain't much at all. Just use a little common sense," at the same time she was laughing, spitting and wiping her mouth.

"We gone see how much you wanna learn. You gonna get up with me in the morning and start."

"I'll be ready. What time do we need to get up?"

"You need to get up by 4:00."

"Oh, okay."

Aunt Eliz got up at 4:30 a.m. and had cooked breakfast with homemade biscuits and washed a load of clothes in this huge silver tin tub. She used a scrub board to clean the clothes, towels and sheets, and hung everything on line in the back of the house. Aunt Eliz even went out and split a pile of wood with an axe.

And by the time I got out of bed, her dinner was almost ready and it was 10 a.m.! She was 76 years old! Even though I tried a few times, I could not get up that early to learn anything. It was just too hard for me.

Section 148
I was honest and told her everything.

I use to be amazed at how she did all of that at her age. One day, she had me to try and split a wood log. I couldn't even swing the axe over my shoulder to hit it! She thought that was so funny.

I got sick one morning and Aunt Eliz asked what was wrong. I told her that I was about two or three months pregnant and that James told me to keep

259

it a secret. My stomach was cramping so bad that it felt like the time I had my baby at home in the toilet.

I got a chance to tell Aunt Eliz about everything that had happen to me and all the bad stuff that I had done. "I already knew that you was carrying a sack. Here, eat this. It will make you feel better and it will help you to hold that little one."

"You mean, I'm gonna lose my baby?!"

"No, chew this, just don't swallow it. Spit it out when you're done." It looked like some odd-shaped tree leaves. She called it shoemaker. Whatever it was, my cramps stopped after an hour or so.

Section 149

He said he was going to make a home for us.

I was pregnant with my first baby, the baby that I was going to be able to bring into this world without anybody telling me that I couldn't. James was so happy that I was going to have a baby.

It was so hot outside! The heat index was reported to be around 101 and Aunt Eliz didn't have air conditioner, only fans! I was sitting on the front porch, shelling peas when James came by. He told me that he was going to go Las Vegas with his cousin to see his brother that lived there. He said he was going to find a place for us and then he would send for me.

I couldn't have been any more than three months pregnant, so I really didn't want him to leave me. He promised he would come back or send for me.

James asked Aunt Eliz if I could stay there until he got everything straight for us. She agreed, saying, "Going up there ain't gonna get you straight cause you as crooked as they come," spitting in her can. "You don took this girl away from her family and now you gonna leave her, knowing she carrying that sack of yours."

"What you been telling her! You know I ain't took you from nobody!" as he walked towards me yelling. Aunt Eliz raised her hand and stood up, "If you lay your hands on that girl I will put something on you that you'll never be able to get off! Try me, boy, if you want to!"

"Ahhh, Aunt Eliz, you know I'm not gonna touch that girl! She's carrying my baby. I love her!" He kissed her on the cheek. "Debra know what I am talking about."

The next morning, James left for Las Vegas. I was glad in a way because I'd never been to Las Vegas. He told me that as long as I was with him, I'd be going places. He was right; I had never been to all these places in Arkansas! We were doing a lot of traveling with hardly any money.

Everybody always took care of him and he took care of me. I did my share, though—washing clothes and cleaning up whichever house we were in at the time.

At first, I thought that James left me because I was pregnant. I asked him was that the case and he assured me it was not. I was satisfied with his answer and knew that all he wanted was the best for us. He had to do whatever it took for us to be happy. He would tell me all the time that he had to make the money for us. How else were we going to survived?

We had been through so much. I knew that if I stuck by his side, everything would be alright. He promised he would take care of us and he made me promise that I would never leave him. He said he would die without me. I believed him.

Section 150

Will you ever tell your deepest secret?

I was 19 and pregnant. We have been together since I was 14. We have lived in two different places—Camden and Fordyce—and now we are in

Lin Ridge. I stayed with Aunt Eliz for a little less than two months after he had left.

Late one afternoon, I went out on a boat ride with one of his cousin. James called him Pretty Boy because he was very nice looking with curly black hair, that good grade of hair like James' mother. It was late and we were drinking and smoking some of that laughing reefers and one thing led to another. Right there under the stars, there I was with my panties down and with him on top of me! It was nothing really. I had my mind on James all the time. It was just something to do at the time.

I cannot believe I told that! I have never told anyone, but the more I write, the more I actually remember the little dirty secrets that are in my closet.

I believe I needed someone to hold me, to tell me I was pretty and that everything was going to be alright.

James never knew what happened. He never knew that I had acted like a trifling tramp and all the other names that I had been called! That is what I thought of myself after that happen. I did it while carrying James' baby. If he had found out, he would have questioned whether or not the baby was his, even though he knew I was pregnant with our baby before he left for Las Vegas!

But, I knew that James was probably with another girl in Las Vegas. He had always done it before. *This is my first time ever saying this out loud.*

His cousin never came back around after that, at least not while I was there. I promised myself that I would never get myself in a situation like that again. I stayed close to the house with Aunt Eliz.

One Saturday, Willie Earl stopped by. James had a lot of respect for him. Willie Earl was much older than James, maybe in his earlier thirties. James had taken me to his house several times to visit him and his wife.

Willie Earl had had just gotten out of jail after a long time and was glad to see James. I never knew nor did I ask why he went to jail. It was none of my business. Before James left, he was getting his drugs from Willie Earl, especially reefer and syrup.

Willie Earl talked with Aunt Eliz for a while.

"Hey, Debra! Girl, you have been in this house since that boy left. Come go out with me and my wife tonight. We will take care of you. We just going into Fordyce to the club for a couple of hours."

I looked at Aunt Eliz, and asked her if I could go and she told me, "That's up to you, but if you know like I know, you will stay at home!" She walked toward the kitchen, mumbling under her breath.

Willie Earl asked, "What you say, Aunt Eliz? Did you say something?"

"No, boy! You need to get on away from here! That boy James is gone up there to Vegas."

I laughed a little and said. "I'll go. What time do I need to be ready?"

"About 7 or 8. If we get there early, we won't be long. My girl do not want to stay out late!"

"Okay, I'll be ready."

That evening, he came by to pick me up. I was glad to be getting out of the house. I was not showing yet, so nobody really knew that I was pregnant, other than Aunt Eliz and James. I wore jeans with a pretty shirt and sandals.

Wait! He did not have his wife with him. One of his friends was with him. I asked where was his wife and he told me that she was going to meet us at the club. I got into his van and sat down in the back.

Section 151

Listen to your first mind. Never go against the grain!

I was a little wary about going. You know how that little voice tells you 'Do not do it." Well, I didn't listen.

On the way to the club, we talked small talk. It was pitch black as we rode on this dirt gravel road. Willie Earl was driving and every now and then he would cut the headlights off. I would scream and laugh, "Cut those lights back on!" Willie Earl teased, "What's the manner? You scare of a little darkness?"

"Yeah! You don't know what's out here in these woods!"

"You right, cause we got mountain cats out here!"

"Oh my God, really?! I am deathly afraid of cats, which you already know cause you put your cat up for me when we came to your house. Please, we do not want to get stuck out here, right?" as I laughed nervously.

"Baby, I am going to take real good care of you. Don't you worry, we will not get stuck."

I eased back in my seat, "That's good. I like hearing that." But, just as those words came out of my mouth, it did not sound right to me. And at that moment, I spotted him looking at me in the rear view mirror. It was dark and all I could see were his eyes. I played it off and kept on laughing as if I never saw that strange look in his eyes.

When we got to the club, he told the bartender to give me whatever I wanted. I asked for a wine cooler. I had never been to this club before. James used to go out all the time and every now and then he would take me with him. This hole-in-the-wall juke joint was nice. It was back up in the woods on a dirt gravel road.

There were a lot of older people there and it was very smoky. They were playing the blues and people were talking loud, laughing, dancing and having a good time. The floor was covered with a little sand, so when you danced, your feet would slide a little.

When we walked in, several people asked, "Hey, Willie Earl, what you got there? That's some pretty little thang with you!" He answered, "Nah, man, this here is my cousin little girl. I'm just taking her out for the night, helping my little cousin out."

Then one of the old men asked, "Where is your wife?" and they all laughed.

"Shut the hell up and give her what she wants!"

"Hey, I got a drink already." I gulped down the wine cooler. "Give her another one and this time, put it in a glass with one of those pretty little straws."

"Come on, girl, let me see if you know how to step!" I got on the floor and danced with Willie Earl. "Did my cousin show you really how to get down?"

"Yeah, he did and I know how to do it!" I was having so much fun that night.

Section 152

Never, ever leave your drink at the bar!

It was time for me to go to the restroom as the bartender poured my next drink.

"I'll be back. Watch my drink." When I got back, I drank the wine cooler. I asked Willie Earl, "What time is your wife coming to the club? I'm feeling a little tired."

"We are going to wait just a little while longer, about 30 more minutes."

Then I got up and was dancing by myself on the floor. All I could hear was "Get it young girl, shake that thang!" I felt dizzy and the room was spinning fast. I stumbled over to Willie Earl and fell into his arms.

"Willie Earl, I do not feel good. Help me to the van." I was sick to my stomach; I needed some fresh air. Willie Earl grabbed me by my waist and said, "Oh yeah, it's time!"

He helped me out of the door. I heard someone yell out, "Nigga, you gonna go back to jail doing that same old bullshit." Willie Earl yelled back, "Mind your own damn business!"

I could feel my knees buckle and I needed all of his help to get to the van. I couldn't walk. I was semi-conscious, but knew what was going on around me. I could not move—I was limp!

When he put me in the van, he laid me down on the back seat. In my mind I'm thinking, he's about to take me back to the house. But, instead he got in the back of the van with me from the other side. "Baby, I know you want me. I been waiting all night for this!"

I tried to push him off me, but my arms and hands were so limp! I was trying to scream NO! I had no strength to even scream!

"I bought you those drinks and gave you a ride! You was up there dancing like you wanted me! Hell, no, I'm not going to stop! You are going to give me some of this pussy tonight!"

He began to unfasten my pants, "Damn I didn't think that shit was going to work on you that fast. I put that little magic pill in your glass! Damn, it's all good now!"

I remember crying and him saying, "Bitch, you don't even know me nothing more than I am James' cousin!"

266

Section 153

You don't know that man!

"Did you know that I went to the penitentiary for rape and murder?! This should teach your fast ass a lesson not to be so quick to get in cars with motherfuckers you don't know! Fooled you, little bitch! All you bitches are just alike!"

I looked in his eyes and I saw the same eyes that I saw in the rearview mirror. I am terrified, but this time, I put myself in this situation. I should not have gone out with him—it's all my fault!

He began to get even more forceful! He managed to get one leg out of my pants and he pulled his pants down! I tried to scream, but the scream would not come out!

I could hear myself trying to get out, "NO! STOP! NO! Please STOP! I am sorry, please do not hurt me! I am pregnant, you are going to hurt my baby!" He never stopped, he just keep right on shoving his dick inside of me!

He said, "James told me you got some good pussy, so I decided to see for myself! I couldn't wait for him to leave!" He put his hands over my mouth as my words kept coming! He went faster and faster until he was finished! I lay there helpless, could not move.

He got up, leaned over and whispered in my ear, "You keep your motherfucking mouth shut before somebody find you and that baby you got in your stomach somewhere in these here woods! Now you lay here until that shit wear off in about 30 minutes and I'll be back! Do not make me cut that damn baby up out of you!" as he put a switchblade up to my neck. "I am not going back to the pen for you and nobody else, do you understand me?"

I just nodded my head and the tears streamed down. He got out of the van and shut the door. I could do nothing! As the time went by, I was able to put my pants on and was about to get out the van, but Willie Earl was coming back. He and his friend jumped in the van and he looked back at me, "Are you okay?"

"Yes, I am okay. I just want to go home, please."

It was so dark and I was crying on the inside. I did not know if his friend knew what he done, or if I said something, he might put me out in the woods and drive off! Or, he might even kill me and my baby. I thought it was best that I remain quiet. I will never tell anybody about this! I will take this secret to my grave, I thought. Maybe I led him on, I don't know. I was not trying to do that. He was right, I should never have gotten in the van with him.

Section 154

A hard head really do make a soft ass!

I should have listened to that little voice in my head. Aunt Eliz even told me not to go. So, it really was my fault. I have to keep this a secret—I cannot tell.

It was late when I got to the house and Aunt Eliz was waiting up for me. When I came in the house, she looked at me and told me to sit down. She turned on the lights to get a look at me.

"Are you alright?" I looked at her and dropped my head, "I'm okay."

"You will listen next time. Go in there and take a shower and clean yourself up. You will be fine. Going to try and get the money together so you can get out of here tomorrow. I want you to get on that bus so you can be with that boy James. I'm sorry that happened. You don't need to tell nobody cause that boy there ain't got good sense! He'll be back for you and I don't want to find you nowhere in them there woods!

"James had no business leaving you like that! Now, do you want a ticket to go to that boy, or do you want to go home to your mother? You need to call your mother in the morning and see if you can go home. You need to be with your mother right now being that you with child."

I cleaned myself up. I prayed that my Mommie would take me back. But, I knew that she would not, not after taking her stuff out of the house. I was too ashamed to call my mother. I did not want her to know that I was having such a hard time. I had James in my life and nobody understands him like I do. I know he loves me and only me. I'm going to James—I'm going to Las Vegas, Nevada. I need to be protected and James said he will protect me.

Section 155

Vegas changed him!

The church paid for my ticket to Vegas. I was on my way to see James and he was waiting for me. At least, that is what I wanted to believe.

The first day that I got there, I got jumped on by one of his super fat cousins! I broke the ashtray on her head trying to protect myself. Then she picked it up and stabbed me on the side of my face!

James didn't help me; he just stood there and let her beat me up! We were at his brother's house. James left me there that day and walked out of the house with a girl that he evidently was dating while I was still in Lin Ridge—waiting on him, getting raped by his cousin, and fucking his other one! What goes around comes around... I did wrong and this is why this is happening to me!

A few months passed and I went back to school to get my GED. I then got a job waiting tables at the Golden Nugget.

I often walked to the store. This particular day, I see James lying in the grass under a shady tree with this girl, having a picnic! I just walk pass as if I didn't know him! The humiliation wasn't enough for him, so he called me over to ask me where did I think I was going.

"James, I'm going to the store."

"It's too motherfucking hot out here for you to be walking! Get your ass back to the damn house! You didn't ask me if can you go to no damn store!" I didn't want him to make a scene as the girl looked at me with a smile on her face like she was really doing something. Well, I guess she was—she had my man, my baby's daddy.

I walked away, but he yelled, "Debra! Debra! Come here! Matter of fact, I need you to get me some beer, a six pack of Schlitz Malt Liquor, tall cans. Baby, give her the money," speaking to the girl who was lying next to him under that shady tree.

I made it up in my mind that day that I was going to work and have my baby so that I could have somebody to love me. I had so much love to give and no one to give it to.

James had started hitting me more often and he was getting high. I could never understand how he could find the people who had the different types of drugs wherever we went.

James came in later that night only to tell me again how much he loves me and that he is only looking out for the both of us. That these women are damn fools who are taking care of us. "I have to spend time with them in order for us to make it out here."

He asked, "You get your check today or is it tomorrow?"

"I get it tomorrow, James." I turned over to go to sleep. I had just gotten paid and was keeping it in a shoe box under the bed. I hadn't cash it yet because I wanted to keep twenty-five dollars, along with my tips, without James knowing it and before I handed over the money. I made at least thirty dollars in tips that night which was a good night.

"Baby, you go ahead and lay down. I got one more thing I got to do tonight."

"What? James, it's late. I thought you were going to lay down with me and feel the baby move."

"Listen, you know I love you, right?"

"Yeah, I know that, but why do you have to treat me like that in front of people, especially other women?"

"Baby, this is for us, everything that I do is for us, and I want you to trust me!"

"Okay, I see you when you get back. I love you, too, James."

Well, that night came and went. James wasn't in the bed when I woke up that morning. I got one of his cousins to take me to work. I didn't want to know if he came home or not. Then, maybe he left early this morning before I got up. I didn't want him to come in the house and I was still there because we might start arguing and I get slapped or something. I didn't want to make him mad. He told me to trust him and I do. I know James loves me and our baby.

I had to go to work. It was my way of getting out of the house and away from everything. I was getting so big and my baby was moving a lot. All I could think about was my baby. Finally, I was going to have a baby, a baby in Las Vegas, Nevada. I was saving money so that I could go and buy my baby everything we would need. I didn't want to ask nobody for anything.

"Jessica, will you drop me off, please? James is not here and I can't be late for work."

"Debra, you gonna have to give me gas money. I don't have gas to take you downtown and then make it back. You shouldn't be working anyways."

"Well, if I don't work, I will not be able to buy all the stuff for my baby. I want to have a baby shower, and I'm going to have one if I have to give it to myself!"

"Okay I'll take you, but I wouldn't put up with that bullshit that James is doing!"

"I know. I got five dollars. Will that be enough for you to take me and pick me up?"

"Hell, yeah, girl, and I could get me a couple of single cigarettes!"

It was a long day and I worked really hard. There were so many orders, but I got about $50.00 in tips. When Jessica picked me up, I felt something was wrong because James didn't come and he knew I got paid today—well, that's what I told him.

Jessica and I didn't talk much, just made a little small talk until we got to the house. It was so hot and I was really tired.

Section 156

Why did he leave me?

I went straight into the bedroom and sat on the bed. The box that I used to save money for my baby was gone! James had taken all the money out of the box! I called out to Jessica!

"Where is James?! He took all my money that I had under the bed! Have you seen him?!"

"Girl, let me tell you! James done took over $3,000.00 from that woman and I see he took yo money, too! And, he done left and went back to Chicago! That girl got the police looking for him and he's gone now! Carmen dropped him off at the bus station this morning, not too long after you left for work! Well, Debra, what are you going to do?"

"Do about what?! I don't know!" I began to cry. "I am going to wait until your father Leon comes home and I will ask him what to do! I have no money, no more than this tip money that I made today! I want to go home, back to Chicago! I need my mother and I am too shame of what I did to even call her now. That's where I should have gone when Aunt Eliz asked me, instead of coming here!"

I went to the bedroom, wiped my face, and began to pack my bags. I couldn't believe he left me down here like this and took the money that I had saved for the baby, for our baby!

James had been getting high a lot, and I just ignored it because I didn't want him to get mad at me and make him hit me. Since we've been here, he's busted my lip a couple of times, but I knew it was my fault. If I had not done something or probably said something really smart, I probably wouldn't have gotten hit.

Are you kidding me, Debra?

James' brother Leon worked for one of the biggest hotels in Vegas as one of the head bakery chefs. He will be home in another hour and I will be so glad. I was rubbing my stomach and praying that he will have some money to send me back home.

When Leon got home, I told him what happened and that I wanted to go home because I was afraid to be in Las Vegas by myself. "James took all my money along with that girl's money."

"Stop crying, everything will be alright. You are more than welcomed to stay here until after the baby is born and then leave."

"Thank you, but no thank you. I want to go home. Can you, please, find it in your heart to help me get home? I will be forever grateful. I got fifty dollars from my tips today, if that will help?"

"No, baby, that's okay," as he placed his arms around me and patted me on my back. Don't cry.

"Jessica, get the phone book out and find out how much the bus fare is for a one-way ticket to Chicago."

"Daddy, the bus people said that if she is more than five months pregnant, she can't ride the bus."

I felt like it wasn't their business how many months I was, so I lied just so I could get back to Chicago. I left in two days.

Section 157
He did what he had to do.

That was the longest bus ride I ever took in my life. I had only been on a bus with James when we went to Arkansas. I was a little scared, but I was going home. I really didn't have a home in Chicago. The only place I could go to was Madear's house. I prayed that she would take me in.

When the bus stopped at different locations, I was able to buy me a few snacks. Leon let me keep my tip money so I could buy food and drink, and to have bus fare once I got to Chicago.

I called and told Madear that I was on my way and she made arrangements for one of her daughters to come to the bus station to pick me up. During the bus ride, I thought about all that James had done, but mostly about the things that he had said to me. Like, the night before when he told me that he have to do what was best for us, and he wanted me to know that he loved me and the baby.

Oh! I get it now! He was telling me that he was going to leave. He probably went back home to get an apartment for us now that we are going to have a baby. See, I knew that James really did love me and he wanted the best for us. I had to realize that I was so much younger than he was and he knew how to make money for us, even if it was getting money from other women.

I convinced myself to turn every negative thought into a good thought when it came to James—he could do no wrong. I loved him and wanted so much to believe that he loved me to. I didn't want him to die like my father did. I knew that I can make him change, to stop using all those drugs. After

274

all, we were going to have a baby. He said he needed me. I need him; no one really loves me, but him. Who was going to watch out for him when he was high off that stuff? Nobody understood James like I did. He really does love me. He left because he did what he had to do! I just sat there rubbing my stomach and daydreaming, looking out the window.

Section 158

Madear protected me.

When I arrived into Chicago that Friday evening, it had taken four days to get there. It was a party going on at Madear's house. Everybody was there, his whole family. I was glad to be back, but I wanted to see James. I wanted to tell him that I understood that he had to leave. I wanted him to see that I made it back, to show him that I'm a grown woman now. I traveled all by myself, crossing many states just to be with him so we could be a happy family— just the way he wanted it to be.

Madear was so glad to see me. She actually said that she missed me and that was something coming from her. I asked James' sister, the one they called 'Got to be starting something', where was James?

"Oh, he back here. Come on, let me show you." I got up and walked to the back of the house.

"He's in there, in that room. Gone in there, he's there." She had this little smirk on her face. I hesitated, looking back at her. I didn't know what he was doing, and I didn't know if I was going to be ready to see what was behind that closed door. I thought that after coming such a long way, he would be happy to see me.

I opened the door and there James was sitting on the bed with this girl sitting on his lap!

"Who are you?" the girl asked me.

"Who am I? The question is, who are you, motherfucker?"

James jumped up, making the girl fall to the floor and grabbed me by my throat! He slammed me upside the wall, screaming, "This is my bitch! Who do the fuck you think you are coming in here asking any motherfucking questions? I told you what the fuck I got to do! Now, get the fuck out of here!" as he tighten his hand around my throat.

I had never seen James like this before! "What did I do wrong? I'm so sorry. I won't do it no more." He scared me!

I heard his sister yelling, "Madear! James jumping on this girl back here! That's a shame!"

I cried, "The baby, James, please don't hurt the baby!"

Madear came running towards the room, "That crazy motherfucker better not be jumping on that girl! She's pregnant and she just got here!"

"Motherfuck you and that baby when it comes to my money!" as he pushed me out the room, down onto the floor and slamming the door shut behind me.

Madear kicked the door in and said, "Don't no motherfucker slam my doors in here. I'm the baddest bitch in this motherfucker! Now, what the fuck is going on? You got to get the fuck out of here, James, with all this bullshit! Jumping on this poor baby like this and she pregnant! What the hell wrong with you? What happen?"

"Madear, Debra came back here fucking with me!"

"I'm not fucking with nobody!"

"Come on, baby," as he grabbed the woman's hand. "Let's get the fuck outta of here! I ain't got time to listen to this bullshit! Debra know what the fuck I told her!"

"Get up off the damn floor, girl!" She stood in front of me to make sure that James didn't hit or kick me! "Bring your ass up here and sit down with me, and let me look at you to make sure you okay! The boy wasn't bothering nobody! Who told you that he was in that room? This shit didn't start until you got here! What the fuck happened? Let me look at you! You okay?"

"Yeah. He grabbed me by my throat and choked me!"

"Let me see! Aw, hell, you still breathing! He didn't hit you in your stomach, did he?"

"No, he didn't."

"Well, then, be glad he didn't beat the hell out of you in that room! That boy been shooting that shit and his mind is gone! Leave that crazy motherfucking nigga alone!" She picked up her glass of beer, crossed her legs and began to shake her foot. "Ain't nobody got time to be listening to all that hollering and screaming that he do!"

I told her who told me that James was in the room.

"Stop right there!" She pointed her finger at me, "You mean to tell me you went back there cause she told you that?! Oh hell, you need your ass choked listening to that trick! Why you think everybody call her that name? Cause she always got some shit going on somewhere! I told you when I first met you don't trust none of these bitches out here in these here streets! They will set you up every time! That's why I don't fuck with none of them."

Madear called for one of her daughters to go and get a cold towel so I could wipe my face. "You gonna have to get your own place because y'all ain't gonna turn my house into no boxing ring! Monday morning, I'm going take your ass up there to the welfare building so you can get some money and food stamps and your own place. Have your mammy changed her mind and willing to take you back home yet?

"No, she haven't."

"Damn trick! I don't see how she just turn her back on her own daughter, but you did tell me what happened. I probably would have kicked your ass to the curb, too, but not before I kicked your motherfucking ass! Steal my shit! It's an apartment about two doors down from me. I know the landlord there, so I'm gonna talk to him first thing in the morning to get you lined up."

Section 159

My first apartment

James never did come back that night. I was kinda glad because I slept well. Madear got me up earlier that morning to go down to the welfare building to apply for assistance.

"Come on, get yourself together so we can be one of the first ones down there."

"I'm ready. I had to lay down for a few minutes. Do you think that they will give me money and food stamps?"

"Yeah, I know what I am talking about. I've been doing this for many of years. We got to get on the bus. Let me see how much money I got cause I got to pay your way down there and back. Do you have any money?"

"Yes, I got about twenty dollars."

"Aw shit, that's all we need, let's go."

"Madear, I really do thank you for helping me."

"That's okay, baby. I know you don't know nothing out here in these streets. You got to be strong out here. You all by yourself and I would want someone to do the same for my daughter if she was out here like this. It's a shame, but I know it's not your fault that you got hook up with my boy."

"Madear, I love James and sometime I don't understand why he do the things that he do to me."

"Well, he do the things that he do to you because you let him! The other thing is he is messed up on them drugs! I know my son love you, and

278

he will get tired of using that shit soon. The thing is will you be with him that long?"

"Yeah, I'm not going to leave him."

"You know what? I believe you really do love him and you will stay with him. Come on, we get off here! Ring the buzzer."

"Stop here, please," I yelled to the bus driver. Madear told me what to say once we got in there. Everything went well. I was told that I was going to get a check within a week or two.

"Now, let's go back over by the house so you can look at the apartment right down the street. This way I will be able to keep my eyes on you and make sure you are okay."

"You got to talk to the landlord?"

"Girl, I done already talked to him this morning while you was laying up there sleep. I told you only the early bird gets the worm. He said you can have the place to start you off."

"Thanks, Madear, thank you so much!"

"Yeah, well, you got that baby coming and you gonna need a place to take it to. You ain't fixin' to bring no baby up in my damn house! No way! I ain't got time to be taking care of no damn babies! I done had my turn of them, and raised all ten of my children by myself! I be damn if I'm gonna start taking care of some newborn babies! She laughed.

"I know, Madear. I'm gonna take real good care of my baby."

"You gonna be a good mother. You come from a good family background, all except for them motherfuckers that want to act like jackasses and tricks."

"I can't wait for my mother to see my baby! She gonna be so happy and proud of me."

279

"Well, don't get your hopes up high. She just might not feel that way. You got to prepare yourself for the worse, then, if good comes out of it, you won't be disappointed because you didn't expected it no way, right?"

"Yeah, I guess you right."

"Hell, I know I am. Turn in here, this is the place."

When we got in the building, Madear talked to this man and before you knew, it she had the keys and said that I can move in!

"Just like that, I can move in? This is my apartment? How did you do that? I don't have to pay no money?"

"Yeah, you got to pay your rent when you get your first check. I told you I got connections! You gonna be alright! James don't need to know nothing about this until you get that check and pay the rent! Otherwise, you gonna be up shit creek, fucking with him. You gonna make sure that the rent get paid?"

"Yes ma'am! I sure will cause I just put my word out there that it was going to be paid. All I got is my word."

"Cause I sho' in the hell ain't got no damn money to be paying nothing extra," as we laughed walking to her house.

Section 160

An unexpected, but pleasant visit...

The weeks had gone by and the rent was paid. James and I were doing real good, no arguing or fighting. I understood now that he had to do what he did to get money and I really needed to keep my mouth shut when it came to his business. Otherwise, he will beat me.

So I see now that my Aunties must have been doing or saying something to make my uncles beat them all the time. I'm not going to be like them. I'm just going to do what he tells me to do. Soon he will stop using the drugs and he'll see how much I love him and how much he really loves me. We were going to have a baby together.

I'm almost eight months pregnant and my stomach is so big. James loves to feel my stomach, and he even lays his head on me so that he can feel the baby move.

I had been in contact with my cousin Beverly and she was also pregnant. I gave her my address and she said she was going to stop by. I hoped that when she did, James wouldn't be at home. I didn't have a phone in the house. Someone was ringing the doorbell and knocking at the door at the same time. "Who is it?"

"Beverly! Lottie! I'm so happy to see you!" We hugged and cried together. We talked in the hallway; I was too shame to let them in because I didn't have any furniture. They didn't stay long at all.

Beverly was delighted to see me, "Look at you, Debbie, you look so pretty! Look how big you are!"

"I know, right? Look at you! Lottie, look how big the both of you are. I'm having a girl and I don't know what name to give her yet. I asked God to give me a sign of what to name my baby, so I'm just waiting on that moment. What are you having, Beverly?"

"I'm having a boy."

"Me, too," Lottie replied.

"I miss you, Debbie and love you so much! Are you okay?"

"Yeah, I'm okay and I miss and love you, too, Beverly."

"Ahmm, I was getting ready to go, I got something important to do. I am so glad you stopped by."

"Okay, Debbie, call me sometime. If you need anything, and I mean, anything… I am your cousin and I will love you always, unconditionally."

"Okay, I will call and I love you, too! See you guys later."

Section 161

I couldn't even help my little brother.

James was using heroin a lot more and he was acting so odd. He would nod at any given time whenever he sat down. If he didn't have that stuff, he was very mean to me, like it was my fault that he didn't have it. I was so afraid of saying anything to him because I didn't want to say the wrong thing.

Time was getting close for me to go in the hospital. I only had one more month to go. James would cook all the time on the hot plate that we had, but for the majority of the time we went next door to Madear's house to eat.

One evening, James and I were lying on the bed watching TV when we heard someone calling my name at the window. It was a cold night after a big snow storm blizzard and the temperature was at least 15 below.

"Who the hell is that? Who did you tell we were here?"

"Nobody, James. Don't nobody know where we live."

"Debbie, Debbie, open the door!" The snow was blowing so hard that I could hardly see who it was when I peeked out the window.

"It's my little brother! It's Chuckie!"

"I don't give uh fuck who it is! You better not open that motherfucking door and let them motherfuckers in here on me!"

"What? Who you talking about? It's my little brother, James! He's cold and he must have run away from home. Something has happened, otherwise he wouldn't be over here this time of night!"

"Do you want me to kick your motherfucking ass!" grabbing me by my hair. "I know your mother is out there with the police! It's a trap! They think that they got me!"

I went back to the window to peek out at my brother, and there he was standing in the middle of the street with the high winds of snow blowing all around him. I don't know if he saw me or not, but I'm pretty sure that he saw the curtain move and the light from the TV.

"Bitch, you trying to send me to jail! Get the fuck out the window!" He hit me in the back of my head!

"James, I didn't do nothing!"

"I will kill that little motherfucker. You won't have a brother! Let the motherfucking police come here! I will find that motherfucker and kill him dead! Do you understand me and what I am saying to you?!"

"James, I understand!" I felt so bad for Chuckie.

My brother continued, "Debbie, Debbie!"

All I could think about if he was okay? What about Nana? Mommie? Something was wrong for him to have come this long way in the cold at night, and I wasn't there for him when he needed me the most. I felt like I had let my brother down.

Section 162

I told him that I didn't tell anybody where we lived.

The next day, I founded out that my brother went over to Madear's house that night. She saw him in the streets, opened her door for him and let him in. One week later, at the first on the month when I got my check, we moved.

James and I lived on 51st in Calumet in a rooming house, and we were trying to move on the North side of Chicago. James apologized for the way he had acted when my brother came by. He didn't know that my brother didn't have anywhere to go that night.

We had the back room off from the kitchen. We shared the bathrooms and the kitchen. It was scary for me there because James would come home real late at night sometimes.

283

After that, I was so afraid for my brother. I never tried to contact him and I surely didn't try to contact anyone else, except Beverly who kept me up on everything that was going on.

It's so cold outside and I don't even have a winter coat to cover my stomach. One afternoon, the sun was shining and it was about 45 degrees. I decided to go see Mama Angie. I had enough sweaters to keep me a warm as long as I got back before dark, before the temperature dropped, I would be okay.

Section 163
The bus ride I'll never forget.

I had got on the King Drive bus to go over to Mama Angie's house. I had a big stomach, I was about 8 ½ months pregnant and it was cold outside with knee-high snow. Since, I didn't have a winter coat, I put on two sweaters, a tee-shirt and a turtleneck with a blue-jean jacket. I was fine. When I got to Mama Angie house, she was so glad to see me and I was glad to see her.

"Come on in, Debbie! Where is your coat?"

"I don't have one."

"Come on, baby, let Mama Angie find something for you." We went to her bedroom. "Debbie, come and try on this coat." It was a big brown coat with six big brown buttons.

It went over everything that I had on. The coat had flair around the bottom and it was heavy.

"Do you like that one, Debbie?"

"Yes, Mama Angie, yes! This fits great!" I gave her a big hug. I was so happy to get this coat! Now I could completely cover my stomach. She then added a scarf, a hat and some gloves. She made sure I was warm!

We talked for a while, but she had to leave. I told her I was going to my cousin Beverly's house because she had some clothes for me.

"Okay, Debbie," and she gave me a big hug and kiss. "Wait, here, take these few little pennies and you buy yourself something." She gave twenty dollars. We hugged again and I thanked Mama Angie as I buttoned up my new coat. I loved her so very much. I walked out of the house with my head held high with a warm coat, scarf, hat, and gloves!

I was so happy. All while I was riding the bus to Beverly's house, I could think of nothing else but what Mama Angie had given me. I rubbed on my coat with a smile on my face... I was so happy. I knew everything was going to be alright, even though it started to snow.

Once I got to Beverly's house, we talked and laughed for a while. It was getting late, so I told her I had to get back home to cook something for James.

It was about 5:00 pm. I figured that I would get back around 6 or 6:30 which wasn't too late. I wanted to get back before it got dark. I had left the house earlier that day and James was gone.

He came in around 4:00 in the morning and was gone by 10:30 a.m. So, I thought he should be home by the time I got there. I gave Beverly a kiss and thanked her for all the nice clothes she had given me.

I took the shopping bag and got on the bus. I was so happy going back home. Today had been a good day. I could take that 20 dollars and buy a bag of potatoes, bread, polish sausage, and a chicken! I had enough to get me some cigarettes and James a 40oz. beer.

My stop was coming up. I began to wrap my scarf around my neck and put my gloves on. I stood up and started walking to the front of the bus. I saw James through the window waiting at the bus stop. I wondered what he was doing. I couldn't always tell whether he was angry or not.

Section 164

Will you turn your head and do nothing?

The bus stopped and the doors open. He began to yell like a crazy man!

"Come on bitch! Get your ass off the bus! Who do you think you are fucking with?"

I looked at him, "What? What's wrong?! What did I do?!" James came up on the bus steps and grabbed me by my scarf and pulled me off the bus! I lost my balance and slipped and fell! The bus driver just closed the door and drove off!

I was crying, yelling, "James, no! Stop!" He kept hitting me!

"Get up, motherfucker! Get the fuck up!" He grabbed me by my coat and broke some of the buttons! "Where the fuck you been, bitch!"

I was crying, trying to reach down and get the buttons that had come off my coat while holding on to my bag of clothes. He hit me in the mouth and I fell in the snow in the middle of the street, hoping that somebody would help me! Nobody did, nobody stopped to help!

Blood was all in the snow from where James had busted my lips. I was crying so hard, "I didn't do anything wrong!" I couldn't understand why James was beating me! I believe I was crying more because he broke the buttons on my coat that Mama Angie had just given me.

"James, please, please, the baby! You are going to hurt the baby!"

"Bitch, I will kick that baby out of you, don't fuck with me! You think I'm a motherfucking fool?!" as he grabbed the collar of my coat and began to drag me in the snow. I tried to get up, I tried to stop him from hitting me, but he kept on! My shopping bag had torn and some of my clothes were in the street. I looked back and the cars just rolled over them. I got on my feet and I walked toward the house with James in front of me.

286

"Yeah, come on bitch, you think you slick! I know you been fucking around! Bring yo ass to the house!"

I just held on to what clothes I could and followed him to the house. I hadn't done anything wrong, as I wiped my eyes. I could feel my baby moving in my stomach. 'Oh, Lord Jesus, please let my baby be okay. Please protect me and my baby Lord.'

I went in the house and walked to our room which was in the back of the house. I could hear James yelling all in the building, calling me out my name. The other people that lived there came out to see what was going on. Once I got in the room and sat my things down on the bed, James slapped me across my face.

"Now, you tell me where you have been?" The tears kept rolling down my face. I explained to him where I had gone.

"Shut up, lying bitch! I know you been over some niggas house!" He jumped across the bed and grabbed me by my throat, yelling and spitting in my face saying, "Don't fuck with me! I will kill, I will kill you, bitch!"

I was yelling and begging him to stop, "James, stop! James, stop! I didn't do anything!"

"Do you have any money?"

I just nodded my head and reached in my pocket and gave him the twenty dollars that Mama Angie gave me. I heard walkie talkies in the kitchen then I heard a knock at the door. James raised the window and went out the window. "Bitch, you better not say nothing!"

I didn't know what to do! I just stood there with my hands over my mouth, crying. It was the police! They began to bam on the door, "This is the police! Open the door! Open the door! I heard people in the background saying, "He's always beaten on and yelling at that girl! She's pregnant, getting ready to have a baby!"

The police yelled, "Miss, open the door! Everything is going to be alright! Just open the door!" I had to pee so bad that I wasn't able to hold it! Pee came running down my legs as I slowly walked to open the door!

I figured James was long gone by now. He'll never know I had opened the door. He's safe. The police won't get him, I thought.

I opened the door and the police looked at me, "Where is he?!" What's your name?" They grabbed me by the hand and led me out of the room with their guns drawn!

Section 165

Living in a boarding house...

The room was so small; it was only a full size bed and a dresser in it. That was all that could fit in this room. The policeman noticed that I had wet myself. I began to have pains in my stomach. I thought it was just because I was scared. When I grabbed my stomach, the policeman said, "Come on, we're taking you to the hospital."

"Well, I'm okay. We just had a little argument. He was just worried about me because I'm carrying our baby and I was on the bus by myself."

"Yeah, the same bus that he drugged you off of!"

"I'm okay."

"Do you want to go checked it out to make sure your baby is doing fine? And if you want, you can come back here. It's up to you. We are just here to try and help you, but if you are not going to help us, then it's nothing that we can do for you."

"Can I change my pants and put some dry clothes on?"

"Sure, go right ahead. We will stand right here and wait for you."

I got some of the clothes that my cousin gave me and was changing my clothes. I heard a noise and it was James at the window peeking from under the debris that was on the back porch! I looked at him and shook my head letting him know that the police was still here.

"Okay, police officer, I'm almost ready to go to the hospital."

I quickly grabbed the two buttons that came off my coat and placed them in my pocket. I was scared for James. I didn't want the police to see him. They had their guns out and they might have shot and killed him—like that policeman killed my daddy. I didn't want him to die. I didn't want him to hit me anymore so we could be a happy family.

I should not have gone anywhere. I should have waited until he got home. It's just that he been working so hard that he can't be worrying about me all the time. He really didn't mean to hurt me or call me out of my name like that and he wouldn't have hurt our baby.

I went to the hospital and when I returned, I was told that I could no longer live there if James was going to be with me! We had only been there a week or two.

I didn't know what to do. I didn't have anybody to help take care of me and the baby! James said that he would hurt my family if I ever left him. There was no way that I wanted my Nana or my Mommie to get hurt. He had already threatened my brother. Hell, he said that he would rather die than for me to leave him, and if he couldn't have me, nobody could. He would kill me.

James always said that there was no place in Chicago that I could hide because he had people everywhere watching me. If somebody tried to hide me from him, he would kill them, too. I believed him.

I believe that if I tried to leave him, he wouldn't have any reason to live because all he had was me. Soon he will stop. He really doesn't mean to hurt me.

Section 166

I finally had my baby, and talked to my Mommie.

We moved to the north side of Chicago off of Wilson Avenue. I went into labor a week after we moved into our apartment. The doctor was two weeks off on my due date. I had a pretty little baby girl and she was born on Valentine's Day! I named her Tyra after a white girlfriend of mine. That was the most painful experience that I had ever felt in my life, but yet it was the most beautiful thing—bringing life into this world! I asked if I could call my mother before they took me into the labor room. I wanted my Mommie with me.

"Mommie, it's me. I'm so sorry, Mommie, I love you. Will you ever forgive me? Do you still love me? Mommie, I'm getting ready to have a baby. They're taking me into the labor room now. I got to go now. I just wanted to tell you that I love you and I'm so sorry for hurting you and letting James take your stuff. It's time to get off the phone now."

"Do what they tell you to do. I know you're sorry. I love you, too, Debbie. Everything is going to be alright. Call me later, after you have the baby."

I was there by myself. You know James was busy… He said he had to go to work, but he will be here. Or, was he with another woman? Madear called him a big time gigolo! Yet, she still talked about being so proud of her boy!

I had the prettiest baby that you ever wanted to see! She loved for me to hold her close to my heart. I didn't have any money to buy too much for my baby.

James made sure that I paid the rent and sometimes he would even go to the grocery store with me. James loved to cook and I enjoyed the good

290

times that we shared together. He was so happy with our baby and really protective of her.

Section 167

She was just a baby. What do you do around your children?

One day, we were in the apartment and James was bagging up the weed he was now selling. He was doing well, too. He had slowed down getting high on those hard drugs and was smoking a lot of weed instead. Of course, he still had his beer for breakfast.

James went to the bathroom and left a pound of loose weed on the table. I was in the kitchen washing the dishes. Suddenly, I heard my baby screaming because James was slapping her little hands! I stood there helplessly, praying that the stuff won't affect her.

"Don't you put this in your mouth! Bad girl, you just a bad, bad, little girl! Motherthafuck! She done knocked all my shit on the motherfucking floor and got this shit in her got damn mouth!" He reached in her little mouth and wiped the weed away as she gagged. "Come and get this little motherfucker before I beat her bad ass!"

I ran to pick up my baby and held her so close to my body. Her little body jerked as she continued to scream and cry. She was only seven or eight months old at the time. From that day on, her nickname was Bad-o-Bad. James never again made the mistake of leaving the weed out.

Regardless of how he treated me, he loved his daughter and never wanted any harm to come to her. Months went by and we were doing really well. He wasn't beating me and stayed close to home. We watched a lot of movies together. I don't know if he was in the house more with me because it was so cold outside, or because of the bond that we were finally being able to forge. I don't know what I'm talking about, we had a bond that no one could break. I knew James loved me and I loved him more.

Section 168

How far will you go for your baby? I have no shame, do you?

When James and I made love, sometimes I would cry because I was so happy to have all of him with me—mind, body and soul. Soon, that changed.

James began to use more hard drugs. I don't know what happened, but things got real bad. He began to break into apartments and stealing so that he could buy more heroin, methadone, syrup and other stuff. We moved to other apartments all the time; whenever he would do so much in one building, we would move to another.

We were on Wilson Avenue in an apartment building that had about 75 apartments. We lived on the fifth floor in a small studio apartment, right by the elevator. One morning, I woke up and there was no food in the house. Tyra didn't have any milk or pampers and I was so hungry.

James was asleep. He heard me stirring and asked where was I was going. I told him that I was going to see if I could borrow some money from a friend. I dressed the baby and left the house. I had no idea where I was going, but I knew that she needed a clean pamper and some milk or juice in her bottle.

I went into the neighborhood grocery store and walked around looking at the food. I didn't want to steal and go to jail with my baby. So, I opened a bag of pampers and took one out and change her right in the grocery cart. I opened a carton of milk and filled a bottle. I took the extra bottle from my purse and filled it up with some apple juice, Tyra's favorite juice. I then proceeded down the other aisle. I stopped and made me a bologna sandwich and shoved it down my mouth, right in the store.

This white man walked up behind me and touched me on my shoulder, "Excuse me, what are you doing?" I looked at him with tears in my eyes, thinking that he was going to call the police.

"I'm hungry and my baby didn't have any milk and she was wet. I don't have any money and I didn't steal anything cause I don't want to go to jail." That man looked at me and I guess he could tell I was trying to swallow the food in my mouth.

"Listen, I understand. You don't have to say nothing else. I want you to go throughout the store and put whatever you want in this cart and when you get to the counter, they'll let me know."

"Okay, thank you so much!" I gave that man a hug. I had the opportunity to get food, milk and pampers, with no money. Thank you, God! I can feed my baby. I got all food that I thought would stretch. I even got two big bags of pampers and some powered milk in case I ran out again. The owner even had me to give him my address and said that he would have the food to go out on his next delivery. I had gotten a total of three boxes of food! I had put so much in the cart that it was running over!

When I got home, I told James what had happen and that the food was being delivered to us. He didn't believe my story!

"Ain't no motherfucker gave you no food or let you go shopping. What did you do for him?!"

"I didn't do anything! The man saw that I had fixed me a sandwich in the store and I had poured some milk in Tyra's bottle! That's when he said that I could go shopping and I didn't have to pay for anything!"

"Yeah, well, you better not open that motherfucking door!" I turned around in unbelief! What the fuck, man? It's free food! The man was nice enough to give us food! He talked for about thirty minutes or so and got dressed. I heard the elevator gate open on our floor and someone knocked on the door.

The delivery person called, "Delivery, I have your food, Debra. Delivery."

"Yes, could you just sit it down at the door, please? I just got out the shower and I'm not dressed. Thank you!"

"You welcome! I'll leave it here for you."

"Okay, thank you again."

Once the elevator doors shut, and began to go down, James opened the door in a hurry and dragged the boxes inside. I started to put the food up.

"Wait a damn minute. let me see what's in here! You don't need all this shit!" He began to put some of the meat in a bag. I grabbed the meat saying, "What you talking about? This is for us!" James slapped me across my face.

"We not gonna eat all this shit! You get your food stamps next week. Fuck, this shit! I'm selling some of this so I can get me a hit! You be all right with what's left!"

I couldn't believe that he was doing this! I mean, it was just an hour ago that there was nothing in the house! Now he wants to sell what we got! He was looking crazy and frantically threw the meats in the bag. He even took a bag of the pampers. "She ain't gonna go through them many pampers that fast before you get your check! If she do, I'll get another bag! This is ten dollars right off the back!"

Section 169

My little baby almost died!

I sat holding my baby, saying to myself that everything is going to be alright. I wanted him gone so I could cook something for us to eat. Once he took those pampers, I knew then it was time for Tyra to learn how to use the potty chair. James didn't come back until late.

When I got my check, we had to move. James said that we had been there long enough. What he was really saying was that he had been breaking into Mexicans' apartments and he didn't want them to catch him and beat the shit out of him!

James said that the people on the North Side were sweet, and they weren't up on no game. I liked that side of town because it was much cleaner and there were Mexicans, white and black people living together, in the same neighborhood. I made new friends of all races and that's what I liked about living up North.

James continued to get high and I think this time must be the worse than ever. I was so afraid that one day I'd find him overdosed, or get a call that he was found dead.

Tyra got sick and I took her to the hospital. She had pneumonia and had to stay in the hospital for two weeks. I thought my baby was going to die. James didn't have time to take me to and from the hospital—you know, he had other things that he had to do.

I didn't want to make him angry, so I packed a bag and stayed there with my baby so she wouldn't be by herself and afraid. They had to keep her under this oxygen tent. I called my Mommie and Nana and asked them both to pray that my baby would be alright.

I felt if I heard my Nana tell me that everything would be alright, then it would be. My Mommie told me not to worry, "Debbie, you have a strong baby. She will be just fine."

My Mommie bought my baby a real pretty, thick pink snow suit. Mama Angie saw that I had those thin receiving blankets, so she handmade me a heavy blanket for my baby. It was black, yellow and white. At the beginning of the winter, I didn't have enough clothes on my baby. So, when I got these things from Mommie and Mama Angie, I think I overdressed her to keep her warm. I don't know, but I thank God that my baby recovered.

Section 170

My Mommie do love me! It's nothing
like having your mother's love.

The nurse told me that my Mommie had come to visit Tyra and brought her an outfit after I left to get something to eat. I was surprised, but happy that she came to see about my baby. I was sorry that I had missed her. She didn't stay long. The fact is she came.

I had an understanding with my mother: She would allow me to come see her as long as I do not tell James where she lived, and if I did, I will never be able to come back to her house. That was fine by me. I was so glad that my mother has forgiven me and accepted me back into her life.

I realize that nobody and nothing is worth losing the relationship with your Mommie. I was even happy to see my uncles and aunties, despite how they felt about me. I was back with my dysfunctional family and it felted so good. I would never do anything to jeopardize the love of my mother and family again.

Sometimes, I would catch the train and bus to visit Madear, my mother and Mama Angie. By now, James really didn't care where I was because the only thing that was on his mind was heroin and methadone. I would leave notes in case he came home and I wasn't there.

Going over to Madear was a challenge for me. When Tyra was a baby, she always cried when she saw Madear's house, heard her voice and even when she saw her.

"Here comes Debra and hollering ass Jenny! That damn girl holler too much for me! You not gonna get nobody to watch her! She holler too damn much." Tyra would cry even louder when she would hear Madear's voice.

"Shut up, little girl, before I come over there and give you something to holler for, hit you in your damn mouth! I know you don't like me and I don't

296

give a damn!" As usual, with her point made, she crossed her legs, drank her beer and shook her foot.

"Come on, don't cry. Let's go see who's in the back," as I held her in my arms with her little hands holding on to me so tightly. "Don't cry, that's your grandmother. She loves you. Shhh, don't cry," I would tell her.

I hadn't been feeling well and had missed my period for last two months. I know that I'm not pregnant! I just had a baby! I talked to Madear and told her what was going on.

"Do you think I'm pregnant?"

"What you asking me for? I'm not no damn doctor! When was the last time you came on your period?"

"It's been about two months now."

"Yep, you done got your ass knock up! Ain't that what you said you wanted, to have some damn babies? Well, you got what you ask for! That's a damn shame! You the only motherfucker gonna be walking around here with all these damn kids. Ain't nobody got time to bother with a bunch of hollering ass babies!" She crossed her legs, drank her beer, shook her foot and waved her hand at me.

"Let me tell you something, having a bunch of kids by a man ain't gonna keep him. Cause they can leave your ass and go make some more babies by some other whore out here in these streets. You the damn fool that's gonna be stuck with them hollering ass babies!"

She paused to sip her beer and continued, "You better listen to me! I ain't gonna tell you nothing wrong. If I can't help you, I sho ain't gonna do nothing to hurt you. You need to take your ass back to school or something, and stop running your ass after somebody that don't give a damn about himself! He is nothing but a damn dope fiend! But, a piece ah man is better

297

than no man at all. Look at my man, he ain't nothing but a drunk, but I bet nobody fuck with him or they gonna have to answer to me!"

"Yeah, well, I'm going to the doctor to be tested tomorrow."

"Let me know what the motherfucker say! I bet yo ass is knocked up!"

True enough, I was pregnant. My babies were going to be eleven months apart. I just prayed that the baby was going to be alright because James was using heavily, more so than any other time.

Things were really hard. James was always in a rage, hollering and screaming when things didn't go his way or if he didn't have the money to get more heroin.

Even in those times when he was at his lowest, we had some good days. He would spend time with us at the house, play with our baby, watch movies with me and he was always in the kitchen cooking up a full course meal. It wasn't always bad. I loved him. He's the father of my baby. He's just having a hard time right now. He's sick and I know deep in my heart that one day he will change. He will see that we can be a happy family, the family that I have always dreamed of having with him.

Madear often gave him money to get what he needed. She said he was really sick and she didn't want to see him like that. Everybody always gave him what he wanted just so that they wouldn't hear his mouth.

Section 171
They really do love each other.

James had seven sisters and they were all different, but a lot like their mother Madear:

When one sister would visit Madear, she never put her purse down. She kept a lot of pills in her purse and sometimes she would give James some of her Valium.

Another sister carried a gun. One Thanksgiving Day, James got angry because no one would give him money to buy drugs. He knocked the entire dinner off the stove! From turkey to pies, it was all over the floor and he tried to run out the door! She shot at him, right there in the kitchen!

There was the sister who carried herself as if she was the prettiest of them all. She wore tight, low cut fitted tops, tight jeans and a belt that she kept pulled tight to show off her small waist. She dated this married man.

The next sister was the one who didn't take shit off of any of them at all. She had the biggest, most generous heart. She, too, was pretty, but in her own way; she didn't wear make-up or fancy clothes like the others sisters. She was more down to earth. James didn't mess with her. She also went both ways, you know. Like the others, she knew how to fight.

She was the one that could use a straight razor like no one I ever knew. They told stories of how this man had slapped her in a bar and before he put his hands down, she had cut his hand up. He never slapped her again. I guess I remember more about her since she protected me from James who never jumped on me around her. He knew she would fuck him up. I appreciated her for that.

There were two younger sisters. They had their own style of dressing and were a lot alike. They made their money by working the streets, standing on the corner waving cars down, picking up men—tricks, as she called them—at different night clubs and local taverns and bars.

Another younger sister was more... What could we call it? More professional! You know, like a call girl. She worked the Navy base and her clients called for appointments.

Then there's Monica, the prettiest of them all. She was the closet to James. He loved her more because they had the same father, at least that's what he said. She talked fast just like James. Monica and I were pregnant at the same time and our children played together all the time. What drew us to each other was that her husband was beating her, too. Monica kept my secrets and I trusted her more than any of the rest.

I loved them all. They were my family; they adopted me into their world. I learned so much from each one of them. They shared their mother with me and became the sisters that I never had. For that, I will always be grateful.

Section 172

What is 'Deception Practice'?

James and I were walking and talking one day. "Here she is," as he went over to a car.

"Come on, get in. Okay, drive!" he told the lady. "Hey, baby, listen! This is Karen and she's been helping me get money for us so that we can pay the rent and keep our apartment. You don't want Tyra and our new baby to be out in the street, do you?"

"Nah, I don't."

"Now, you trust me right?"

"Yeah, I trust you, James."

"Well, dig this. I need for you to go into this bank," as his friend parked across the street from the bank. "I want you to go in and give them this check. Let them know you want to cash it and when they give you the money, you come back out here to this car. We are going to be parked on the next block. I'll be able to see you when you come out. Okay? Do you understand what I just said?"

"Yeah, I do. Whose check is it?"

"It's your check; she made it out to you. See your name is on it?"

"Oh, okay, I see. This gonna be my money?"

"Yeah, baby it's gonna be our money so we can keep our place. You want our apartment, right?"

"Yeah, I do."

"Well then, you got your ID with you?"

"Yeah, I do."

"Well, go head into the bank and just give the lady this check. Sign the back of it," pointing to where I had to sign. "But, make sure you sign it in front of the lady, and don't be asking a lot of motherfuckin questions. Just do as I say. She's not going to ask you any questions at all. Just sign your name, show you're ID and that's it."

"Okay I can do that. I'm not going to get in any trouble, am I?"

"How you gonna get in trouble when the check is in your name?! Damn! Give me more credit than that! You think I'm gonna send you in there for you to get in trouble?"

"Oh, yeah, I forgot. You just said that it was in my name," smiling at him as I walked toward the bank. I stood in line when I got inside.

"May I help you?"

"Yes." I took the check out of my purse with my ID and picked up the pen and signed the check like James told me to. I gave it to the lady at the window. The lady looked at me as I smiled at her, waiting for her to give me the money.

"Hold on. I'll be right back."

"Okay." I thought she was going to go get the money. I could only think about us paying the rent three hundred dollars for our rent. The check was for four hundred, so that was good.

A man came back with the lady and he looked at me and said, "Debra, could you come with me? I need to ask you some questions."

"Okay, is it a problem? The check is mine. It got my name on it."

"No, ma'am, it's not a problem. We just need for you to answer a few questions before we give you the money."

"Oh, okay." as I followed him on into the back room of the bank.

I felt so important because I was going to the back of the bank. Everybody was looking at me and I just smile right back at them with my head turn up.

There was a lady police in the room and another plain-clothed policeman. He showed me his badge. "Will you tell us whose check is this?"

"That's my check. It got my name on it."

"Yeah, we see that. Now, tell us where did you get it from?"

"I got it from my boyfriend and a lady friend of his. He gave it to me and told me to bring it in here so I can cash it. He said that it was going to be the money for us to pay the rent at our apartment. That's if he don't decide that we have to move. I hope that it is enough."

"Okay, now where is your boyfriend and this lady?"

"Outside waiting in the car on the corner. He told me to come to the car when I got the money. Could you please tell me how much longer it is going to be before you can give the money to me because he said that if I take too long that he was going to have to leave?"

"Well, Debra, what you are doing is wrong. You just let your boyfriend get you in a whole lot of trouble."

"What he do? He didn't do nothing!"

"Yeah, you right, he didn't, but you did! Call her mother. We are going to take you down to the Cook County Jail and you are going to be charged with a Deception Practice."

"What! The check got my name on it, so how did I do something wrong?! I don't even know what Deception Practice is!"

"Turn around so you can be handcuffed."

"My name is on the check! It's my check! His friend gave it to us! She was trying to help me!"

"Okay, we hear you loud and clear, thank you. Here, take this, get her information and take her down to the station. Book her and call her parents so somebody can be down there to pick her up so she won't be put in a cell. She really don't get it."

He continued, "Another young girl got hooked up with the wrong person, so young. Come with me." The lady police grabbed me by my arm and we walked out the back door of the bank. "Watch your step in the police car."

My mother and Auntie DD came to get me out of jail.

Soon as my mother saw me, she yelled, "What the hell where you thinking? Taking a check into the bank like a damn fool!" as she hit me in the back of my head.

"Get in the car! I am through with you with this shit here! If you wanna keep on acting like a damn fool, then you are on your own! I am done! Keep fucking with James and see where it leads you! This is the first, and it will be the last time! Do not ever call me if you come back to this place!"

Rolling my eyes and folding my arms, I thought 'You don't have to worry about me cause I'm not coming back here and I didn't do nothing wrong. Besides, I didn't ask you to come to get me no way!'

Bam! My mother slapped me across my eyes!

"Roll your eyes one more motherfuckin time and see don't I kick your stupid ass out this car, right the fuck now! Roll them again!" Bam! She hit me again.

I could have sworn she knocked my eyes out! I couldn't open my eye for the whole time we were riding! I just kept my hand over my eyes and wiped the tears from my face. I couldn't understand what I had done wrong. I was three months pregnant.

Section 173

My second baby is coming out and I'm all alone.

The time came to have my baby. James was there this time; he even took me to the hospital. I was in the room screaming that the baby was coming. He ran to go get help and I lay down on my side. I could feel the pressure of my baby moving down. I was alone in the room on the table.

When the doctors came in, they saw that my baby was coming out sideways and they had to turn her head up right. Because of that turn, she was born with facial paralysis. She was a tiny little thing and I named her Ericka. Later, I was told that she was born without a corpus callosum, which is the pathway of the brain that gives signals to the left and right side.

Ericka was born two and a half weeks early, coming into this world so very strong. James gave her the nickname 'Airframe' because she was just a frame, so tiny. And she was daddy's little girl.

Nothing too much happen after Ericka was born, nothing more than the usual highs and lows of being in love and living with a drug addict and a gigolo. However, I must say that he was a good father.

Madear was right—a piece of a man is better than no man at all. So, I settled for what I had. He's the father of my girls and I don't know anything but him.

Section 174

The pretty cookie jar!

Again, we were in the situation of no food. It was the end of month and I was waiting for 'the eagle to fly', that is, waiting for the mailman to bring the checks. James came home in a panic with a whole lot of stuff.

"Hurry up, close the door behind me and don't open it!"

"What happen? What you do? Whose stuff is this?"

"Shut up, Debra, damn!" I immediately noticed this pretty cookie jar in the pile of stuff.

"Can I see this, James? It got cookies in it! I reached and picked it up.

"Okay, this can get me seventy-five dollars! Don't be fucking with shit! I be back!"

"James, we hungry! Will you please bring back some bread and potatoes! Can I have this cookie jar with these cookies in it?"

"I don't care about no damn cookies! Here take it! Eat on this until I get back!" and he ran out of the apartment with all that stuff.

I thought to myself that sooner or later somebody is going to catch him doing all these burglaries. Everywhere we moved, he's got to robbed somebody! It is so wrong.

I was so glad that I have babies now because one time he made me go with him when he broke into somebody's apartment. I had to watch his back and make sure no one came in. One time, he was in for a surprise as he walked into this apartment! I was at the door and whispered as he was trying to unplug the television, "James! There's somebody lying on the couch, somebody is in the house!"

"What?" running back to see what I was saying.

"Look, that's somebody lying there!"

"Come on!" as he pushed passed me out of the apartment and told me to keep up with him. We ran out of the building.

"In all my years of doing this shit, I never ran into nothing like this before! It's your motherfucking fault! You jinxed me! You won't bring your ass with me no damn more! You almost got me killed!"

Thank God! I got kids now and don't have to go through that shit with him! I sat down with my babies on the floor and we ate those cookies while watching Sesame Street.

"Yes, who is it?" I heard someone knock at the door.

"The police! Open the door!"

"Yes, what can I do for you?" I looked this police officer with this white lady standing there next to him yelling, "It's her boyfriend that broke into my apartment!"

"Ma'am, I need for you to stand back." He took a step into my apartment and looked around. "Are you here by yourself? Do you have a boyfriend that lives here with you? Did he black your eye?" He then unsnapped the gun hoister and kept his hand on his gun.

"Yes, James do live here. He's the father of my girls, but he just left."

"Do you know anything about him breaking into this lady's apartment?"

"No, I don't, but he had a lot of stuff with him when he left and I don't know where he got it from."

"She's lying! That's my cookie jar over there on the floor!" pointing and describing the type of cookies that was in the jar, as my girls ate them.

"Where did you get that cookie jar from?"

"James just gave it to me, before he left!"

"Whose name is on the lease to this apartment?"

"Mine."

"You are going to have to call someone to come and get your children, otherwise we will call DFHS. You are under arrest for burglary!"

"What! I didn't do anything, I didn't do it! Here, you can have your cookie jar. I only wanted the cookies out of it to feed my kids! That's why I asked him for it."

"So, you are admitting that you did burglarize this lady apartment?"

"No, that's not what I'm saying!" crying and feeling so scared, not knowing what to do. "Can I ask my neighbor if she can watch my kids for me?"

"Sure, lock up. We got to go. Get word back to your boyfriend that we are onto him. This is a good way to get killed, breaking into someone's place."

Crying and locking up the apartment, repeatedly I told the officer, "I didn't do it! He was the one that did that!" kissing my girls bye-bye. "I just wanted to give them something to eat they were hungry."

I remember being in the courtroom and the public defender telling me that if I want to see my children again and for them not to go to a foster home, my best bet was to plead guilty to the charge. I would be able to go home, not go to jail or lose my kids.

I knew that I couldn't call my mother or anyone in my family, and James' family couldn't help me. I was all alone, afraid and not knowing what to do. I did what I was told so I could go home to my babies. They would not go to a foster home and I could get them back. I don't ever remember seeing the judge again to explain! I did not realized that I had admitted to committing a felony, which would come back to haunt me! I didn't know what a felony was! I just want to go home to my babies! Damn cookie jar got me in so much trouble!

Well, so much has happen to me thus far—things have got to get better! I know my life is not going to be like this forever. What am I doing wrong? God, please show me what am I doing wrong! I did not want to go to jail! Fortunately, I received three years' probation, and never went back there again! I didn't do anything but eat the cookies!

Section 175

He kept me barefoot and pregnant. Three babies, so young.

I had been drinking beer since Tyra was born. When I drank, the pain in my heart and the physical pain were numbed out. I said things that I wouldn't have the nerve to say if I were not drinking. I began to love that person more and more each and every day. I tried to be like so many people, trying to fit in, wanting people to like me…when I didn't even like myself.

I came to realize that my life with James is going to be until death do us apart. He's not going to let me leave him; I don't want to leave him, I love him too much and I'm afraid to be on my own. After all, I have his children, so let the good times roll—as Madear would say.

Every day I was at Madear's house. I would sit and listen to her tell me stories, watch who came in and out the house, and talk with family members that were now my family.

There were times I would not see James for two or three days, but I was used to it by then. I no longer said anything about it. *I crossed my legs, shook my foot, drank my beer and smoked my cigarettes!* What a life! I believed I was happy.

I was feeling so good. In and out of bed with James, whenever he came home, I was pregnant again two years later. Even though I got an abortion, it didn't help because I got pregnant again almost immediately. I felt that God wanted me to have the baby, so I did… another little girl, Patrice. I gave her James' mother's middle name.

We were still living on the North Side, and being there was really nice. I got a lot of help from the landlord that I was renting from. I told her up front what James had done in the other apartment buildings and I didn't want anything to happen that would have her call the police on me. She still allowed me to rent one of her apartments and she became a good friend of mine.

Nothing had changed with James. He is still getting high. Sometimes he stops using heroin and just drank syrup or methadone. But, he was so smart in so many other ways.

He loved being at home playing with the girls and telling us stories as he prepared our meals. He didn't like company in the house other than only some family members who would stop by. Usually, we'd see everybody at Madear's house.

I had been in the hospital for a week already and the first of the month has come and gone. I was praying that James had paid the rent with my check. He's been doing good except for smoking weed. The day before I was supposed to come home with my baby girl, I called my landlord Gail to have James come and pick us up. That's when she told me that she had to sit all of my belongings out in the street that day! James did not pay the rent and he cursed and threatened her husband! Besides that, we were two months behind on the rent!

"Yeah, I know. I'm sorry that happened. It's really nothing I can do right now, I just had my baby. Who has my girls Tyra and Ericka?"

"I got them, don't worry about them. I will keep them until you come home."

"What? James just left them?"

"No, I was watching them for him already while he went to the store. Then that's when everything happened. This was last night."

"Oh, okay, thank you, Gale. Is there any way that you could, please, just get my pictures and my kids' clothes for me? I should be home maybe in the morning." All I could do was pray. I had no idea where I was going to go now that she has put my stuff out on the streets.

Social Services called a cab for me and said that my Medicaid card would pay for my trip home. The hospital gave me some milk for my baby. There I was in the cab with my new baby girl. As I rode home, I prayed that my stuff really wasn't put out.

Section 176

Coming home with my newborn baby

When the cab pulled up in front of the building, I saw that all my furniture outside. James was nowhere to be found. I got out of the cab and went to Gale's apartment to get my girls. You could see that people had been picking through all my stuff. I couldn't believe this was what I was coming home to. Why, I kept asking myself, why didn't James pay the rent? Why and how could he let our stuff be sat outside?

"Sorry, we had to sit your stuff out," Gale said so apologetically.

"Yeah, me too, but I understand."

"We put your pictures and the children's clothes in the basement."

"Okay, thank you so very much." Tyra and Ericka ran to me hugging and kissing.

"Let me see baby," Ericka reaching out her little arms. I sat down and to let them see their little sister.

"Gale, I don't know what I'm going to do now. Where am I supposed to live? What am I going to do with my children?"

310

"Well, Debra you can stay in a shelter if you can't stay with nobody in your family." I got up and put my baby down on the sofa and told the girls not to let her fall.

"Can I see your phone book to find a shelter? Will you help me find one?" The first place I called was the Pacific Garden Mission. I spoke with a lady there and explained to her what had happened.

"I have a newborn baby with two other small daughters and I don't have no place to live. My children's father didn't pay the rent and they sat all my stuff outside. My family won't let me stay with them and I don't know what to do." I was crying through the entire conversation.

"I have a bed for you and your children. Write the address down."

"Thank you, I will be on my way."

"Don't worry about anything. Come here and we will help you with your children."

"Thank you," as I hung the phone up. "Gale, will you hold my stuff for me until I get settled? The mission will help me get back on my feet."

"Let me ask my husband, Debra. I will hold your items for 60 days and after that I won't be able to keep it."

"Okay, thank you. Am I asking too much for you to drive us to the mission?"

Section 177

Living on skid row with my friend Gee-Gee

When we got to the mission, there were a lot of homeless people hanging around the building. They looked like bums and you could smell the odor coming from their bodies and dirty clothes. I rang the doorbell and someone came down the steps to help me with the kids and my bags.

"Goodbye, Gale, thank you for everything. I'll be back to get my pictures and stuff."

311

"That's fine, Debra, I know you will. You take care of yourself with them babies."

When I got in the place, they asked all these questions and I had to fill out a lot of paperwork. I was really nervous because I never been in a place like this before.

The lady took me to where we would be sleeping. We walked into this big room that looked like a dorm with rows of beds and bunks beds on both sides of the room. There were lots women and children in this room. Everybody was looking at us when we walked in, but I didn't care because they weren't any better than me. They wouldn't be here if they didn't have problems, too.

The young lady explained, "Now, every day you will have a chore to do," as she showed me where the list will be posted. "Church is every night before you are allowed to have dinner. Oh, very important. Any time you leave the building, you have to take your children with you and you have to go outside to smoke, no smoking in the building."

I didn't have a problem with any of this. I was just happy that my kids and I had a place to stay, for now. She did not have to worry about me letting anybody in here to watch my babies.

I began to look down my nose at the other women and children, as if I was better than they were. I thought 'I mean look at them! They smell! Looks like they haven't taken a bath in years! Their clothes! They just look so nasty! I know I'm better than they are. I come from a good home. I came from my Nana's house and my Mommie bought me nothing but the best!' I walked around like I was the cake and they were the shit.

I began to unpack stuff and get the kids situated.

"How old is your baby?" this older, heavy set lady asked me.

"She's a week old. Her name is Patrice."

"What's your other daughter's name?"

"This is Tyra, she's four and this is Ericka, she's three."

"Are they twins?" looking at them with the warmest smile on her face. "I'm sorry, what is your name? My name is Gina."

"My name is Debra."

"You don't look like you belong in no place like this? What happened, if you don't mind me asking?"

"You don't look like you should be here neither. Why you here?"

"Well, honey, I fell on hard times. I lost my place."

"That's what happened to me."

"But, you see I just recently lost one of my daughters. She got into a fight with her boyfriend and they stabbed each other to death. I had to take in her two small children. Those two girls over there are my other daughters and I have four of my grandchildren here with me also."

"Wow, I'm sorry to hear that, I mean, about you losing your daughter like that. I'm here because my children's father took my check and spent the money and didn't pay the rent. When I got out the hospital from having my baby, all my stuff was sitting out on the curb. That's how I ended up here."

Gina was very heavy set and her legs and feet were swollen to the point it was hard for her to walk. "Do you have a cigarette?" one of her daughters asked. I really need one right now."

"Yeah, I do, but the lady said we can't smoke in here. We have to go outside."

"That's fine. Do you want to go downstairs with me and smoke a cigarette? Let me get my little boy."

"How old is he and what's his name?"

"He's four and his name is Johnnie."

"He's the same age as my daughter Tyra."

"Come on, we have to sit over here to smoke."

We sat down on the bench and we shared our lives with each other. In that short period of time, we became the best of friends.

"Why all these homeless people hanging around here like this," trying to sound all superior.

"They come here to eat and they have nowhere to go," she replied in such a humble voice.

"Oh, I didn't know that."

"Here comes my friend. I know she is going to ask me for a cigarette. I always give her one."

"Hi, Miss Gee-Gee, do you have a cigarette for me today?"

There stood this bag lady. You know, the lady that walks around pushing a grocery cart with everything that she owns in it—with layers of raggedy smelly clothes on, hair matted brown and missing teeth. She reminded of the homeless people who ask for a quarter or a cigarette, and then we reply 'no, I don't have any money' or 'cigarettes cost too much to share.' We were probably on the way to the store to buy beer and more than likely have a whole pack of cigarettes in our pocket. Something about the way she said 'here comes my friend' touched my heart.

"No, Miss Hollywood, I don't have any today, but you can have the short on this one."

"No, you don't have to do that. I have a cigarette for you. Here, you can have these." I took out five or six cigarettes and gave them to her.

"Thank you! You must be new here. Haven't seen you around before."

"Yes, this is my first time here. I never been to a place like this before." I wanted to make sure she knew I was too good to be there.

"Yeah, well, it happens to the best of us. Can you give me a light?"

"I can do that for Miss Hollywood. Here's a light. Miss Hollywood, this is my friend Debra."

"That she is, a true friend. You won't find many in your lifetime. Hold on to her. Thank you, our new friend Ms. Debra, thank you! Don't worry, when you leave here, you would have learned what you need to know, what you need to go further in your life. He has given you favor; you have been chosen. Well, I must push on… I got a date with Mr. Hollywood! I'll see you tomorrow. The Good Lord say the same!" She pushed her cart on down the street.

"What she mean by that?"

"I don't know. She always saying something odd."

We went back upstairs and continued to share with each other about our lives. Gee-Gee shared with me that she had an enlarged heart. She lived on 47th street and was tired of living in that type of environment. She wanted more out of life for her and her son. She saw no way out. I shared with her where I lived my mother and grandmother and about the life I have had with my children's father.

As we talked and shared more, I came to realize that there are no little you's and big I's. I am no better than the people that I was sitting down at the table with. I got a real reality check when there was a roach in my baby's milk and I had to pick it out and still give it to her because that was the last of the milk until morning. I learned that it's not about what material stuff you have; it's about what's in your heart and how much do you care about others. Are you willing to give a quarter or that extra cigarette and a helping hand without turning your nose up at someone's misfortune? Do you think that you are so much better than they are? You never know who you are helping.

We never saw that bag lady again. We heard days later that she was found dead sleeping under the overpass. Gee-Gee took the news hard.

315

I stayed at the mission for 45 days. Sometimes when Gee-Gee and I would sit out and smoke cigarettes, I used to look up and watch the Dan Ryan train go by, wondering if my Nana could see me. I would wave my hand just in case she was sitting at a window looking down at me on skid row with all the homeless people. 'Bums' is what we were called. I was just fortunate enough not to look like one, but I was one of them.

Gee-Gee became a long life friend. For so many years, we would often see each other since we both lived on the other side of the track. We had so much in common in our life path.

But, my dear friend had no idea that later in her life she would die a Hero. She died ten years later saving her mother, son and nephew from a burning building. She was five months pregnant. She collapsed on the railroad tracks off of 47th Street.

People can find themselves in bad situations, making all the wrong choices, living in the wrong environment, and as part of a dysfunctional family. It doesn't matter whether we have lived high, low or somewhere in between—there are good people everywhere, even those who come from bad situations, like Gee-Gee! I'm so grateful and blessed to have had a best friend by the name of Gee-Gee.

Section 178
I married that old saying.
'A piece of a man is better than no man at all'!

After I got out of the mission, I stayed with my mother. I needed help. I needed my mother to help me. For the time that I was with my mother, James had no idea where I was, but I knew it was a matter of time that he would find out. I couldn't take the risk of him doing something crazy again when it came to my Mommie.

I started missing him, missing the excitement at Madear's, his sisters and the freedom that I had when I was over there. I stayed with my mother no more than two months, just long enough to save up a few checks to rent an apartment. I convinced myself that James needed to be with his children and they truly missed their daddy. I knew by me being gone for a while, it would give him something to think about.

James and I reunited; he gave me this whole spiel about how sorry he was. I forgave and believed him.

"Debra, I'll prove to you that I am sorry. Will you marry me? I mean, right now, let's go down to city hall and get married. I can't live without you and the kids. I do love you. Don't leave me no more. I'll leave the drugs alone."

I was happy to hear that he wanted to give up everything just to be with me and the kids. I knew James really loved me!

Yes, we got married. After we left City Hall, we went to his old friend John's apartment. I cooked some large lima beans, rice and hot-water-cornbread, with a pitcher of Kool-Aid.

James and John went in the bathroom to do their thing. Would you believe that John gave him a bag of heroin for his wedding gift?! He's going to stop, he promised me! We just got married and I sat in the front room looking out the window. As the kids played, I thought to myself that this will be my life. He finally realized that he needs me! I crossed my legs, shook my foot, took sips on my bottle of White-Poke w/lemonade chasing it with a beer, and smoked my cigarettes. This was the good life.

Down deep inside, this was not the way I wanted to get married, but remember… I live a fairytale dream life in my mind—a dream that will never come true.

I guess Madear was right: A piece-of-a-man is better than no man at all, and the piece of a man I had is my children's father. I just vowed 'for better or worse, til death do us apart...'

Section 179

Seeing old friends and meeting new ones is always a blessing.

I looked out the window and I saw my old friend Bobbie walking down the street.

"I be back, I'm going downstairs to see my girlfriend Bobbie," I yelled running down the stairs. I hadn't seen her in some years. It was so good to see her. She was still pretty as ever.

Bobbie had four children now. Three by Patrick and the other by a guy she was with. She and I talked about what was going on in our lives at that time. I told her I had just gotten married. She was living right around the corner from John. I didn't mind going over to John's from that point on because I was able to visit with my long-lost friend.

We both came to realized we were with someone that was abusive and controlling and we didn't like it, but felt like we were stuck. We were both waiting for that opportunity to make our move.

I founded out that her guy got killed on Lake Shore Drive on his motorcycle with another woman riding with him. Now, Bobbie is happily married and doing so well. We keep in touch to this day.

Anyway, James was willing to give it another shot by letting go of the drugs and moving back to Arkansas to raise our children as a family—and we did.

Living in Arkansas this time was so much better. We were away from everybody and all the drugs that he was accustomed to using. There were some withdrawals, but he handled it with surprising ease. James had a cousin there in Fordyce and her name was Lillie Mae. She drove a light blue pick-up

318

truck and was in love with us as a family. She did all that she could to help us in every way. She would come by every day to pick me and the girls up so we could get out of the house, even if we were just going to the store. James had a job that he worked for a while.

Lillie Mae used to tease me all the time, "Ohhh, wee! That girl know she love herself some James!" I've never had anyone to take a liking to me and my girls the way she did.

She surrounded us with nothing but love and a helping hand. Lillie Mae's whole family was so good to me and my children.

I found out I was pregnant again. This time, in my sixth month, I was told we were having twin boys! Tyra had just started kindergarten. That was such a good day for all of us. The principal of the school was James' cousin. He was one of the wealthiest black men in Fordyce and his wife was Tyra's teacher. We only moved two times in Fordyce while we were there.

In the last house, Patrice found some kittens and was feeding them! She was too young to understand why I was so afraid of cats. Patrice loved the kitten with gold color fur and did her best to help me overcome my fear. I do believe if we had stay on at that place any longer, she would have had me touching that kitten. It never happened!

We struggled, but life was still good. I liked living in the south, you know, a much slower pace and people seemed much friendlier. I was still so young and was on the verge of having twins with three little girls!

James was pleased to know that he was finally going to have a boy, two at that. He didn't beat me too much, not really. I had been with him long enough by now to know what pissed him off. I did my best not to get on his bad side, but I still did what I had to do to get by. I didn't care, or should I say made myself believe that I didn't care, about who he was with or what he was doing, just as long as he was happy when he came home to me and the kids.

He would take a few pennies from me and got more from other women. He did his own thing which was scouting for a new bait, drinking his beer, smoking weed and hanging out in all the clubs.

We had an older male friend that would come by every now and then just to see if we needed anything. For instance, our friend made sure that I didn't run out of pampers. He worked as the janitor at the courthouse for many years.

What James didn't know was that he was really coming by to see me— two could play that game. James didn't know that I learned from him, and that I was in the game, too. I just didn't have to sleep with him. So, living here in the south seemed to be good for James and me. We weren't living in that rat race in Chicago! With James hanging out with his old friends, it seemed to make him more of the family man that I have seen in him so many times before.

Section 180

Did he say 'sell' the boys?

There are a few things stand out in my mind about Arkansas, one being about James wanting to "sell" the boys!

After the boys were born, James came to me and said, "Debra, I done met this old ass bitch and she can't have any children. She is willing to give us five thousand dollars!"

"Why, and for what?"

"Listen, this is just a scheme and all you have to do is let me give her the twins and get the money, then you call the police and say she kidnapped the boys!"

"Hell, no! I'm not gonna let you sell my babies!"

"See, that's what you don't see! It's not selling them, you gonna get them back!"

"Well, James this is one ass whooping that I'm gonna have to take because these boys not going no damn where," and I put them both in my arms. They were around four or five months.

"Ain't no motherfucker gonna take them boys from you! I don't see why you would say that! It's like that you done took this shit all out of proportion! I'm just trying to get some money. You got any money?"

"Yeah, go look on the dresser in there. I think there's twenty dollars in there."

After that I kept a real close eye on the boys. I knew he wouldn't do anything so stupid like that, like sell our babies. It's the fact that he even said it gave me the creeps.

We moved to Camden into the prettiest house that I had ever lived in. It was a huge canary yellow house that sat on a hill. We had four bedrooms, one and a half baths and the kitchen was bigger than any kitchen I'd seen before. The backyard had a swimming pool and a guest house. Yeah, I couldn't believe it, it was our dream house. We were so happy.

"Come on, Debra," James yelled. "I told you we would have a house. Is this what you wanted baby?" as he grabbed and kissed me.

"Yes, it's so huge and pretty! James, do you think we can buy this house?"

"Hell, yeah! Didn't you hear the man say all we have to do is stay here for a year and he'd let us rent with the option to buy?"

"Yeah, that's right, he did."

We didn't have any furniture, but as the week went by, I was able to get some on credit. Things were really going good for James and me. We weren't fighting anymore and all the kids were in school. Everything was going just fine—my dreams were coming true. It was the life, or so I thought.

The days and weeks flew into the years. James had gotten a real good job, but that didn't last at all. After that, James did yard work, painting, cutting grass and little odd jobs. This time we stayed down south for at least four years. I had no idea that we would ever move out of that home. It was in this home that James developed a bond with the children. They were at an age to understand him.

We enjoyed the movies, stories and he would play games with the kids. They really love their father and he loved them more. I often sat back and watched them as they interacted with each other. You could hear it in their voices and see it in their eyes how much they loved each other. The lady that lived in the guest house helped James get a real good job at the bomb plant, right there in Camden.

James had an interview that morning. He decided he wanted to smoke a joint before he left for the interview. I thought it was a bad idea and expressed that to him, "James, you have to take a drug test and you are smoking. Don't you think you should not do that?"

"I know what the fuck I'm doing!" He went out the door, smelling like weed, to an interview at a bomb plant.

A few hours later, he returned. "You jinxed me, motherfucker! It's your fault I didn't get the job!"

The kids were running out of their rooms. I could hear them crying and yelling, "Mommie, Mommie!"

James and Jerome rushed up behind James hitting him and crying, "Leave my Mommie alone!" They were around seven or eight years old at the time.

I grabbed them and held them close as I curled up in the corner of the hallway. James grabbed the boys away from me and threw them on the floor shouting, "Don't you ever in your motherfucking life run up on me! I'll gut you two little niggas like a hog! Do you understand me?" Well, the fight was on.

I really didn't do anything that time. James just wanted to blame someone other than himself for losing a good job. He never got that opportunity in his life again.

It was a pretty bad fight. I ended up with black eyes, the whole nine yards. Looking like 'what's love got to do with it'. He was too shame to stay there, so we moved into a smaller home only to stay there for a few months.

One day, James came in the house and told us that we were moving on the first and going to Racine, Wisconsin where Madear was now living. The first of the month was just a few days away. I had to get boxes and try and pack the things that I wanted. We had accumulated so much stuff in four years.

Section 181

These were all warning signs. We should have stayed in Arkansas.

It unfolded from that point for us...downhill!

We rented a U-Haul trailer and down the highway we went with just the check that I got once a month in his pocket.

We were driving through Memphis when we started having trouble with the car. The U-Haul trailer was too much for the transmission. We pulled over at a hotel and the girls and I had to go through our belongings to get what we could pack in and on top of the car, and sacrifice all the rest.

323

While we were inside of this trailer in 99 degree weather, James had the twins in the outdoor pool. We abandon most of our stuff right there at a hotel.

When we got into Illinois, about 4oo miles outside of Chicago, the car began to give us problems. I had to call Mama Angie for help because I didn't have enough money to get to Chicago. We had to take the Amtrak train. Again, we are going through our stuff that was in and on top of the car to filter out only what we could carry in our hands. Again, sacrificing the rest.

Once in Chicago, we went to Mama Angie's. She welcomed James into her home and she loved me unconditionally as she always has, with all five of my children. We stayed there for a few weeks, but James was trying to get to Racine, to Madear, because he was feeling uncomfortable at Mama Angie's.

It was not because she made him feel this way; she was the only person in my family that accepted him into their home, and he had never been treated so kindly before. Mama Angie found plenty of work for him to do around the house—cutting grass, painting, etc. And she paid him very well.

I asked Mama Angie if it was okay to leave the children with her so I could go to Racine to look for an apartment.

"I would only be gone for the weekend."

"Sure, just make sure you come back when you say."

"Okay, I will."

We were gone until that Monday. When we got back things turned real ugly. My Aunt Lilamae had gotten our children. When I called her to let her know that I was back, she told me that she was going to keep them until I got on my feet, which would allow her to get the check for them.

Well, I don't have to tell you what James was feeling at this time! We went straight to the police station and made a complaint, stating that my Aunt wouldn't give our children back to us.

The police called her, "Ma'am, if you don't give these people their children back, you will be charged with kidnapping." She got escorted to the police station with our children.

Mama Angie was real disappointed in me, but soon forgave me. My Aunt Lilamae, on the other hand, I don't believe ever forgave me.

We moved to Racine and the life there became so unbearable. His sisters were not little girls anymore. They were all grow and doing their own thing and at times making me feel like I was the fool, which I felt I was not.

The only way that I was able to deal with my life, I drank more and more, each and every day. James got with family members in Racine and started the drugs again and became involved in open relationships that he was having with different women. It was so embarrassing and humiliating that I drowned myself even more in alcohol.

Nothing too much changed than what had been going on my entire life with him. Sure, there were plenty of times that we went through the honeymoon cycle, but soon as it was over, I caught hell. I always was told that I talk too much and just maybe if I would shut up, then bad things wouldn't happen to me. Hell, I was drinking and getting drunk so much that the word 'shut up' meant nothing to me!

There are two incidents that happen that I must share with you. Who am I fooling? There are a whole lot more than two, but I will only share these two. You can read between the lines as to what must have happened along the way. I'll make it as brief without going into every little detail. Still, when I think about it, I don't know if I get upset at myself, or if I blame James or the girl that said she was my friend.

325

Tyra's birthday was coming in three days and I was planning a big birthday party for that Saturday. I always gave huge birthday parties for all my children. I didn't have to worry about inviting other kids because they had at least five or six cousins which were enough for a party.

Her birthday is on Valentine's Day, so she got extra gifts and the decorations and cake were so pretty. Tyra always felt like her birthday was a curse, at least this is what she shared with me years later. Maybe this will explain why she would think that way.

On this particularly birthday, we were all in the kitchen putting up the decorations, getting ready for a big fun-filled day. The children didn't mind helping out because they knew that they were going to have a good time, with all their cousins at the house.

Tyra asked me, "Mama, do you think I'm going to have a good birthday party?"

"Sure, Tyra! Why would you ask that?"

"Because it seems like every time my birthday comes, you and daddy have a fight. I be afraid for you when my birthday come."

"Oh, baby, Mama's big girl. You have nothing to be afraid of. This is going to be the best birthday ever. I promise it will be alright, now, hand me those streamers so I can put them up."

Section 182

Don't be so quick to say friend. Know who you call a friend!

There was this woman Tessie who had three boys. I met her through one of James' sisters and we became really close, at least I thought so. Tessie came by the house that Wednesday before the party and brought some beer. Less than 30 minutes later, James came in with Tessie's boyfriend. We listened to music and had a good time.

James changed his clothes to go out to the club, and Tessie asked me if I mind watching the boys. She wanted to go out and hang out with them. I didn't have a problem with that because she gave me twenty bucks.

She left them with me for three days! No phone calls, nothing! James was with her! All kinds of thoughts ran through my mind. I didn't want to think the obvious because she did have a boyfriend. Little did I know, she was sleeping with them both and selling her ass at the Navy base with James youngest sister! I was the babysitter! Ain't that some shit!

Part of me couldn't believe that I had been played for the fool! I called Monica and told her what had happen.

"Damn, Debra, I thought you knew! Everybody know that they been kicking it! Where you been?"

"How was I supposed to know? She got a boyfriend!"

"Girl, that shit don't mean nothing. She ain't nothing but a tramp! That bitch is fucking both of them. Damn, you watchin her kids? That's fucked up!"

"Yeah, it is fucked up! She been gone for three days now, but I am going to whoop that bitch ass whenever she come back to pick up these damn kids, and Tyra's birthday party is tomorrow!"

"Yeah, well, that's on you! Now you see why I don't fuck with no bitches, I be by myself!"

"Yeah, I know. Talk to you later."

How could she? How could she come and smile in my face while sleeping with my husband the whole time? I started reflecting back when I was at Madear's house and James and Tessie was sitting in the kitchen at the table talking. Everybody knew something was going on but me! That made me feel and look like a bigger fool!

I drank more beer, chasing it with Gin and juice. James' two youngest sisters stopped by the house to give Tyra a gift. "What's wrong with you? Damn, you mad!" as they both laughed coming in the house.

"Oh, y'all, know why I'm mad! Everybody know about Tessie and James but me!"

"I was with them last night and made $300 dollars at the Navy base. Girl, Tessie out there making money! Why you so upset? You should be glad that James got a bitch like that out there making money cause he was gonna give some to you."

"I'm gonna beat her ass! Left her kids on me like that!"

"You a square and that's why James don't tell you the truth."

"Whatever!"

"Hey, it ain't my business! I just came to give Tyra something for her birthday." She called Tyra into the room and handed her a twenty dollar bill.

Tyra was so happy. "Thank you, Auntie!"

We talked and laughed while we finished cooking. We made fried chicken, spaghetti, potato salad, deviled eggs and more. Tyra asked me what time was the party going to start and I told her in a few more hours. I had combed her hair the night before, so I was glad that was done because I had been drinking. I showed her where put her gifts when her guests arrived.

"I be back. I have to use the bathroom. The party will start in about two hours, so make sure that your room is clean."

I heard the key turn. It was James, Tessie and her boyfriend. James called for me, "Debra, where you at?"

They went up front, turned on the music and began laughing and talking as if they just came back from the store. Well, you know I acted a complete, damn fool! I wanted to fight and started calling them out of their

328

names! James had to show off by telling me that this was his bitch and I better not talk to her like that! He had the nerve to slap me!

Section 183

A breakdown... Fed up or paranoid schizophrenic?

I was so angry, and had no other way of releasing my frustration other than throwing plates, glasses—anything that would break against the bare wall in the kitchen! I opened the refrigerator and threw everything out and onto the wall! James came running at me and I grabbed a butcher knife! He called the police and said that I was going crazy! That he needed for someone to come get me!

"You think I'm crazy?! Come on, motherfucker, I will kill your ass today! Come on! Fuck with me now!" I grabbed the phone cord and bit it in half, yelling, screaming, and crying uncontrollably! I couldn't believe he hit me because of her! I was so hurt that I didn't know what to do! I heard them talking and laughing in the room and I felt they were laughing at me!

Before I knew it, the police was at my house. James had told them that I was crazy and that he had been home all day, but when his friends came over, I started acting like this. He also told them that I became even angrier, and started throwing plates and glasses at him, calling him a liar!

I just wanted to keep throwing stuff at him! I heard the police say something on the radio, and the next thing you know, there were more police in my house covering their face from flying glasses and plates.

The police grabbed me and knocked me down as I screamed, "Stop, Stop! I didn't do anything! It's James! He's the one that caused this, not me! I continued to scream, fight and kick!

The police had this white jacket that they put me in, where my hands were tied in the back! Then they put me in a black body bag! I was screaming and yelling, "Why you are doing this to me?" They picked me up and took

329

me out on the stretcher—kicking, yelling, crying and screaming like someone who just lost their fucking mind!

James leaned down like he was going to kiss me and whispered, "See, crazy motherfucking bitch, what you did?! You not gonna stop shit! I'm still with my bitch!"

When I got to the hospital, I remember them throwing me in a padded room with what looked like mattresses on the wall. All I could do was sit in a corner and put my head down and cry. Later, two men and a nurse came in and gave me a shot in my arm.

I was crying out, "Oh my God, what's wrong with me? How did I let this happen! It's Tyra's birthday and look at me? I messed up my daughter's birthday! I am such a bad mother! GOD, WHAT'S WRONG WITH ME?!!!"

The medicine made me stop crying and go to sleep. I think I was there for one week. I was diagnosed as a paranoid schizophrenic, whatever the fuck that means. I just wanted out of this place! Ain't no paranoid shit wrong with me! James is the paranoid motherfucker, not me!

I was assigned to a white social worker named Terri. She listened to me. She was concerned about me and my kids and wanted to start coming to my home once a week to make sure everything was going smoothly. She offered to help me with anything I needed, like finding a job and transportation.

She wasn't afraid of James. She knew that I was, so she made it mandatory for her to come to the house. James was pissed because he didn't trust white people. It was fine by me because I enjoyed her and looked forward to her every visit.

The doctor's put me on Valium for my nerves and Anitbuse medication for the alcohol abuse so I wouldn't drink while taking the Valium. You already know that the majority of the valiums went to James. I stopped taking the other medication because it made me sick as a dog…when I had a drink!

Drinking beer was the only thing that eased the pain and put me in a world where I rather be. I became a beer alcoholic which led to hard liquor. Hell, I was just a damn alcoholic in denial. What a combination!

I would go out sometimes with my friend Tiffany. She worked at the police station and would come around just to go out at times, even though she didn't drink. She drove a small sports car and my manger of the apartment building had a crush on her. She was a lot of fun.

Tiffany was only in my life for a season, mostly during the time James was locked up for domestic violence. Just the fact that she worked at the police station made James a little bit uncomfortable. I was glad because James would stay out of her way. I often wonder whatever happened to her. Honestly, I was too much of a mess to be anybody's friend at that time.

Section 184

Jesus is the answer… He will send a ram in the bush.

I walked into a small corner church and met some really nice people. There was a lady there by the name of Sister Carter. She had six children and fell in love with me and my kids. She came to my home to get me for church, even though the church sat at the corner from my house. She didn't care about James and all that loud talking. When she came by, he backed down. She always told me that Satan runs from God. She must have been God-sent because James got out of her way whenever she came around.

Sister Carter was the world to me. She was awesome. She knew the Bible and how we are to live right. She was a lifesaver for me. She took me under her wing and I was holding on for dear life. It almost felt like she was my life support, but she told me many of times that it is the Lord that I had to look to, hold onto and not man. I had to learn that and I did.

Oh, my Lord. That is a place that I'm still trying to get back to. The closeness with the Lord is like no other experience. There's peace, rest, and at the same time, it feels like fire shut up in your bone! My, my, what a feeling it is to be close with the Lord!

All I had to do was repent and ask the Lord to forgive me for all of my sins—and he did! I acknowledged that Jesus died on the cross for my sins and believed that he is the Son of the living God. It was that simple.

This was a Pentecostal church. There were only three families there, besides the pastor and his wife. The sweetest lady in the church was the one that had three daughters and they all cared for and about me and my children. Each one of her daughters took one of my girls and bought for them, and even took them on outings. They taught them how to behave in the House of the Lord. I became very close to the oldest one and her husband.

She became what you call my sister in Christ. Every time the church doors opened, I was there, trying to do all I could to change my life by changing my mind. I began to transform into a person who I didn't even know existed inside of me. I had no fear, not even of James.

I trusted in the Lord, prayed on a regular basis, and most of all, I had faith and love for the Lord. It didn't matter what the next person thought or did; I knew in the depths of my heart that I was walking in the path the Lord would have me go.

Know this, when you take your eyes off of Jesus, you open the doors for all of Satan's demons to come into your life and try to destroy you. Believe me, I know!

Sister Carter went to Chicago with me one time to meet Nana, my mother, Mama Angie and Auntie Lilamae. I wanted my family to see that I had gotten my life on the right track. Sister Carter shared with them how much I had changed. My mother still had her doubts when it came to James

332

who was in jail for domestic violence at the time, and he had a warrant for driving with no license.

Section 184

The Big "C"

Monica told me about a shelter called the Women Resource Center for the Abused and Battered Women. I was going in and out of this shelter. That was where I started to learn what the true meaning of abuse was. I had a choice to stay or leave. I wasn't ready to stay yet; I was still doing my thing. I mean, James was locked up and I was free, for now, so I didn't need them— so I thought.

I went back to school for a Nursing Assistant certification. I was determined to do something other than be barefoot and pregnant, and continue to get my ass kicked for breakfast, lunch and dinner. Monica and I were in school together. She started before I did and it inspired me to do the same. I felt if she could do, so could I.

Things were looking up for me; I was able to buy more stuff for the house and for my children. I was doing something with my life, while James stayed at the house cooking and making the kids clean the house. I didn't care, I was out of the house.

My mother and I now had a good strong relationship that no one could come between and I was happy about that. My mother even came to visit us several times in Racine.

. I was taking my finals at school and I called my mother just to let her know and to hear her voice.

"Hey, good morning, Mommie."

"Good morning, Debbie, are you at school now?"

"Yeah, today is my finals. I have to past this test. I know I will."

"Sure you will, Debbie. Just stay focus and do what you were taught. I need for you to call me after you take your test. I have something that I want to tell you."

"Tell me now, I'm listening."

"No, I'm going to wait until you pass your test, so call me when you get done, okay?"

"Okay, Mommie I will."

Section 185

Why my Mommie?

I called my mother only for her to tell me that she had cancer—lung cancer. That was September 19, 1989. That was too hard to believe. I cried in fear, thinking that my mother was going to die, to leave me.

"Mommie, do you need me to come there with you now?"

"No, Debbie. I'll let you know if I need you. You stay there with your kids, and take care of them."

"You promise, Mommie? You will tell me."

"Yes, I will. I'm okay."

It was scary because Auntie DD had died a few years earlier from cancer. I was taking the train every weekend to be with my mother and giving Nana, Auntie Eunice, Uncle Tom and Auntie Janice a break. It was hard to leave Mommie and then have to wait a whole week before I seeing her again.

Within the next month or so, I called my mother just to check on her as I did throughout the week. She said, "It's time, Debbie, I need for you to come." I told Nana that I was on my way. When I left that weekend, I left my children to go take care of my mother and didn't care how no one felt.

When I got there, my Mommie was in the Cook County hospital where some of the best doctors practiced. But, at the time my mother was there, the care there really sucked, big time! She was lying in a puddle of urine and feces, and it looked and smelled like she had been in it for some hours! I began to clean my mother, and making her comfortable, all the while raising hell and crying, "No one cared!" I looked at my mother and felt so helpless.

My Mommie wanted out of there, and so did I. She was in a ward way back in a corner at the end of the room that reminded me so much of the mission on skid row—one big room with a row of beds with only the curtain to separate the beds.

People, were moaning, crying in agony, yelling for pain meds, to be changed, and just calling for help! It was an awful sight!

The doctors came to see my mother and the family was there. Mommie had been taking chemo and radiation which was not as effective as doctors had hoped.

"She needs to have an operation to remove the spots on her lung," the doctor advised. My Mommie began to cry and Nana cried even louder.

"Come on, Mama, stop crying." Uncle Tom helped Nana up and walked her out of the area.

I tried to console my mother, "Mommie, don't cry it will be alright. It will Mommie. Don't cry."

I have never seen pain and fear in my mother eyes before. That day, I saw more than I wanted to. I cried, but tried to convince her that things were going to be alright, but I think she saw the fear and devastation in my eyes. Her daughter was afraid for her mother's life. I laid my head on my mother's stomach and held so tight.

There were three or four doctors standing on the outside of the curtain. I could hear them talking to Nana and the rest of the family.

"You're her daughter? Don't cry. The doctor would like to speak to you all if you could just follow me, please." I looked at my mother and wiped my eyes.

"Go on, Debbie, find out what the doctors have to say and let me know." She already knew what they were going to say. I could tell from the look in her eyes.

We followed them into the counseling room and sat down. I began to ask so many questions, but the doctor interrupted me, "How about I explain to you all what's happening, and then if any of you have any questions, you can ask at that time."

"Okay, that's fine because I have a lot of questions." Nana and I both wiped away our tears as we readied ourselves for the doctor to give us a clear understanding of what was going on with Mommie.

"Here's the patient's x-ray," as he placed it on the light. This is her right lung. The cancer has progressed," pointing to the dark spots on the x-ray. "The radiation and chemo are not working fast enough, so she's going to have to have an operation to remove them."

We asked more questions and the doctor answered them all, to our satisfaction. All I wanted was for Mommie to get better, as I continued to cry.

The doctor tried to ease our concern, "Your mother's chances are real good and I've made the arrangements for her to have the operation in the morning." Everyone agreed that the surgery was the best thing for my mother.

"What does Mommie want? Did she say she wants to have the operation?"

"Yes, Debbie, it's what Marian wants," Nana replied.

"Okay," wiping my eyes and looking at the doctor, "is my Mommie going to be all right?"

"Your mother has a 10-40% change of things not going well and the 70% is in her favor."

"What are all the bags of blood and the tubes in my mother for?"

The doctor explained that my mother had to have a blood transfusion because she was so weak.

"Okay, is that all? I wanted to go back to see my mother. "Will you please put her in a room? She doesn't like being in a ward. She was soaked with urine and bowel movement, and no one came to change her bedding. Please don't do my mother like that," I cried.

"Don't worry. I'll have her moved right now."

"Thank you, doctor. Please take care of my Mommie. She's all I got," as I walked out of the room.

The doctor placed his hand on my shoulder and looked me in the eyes, "Don't worry, your mother will be fine. I promise, you have nothing to worry about."

I walked back to my mother in tears. I was really afraid for her. I prayed as I walked, 'Oh, please, Dear Lord, my Heavenly Father, please watch over my Mommie. Please take care of her.'

"Hi. Mommie, how do you feel now?" I leaned down to give her a kiss.

"I'm weak, Debbie, and I am tired. This chemo and radiation is killing me."

"No, it's not. Don't say that, Mommie."

There was a nurse in the room taking the blood bags down. They had just given her and transfusion.

"What are you doing?" I asked the nurse.

"The doctor ordered that your mother to be moved and she's finished with this anyway."

"See, Mommie," smiling at her, "you're going into your own room

337

now. The doctor said you're having an operation in the morning. Did you want to have this operation?"

"Yes, Debbie, I just want this to be over with. Mommie is tired, I'm just tired now."

"Mommie, let's not talk about being tired anymore. You will be okay. The doctor promised me that you are going to be fine. Just try and get some rest." I kissed her on the forehead.

Once she got settled in her room, I stayed the night at the hospital with her. She had lost all of her beautiful hair and she was on Morphine for the pain. Mommie didn't look good at all. The next morning came and my mother had the operation, but it didn't go well at all.

The doctor said when he opened her up, her right lung was covered with cancer. He said he couldn't remove the lung because her left lung wasn't strong enough to keep her alive, so he closed her up.

The doctor went on to say, "It's just a matter of time now. I'm really sorry. There is nothing else that we can do."

"You sorry?! What the fuck do sorry have to do with it! You promised that my Mommie was going to be alright! You looked me in my eyes and said don't worry! What about that? I don't understand what the hell you are telling me! That my Mommie is going to die? And all you can tell me is that you are sorry?!" I was completely and utterly devastated!

My mother was going to die and there was nothing we could do about it. I knew a Man that could save and heal my mother and his name is Jesus! He can work miracles! I prayed, pleaded with my Lord, "Please don't take my Mommie away from me."

Section 186

I made a promise to my Mommie.

The days went by and it was time for my mother to leave the hospital. As I put her sweater on and helped her into the wheel chair, she whispered, "Debbie, promise me something."

"Yes, Mommie, I'll promise you anything. What is it?"

"Promise when we leave here, you won't let them bring me back. I'm tired of all of this. I can't go through this anymore. Promise your Mommie. Can you do that for me? No matter what happens, don't let them bring me back to the hospital." She held my hand tightly and looked directly at me with tears in her eyes.

Trying to speak through my own tears, I promised. "Yes, Mommie, I promise. I promise you won't have to come back to the hospital no more. Do that mean you don't want your treatments anymore?"

"Don't let them admit me in the hospital no more."

"Okay, I won't."

A lot happened after Mommie left the hospital. They continued to give her Morphine for the pain and she went back and forth every day for her treatments. It made her very weak and it had gotten to the point where her pain was unbearable.

The last time that we were there, waiting for the elevator to come, Mommie was lying on the stretcher. I felt so sorry for my Mommie; she was in so much pain and there was nothing I could do about it. She moaned and groaned because the pain was so bad. I just stood over her praying like I never prayed before.

Her eyes were closed and tears ran down the side of her face, "I see Jesus, Debbie. I see, Jesus."

I fell on top of my mother trying to cover her with my body. I waved my hands over her face saying, "No, Jesus, please don't let Mommie see you right now! Not now!" I continued to cry as I begged my mother to open her eyes!

"Look at me, Mommie! Look at me!"

That's when the doors opened, frantically pushing my Mommie into the elevator thinking, "Well, now she won't see Jesus! It's not time!"

I figured if I could only get her back home, she would be alright. For a few days it seems as though Mommie was getting better. I had the cancer support organization send an egg crate for her bed, a walker, a wheelchair, a potty chair and an oxygen tank was coming the next day—I wanted whatever was needed to make sure she was comfortable.

I called Miss Betty and asked her to tell Patrick what was going on and to give me a call. He made sure that he came to see my mother. He came often to see her.

"Thank you, Patrick for coming."

"Remember, friends for life," as he smiled.

"Yeah, I remember, friends for life," crying, as I reached out to him. "I'm so scared my Mommie is going to die."

"I know, I'm here for you if you need me. Where is Chuckie?"

"I'm in the process of trying to get the state prison to let Chuckie come see Mommie. Chuckie is serving a five-year sentence. I pray that they let him come to Mommie."

"Just keep trying, Debra."

Section 187

My Mommie died and her last words were... He will?

That night, Mommie and I talked for a long time. She was telling me all the people she wanted to see and/or talk to, so I got her phonebook and called them. Some of her friends came and some didn't.

I tried to do whatever Mommie asked. She asked to see her oldest brother, but when I called him, he told me he didn't have time to come see Mommie. I explained how her health was failing, that she wanted to see him.

"Won't you please come see my Mommie, your sister?"

"I don't have the time."

I sat there trying to take her mind off of her illness, but her mind was on something else—me!

"Debbie, I need to talk to you and I need to tell you this."

"Okay, Mommie, what is it?"

"You know James ain't shit! He'll never be shit, and as long as you're with him, you won't amount to anything! Do you understand what I am saying to you?"

"Yes Mommie, I do." I put my head down on her bed as she continued to express the things she needed me to know.

"Debbie, when I leave you, I want you to know that you won't have a family anymore."

I held my head up looking at her, "Mommie, you're not going anywhere, so don't worry about that, it's okay."

"You need to know that you truly will be on your own. You won't have a family anymore. No one in the family will be there for you. They will not have anything to do with you or your children."

"Okay, okay, Mommie, I hear you," not knowing the true depth of what she was really saying to me.

I helped Mommie get comfortable in the bed. I went to turn the lights off.

"Leave the lights on; I don't want to be in the dark. I'm tired Debbie, Mommie is tired."

"Okay, Mommie, you can rest now. Remember, Chuckie will be here tomorrow. Chuckie will be here tomorrow, Mommie."

She turned to me with this warm, peaceful smile on her face and asked, "He will, Debbie? He will?"

"Yes, Mommie, he will," as I curled up at the foot of her bed and drifted off to sleep.

Early the next morning, I woke up and turned to my mother. She was sitting straight up in the bed, staring straight ahead.

"Are you okay, Mommie? What's wrong?" She didn't say anything.

"Mommie! Mommie, what's wrong?!" I began to cry as I sat there looking at her—so scared!

"Mommie, Mommie," I cried. "Oh God, please watch over my Mommie!"

I kissed her and whispered, "I love you Mommie. I'm going to call Nana, okay?"

I went to the phone and called Nana at work. When she came to the phone, I told her Mommie was paralyzed and was blind. "She can't move or talk."

"Is Marian okay?"

"Yes, Nana, she's okay, but she can't talk or move right now."

"Oh, my God. Okay, Debbie, I'll be right there."

All I could do that entire day was make her comfortable and keep her dry until Nana got there. I talked to Mommie the whole time because I learned in school that your hearing is the last thing to leave you.

Mommie's last words were, "He will, Debbie? He will?"

My brother was calling every thirty minutes to check on Mommie. When Nana made it to the house, she had some of her co-workers with her. Uncle Tom was there; Beverly and Auntie Eunice and Auntie Janice, and my children.

James had dropped my children off the other day. Ericka was soaking wet! He didn't bother to stop and let her use the bathroom on that hour and forty-five minute drive from Wisconsin. He dropped them off with no clothes, knowing I was caring for my mother.

Mommie was comfortable and things were going fine until one of Nana's co-workers came in the room, "Marian needs to go to the hospital. Look at her. It's hard for her to breathe!"

I was sitting next to Mommie when Uncle Tom told everybody to come in the room to see how Mommie was breathing. The co-worker called for the paramedics because she felt like Mommie wasn't getting enough oxygen.

The Cancer Society was bringing an oxygen tank in the morning, so I knew she would be okay. When the paramedics arrived, it was a mess because Uncle Tom got mad telling the co-worker that she should mind her own business, that it wasn't her place to make that call.

The paramedics came into Mommie's room and examined her. "She needs oxygen and we have to take her to the hospital."

"Are they going to admit her?" I asked.

"Yes, they will be admitting her."

"Well, she will not be going. I promise my Mommie that I will not let no body take her back to the hospital, so you can't take her."

Mommie was lying down while everybody argued at the foot of her bed. The paramedic asked Nana who was she to the patient? "I'm her mother."

343

He turned to me and asked, "Are you the daughter?

"Yes, I am."

The paramedic stated that he would have to honor what I was saying because I was her daughter. "If that was her request and her daughter promised to keep it, there's nothing I can do."

He put his equipment away and headed out of the room. Uncle Tom started arguing with Nana about her friend calling the paramedics. Suddenly, Mommie raised up staring toward their voices.

"Nana, Mommie is getting ready to leave us." Nana rushed over to the bedside, sitting next to Mommie and held her close. Mommie looked into Nana's eyes without a word.

Nana asked, "Debbie, how do you know my baby is going to leave me?" She was crying so hard she could hardly speak as she held onto Mommie. Then Nana leaned down and kissed Mommie.

Uncle Tom grabbed Nana, "Come on, Mama, come on!"

I put my arms around my mother and she turned to look at me. "I love you, Mommie. I love you."

She blinked her eyes as a tear rolled down her face and then closed her eyes. That was it; she was gone.

I could not believe it… My Mommie had just died. I didn't have a mother anymore. I held onto her tightly as I cried out, "Oh God, please, no! Mommie, please don't leave me! Please don't leave me!"

At that point, the phone rang. Everybody got real quiet and turned to look at me. Somehow we all knew it was Chuckie.

"That's Chuckie calling. Oh, my God! How am I going to tell my brother that Mommie is gone?"

"Answer the phone Debbie. You should be the one to tell him," Auntie Janice spoke up.

I laid Mommie's head down on the pillow carefully. The phone continued to ring. I went to the kitchen to answer, "Hello."

"Will you accept a collect call from caller, your name is…"

"Chuckie." My knees buckled so I sat down at the kitchen table.

"Yes, I do."

"Debbie." For a brief moment, there was silence.

"Debbie!"

I moaned, "Oh Chuckie, Chuckie!" I heard his voice tremble .

"No, Debbie, please don't tell me Mommie is gone!" We cried together.

"Yes, Chuckie, Mommie is gone." He cried with so much pain and hurt.

"Her last words were 'He will, Debbie? He will?' I was telling her that you would be here tomorrow." He couldn't talk any longer. I heard the phone drop. I went back into Mommie's room and gave her a kiss.

Section 188

I released it all.

"You're no longer in pain; it doesn't hurt no more Mommie." I got a pail and I began to washing her up. Then I got some clean clothes to dress her and that pretty red polish that she loved to wear. Beverly polished her nails. Uncle Tom had called the police to come pick up Mommie's body.

Nana cried. Oh, how my Nana cried! The coroner came with the police for Mommie. I got her false teeth and put them in the container to send them with her. Uncle Tom picked Mommie up and carried her down three flights of the stairs. At that moment, I forgave him for all the mean and hateful things that he had every said or done to me.

345

When we got outside, I thought there would be paramedics, but there was a patty wagon waiting instead. Uncle Tom laid Mommie down carefully making sure her head was straight.

"Fix her head, Uncle Tom. Here, put her teeth in. She's not going to want nobody to see her without her teeth." He shut the door and the police drove off.

That was it. Mommie was gone. We went back inside the house and everybody continued to cry. I said to everyone, "Let's not cry for Mommie anymore. Let's be happy that she's with God. She doesn't have to be in pain no more; she doesn't have to suffer no more."

"Yeah, that's right. Marian doesn't have to suffer anymore." But, Nana couldn't stop crying. She just lost her baby girl that she was so close to.

"Nana, Mommie's not in any pain or suffering. She was ready to go." Uncle Tom offered to drive her. "Come on, Mama I'll take you home now."

Nana's co-workers left right away to give us that privacy that we all needed.

"Debbie, are you okay?"

"Yeah, Beverly, I'm okay. And you?"

Everybody left and I was all alone. I got in Mommie's bed and cried. I held onto her pillows and cried like a little baby. The phone rang; I thought it was my brother calling back, but it was Patrick. I told him Mommie was gone and he came right over.

We sat in the front room and talked for a while. He didn't leave me. He kissed me on my forehead and told me to rest. I fell asleep resting in his arms, right there on my mother's couch. He was the friend that I needed.

A week is a long time to wait to bury your mother. I couldn't understand why they had to wait so long. I think just black folks do that, you know, wait a whole week before you bury your love one.

346

I had to pick out a picture for my mother's obituary. It was a pretty picture of Mommie. She was smiling and looked really happy. Everybody said it was nice.

Nana picked out what she wanted her to wear and Uncle Tom made all the funeral arrangements—and paid for it. Mommie didn't have an insurance policy. I was only receiving a government check, so I surely couldn't help to even pay for flowers, let alone the arrangements. It got even harder as time got closer.

The day had finally come. It was time for the funeral. I was dreading that moment and didn't want to go. I got dressed at Mommie's house and was crying the whole time I was getting ready. I told myself that Mommie was in a better place.

'She's with God now. Mommie is no longer in pain, she's not suffering anymore,' I kept telling myself so I could get through it. But when it was time to walk out that door and get in that long black limousine, I couldn't do it.

I begged Nana, "Please don't make me go. I don't want to go! Why do we have to get all dressed up and go ride in that car? Why Nana? Please, Nana, please!"

"Debbie, listen to me. You don't have a choice here, you have to go. You have to go out of respect for your mother. You have to be there on Chuckie's behalf."

I came out of the house and got in the limousine. It was the longest and the loneliest ride I'd ever taken in my life. I remember staring out the window at nothing in particular. I don't remember talking to anyone.

Section 189

We will always be friends.

I just kept mumbling, "Why Mommie? Why did you have to leave me? I miss you already." When we arrived at the funeral home, lots of people were standing around. I remember wiping my eyes and holding my breath when I got out of the car.

'Lord, please give me the strength. I need to get through this.' I walked into the funeral home and my best friend Patrick was standing at the door waiting on me. I was so relieved to see his face. He wrapped his arm around my waist and asked, "Are you ready to do this?"

I looked up at him, "No, I'm not. I'm not ready for this, Patrick. I don't think I can do this."

"Come on, Debra, you have to be strong. I got you," as he held me tight. "I'm going to walk with you."

I held his hand so tight and as we walked toward the casket. My eyes were locked on it and then I focused on my mother's body. Before I knew it, I was standing over my mother looking down at her. My knees buckled as I leaned over and kissed her. She was so cold and her face was so hard, I couldn't take it.

"No, Mommie, don't leave me! I love you!" Everything became a blur. I turned to look at everybody, then shouted, "What are you here for? Why did you come? When my Mommie wanted y'all to come see her, you didn't! But now, here you are sitting here!"

I continued to yell, "Oh, my God, Mommie, please don't leave me. I don't have nobody else, Mommie. Please don't leave me!"

"Come on, Debbie, come on." They walked me away from the casket. I really don't remember much after that. Next thing I knew, we were at the burial site. I didn't get out of the limousine. I could not watch them lower my mother into the ground!

Then it was over. The state prison never let my brother come. They called and said that my brother was a high risk and they couldn't allow him come to the funeral. I feel so sorry for my brother.

The family was at Nana's house drinking. My Aunt Esalemia, my mother's oldest sister, came from New York for the funeral. Somebody had to pay her way because she never has any money, according to the family.

She was the aunt that whenever she came to Chicago, Nana had to buy new pots and pans because she didn't eat pork and she didn't want any of her food cooked in Nana's old pots and pans. After she goes back to New York, they would talk about her and say she was one of the neediest children that Nana had. She begged a lot, in other words.

Aunt Esalemia picked up Mommie's obituary and made a very nasty comment.

"Who picked out that picture of Marian?" and turned up her nose. That's such an ugly picture! She looks sick."

"You look sick, bitch, and you ain't even dead! Don't talk about my mother!" Boy, was I hot!

"Debbie, don't talk like that. She's your aunt."

"Man, fuck her! She never liked me no way! Talking about my mother! I'm leaving!" I packed up the liquor since I had bought drinks for everybody, whatever they wanted. I took the Crown Royal, the beer, the scotch, cigarettes—everything. I was just so angry.

I cursed up a storm and told them, "Y'all don't have to put me out, I'm leaving!" I knew that I was speaking out of angry, but I meant everything that I said. I didn't want Nana to ask me to leave her house, so I left before her children made her ask me to leave!"

349

Section 190

She said it on her death bed.

I went over to Brenda's house for a while, then back to my mother's—with drinks and all—crying, crying, crying!

"She's a lowdown, begging, nothing-ass-having bitch! How could she talk about my mother like that?" I got pissy drunk that night all by myself.

The next day or two, I began to pack Mommie's belongings to take back to Wisconsin.

Uncle Tom said he was taking her bed and the rest of the furniture. My Aunt Eunice wanted Mommie's black raincoat, but I didn't give it to her. Had I known she would never speak to me again because of it, I would have wrapped it up and given it to her with a ribbon on it! Hell, she couldn't fit it no way! I took all of Mommie's clothes and other items back home with me.

I was really upset with James. I was really hurt because he didn't come to my mother's funeral. What hurt me the most was he didn't even bring my children, but it was okay. I got over it.

I put everything in its place once I made it home. I even tried to set everything up just the way Mommie had in her apartment. One of my favorite items was the lamp that would come on when you touched it. My apartment looked really nice after that.

I continued to go in and out of the shelter. I always kept in the back of my mind the things that my mother told me on her dying bed. Things had gotten worse and James didn't show any compassion for my mother's death. "Every motherfucker gonna die, so that's not no big deal."

From that point on, I began to look at him in the way my mother needed me to. With each visit to the shelter, I learned something new. Let me tell you about the last time I was there:

350

I had a beautiful home. I had everything in my home from white carpet on the floor to the picture mirrors on the walls. It all ended when he jumped on me again.

I left and went back to the Women Resource center. On the third day, I went home to get some of my belongings only to find that he had sold everything. When I walked into the house, I just fell to my knees! I couldn't believe what he had done! At that time I thought, this is it! This is the end!

I got a restraining order and filed for a divorce. I even started putting my life back together again. But, when it came to sign the divorce paper, I couldn't do it! I was still holding on to a dream…being with my husband, my children's father, growing old together and sharing the joy of our grandchildren when the time came. Yet, James had managed to destroy the love that I had for him.

Section 191

What's done in the dark will soon come to light!

In fact, James brought it to my attention that when our home got broken into and everybody thought it was Chuckie, well, it was him! Ain't that some shit! I had to call Nana and tell her this. I didn't want her to die and go to her grave thinking that Chuckie did something when he didn't.

When Auntie Eunice got wind of this, she immediately blamed me and said that she did not want to have anything to do with me ever because I stole from her mother.

Now I understand her statement at Papa's repast. But, I have never taken anything from my Nana.

Who would think that twenty-five plus years later, Auntie Eunice has taken, or "used" way over $50,000.00 from Nana's bank account. Yet, she is so righteous and don't speak to me. I pray for her.

351

Section 192

The wrath of my brother's hands

James was afraid of my brother, but really didn't have too much concern because he stayed in jail all the time. Years went by and my brother was still going in and out of jail, so he was never there to protect me.

Chuckie joined a gang at a very young age. Other than the Black Stone Rangers, he was in the most treacherous and ruthless gangs in Chicago, the Disciples. He rose pretty high in rank and was now commanding those under him.

After doing over ten years in jail, my brother got out and came to Racine to be with me. There, he met the drug kingpin of Racine, Wisconsin who also had just gotten out of prison also. I think he did ten years straight.

These two cons were inseparable. The kingpin was my brother's friend, the brother he never had. A big time drug war was going on, so my brother and this drug kingpin joined together and there was no stopping them. They were the most dangerous persons walking the streets. They took over Racine, from the North Side to the South Side and so many people lost their lives and so many families were destroyed.

Everybody knew who the drug kingpin was, but they didn't know who his right hand man was.

Stories have been told that my brother was called the Enforcer, the hit man! Case in point, one day I got with some ladies and experimented with smoking crack cocaine on the pipe. I had been lacing and doing primes.

"Here, try to smoke the pipe. Do it like this. Hold it in for a few seconds and then blow it out. Hold it! Hold it!"

She held it for me, helping me out. I did not know that I was being fed rat poison! I started having seizures and went into convulsions! I was rushed to the emergency room. I could have died.

352

My social worker came to see me. She protected me and my children by sending us to Sister Carter's house to make sure that the system didn't take my children and put them in a foster home and me in jail.

Sister Carter saved my life. I thank God because she was a license foster parent and cared enough to take us into her home.

Nothing ever happened to the girl that tried to poison me. I had no idea that she was out for revenge because my brother had done something to her brother. She was trying to kill me.

After a week or two, I got myself together and James was getting out of jail. With him being locked down for about two months, I just knew he had gotten his act together. Just in case, I knew that the shelter was there if I needed them.

Section 193

Let's pause for a moment...

I had to grab your attention and take you back so many years just so you will have an idea and understanding of how and why I ended up desperately trying to get away and fearing for my life.

I tried my best to describe in every detail what went on behind those pretty curtains, after the street lights came on, and on the other side of the street that some of you wouldn't bother to go near what it was like on the streets at fourteen years old.

It was the type of life that you only see or hear about on TV and the newspaper. It's real! This was not a joke!

At this point, this should be a wake-up call to all rebellious young girls who feel their mothers suddenly don't know or understand you, and, of course, you know everything. Wrong!

Please listen to your mother or grandmother. You don't want to fall in the hands of a wolf dressed in sheep's clothing. He's out there just waiting for someone like you!

Mothers, don't be so quick to give up on your daughters and declaring 'let her go, she'll learn the hard way.' Don't give up on your child no matter how hard the task of raising her may be.

Be careful of dressing them up in short, tight-fitting clothes—'Don't my baby look pretty!'—and sending her off with a guy you don't know, don't know his folks, and your gut told you something wasn't right when he walked in!! Get to know who your daughter's friends are and her whereabouts.

Ladies, you may be experiencing some type of abuse. Throughout my testimony herein, I attempted to share with you what abuse looks like in hopes that something will be triggered in your spirit to seek help. I hope you find the strength to say 'I am sick and tired of being sick and tired.'

Section 194
Now, we're back at the beginning where
she finally got away... Or did she?

The Women's Resource Center put us up overnight while they located other facilities that could provide a safe place for us to stay. At the first shelter, we were referred to the Sojourner Truth House in Milwaukee, Wisconsin which was about forty-five minutes from Racine. We stayed there for two months under assumed names.

The staff went out of their way to help me get settled in, but my main concern was the kids. I wanted to get them settled into a regular routine so the first thing they help me do was enroll them in school. Of course, it had been a hard transition for them so it was important for me to give them as much of a normal life as possible. After about two months and with the help of many

354

agencies, I was able to secure an apartment, clothes, food and a peace of mind. I was now making progress towards being my own person.

It felt good to be in an apartment without having to worry about James trashing the place, taking whatever household items that weren't nailed down and selling them or beating and raping me. If I said 'no' and he said 'yes', that is rape! No means NO!

The kids were happier, too—it just felt like home. For the first time, I could breathe and I felt like I was finally living, living without fear.

The only thing that bothered me was I was still worried that James could find me. There were many days that I found myself looking over my shoulder because I was expecting him to pop up out of the blue and grab me. I kept trying to convince myself that I was overreacting and there was no way he could know that I was no longer in Racine. Even if he did, I was sure he was telling himself, 'She'll be back, she needs me, she don't know any one that would take her and them kids in no way.'

Once we settled in, I kept reflecting on my past relationships and how stupid I was. There was still a void in my life and I didn't know what it was. I realized that I don't know how to be by myself, to be Debra. I wanted things to be like they were long time ago.

I wanted to rekindle with Mack or Patrick, who always made me feel safe again. I blew off how Mack treated me, how Pat had disked me. I was still looking for a real love, that fairy tale love—when someone comes into your life and loves you for who you are. That was the love that I was praying for, but instead I became bitter.

There was a part of me that hated all men. I felt like they were all dogs and I didn't trust them. I hate to admit it, but I wanted to get even and destroy them all! I had become very bitter after the hell James put me through. I was a manipulative, uncaring person that used men for whatever I could get out of them. I didn't care about them, it was all about me.

I continued to drink more and more and my apartment had become party central. I always had a card games going and the liquor and food flowed freely. I had all different types of men at my disposal. I felt like men could only be in my life for whatever reason I needed them and I would dispense of them as I chose to do so! I had several men in my life and I didn't have to sleep with them; I was that good.

Section 195

This is not me.

I learned that I didn't have to sleep with every man that came along. All I needed was the gift of gab. I had to be firm like James was with me. I just sweetened it with some womanly wiles! Hell, I figured if James could get me to do all I did for him, why couldn't I do the same with other men? And guess what? It worked!

My favorite line was 'You gotta pay just to talk to me baby! I was a hot mess!'

You couldn't tell me I wasn't a bad girl. After all the shit I had put up with, I had to be this way. Things were getting sweeter and sweeter. I used all those years of James calling me a bitch and whore to my advantage! I had to do it for me and the kids. I spent years giving my body and soul to James with nothing to show for it, so I was determined to turn the situation around and let it work for me.

The one guy who cleaned my house didn't have a problem washing the dishes or mopping the floors. He was really sweet. Whatever I wanted him to do, he did it!

My children didn't like him, or his son, but he was so nice to me. Sometimes I would feel bad the way I treated him because I'd flashback to

James treated me and that was not good at all.

One day, we were looking for his son and realized my kids had put him in the clothes dryer, and turned it on! My children were very active, but in my eyes, they really hadn't done anything wrong. They had lived such a strict and fearful life with their father that I felt they deserved to do whatever they wanted to do. I didn't realize that I was not being a good example for them. I thought I was doing rather well for them.

I received $2,500.00 per month assistance with plenty of food stamps. I had the meat deal man, fruit and veggie man... I felt I was showing them how strong I was, how we could get along without their father. I didn't know that I was still selling my soul to the devil. I thought life was grand! But, I continued to drink heavily.

Section 196

My two guardian angels

Brenda and Edna

The Lord had a ram in the bush, and her name was Brenda Potts. I believe the Lord placed her in my life to be my guardian angel. She didn't drink, get high or nothing. She was one of those friends that you could count on. Brenda watched my back and made sure that I didn't get hurt, kept me out of harm's way, and she never let me drive when I had been drinking.

She would always tell me over and over again, "Come on, Debbie, give me the keys! Girl, you know, I'm not gonna let you drive and you been drinking. I love my life and I'm not gonna let you kill me, or you. You got them kids to live for. So, you just go ahead and get over there in the passenger seat...I got this!" We'd laughed and I got into the passenger side.

357

I never exchanged words with her no matter how drunk I was. I knew that she was that God-sent angel.

Just like my family and all my childhood friends, she always called me Debbie. It was the way she said my name. She was so special to me; a friend for life. We promised to keep in touch and to this day, we talk often.

Then there was my best friend Edna. We travel to the prison to visit our boyfriends. Well, it was my so-called boyfriend and she was just visiting someone she was close to—nothing more than that.

The road trips were a lot of fun and we figured it was our way of supporting the men we thought that we loved, in their time of need.

Edna would take me to church with her all the time. She was one of the lead singers on the praise team. When Edna sang, her voice was so sweet to your ears. It seemed like Heaven opened up and all the angels with their golden harps were playing for her. She was a bad girl, but there were none that could top that gifted voice, at least I haven't heard them yet!

Going to church with Edna helped me to reach out to the Lord and try to rebuild my faith. Edna was an important part of my life; she didn't drink, smoke or chew so she was a very positive influence on me.

Edna did have a warped sense of humor that few people in my circle could understand, or even like. She was blunt, firm and had a sweet, soft-spoken way of getting her point across. She was very intelligent, and didn't take crap off anyone. Maybe that's why we got along so well—we had so much in common.

Edna never judged me about anything I did; she just accepted me for who I was and cared about me and my children. She had a daughter and a son and there was no denying how much they loved her; they were inseparable. When you saw Edna, her children were close by. I envied that because while my children do love me, they never wanted to hang out with me like that. I sometimes wonder why.

Some fifteen years later, my best friend's son died in her home. Four years after that, she died from cancer. Her favorite quote to me was "If the Lord says the same." (Sounds familiar?)

I didn't really know when to stop when came to drinking. I'd have a few cans of beer, but then because it was there, I'd drink until the beer was all gone. Sometimes I wondered how my children ever made it out of the hell they saw their mother go through with their father, and now watching me on such a self-destructive path. What I didn't realize was that it was all about the choices I was making.

I was totally bent on trying to regain everything that James had taken from me. I wanted power...I wanted to be in control! I felt I had to be lowdown and dirty to men, just like James was to me. I was like a wounded, wild angry female in heat and on the prey. Like the old folks would say 'a dangerous Jezebel just got lose after being locked up'. I was nothing nice at all!

Section 197
After twenty years, we meet again.

My life had been going just great for me. I had everything that I wanted—the fast life, easy money and the freedom to go as I please. But, deep in my heart, something was missing and I had no idea what it was.

One evening I was on the bus going home and Tyra and my brother's wife were with me. My brother had gotten married while he was in jail, doing a twenty-year bit. I noticed a man getting on the bus. He had on a green and black jacket. I recognized his face, but I had no idea from where.

"Do you know that man? I mean, have you seen him somewhere before?"

"No, Ma, I never seen him before."

"I haven't neither. What, you owe somebody some money?" my sister-in-law teased and we laughed.

"Shut up, nah. I have seen his face from somewhere before."

Then, out of the blue, "Debra Dent, old Debra Dent!" he shouted walking towards me with this great smile on his face.

Okay, where does he know me from? It has to be from Parkside because nobody knows me by that name here in Milwaukee.

"Hey, how are you?" I replied, still trying to figure out who he was.

"Piggie! You don't remember me?"

"Yeah, I do. Hey!

"What you doing up here in Milwaukee? You live here?"

"I do. This is my daughter Tyra, and this is my brother's wife."

"Oh yeah, damn! How's ole Chuckie doing? I thought I heard he was dead."

"Nah, you ain't heard nothing like that. He's in jail, but will be coming out soon."

This conversation went on for the whole ride home. As we talked, I was checking him out and he was doing the same thing to me. 'Nice looking, he is that!' I thought. And he talked like he had game. He knows me from Parkside which means we have some history together. He might be worth checking out. I gave him my phone number and told him to give me a call when he get some time.

"You married yet, I don't see a ring?"

"Nah, been there, done that. I'm divorced, just me and my kids at the house."

"Yeah, I'm divorce also, but I'm up here visiting my daughter. Her mother lives off of 87th Street. That's where I'll be."

"Well, I don't want to get in between nothing, but stop by if you can. I'm having a card party at my house this Saturday. You are more than welcome to come and bring your girl with you—giving him a sly look."

"I got you, I'll be there. And do I need to bring something?

"Nah, just bring yourself. I got everything you gonna need." He got off on 87th street and we went on to 107th street.

"What, you are flirting now?" asked Tyra with a grin.

"Man, I'm just trying to see what he's working with. I just invited him to the party, that's all."

The weekend came and the party was on. Brenda was there and the kids had a few of their friends over. It was a party for them, too. I had gone to the store to get more beer when Piggie arrived.

"Who is that, Debbie? He's nice looking?"

"What? Who is who? putting the bags down on the table. "Hey, Piggie!"

"Hey, Debra, let me talk to you for a minute," with this suspicious look on his face. We went into the bathroom.

"What's up?"

"You know all these people in your house? You know how we play it in Chicago. Girl, you ain't supposed to have all these niggas in your house and you not at home. What's up with all this?"

"Yeah, baby, you ain't got to worry about them. Brenda Potts is here, the kids and these are my kid's friends. The card players ain't even got here yet. That's sweet of you to look out for me like that. I got this. Ain't no motherfucker gonna try nothing up in here. But, come here," as I pulled him closer to me, "do you mind if I give you a kiss for being so nice?"

"Nah, I mean, yeah, you can kiss me if that's what you want to do."

"Oh, yeah? You gonna let me do what I want?"

361

"Whatever makes you happy!?" I gave him a kiss like he never had before. "Make you wanna come back for mo!!" People were coming in, so we exited the bathroom.

I greeted them all, "What's up, everybody! You ready to get this party started?"

"Yeah! Debbie, you gonna be my partner?"

"Brenda, I'm gonna see what Piggie got."

"Piggie? That's his name? That's funny! What kinda name is that? Piggie! I mean, what's yo name yo mama give you at birth? What's your real name? We all laughed.

"Ronald is my name. People call me Piggie."

"Oh, okay then, Ronald. I'll call you Ronald. I ain't calling you no Piggie. Where you get a name like that from? You from Chicago, too? Come on, let's play some cards. I'm just messing with you."

"Don't pay Brenda no mind! That's my friend. She don't mean no harm."

"Let's see if you know how to play cards, Piggie. I mean Ronald," as she laughed and shuffled the cards.

"Hand me a beer."

"I got you, baby." I like him.

"Come on and put your money where your mouth is. I see you like to talk a lot of shit! Debra, how long have you been knowing her?"

"Hey, let's play."

Section 198

He's fun to be around and he makes me laugh.

We had fun that evening. Ronald had to leave at a certain hour since he was staying with someone. From that night on, every weekend the card party was the same. We all had fun and it was pretty much the same people that

362

came over to play. Ronald knew how to play bid whiz! He even helped me brush me up on my game. I hadn't played that in years.

Ronald couldn't believe and was somewhat amazed about how I really had things under control, as a single mother—even with all these people in my house.

He came by just about every day after that whenever he wasn't in Chicago. We began to share our intimate stories and secrets from our past relationships. I saw him on weekends because now he was making trips back and forth to Chicago. He was still living with his little girl's mother and experiencing a whole lot of drama, as he said. I didn't want to get involved. I began to have feelings for him and I tried to fight it because I never felt like before.

We both worked at Labor Ready for some quick cash. You know, work-same-day cash. I didn't go into work this one particular day, but instead went to Ronald's job dressed sharp as hell, driving my black short-body Cadillac. I had on a brown pants suit with my long brown suede coat with the fur lining and the matching wide-brim hat.

"Hey, you! Ronald! What they paying you for the day? How much you gonna get?

"What you say?"

"You heard me. How much you making for the day working here?" as I pulled out my money looking at him laughing.

"Forty-five dollars."

"Here. You just been bought! Come on and go with me, I got something for you."

"Are you serious?"

"What you think, I'm playing with you? Here's something a little extra for yourself," and I gave him more money. "Let's go."

"I'm outta here!" he told his co-workers.

That day was awesome! We had so much fun. It was all on me, but it was worth every penny. He was so much fun. He kept me laughing and I never knew what he was going to say next. I did find out that he loves to work and help around the house. He knew how to fix stuff. He loved to fish. And…he didn't hit women! We got that straight real quick.

Then something happened between him and his baby mama, so I told him to come and stay with me.

Section 199

He's a challenge! I love a challenge!

I was not ready to settle down. I had just gotten out of a cage and was not going to be put back into one—by no man. But, it was something about these feelings that I was having for him I couldn't explain.

Ronald had some issues going on back in Chicago; he still had feelings for the woman he was with previously and he hadn't let those feelings go yet. He said he wanted to give it one last shot with her and if she didn't want to be with him, then we would be able to move on with our relationship and his life.

I had been to Chicago with him and met his family. Oh, my God what a big family! I thought James had a big family—Ronald's was bigger! Later that night, we sat around getting high and drinking, of course. I was smoking my primos and he was smoking the pipe.

He agreed that none of his previous relationships worked out because of his drug use. I saw something beyond that. It was clear to me that he was a good man, but I didn't want to change my thinking when it came to a man, nor let go of the different men that I was holding on to. But, I knew in my heart that there was something I liked about him. I just couldn't put my finger on it at the time. I recalled my Nana telling me that he was a good man, and I would be a damn fool to let him go.

Out of the blue one day, Brenda said, "Debbie, that's gonna be your husband, you gonna marry him."

"I don't think so."

That was the farthest thing from my mind and his, too. We both had just gotten out of really bad relationships and he wanted to see if his last relationship could work out. He was willing to put aside the fact that she was sleeping with a guy down the street from his mother's house. He saw the car that he was paying for parked outside, knowing that she was sleeping with another man.

He said that's what sent him to the drugs even more, knowing she was a cheating, lying, manipulative, crazy motha…let him tell it. He claimed his family never liked or accepted her. Hell, she either wants you or she doesn't!

I used to tell him all the time, "It don't matter to me. I really didn't think it was gonna go as far as it did. Hell, if they don't want you, just bring your ass back and I'll keep you, but we gonna get this straight first thing in the morning!"

I saw something that they were throwing away and it was gonna be for my good, at least that's what my Nana said. I had a plan.

Section 200

Drinking and drugging was my out!

This was our plan: The next day I bought him a new outfit. I dressed him from head to toe—suit, shoes, everything. I cleaned him up real good, like a new shiny penny. We went to Chicago to his mother's and I gave him one hundred dollars.

"Now, go over there and let her see how good you look. If she decides to take you back, then you'll have your answer. We both will know." I laughed as I reached out to kiss him and he headed for the door. "Hey, just remember, I love you with all your faults, no matter what. Now, go to her, and dig this, that bitch is crazy as hell if she don't take you back!"

We laughed and then he was gone, gone to be with someone that he says didn't want him anymore. I remember thinking 'Oh well, if he's for me, Lord, bring him back. And if he's not, then let that bitch keep him as far away from me as possible.'

"Hey, let's go get some more beer, I'm paying. Let the party begin!" as I walked back into his mother's the house.

In my heart, I was hoping he would come back to me, but I didn't want to show him how much I cared because I didn't want to get hurt again. We've been together for over a year now.

By the way, she sent him back to me! They say a person's garbage is another one's treasure...And treasure he is...Stupid b...!

We were getting high almost every day, you know, functional addicts. Ronald was a truck driver, so having a good job came easy for him, and he didn't mind helping me with anything around the house.

My girls really didn't care for him. Let me explain... They didn't like that we stayed in the bedroom all the time getting high off of crack cocaine, and my drinking had gotten even worse. Some kind of way I convinced myself that drinking beer leveled out the primos. So, the more I smoked, the more I had to drink. They thought that he was the one supplying me with the drugs, but he wasn't. I was buying it—he went and got it for me.

I would send him to pick up the stuff from the dope man. He started keeping a bag on the side, not being honest about how much he got. That used to piss me off because I'm the one paying for it, and he wants to steal from me?! Man, a crack head ain't no joke! Believe me, I know. I was a primo smoker, not a crack head! *Really?* I had the nerve to look down on him as if I was doing better than he was.

Anyway, Tyra got pregnant at sixteen from her first time. She fought me tooth and nail to have an abortion! I pleaded with her not to do it because I knew what it felt like! I didn't want her to have any regrets when she got older. She was adamant about going to school, to college and she didn't want anything to stop her, she was only sixteen years old.

"Please, Tyra don't kill the baby. Mommie will take care of it and you can go to school. You won't have to do anything at all for the baby from buying pampers to milk, clothes, nothing! I will do it all, just don't get rid of the baby. Give the baby to me, you can go to school."

That reminded me so much of what Mack's mother said to me.

She had the baby and gave him to me. She named him Notorious James, and I took care of him as if he were my own.

There I was with a new baby and my four children at home. Tyra went off to college and now we have Ronald's daughter staying with us because she had run away from home.

Now keep in mind—the drinking, card parties and getting high never stopped. Oh, don't let me forget, my cousin from Chicago on my daddy side came to one of our cookouts, and she never went home. Yep, she and her son moved in with us, too. We welcomed them with open arms.

My brother wanted to keep close tabs on his wife, so he asked could she stay with me. He gave me some sad story about she needed help to get back on her feet. Sure, why not? The more the merrier!

She became more of friend, you know, a get-high partner rather than my sister-in-law. That worked out pretty good for the both of us and we kept it from my brother.

Wait! Not done! I failed to mention the two rebellious children of Ronald's from Chicago. They joined the tribe, too!

We now have thirteen people and a dog, Coco, living in a four bedroom house! Don't ask me how we did it, but we did!

We had to deal with jealousy among the children, but we decided early on that we wouldn't let any of our children or family member come between us. So, we made a vow not to waver, to stand firm and strong and not let them divide us.

During this time, I was so caught up in taking care of my grandbaby. I put my own children on the back burner. I was so determined not to make the same mistakes with this baby that I had made with my children, but I took it too far.

For example, his first Christmas was just for him—I didn't buy my children much at all. My grandbaby had everything that a baby could use or need at his age—a walker, bike, playpen, etc. Whatever I thought I wanted him to have, I bought! Maxed out all my credit cards!

Section 201

You can never see what's in front of you if you're looking back!

It took time for me to let go of all my bad habits and Ronald hung in there with me through it all. I had to let go of things like talking to these two guys that were in jail, my brother's associates and the jail house lawyer/drug dealer that I was considering marrying at one time. I was still looking for love in all the wrong places, but came to realized that the jailhouse lawyer was only placed in my life to help me get the divorce from James.

The other guy was calm and easy going. I talked more on the phone with him when things got too much for me to handle. I had to let them go. I actually had the perfect person right there with me, willing to place my head on his shoulders and wrap his arms around me. I still didn't see that Ronald was 'the one'.

Ronald asked me over and over not to take calls from my male friends, but I didn't feel like he had the right to ask that of me. I told him that it was my phone, my house and I paid the bills, so I could do whatever I wanted. I just couldn't see him telling me what to do when I had been on my own for so long and he was just coming into the picture. At the time, I didn't realize I was disrespecting him which made it easier for my children to disrespect him, as well.

I went through a lot with his baggage of two baby mamas' drama. Taking care of his kids, which really wasn't a problem, but it was something that I had never done. It was still all new to me, and everybody was all in my space—a space I didn't want to give up completely.

I thought I would be giving away my power to yet another ma; a power that I hadn't fully understood how to control.

Ronald finally got fed up with my jailhouse friends and their phone calls, so he decided to move out. I didn't take him seriously until he packed his clothes and told me he had gotten an apartment. I thought he just needed some space. I was relieved because he wouldn't be around to complain about the calls. And besides, I wasn't sure that I was ready to settle down because of the hurt that I had been through. Hell, he said the same thing, so what's the difference? His baby mamas didn't want him, but I had plenty of men that wanted me.

I thought Ronald's move would actually be good for me. I felt like I needed the space and figured I could see him on my terms. As time passed, I realized how wrong I was. I missed him so much; his laughter, his smile and the way he held me close as we slept. I even missed his smelly socks when he kicked off his work boots!

We soon decided that enough was enough, and it was time for us to move back together! "If we were going to move forward and be together, we have to move into a place that would be ours."

Ronald agreed, "I don't care I just know that I want you in my life."

369

"And I want you in mine. I've wanted you since Parkside." We both laughed.

Ronald moved back into the house, but we looked for a new place that we could call ours. We knew we would have to downsize, but we didn't care; we just wanted to be together. That meant going from a three level, four bedroom house to a two bedroom apartment.

We had come a long way with the kids and I was glad they had finally started to come around. Early on, Tyra had tried to get one of her boyfriends to jump Ronald because she thought he was the reason I was getting high. The twins never wavered when it came to Ronald; they liked him and never wanted me to be with anyone else.

Ronald came into the relationship not only wanting to be with me, but hoping to bond with my children, too. They began to see that.

I have done some really dumb things in my life. I almost lost my man that I know God had blessed me with. The man that could make that fairy tale dream come true. *I allowed my past to come back into my life. I open the door and invited Satan in!* Yes! I let James come to the house after all this time!

Don't ask me why, but he wanted to see the kids. To be honest, I think I allowed him to come over because I wanted to see if anything had changed. I had deep feelings for Ronald and before I could really let myself go and give him my heart, I guess I had to make sure that it was truly over between James and me. I had to be sure that I didn't have any sick, corrupted feelings still lingering around deep down, imbedded in my heart for him, and the only way I figured I could do this was to come face to face with that demonic spirit itself!

THAT'S WHAT HAPPEN!

Wow, this is the first time that I really was honest with myself—right here, right now as I write. Being a damn fool is what I was doing, going back to my old habits that I never had control over. Please be the jack-ass that I know you are, so that I can validate my love for Ronald and move on with my life!

This was all new to me—realizing that I could control my own feelings, thus my life. That loving someone with all your heart is fine, but you must have trust and honesty. I had just broken that between Ronald and me.

That was a kick in the face to my best friend, my man that has been there for me all this time. He helped me with bills and my children, fixed things around the house, loved and cared for me, showed and gave me respect, never put his hands on me, and I must say, got high and drank with me. My partner.

I literally kicked him to the garage, not the curb. He stayed in the garage for two or three days getting high, trying to smoke away the pain of James being in his house with me, where he should have been.

He stayed there by his own choice in hopes that I would come to my senses. He was in so much pain, but he couldn't move because he didn't want to leave me.

That was a hurt that took years to overcome for him, and all the trust that I had gained with him went straight out the window.

The twins stayed close by him; they never left his side. They made sure that Ronald knew that they did not agree with my decision and that it was the girls' idea, not theirs. They took food and blankets to Ronald to make him comfortable. They could not understand why I would do something like this—to Ronald. Yet, my children were happy at the thought of seeing their father. It had been a few years since they last saw him.

Once James was in the house, the wolf took off those sheep clothing, and the horns came out, again! He slapped me, only to see if he still had

371

control and if the fear was still there! It was not! I pulled a knife out! The twins heard the slap from the next room and, they came out in force saying, "Not today! You're not gonna hit our mother no more!"

I got rid of him, and never, ever looked back at that wolf. Did you know that you can invite Satan into your home and all hell will break loose? You got to plead the Blood of Jesus throughout your home and be mindful of who you let come in. That was a scary situation, but I held on to my power and the demon had to flee! Not today, or any other day in the near future, will I surrender it again. I had and made a choice that day!

Ronald went back to Chicago with his mother. I had to explain, tell him how sorry I was and that I didn't mean to hurt him.

When I looked in his eyes, I saw a reflection of me. I saw hurt, pain, humiliation, unbelief and worst of all, I felt his withdrawal from me.

I knew what pain looked like because I had been through it just a few years ago. It hurt me so deeply, deep down in my soul and spirit to see the pain I caused. I never would want anyone to feel the hurt that James had put me through and here I was doing the same thing. I was no better than James; I just did it in a different way.

"Listen, I don't want to lose you, but it's really hard for me to trust men. I need you to show me how to trust you, how to love you."

I explained that I wanted to be with him, but I needed him to meet me half way.

"It's hard for me, too, Debra, because of the cheating I went through in my last relationship. I don't know how to deal with that, so I run from my problem instead of facing it. We both got some work to do."

We agreed to work it out because we loved each other that much. We realized that it was best to find somewhere else to live. This house held too many memories from my past.

Section 202

We got married.

Ronald and I have been through some storms together, and we made it! Oh, God, we couldn't have made it without your grace and mercy! We got married, promising that we wouldn't cheat or lay hands on each other and that we will trust and be honest with one another. We both had been down that path and weren't willing to turn back.

Our wedding day was on Tyra's birthday, Valentine's Day. It was to remind her every year that her birthday was no longer cursed. Instead, it will always be a day that we will cherish, just like the day I was blessed with my first child! My dreams have finally come true!

As time passes, Ronald and I realized the drinking, drugging and partying every weekend wasn't the life we wanted. It went from a everybody's party to our party. Ronald's older brother Lem and his girl Cynthia had been clean for many years and was doing everything they could to set a good example for us.

Lem would always say, *"Pig and Deb, once you get sick and tired of being sick and tired, along with the people, places and things, ain't nothing going to change in your life. When it's that time, you won't even try and stop, you'll just STOP! Keep praying, Deb and Pig. You know we love you and we are here whenever you need us."*

"We know. Thank you."

I started having severe, unbearable migraine headaches whenever we were getting high, at least that's when I really began to take note. We got high every day—we couldn't and wouldn't stop. When I got that check on the first of the month, I paid all the bills and bought plenty of food with my food stamps. Any extra was for my beer and we blew it up in smoke...puff-puff-pass!

373

I wonder does anyone know what that feels like, you know, the taste, the craving. "I promise just one mo'…then I'll stop…" Have you ever heard that before?

I would stop for a while just to let the headaches subside, and then that demon jumped on my shoulder and whispered in my ear, 'You did it. See, you can stop whenever you want to. Now, let's go get 'just one mo'…'

My children never wanted for anything at all. I bought and gave them what they wanted as opposed to what they needed. I'm certain I was trying to make up for all the things that their father took from them and sold.

You can't buy your children's love. You must spend time with them, listening and teaching. I thought that I had learned that from the relationship with my mother. Evidently, I didn't get it. I wasn't ready. At the time, all I knew and wanted was Gimpy beer and puff-puff pass.

A year or more went by and the same thing was going on. We couldn't shake those monkeys off our backs called alcohol and crack cocaine. We had a tiger by the tail and didn't know how to let it go. We were lost in the pit of destruction and became our worse enemy. Then, after a three-day binge, my head was hurting so bad that I couldn't get out of bed. All I could do was cry because of the pain.

I cried out to God for help. "Lord, I can't do this anymore! I confess to you, my Lord Jesus, that I'm not strong enough to beat this drug and alcohol on my own. I need your help.

"Lord, I know the devil is trying to kill me, but you didn't bring me out of all what I've been through just for me to go out like this! Please help me, Lord. Don't let my words go unheard. Whatever you want me to do, I'll surrender, Lord. I truly surrender! Take the desire for drugs and alcohol away from me. Whenever I'm around smoke, make it feel like my airway is closing up! Every time I drink a beer or any other type of alcohol, I will get sick to my stomach." *God answer prayers. Stop playing with God! Stop playing with your life!*

Ronald went to get some more crack cocaine. When he came back, I told him I'd had enough and couldn't do it anymore. He looked into my eyes and saw that I was serious.

"Okay, right after I do this last bag, and take this hit, I'm gonna stop, too. I'm tired of this shit!"

A few days passed and it seemed like things were going good. We both knew our drugging and drinking wasn't going to stop until we did something about it.

The kids were glad to see us making an effort to stop. They would say stuff like, "Mama, I'm glad you're not drinking," or "Ronald, you look good; we're glad to see you sober."

Ronald and I both wanted to believe that we were on our way to a better life, but we still found ourselves drawn to the same people, places and things.

I had a new job working for an optician and things started to look up. I was doing so much more with my life and I felt better than I had in a very long time. Still, I couldn't shake the alcohol or the drugs.

The job only gave us more money to get high. We were bringing in $3,200.00 plus Ronald's check. We could maintain our home and be functional addicts at the same time. We would go to Chicago every weekend. That way, we could get high and not be around the kids, in the house.

I would take Notorious with us because it was so many other kids his age to play with. We pretty much stayed on the lower level at his sister's place, which was the grand central get-high spot.

Just one mo' bag... We didn't have to go anywhere; they sold it and we all used it! Crack cocaine and alcohol are no joke and have no respect for anyone. They do not discriminate! They are tools that Satan uses to destroy the best of us—if you happen to fall and decide to play his game. I'm here to tell you, DON'T PLAY THE GAME!! It's a trap! Oh, not unless you call yourself an occasional user! Yeah, right!

I became very close to Ronald's mother, in part because I had lost my mother. I couldn't go around my Nana in the condition that I was in, so I clung to Mama Bell. She had the biggest heart that I have ever known. She was even kinder than my Nana and Mama Angie in certain ways.

She would feed any and every one who was hungry. It was almost like a miracle going on in her kitchen. She didn't have much, but if she could help you, she would. Mama Bell wasn't a fool either. She knew that the people she fed were on drugs and/or homeless. She knew that we were downstairs at her daughter's apartment getting high, but she never said a word. She kept her door unlock and didn't fear any one.

On Sundays, everybody knew that the meal was cabbage and with potatoes, fried chicken and cornbread. She would scoop endlessly servings on to a plate. The food kept coming until everyone was fed.

Section 203
There will never be another Mama Bell.

Ronald's mother became very ill. She had lung cancer and never smoked a day in her life. The second-hand smoke killed her.

Before Mama Bell died, she told us both, *"A drug addict and an alcoholic will never make it. You both will have to work on your issues if you really wanted to be together. I know that you are meant to be with one another, but love will not be enough. You have to get your acts together first."*

She asked me to take her son Tennessee with us when we moved, to get him out of Chicago, and we promised that we would.

376

Mama Bell

We were there when she went to the hospital, but we left to go get another bag. "We'll be back," we said. She died before we made it back. We never really said goodbye!

We love you and miss you dearly, Mama Bell—my sweet ole Sadie!

Section 204

A new start

We decided shortly after her death that it was time to move. There was too much holding us back—a lot of hurt and pain from both our past that we didn't know how to let go. Whenever we were around others, it was like we were sad and looking for comfort, which meant more alcohol and drugs.

We decided to move down south, but couldn't figure out exactly where we wanted to go. We pulled names of cities and states to see where our new life was going to begin. We didn't care where, just as long as we were together.

It was bad enough that I could not shake these drugs, but now this cold weather was getting to me. It had gotten so cold that year that the temperature spent more time below zero than above, not to mention the knee-deep snow. I'd simply had enough! Winter was ending and I couldn't be happier.

"Where are we going? Do you know anybody who lives in Atlanta?"

"I got a cousin down there. Let me call him to see what he thinks about us moving there."

Ronald got in touch with his cousin who said he'd be more than happy for us to come to Atlanta and offered to let us stay with him and his girlfriend until we could get on our feet.

That was all I needed to hear. It finally seemed like there was hope. I told Ronald it was a blessing for us to move away from the people, places and things that have kept us connected to the drugs and alcohol. I felt like we wouldn't have to deal with the urges to get high once we removed ourselves from the temptation. Great! I was relieved that we had a plan.

Within days, I was gathering boxes to start packing. I told the twin boys we were moving to Georgia. They had two more years of high school and would finish up in Atlanta. They were the only kids still at home with us because the girls had moved out. Patrice was living across the street from our apartment and Ericka had her own place. Tyra was away at college and had taken Notorious with her.

I was so excited because I knew Ronald and I would be able to make it if we could get out of Milwaukee. We needed balance and stability and that's what this opportunity offered us.

It was the beginning of summer and the twins were out of school. Now, all we had to do was move to Atlanta, find jobs, a house and the twins would be able to start school in the fall.

My girls couldn't understand how I could just up and move and leave them behind. I figured since the boys spent most of their time across the street at Patrice's place, Ericka had her own apartment and Tyra was away at school, that there was no better time to make a fresh start.

That was it! It was going to be the start of a new life for me, for us. It was what I had been praying for! I gave a lot of my stuff to the girls and told the twins that they'd have to come to Atlanta with us to finish their last two years of high school.

"So, you're leaving us?"

"No, Tyrone. We need to find jobs and an apartment, and then I'll send for you and Jerome. You guys can stay with Patrice until we get everything worked out. This is it!"

Section 205

We're gonna make you proud, you'll see.

I explained that it was my chance to get my life together so I could be a better mother. I began to cry when I realized I would actually be leaving my children. I wondered what kind of mother would leave them, thinking that I was no better than their father James.

I felt like I was abandoning my babies at such a young age. I even wondered if I was leaving my children for Ronald. I realized I couldn't beat myself up about it; I was doing what was best for all of us.

"Sons, listen, look at it this way: Your sisters have children now and have moved on with their lives. It's time for me to go ahead and make this work for us. Mama needs to get you boys in a better environment. I need to be in a better environment!"

I continued, "What? Y'all don't want Mama to go? You don't think that if I move, it won't be for the best for us?"

"Oh no, that's not it," Jerome explained. "We want you to go and get a place for us. That's gonna be what's up living in the ATL.

"Yeah, Jerome it will be."

"Ma, we're just gonna miss you."

"I know, Tyrone. Mama gonna miss you all, too."

"We're moving to Atlanta!" they shouted. "That's what's up!" They both gave me a hug and whispered, "Mama, we love you. We know you can do it. You, too, Pops."

"Listen, all I ask is that y'all stay out of trouble while I'm gone. Don't do anything to get locked up because we'll be too far away to help you! Understand?"

"We not, Mama. Don't you worry, we straight."

"They will be okay. They will be with me."

"Thank you, Patrice. Give me a kiss."

"They gonna be with me, too. I'll make sure they little butts stay out of trouble!"

"I know you will, Ericka. You just make sure you stay out of trouble and be careful, as well. All you have is each other, so look out for one another. Remember my old saying, 'Never go against the grain, follow your first instinct, don't take no wooden nickels and stay out of harm's way.'"

They all said simultaneously, "All the time."

"All the time, Mama babies, all the time."

It was hard to believe this was moving day and we were loading up the truck. I was excited about moving to a new city and getting away from the people who we used to get high with. I knew in my heart that Ronald and I were doing the right thing. It seemed like we finally had a chance to make things work.

The move was going to bring us much closer because we only had each other to depend on. We were married and our love was strong enough to endure anything that came our way. Hell, after what we been through in our past, we were ready for anything.

I knew the kids were happy that Ronald and I were leaving because they wanted us to stop drinking and doing drugs, but sad because this was the first time that we have been separated.

I said a prayer for my kids and asked God to protect them and kept them safe until we were together again. I covered them with the Blood of Jesus because I knew the Lord would watch over them.

Ronald told the boys to look for out each other and to take care of their sisters.

"As soon as we get a place, we'll come back to get you so you can finish high school in Atlanta."

He hugged them both as he whispered, "You know I love you; it's gonna be all right. I'll get a job real quick so you guys can come home and be with us. We gonna pull it together! You'll see!"

"Be safe and I love you all," as we got in the truck.

I cried as we drove off, but they were tears of joy because I knew things were going to be different. I guess I was a little nervous about facing the unknown, but I was happy about the idea of a life free of pain and drugs and alcohol. I looked over at Ronald driving,

"Well, what do you think? We're going to do this and we will make it. right?"

"Baby, as long as we have each other, we will make it." And he kissed me.

All I needed was a little reassurance and he gave it to me. We were towing our car behind the U-Haul truck. We had about $2,500.00 in cash to get started. I gave the kids $75.00 each and told them I would send more once we got settled in.

Section 206

We fell for the Okie-doke! Just one mo'!

We decided to stop in Chicago to visit the rest of the family and let them know we were on our way, but the tables turned once we got to there.

We let our guards down and allowed our friends and family to talk us into celebrating our trip by getting high…one last time!

We should have known that one bag was going to lead to more, but we figured just one mo' bag for the road was no big deal. So, we gave in, knowing that we really wanted to get that last primo, that last hit. Just one mo'—that's all.

Soon, the beer and alcohol was flowing and one bag of dope led to a couple of eight balls that we even tried to sell, and everybody knows 'monkeys can't sell bananas.'

We must have spent at least $1,000 getting high over a three-day span. Yes, we got stuck in Chicago after blowing so much money getting high like damn fools. Ronald even sold his shotgun and I sold our bedroom set to get some of the money back that we had spent. We were getting down to dust.

By the third day, I'd finally had enough. "Come on baby, let's go. This isn't what we planned to do! We're spending all of our money, selling shit off the truck, and at the rate we are going, we not going to have enough to make it to Atlanta. Look, nobody cares or gives a damn if we go to Atlanta or not because we're buying this shit! Look at us, the kids are counting on us, and my head feels like it's killing me! It hurt so bad, I got to lie down for a while!"

"You're right, Debra. It's time to go."

The next morning, Ronald was still being called by that just-one-mo' bag. I knew he really didn't want to leave because he had already bought more crack cocaine.

"This is the last bag. When I come down off this, we are going to leave. I promise."

The kids were sure we had made it to Atlanta and called to see why they hadn't heard from us. When I told them we stopped in Chicago to say goodbye to friends and family, they immediately started in on me.

"I thought you were trying to change! Chicago is the last place y'all need to be," Tyra yelled."

"Why are you still in Chicago? It's going on three days now!" Tyrone shouted.

"Mommy, why are you doing this to yourself?" asked Patrice.

My brother was still locked up and he even called to ask what the fuck was wrong with me. He told me he felt like the slip up was Ronald's fault.

"He should have been the real man that you needed! It was his place to take control of the situation, but he did what he wanted to do!"

"Hey, don't go there! It's both our fault and we got this! Worry about your own life! I have a real bad headache and I do not want to talk right now! We are leaving today! You can't blame Ronald for nothing that I do, it's on me. I'm smoking the primos because I want to, not that he's making me!"

Ronald finally realized I was right and it was time for us to leave. We both saw ourselves living to get high and I knew if we could just get away from the people, places and things here in Chicago, we would be free.

Section 207

We got sick and tired of being sick and tired!

That one more bag kept calling our name… Just one mo'bag!

When he showed signs of coming down off that high, we had to leave right then.

"We could always pull into a rest area, baby, to get some rest if we needed to. Come on, we got to get out of here. At least, we will be on our way." I was surprised and relieved when he agreed, reluctantly.

We were practically running to the truck as we said our goodbyes. We both realized we had to get out of there before we were tempted to get one more bag. If we did, we knew it would be over!

There was an awkward silence in the truck as we drove away. We both were ashamed that we had spent so much money getting high and we almost let drugs and alcohol derail our plans for a better life. If we had stuck to the plan, it would have put us in Atlanta two days ago with a lot more money in our pockets!

The drive gave us plenty of time to talk about what happened.

"I'm sorry, baby. You know how I am when I get started on that stuff," Ronald apologized.

"I was right there with you and I could have said no, but I didn't. Let's just look at it as a blessing that we got out of there when we did,"

"How much money do we have left?"

I really didn't want to count it because I didn't want to be reminded how close the reckless binge in Chicago came to ruining our plans.

After counting the money, I sighed, "We got nine hundred left."

"Damn, we really messed up this time!"

"Do you think this will be enough money to make it there?"

"Yeah, baby, we ain't got no other choice. I messed up so I'm gotta fix it. You know I'll get a job. I gotta take care of you. Don't even think about it, we gonna make it. Do you believe and trust in me?"

"I do, you know that. I'm going to get a job, too. We're gonna be alright," as I patted him on the leg.

He held my hand and declared in a strong voice, "It will be alright, okay?!"

"I know it will! Hell, we can't do nothing about what just happened. We are on our way to bigger and better things! Watch! God got something for us! What it is, I don't know, but it will be alright!" We both laughed.

About halfway through Indiana, we pulled into a rest area for a bathroom break and to catch a little shuteye. We had only planned to take a little catnap, but those few minutes lasted six hours. That shouldn't have been a surprise just coming off a three-day binge.

It had to be eight or nine that night by the time we woke up, so we hit the road again. The night driving didn't bother Ronald because he was used to it since he was a truck driver.

We were pulling over throughout the night because Ronald was so tired that he could hardly keep his eyes open. I can't drive at night, so that left all the driving to him.

"I'll drive once the sun came up."

"I know, baby, I got it. We just have to keep stopping."

I called to let the kids know we had left Chicago and was on our way to Atlanta. They were pleased to hear that, but you could still hear the disappointment in their voices. That hurt more than anything. At that point, I was determined to make my children proud of me.

We told each other all of our darkest secrets as we drove to Georgia. I felt like we were in a world all to ourselves; some place where two people were forced to test their love for each other. I was so glad we passed the test. We may have suffered at the hands of one another, but not to the point where we would want to end it. Those tough times made us stronger and our marriage stronger.

I got out a piece of paper and began to write.

"What are you writing?"

"Well, for many of years I've been writing down different things that have happened to me on scratch paper. When I shared some of the stuff that happened to me with different people, they would always say, 'What book you get that out of? That's good. Who wrote that? You should put that in a book.' So I'm writing down what we just went through."

"Oh, yeah? You never know, you might write a book."

"You right, I just might do that cause I sure do have a lot to tell. You never know, what I went through might just help somebody if I put it in a book."

"You never know until you try." I kept writing.

When daylight came, I was able to drive so Ronald could get a little more sleep. The scenery was awesome—the trees were full of beautiful green leaves and you could even see the mountains as we drove through them. It was simply beautiful. I was a little uneasy driving around those curvy roads going through Tennessee, but I held it together.

Section 208

We made it to Georgia. Thank God!

When we made it to the state of Georgia, Ronald decided to drive. It was hard to believe what should have been a twelve-hour drive had become a 22-hour trip! You could smell the cocaine, alcohol and musk coming out of our pores as we drove, but we didn't care. It didn't matter because we had each other and that was all we cared about. We knew we would be in Atlanta in a matter of minutes! We made it, thank God, we made it!

Once we were in Atlanta, we pulled over for gas and directions. We knew we were not that far away. It turned out that we were right where we needed to be. Ronald needed to take a leak, so he said he was going to the restaurant next door to see if they would let him use the restroom.

I figured it was a long shot, but I went with him just to see if they were hiring. I used my fingers to push my hair back into my cap, and took the end of my shirt and wiped my teeth off.

When we walked in, I noticed that they were short of help. I took it as a sign and asked the manager if he was short-handed.

He seemed a little surprised by the question, as he looked me up and down.

"My name is Debra and we just got off the highway. Me and my husband are moving here. That's our U-Haul parked right outside," as I pointed toward the window. "I hope you don't mind me saying, sir, but I see that you're busy and you're shorthanded.

"I have experience waiting on tables and I am great with customers, and my customer service skills are outstanding. I need a job like yesterday! Our family member lives about a mile away from here. I can go and freshen up, come back and help you out. What time would you like me to be back here?"

Man, I was talking fast! All that smack I talked in Milwaukee, I had to put it to use here! And it worked!

The manager looked at me and said, "You know what? I can tell you know how to sell yourself just by the way you approached me. You know how to go after what you want and that is just what I am looking for. You think two hours is enough time for you to come back and start the evening shift?"

It was a struggle to control my excitement as I reached out to shake his hand.

"Yes, sir, I'll be back! You won't be sorry! Thank you!"

I couldn't believe it! Thank you, Lord! We were just driving into Atlanta and I already got a job. Damn, I'm good! I couldn't wait to tell Ronald! I did all of that before he even got out the restroom! I got a J-O-B!

"Baby, guess what? I just got myself a job!" Ronald couldn't believe that I had talked myself into a job so easily.

"It is going to be good down here! That's good luck!"

"Hell, that ain't no luck! That's a blessing."

He seemed really happy as we climbed in the truck. I couldn't believe it! We had money coming in already! I got a job! I was sure things would be okay from that point on.

When we arrived at Ronald's cousin's house, we were glad to see him and he was really happy to see us.

"Hey, man, good to see you! Guess what? Debra done got a job right up there at the little restaurant! See, we came down here straight on business!"

"Hey, where's the bathroom at? I need to wash up and change my clothes." I was so excited about my new job!

Ronald unhitched the car and took me back to the job. It was only six blocks away. At first, I was leery about the environment that his cousin was living in, but I didn't give it a second thought since I now had a job!

I only worked four hours that night. I called for Ronald to come pick me up. When I got in the car, I could tell that he was high. I didn't want to believe it, but when we got to the apartment, that's exactly what they had been doing.

Ronald's cousin was so happy to see him that he bought some crack to celebrate. A free high is the worst high ever! That's when you start hearing things like 'just one mo' bag'! The problem with that was now Ronald was spending our money.

388

The first thing I thought was, *'What a jackass!'* We were already in the hole. I'm out trying to make money to replace the cash we blew in Chicago and Ronald's cousin is encouraging him to get high. He really didn't go overboard with it, because he was tired and all he wanted to do was go to sleep. And besides, the crack that Ronald's cousin bought was garbage anyway.

What the hell *'just one mo' bag'* won't hurt. I just got a job, we can afford it. Now, here's *two jackasses—dumb and dumber!*

Ronald and I went to bed, but he kept getting up to look out the window checking on the truck.

The next day, his cousin's phone was cut off. That was a problem because Ronald could not receive calls about jobs. The third day, their lights were turned off!

"What the hell is really going on up in this motherfucker?!"

"It's time to go!" That was it. Ronald knew we had to go. We couldn't stay there any longer.

Ronald called his friend Eddie C back in Chicago. He had a sister who lived down here. Ronald told Eddie C that we left Milwaukee, and what was going on. We needed help, right now.

"Do you think your sister could put us up until we got on our feet?"

"I'll call you back, man. Let me make a phone call. I got to holler at old girl and I will hit you back up."

Of course, I thought he was just brushing us off. I wasn't expecting to hear from him, so I was shocked when the phone rang a few minutes later.

"Man, I talked to my sister and she wants you to give her call. She feels bad about your situation so she and her husband are gonna let y'all stay there until you get on your feet." I couldn't believe it! They said we could stay with them.

389

I had to let that job go, but that was not for us. I was relieved that we were able to move out of Ronald's cousin's house. I was grateful that he invited us into his home, but we were no longer on that page anymore. We couldn't keep giving in to the people, places and things that were blocking our progress. The same things that we were running from were in Atlanta, waiting for us. It was up to us to control our lives because crack cocaine and alcohol are everywhere. We couldn't run from it.

What we realized was that we will never win at that game. So, the best way to win is don't play the game! We are just one bag away from 'just one mo'! One can of beer, away from a never-ending binge. We chose not to play the game! Ask yourself, why play?!

The man had given me fifty dollars just for those four hours I worked, so I was good. We moved out to Riverdale, a suburb south of Atlanta. The area was much nicer, cleaner and safer than where Ronald's cousin lived. Eddie C's sister Ly'Pattie had a beautiful home and she allowed us to stay in her finished basement.

Being with Ly'Pattie and her family was the best thing that could ever happen to us. She and her husband were wonderful people. They only asked us to pay the phone bill, so we could save money to get our own place. I'm sure they didn't want us living there any longer than we had to. They probably wanted us there long enough to get jobs and move into our own place. We felt that was fair and really appreciated their help.

Section 209

You can only do so much for your children. Then, pray.

I got a job with the same optical company that I worked for in Wisconsin. We had a car, so Ronald would drop me off at work and sometimes Ly'Pattie or her husband would pick me up.

We realized we were running out of time because we hadn't gotten a place yet and school was starting soon.

While we were living there, Ly'Pattie gave me a book to read. The name of the book was 'Woman, Thou Art Loosed' by T.D. Jakes. I couldn't put it down. Actually, that was the first book that I ever read in its entirety. I was so moved while reading the book that I stopped smoking cigarettes. .

Within two months of moving to Atlanta, we were doing well at work and had found a place to live. We were really happy because as much as we loved our new friends, we needed our own place. Ronald and I put our money together so we could get the house.

It was a three bedroom ranch house in a very nice neighborhood. It was nicer than anywhere we had lived in Milwaukee or Chicago. It was really nice.

Soon, the twins and one of Ronald's brothers came to live with us. All three of them got jobs at Burger King so they were able to help out with the expenses. We were doing pretty well and things were going great.

Jerome had problems in school and ended up going to an alternative school. He wore his brother's jacket to school one day, but didn't realize that there was a fingernail file in the pocket and they charged him with bringing a weapon to school. That was the last straw for Jerome and he ended up going back to Milwaukee during summer break to visit his sisters. His girlfriend was pregnant and he never came back. She gave him a son. He wanted to be with his baby boy and even though he was near the end of his senior year, he never finished high school.

By this time, Ronald's rebellious son came to live with us. We did everything we could to help him, but you can only help somebody who wants help. Ronald never gave up.

Tyrone had it hard in Atlanta, as well, but I was determined that at least one of the boys would finish high school. The day before Tyrone's graduation, Ronald's son rushed in shouting that the police had him in handcuffs! I ran like never before to go rescue my son!

When I got there, I saw my son on his knees in handcuffs. I asked what happened and the police told me they were taking him to jail for breaking into a vacant house where they caught him smoking marijuana and having sex with his girlfriend.

I pleaded with the police not to arrest him.

"Please don't take him to jail, sir! He's graduating from high school in the morning. Officer, I give you my word, you won't have any more problems out of my son."

Then I popped Tyrone in the back of his head and insisted that he apologize and promise not to get in anymore trouble.

I guess the officer felt sorry for me or he just got tired of my blubbering. Either way, he let Tyrone go with a warning.

"Say 'thank you' to the policeman, you damn fool!"

I kept thanking the officer over and over again as I hit Tyrone upside his head once more for good measure.

"That's okay, ma'am," the officer said. He turned to Tyrone, adding, "Just don't let me see you around these vacant houses again, young man. Do you understand?"

Tyrone respectfully muttered, "Yes, sir."

My heart was beating a mile a minute as we walked away. If the cop hadn't been so nice, Tyrone would have missed his graduation. I remember thinking, *Something's gotta change with these boys. I can't be stressed like this! They gonna have to learn the hard way. I can't do this anymore!'*

Later that year, Tyrone's girlfriend became pregnant. When her mother forced her to get an abortion, he decided he'd had enough of Atlanta and went back to Milwaukee to be with his brother and sisters.

We decided to let Ronald's son live with us since he was having too many issues in Chicago. We thought that by changing his people, place and things that it would help him. We had to learn the hard way that when you have a rebellious child, nothing is going to change, not unless that child wants it to. He was so rebellious and resentful to his father and me. He had to get his act together. If he didn't, he would be back in Chicago—in and out of jail—to live with his mother.

We decided to turn all of our children over to the Lord. Because of our own issues, we felt there was nothing we could do to help them. We was still fighting the battle of staying sober and clean without going back to the mess we were trying so hard to stay out of.

As time went on, Ronald and I started making friends who weren't into drugs and we realized staying sober was the right thing to do, and it felt so good!

If you want to make a change in your life, you must first have a made-up mind and remove yourself from the people, places and things. It really can work if you want it to.

I was still working at the optical place. Soon, I decided to go back to school, major in business administration and then take a real estate class. One of my instructors was an awesome motivational speaker. She tried to help me build my self-esteem and encouraged me to speak in front of a group of people.

I have never spoken before a group of people, no more than the ones who used to come to my card parties. She encouraged me in a lot of different ways. I even felt comfortable showing her some of the things that I had written down for my book.

"You should write a book. Someone will get a lot from this."

"Who would want to hear all of this mess?"

"Think about it, okay? Just think about it."

Now, it has been about six months since I'd had a drink. I decided to stop drinking beer because I was told I turn into a mean, cruel person who took a lot of bottled up stuff out on my dear husband. Well, I say he brought on or pulled that old person out of me with his flirtatious behavior.

Ronald and I started giving parties again—that was my specialty. We still get calls wondering when we gonna give the next one. I thought it wouldn't hurt to have a glass of wine since I hadn't had a beer in six months. You know, since beer was my drug of choice—a beer alcoholic—I figured that a small glass of wine wouldn't hurt anything.

Well, that glass of wine led to the whole bottle and soon I was back in my comfort zone drinking cases of beer.

I know the parties triggered it, and not to mention Ronald's flirtatious bullshit started up again. Yeah, he used to flirt and flaunt around woman, always wanting to be the center of attraction! It reminded me of when I was in heat back then!

Who am I fooling? It was me with the low self-esteem, consumed with a spirit of jealousy. That's a bad combination—alcohol, low self-esteem and insecurity, mixed with jealousy. Then, add a flirtatious husband. You got yourself a real live, fighting, ignorant, don't-give-a-damn bitch!

You never know what can happen when you're hanging out with friends and associates. It's funny now, but looking back on it, the situation was serious.

Section 210

She's my friend, and that's my husband. Was I wrong?

One night, we went bowling with a few friends and we were having drinks. Everything was fine until I noticed my husband paying my cute college instructor a little too much attention. He wasn't her type, so she didn't give him a second look. She thought Ronald was being his typical flirtatious self. She wasn't the type to cross the friendship line, anyway. So, I wasn't worried about her.

Well, my husband insisted on showing her how to hold the bowling ball. You know, get up all close on her. I just sat there watching the situation unfold as I continued to drink even faster, bottle after bottle! The more I drank, the tipsier I became.

Finally, I said, "Ronald, just let her bowl. The gutters are there for a reason! Just leave her alone!" (Jealousy!)

We had played two or three games and Ronald was out of control with his bullshit. He was sitting with her talking about how I had had too much to drink. Ain't that a bitch!

At that point, I was mad and drunk, so I started yelling at both of them. I turned to my dear loving husband and shouted, "What the fuck? You trying to talk to my friend right in front of my face? Ronald, you're full of shit! She don't want your ass!" (Alcohol!)

Then I looked at her and snapped. "And I thought you were my friend! You ain't shit either!" (Ignorant!)

Ronald had the nerve to ask what the hell was wrong with me!

"Why can't you be more like her?" as he grabbed my hand. (That's where you've called for the bitch to come out, and you grabbed my hand! Flashbacks!)

"Come on, let's go!"

395

"I'm not going anywhere!" I slurred, spilling a little of my beer.

"I'm out! Find your own way home! I don't have time for this shit!"

It was bad enough that he was about to leave me, but I couldn't believe it when they left the bowling alley together with me standing there drunk as hell! I cursed both of their asses out as they walked out together.

"Who needs you?! You better not leave me, I know that!" I screamed. "Well, no need to let good cold beer go to waste," I slurred as I sat down to finish what was left of my pitcher of beer.

I headed for the exit because I was sure he was waiting for me. When I didn't see the car, I grumbled, "I know this motherfucker didn't leave me with that won't-you-be-more-like-her bull-shit! He know I'm drunk!"

Just as I stepped outside, I saw our car pulling off with my girlfriend behind the wheel! "Motherfucker, you better not leave me!" I yelled. "I'm gonna get your ass!"

Ronald didn't bother to tell her to stop. She kept driving and all I could see were the taillights getting dimmer as they drove away. I found out later that Ronald asked her to drive simply because he'd had too much to drink.

I was mad as hell, I mean, furious! I was so mad that I started out walking without thinking about the long haul I had ahead of me. I was determined to get home and couldn't stop thinking about all of the shit I was going to do to him when I got there. I knew he had to drop her off before going home.

More than once I mumbled, "That bastard better be home when I get there or it's on!"

I walked so long that my buzz was gone. I had taken my shoes off and was walking along the road because there was no sidewalk. It's a wonder that I didn't get picked up by the police for walking the streets drunk at one o'clock in the morning.

I was finally able to hitch a ride with an old white man in an even older pickup truck looking for a quick trick. He was in for a rude awakening when I got in that truck.

"Hey, you need a ride?"

"Yeah, baby, I do," as I stumbled getting in the truck.

"You okay? What a pretty thang like you doing walking these streets this time of night?"

"Thank you so much, baby, for stopping. That motherfucker just left me here! I live over on Cedar Creek. You know where that's at? I'm gonna pop his ass!"

I kept my hand in my purse. All I had was a beer bottle that I bought before I left the bowling alley. I had to convince him that I was messed up and this was not turn-your-trick-night. Old, nasty ass, white mother....!

When I finally made it home, I eased the door open to see if could see him. I didn't hear anything, so I opened the door wider and saw him wrapped in a blanket on the floor. There was someone with him! For a second, I thought he had the damn balls to have her in my house! She wouldn't do that, I thought—not my friend! Then, I realized it was his son.

I couldn't believe he was sleeping like a baby after leaving me at the bowling alley at one o'clock in the morning. He knew I was drunk and didn't care how I was going to get home.

"So, you sleeping on the floor with your son, you think that is going to save you! That's bullshit!

I got some matches and set all four corners of the blanket on fire!

"Now, who's crazy?!" as I stood there watching the blanket go up in flames! I didn't care—I had completely lost it!

I saw James laying there, not the man that I was so in love with. Nothing but flashbacks!

397

Ronald jumped up screaming like his life depended on it! Well, I guess it did.

"Bitch, what the fuck is wrong with you? Are you crazy?" he yelled, putting the fire out.

"Yeah, motherfucker, I'm crazy as hell! You'll know the next time to leave me at some damn bowling alley at one o'clock in the morning!"

"I figured you'd get one of our friends to bring you home! I just thought you needed some time to cool off!"

Later that morning, after I sobered up, and the seriousness of my actions set in, I couldn't stop thinking about I tried to set my husband on fire. I finally admitted that I had a problem—I was an alcoholic and I needed help.

Section 211

I went to AA. I need help; maybe I am crazy.

I found a local Alcoholics Anonymous meeting and stayed with that for a while. My health took a turn for the worse, and I found myself in and out of hospitals for two years. I was having seizures, but the doctors didn't have a clue about what was causing them.

I would pass out or drift into a catatonic state with no warning. I'd just sit there staring into space, unable to respond. I didn't have control of my bladder. There were times when I wouldn't be able to walk, so Ronald had to carry me to the bathroom. He even cleaned me up after menstruation. Yes, I love my husband and there's no question that he loves me.

I remember driving on Riverdale Road and the next thing I knew, my car was sitting on the median. I'd just had a seizure and had no idea how I got there or where I was going. Somehow, I made my way home and told Ronald what happened.

Ronald took me to Grady Hospital where they admitted me for intensive testing. You name the test and I had it, everything from CT scans to

MRIs, only for them to tell my husband that it had to be a mental issue. They thought there might have been some damage because of the many blows that I had taken to the head from James' abuse. There was a time that I had seventeen stitches in my head, so they suggested I see a psychiatrist.

I was sent to several psychiatrists and once I began telling my life's story and all I had been through, I was diagnosed as a Paranoid Schizophrenic. All I could think was, 'What the fuck is that all about? Really!'

So you mean to tell me that I've survived all of these trials and tribulations in my life and now that my body is shutting down on me? All they could come up with is that I'm a paranoid schizophrenic?!

I started seeing a psychiatrist weekly to talk about all of the crap that happened to me. He thought it would be a good thing to get over all the hurt and pain that I had bottled up inside me. The doctor couldn't believe someone could endure the extent of my abuse and still be alive. The problem was they still couldn't find anything to explain the seizures.

I was prescribed several types of psychiatric medications only to find out I didn't need any of them. I knew my faith was the answer and I asked God to show me the way out of this web.

After several weeks of unnecessary drugs and counseling, I was told that I was misdiagnosed and they couldn't understand how the doctors at the hospital came to the conclusion that I was a paranoid schizophrenic. I was told there was nothing wrong with me and that I was of sound mind. Really!

Section 212

When temptation comes, will you pass the test?

We tried to rent with the option to buy, but that didn't work out. In the meantime, Ronald tore his Achilles tendon playing basketball and couldn't work for a while.

That put us in a very bad financial situation. We had to move to a low-income housing project in an area that we thought we'd never live. Don't get me wrong, it was fine for the time being because we really needed the help, but the downfall put us right back in the midst of people, places and things again.

When you get force to be in a situation you know you should not be in, will you overcome? How strong is your faith?

We were there for two or three months and temptation was everywhere. We weren't strong enough to ignore the drugs; it was just too hard to say no. We got some of those freebies. But, as we saw ourselves drifting back into the life that we came to Atlanta to get away from, we both realized we couldn't run anymore. We had to take a stand, but this time we had to stand with God. He knew our hearts and yet again, he was right on time.

By now, all of my children had moved down to Atlanta and gotten an apartment in the housing project. We couldn't let the kids know that we were doing crack cocaine again, so we had to sneak around. We knew it was wrong and we were so ashamed of our actions.

One late evening, I was so hurt because of the way Ronald had been verbally treating me. He complained all the time, about how he took care of me when no one else would and how I needed him and he wasn't going to be there for me anymore.

Eddie C was over to the house and he was just showing off in front of him, yet he was speaking his true feelings that went deeper than I thought. It hurt real badly, so I walked out the room and headed up stairs.

I heard him say, "I'm not taking care of her ass no more! She ain't got no money now and I remember how she did me, when she let that nigga come back in her life and put me in the garage. Payback is a mother…"

How soon do we forget where we come from? I have apologized over and over to him. What more can I do? He even married me after that.

I tried to blow it off and tell myself that Ronald was just being an asshole, a real prick! He was dealing with a lot of baby mama drama, also. I should have expected it—he wasn't working, so I guess he was lashing out since our financial situation was spiraling out of control and there was nothing he could do about it.

I'm sure he felt like the situation was his fault since he had hurt himself and couldn't drive. The money I was making wasn't enough to keep the household going until he went back to work, so who better to lash out at than the one he loved.

I couldn't stand the pressure that he was putting on me, and I couldn't shake what I heard him saying. I took it to another level. I went to my old comfort zone as I have done in the past—I couldn't take it anymore!

"Oh, just get one, you'll be alright. All you need is one."

Have you ever had that monkey to just jump on your back when you have been trying so hard to do the right thing? Have you ever had anyone that you love and care about keep bringing up your past in your face to make you feel less than the person that you are today—to stroke their ego? It's not a good feeling...

I confronted him when he came upstairs and asked for some money. Well, he knew that it was late and the only thing that I wanted money for was to go get one.

"Why are you doing this? Don't do it! We said we were going to stop!"

"What you mean 'we'? I said give me some money for me, not you! I heard what you said about me, and I thought you had forgiven me for that!" as I cried.

"Debra, it doesn't make a difference what I said! Don't do this!"

"Give me the money!" holding my hand out. "I don't want to hear nothing you have to say! It's your fault!"

Reluctantly, he gave me the money, but pleaded with me not to go.

"You don't care about me. You just been waiting to get back at me! Ain't that what you said?" I walked out the door.

When I got back, I sat downstairs in the living room and rolled my primo. I couldn't even finish what I had for the tears rolling down my face. I asked God why so many bad things continued to happen to me. I had a big pity party that night and nobody showed up but me. I didn't have anyone to blame for my actions but me. Ronald was upstairs in bed doing everything in his power to resist coming downstairs to join me. I was surprised that he didn't come to my pity party—I was all alone. I sat there looking and feeling so helpless to the trap I was about to walk into all by myself.

Section 213

Why do I feel like I did when my life was at its lowest,
when all I had was one pair of panties?

I remember thinking that wasn't the way I wanted our marriage to end. I love my husband and know deep down inside that he really do love me. It can't end like this; I knew we could make it work.

All I had to do was step out of the way and let God do the rest—to trust Him when my faith was so little. Sometimes we have to stop trying to do it by ourselves and realized that we/I can't do anything without God. If God kicked Satan out of heaven and cast him into hell, then surely He can cast him out of my life and tell him to leave me alone with these drugs.

The key is through Christ. I asked myself, 'Where is He in your life'?

I was crying as I went upstairs. I fell to my knees and asked my husband to forgive me. "Please pray with me, pray with me. God said he will

402

hear our cry. Let's pray for our marriage, for our life, for our salvation." We cried together and my husband wrapped his arms around me and knelt.

"We can't beat this by ourselves, we need help. I need help. We need God in our lives."

That night, Ronald and I were on our knees together crying out to the Lord for forgiveness and asked Him to have mercy on our souls. We confessed that we didn't want to play the drug/alcohol game any longer and that we weren't strong enough to fight Satan like we thought we could in this war.

"Lord, we need you to come into our hearts and save us from the destructive trap that Satan has set for us," I prayed. "We've found ourselves in his web. Lord, let it be Your will, not ours, of what is to come. Please protect us from the temptation that's all around us.

We acknowledge that You are Lord of Lords and King of Kings; that You are the Father and we can't come by You unless we come through Your Son, our Lord and Savior Jesus Christ, who died on the cross for our sins. You are One with the Father, the Son and of the Holy Spirit.

We love You and trust in Your Word that it shall be done according to Your will. We can do all things through Christ who strengthens us. Thank you Lord for what You have already done."

To this day, it has been thirteen years that I am free from alcohol and drugs and thirteen years that my husband been free from drugs.

We truly know now, without a shadow of doubt, that God gives us a choice to do what is right. If you keep doing the same old thing, you will keep getting the same results. Only you can make that decision. Just have that faith of a mustard seed and act on it! You have a choice today,

We looked into each other's eyes as tears rolled down our faces. We wrapped our arms around each other and kissed before we got up to get in bed. We held each other as we drifted off and from that day, we never looked back. Praise God!

Section 214

We moved to Mobile, Alabama.

Ronald got a contract job as a driver with the post office making nightly runs from Atlanta to Mobile. The Lord blessed him with double the money he was making before. Some nights, I would ride with him just to get out of the house so I wouldn't be alone. I thought it would be a good way for us to spend more time together.

He loves to fish and there's a pier on Dauphin Island, so many times we would drive to Mobile to spend the weekend with his Aunt Dorothy. Even though she may not be his biological aunt, she has known him since he was a little fellow.

My Aunt Dorothy

She and his mother lived in the same apartment building and were very close friends. It was a pleasure meeting Aunt Dorothy. She's in her late seventies, but swift on her feet and very intelligent. She speaks in an elitist, but humble tone with clarity, understanding and wisdom.

Aunt Dorothy is petite with beautiful hair that frames her face with a hint of gray, piercing brown eyes and a smile to die for. She's everything in a woman that I've always wanted to be. She's my Nana, my mother and Mama Bell all rolled into one. Best of all, she's truly a Christian woman. You can look at her and see the glow of the Lord—at least, that is what I see.

Sometimes during the visits to Mobile, we would take our grandson Notorious. Ronald and Notorious would go out while I sat with Aunt Dorothy at the kitchen table. Her level of wisdom is unbelievable and she makes so much sense when she speaks.

I told Aunt Dorothy I was thinking about writing a book. When we went to visit, I would sit at her table and write for long periods of time. I'd tell her some of the things that I'd been through in my life. She would look at me in disbelief and asked how I survived the drama that I'd gone through.

"God has had favor on your life, my Lord!"

Ronald would fix things around the house for Aunt Dorothy and Notorious would clean and cut the fish they caught so she could fry it. Notorious was in love with Aunt Dorothy. He was around eleven years old and she called him *Victor Victorious.*

We visited Mobile regularly for a year. I fell in love with the city and finally told Ronald that I wanted to live there. It was a lot slower than Atlanta and I wanted to live closer to Aunt Dorothy. She had so much to offer and I could learn a lot from her. She was that positive person that I needed in my life.

We had begun looking for a place to live, but his job was the determining factor. We combed through the newspaper and had a real estate agent show us available homes. We didn't like any of the ones we toured.

One weekend, we drove pass a small house that we liked right off Dauphin Island Parkway where Aunt Dorothy's granddaughter had just purchased a home in a wonderful, quiet sub-division.

"Stop! This house is for sell."

"This is the house."

"Yeah, baby, I think this is the house, too!" We call a realtor and the lady came out to show us the inside. When she opened the door, I knew this was it and as we walked through the house, I began to pray.

Ronald went to the back of the house to look out at the backyard. I heard him call out, "It's huge, baby! I mean really huge!" He was even more excited when he added, "Look, baby, there's a shed connected to the house! I can use it for my tools and stuff!"

We loved the house and decided it was the one we wanted. We went to the realtor's office and completed the paperwork to submit an offer. She said she would get back to us before the weekend was over.

We got a call from her later that day to let us know Ronald's credit score wasn't high enough to qualify for the house.

I wasn't about to accept that because God told us if we had faith the size of a mustard seed and believed in Him, we would be blessed—with the house we wanted.

Ronald and I went back to the house to get the name and phone number off of the yard sign then called as soon as we made it back to Aunt Dorothy's house.

"What the hell, if they don't want us to have the house then it must not be meant for us to have it."

I got someone on the phone after a couple of rings. The lady that answered was really kind and had a pleasant voice over the phone. I told her that my husband and I had just looked at a house she had listed and another realtor told us we didn't qualify for the house. I was calling to see if that was final or if there was any other way we might be able to get the house.

"So you like the house?"

I quickly answered, "Yes ma'am!"

"Why don't you and your husband meet me at the house? You can take your time and look around to make sure it's the house you truly want to be in and we'll see what I can do."

I was so happy. "Yes, ma'am, we'll be right over."

"Okay, great. I'll meet you there."

"Come on, Ronald, the realtor wants us to meet her at the house." He wasn't moving fast enough, so I shouted, "Come on, she wants to see if we really like the house!"

"Don't get your hopes up," as he reluctantly got up.

"What, you don't like the house? That's our house. God has already blessed us with it. I know he has!"

"Come on, Debra, you know I like the house. I hope we get it, also. I guess it won't hurt to try one more time. What have we got to lose? It's either that or stay in the projects until we can do better."

As far as I was concerned, staying in the projects wasn't an option. Aunt Dorothy gave me a hug and whispered in my ear, "Just pray, baby, it'll be alright." She sounded like my Nana when she said that, so I knew this was the house.

When we arrived at the house, the realtor showed us around, then asked once more if we were sure it was the house we wanted.

Ronald and I laughed after responding, "Yes ma'am!" at the same time.

She was pleased hearing that, and she assured us that she was going to work everything out.

"We don't live here; we're in Georgia."

"That won't be a problem. Do y'all believe in God?"

"Yeah, we do, and I believe God is going to bless us with this house."

Section 215

Some place we can call home...Mobile, Alabama

It turned out that the realtor's sister owned the house. She was anxious to sell and more than willing to work with us. After a couple of rounds of faxing various forms back and forth between Atlanta and Mobile, the realtor made it happen. We got the house with no down payment and the owner paid the closing costs!

You can't tell me that God ain't good! We had poor credit, no money and lived in another state and we were still blessed with a house! God will give you favor if you only believe in Him and want to do right in life. If you confess with your mouth that He is Lord, the blessings will come.

I kept screaming, "We got the house! We got the house!" From that point on, our life went in a direction I never thought it would—peace. Peace is what it was all about.

Ronald and I were so happy that we started packing right away. We decided to leave a lot of our stuff behind because we were starting a new life and we wanted a fresh start. I had been keeping Aunt Dorothy abreast of what was going on and she was so happy that we had gotten the house.

Within a month, we were moving to Mobile and into our very own home—our first home. The realtor had given us the keys so we could start bringing our stuff to Mobile on the weekends.

Man, I get happy every time I think about how the Lord blessed us with this home.

We didn't know that we had moved into Hurricane Alley! We had no idea. Since we have been here in Mobile, we have experienced five hurricanes.

We were blessed not to have suffered any deaths of family members or severe damage to our home like many others. So many people lost their lives with Hurricane Katrina. We have family in Pascagoula, Mississippi where our cousin Diane and other family members lost everything. We thanked God over and over that each of them came through that massive hurricane alive. We love them all dearly.

The years are going by so fast and life is grand. I got a job working for the same optical company that I worked for in Milwaukee. I really love working there and the staff that I worked with was awesome. I've learned so much from them all, particularly from my immediate supervisor.

Section 216
Yeah, I'm saying it. There are cliques in church!
What's inside of you will come out!

Once we got settled, we started going to church faithfully. Ronald and I joined a Baptist church where I fell in love with working for Christ. It was Ronald's first time attending church on a regular basis and he learned a lot about church protocol.

The Pastor was so nice and I shared with him all of the things that the Lord had placed on my heart to do to give back to the community. He was very supportive. All I wanted to do was help in giving back.

"If you feel the Lord has put it on your heart to give back, then go for it and I'll stand behind you. You have my blessing to do as you please. Just let me know what going on."

I loved the fact that I would be able to help people in need. The first thing I noticed was the church didn't have a ministry to feed the hungry. I got three other members to agree to start a food pantry for the needy and we gave out food to people in the community monthly.

Once I had the Pastor's permission, I set up a table to provide free vision screenings when people came to get food. I didn't do anything without the Pastor's permission.

At that point, life was wonderful—we had moved to Mobile, found a church family and I was able to work in the community helping people in need. I couldn't ask for a better life. I couldn't stop thinking about how the Lord had blessed me in so many ways and realized it was time for me to give back.

The members of the church seemed pleased with the idea of a food pantry, even those known to be part of little cliques. You know, the ones that sit together and talk among themselves, criticizing.

Yeah, I'm saying it. There are cliques in church!

These members made it hard for the Pastor with all that voting on this, that and the other, on whether or not you can do something in the church.

Even these cliques liked the idea of a food pantry. It was obvious because they would be the first in line to get free food and would sometimes ask for extras! There were other members who didn't mind going to the food bank to get a food supply when that time came around every month. They needed it.

The Pastor was pleased to see how the Lord was using us to bring new believers to Christ and how our church was helping people in the community.

Our church congregation wasn't very large, but there were some members that have been there since their grandparents and were set on things going a certain way.

We began implementing new ministries at the church like a summer lunch program where the kids could get a free lunch and activities for a few hours. The local food bank was providing the lunches at no cost to the church.

We were in the process of starting an educational program with computers to teach elderly members the computer basics. We also planned a tutoring program to help people study for their GED.

I contacted an organization called Volunteers of America and they donated a computer to the church to help us get started. They were willing to help us in whatever way they could so we could do for people in the community as well as the members of the church.

We brought together different organizations outside the church to develop a network, offering helpful solutions for those having difficult times in many areas of their lives. The workshops were open to anyone that wanted to attend.

Section 217

Who broke your spirit in the Lord?

The Lord showed me that there was a need for new ministries in the church because there were plenty of children and senior citizens in the community that could benefit from our help. But, implementing the new ministries with the Pastor's permission brought on a lot of animosity from some of the members. There were people within the cliques of the church that began to change toward me and the members we were assisting.

The summer lunch program never got off the ground. I'll make this short and straight to the point: The day before the children's summer lunch program, I received a call from the lady that agreed to be there that morning to welcome the kids. She called to let me know she wouldn't be able to help me because she was told if she did, she would lose her job as musician at the church.

"I'm sorry, Debra, I really wanted to help you, but I can't afford to lose my job. I have my children that I have to think about. You understand, don't you?" I tried to stop her from hanging up the phone, but I was too late.

A little later, I received a conference call from two of the members in one of the cliques. I was told that they didn't want the summer program and I should stop trying to bring new ideas to the church.

"Who do you think you are? We were doing just fine before you came

411

along, and gonna do even better when you leave!" I told them the Pastor liked the idea and said it was okay to have a summer lunch program for the kids.

"It's not costing the church a dime so what's the problem? Y'all need to talk to the Pastor if you have a problem with this or anything else that he's allowing us to do to help the community, but in the meantime, the lunch program starts Monday in the morning!" I could tell neither one of the ladies liked what I had just said to them.

"Let me tell you something! I don't know where you come from, but that 'Pastor', as you call him, ain't nothing but the hired help! He can't do nothing in this church without asking us first! And if you keep insisting on doing things that he's telling you to do, we'll put a chains on the fence and lock you and that man out! And furthermore, this was my great grandfather's church before he came along! We hired him to preach, not to tell us what to do! And if he don't like it, we will get rid of him, too!"

She was yelling into the phone like a mad woman. Never in my life had I heard someone speak about a minister/pastor with such disregard and disrespect, let alone someone that was in the church.

At that point, I was afraid of what might happen. It wouldn't have surprised me if she had just dropped dead, right then and there, by speaking about a man of the cloth in such a blasphemous manner.

What and who gave us the right to judge the next man, especially the man of the cloth?

Hey, I'm not perfect, nor do I claim to be holier than Thou, but I know that the Lord is still working on me! There one thing I can say—I am not a hypocrite! You so-called church people better be careful of the way you speak about the man of God. If he does anything wrong, that is between him and the Lord.

I just want to ask a question: How do you know what kind of

412

relationship a pastor has with the Lord Almighty? You don't.

Section 218

The Lord sees all and one day... Am I talking about you?

Be mindful of the way you treat the people who are new to the church family who are seeking after Lord and trying to change their lives. You never know what path a person has been down when they walk through those church doors. Some may be broken spirits, on their last hope of life and maybe on the brink of suicide with nowhere else to turn. They are seeking peace, guidance, love and compassion in God's house.

Now, you know who you are, the ones that are so quick to say, "My grand- and great- family was/are members here, and this is my church! We've been here for ump-teen years. We have seen the pastors go and come. We run this church!" Surely, surely, I just know, I'm not talking about you!

Wrong answer! It's God's church, you foolish people! I wonder what God would say if you told Him that the church belongs to you and your family and not to Him? Why don't you go so far as to tell the Lord if anything gets done in the church, it has to have you and/or your family's vote of approval, not by the pastor's! But, surely now, I'm not talking about you!

I would like someone to show me where is it in the Bible that if your grand- or great- family member was the pastor, or had the church built, that it becomes an inheritance to a family and their generations. I thought it said somewhere in the Bible, don't quote me, that all churches are the houses of the Lord, and that everything in the universe and beyond belongs to the King of Kings, Lord of Lords, our Lord and Savior Jesus the Christ.

Shame on you and beware all you pretenders, perpetrators, pseudo, demonic, lying, mean-spirited, hateful and unforgiving hypocrites sitting in the church house! Whoa, wait a minute! Surely, I know I'm not talking about you! You wouldn't happen to know anyone like that, would you?

Don't you people know that God sees all?! You don't know you who you are messing with... I mean, I'm just saying... I was really trying not to go into my old ways, and curse that woman out. I could have given her a real good, old-fashioned, straight from the low end, back alley streets of Chicago cussing! And people said that I was crazy! Man! You are crazy! But, wait a minute! Surely, I'm not talking about you!

Section 219

You never know who you are mistreating in God's house!

That really hurt me to hear her speak like that. Oh, but God...

After the horrifying call, I couldn't believe it. I cried because it felt like my little world had just come tumbling down. My spirit was broken and I was only trying to do what the Lord had put on my heart to do. I tried to call the pastor to let him know what they said to me, but I didn't get an answer. I decided to leave a message, but I never got a call back.

The pastor had given me a key to the church, so that we could come and go when time came to stock the food pantry. So, the next morning, I opened the doors of the church, getting ready to receive the delivery for the children summer program. I notice that one of the women that called me was sitting in the parking area behind the church, waiting to see what I was going to do.

No one showed up to help; I stood there all alone. When the delivery truck came with all those free meals for the children, I had to tell them that the program will be on hold and to take the food back. I called the members that volunteered to help to let them know that there was a problem and we would have to put the program on hold. No one showed up, no one was willing to stand. This was all new to me. I was in shock and couldn't believe this was happening.

When I saw the Pastor, I told him what happened.

"Don't worry about them, I'll handle it."

After that, the majority of the members in the church stopped speaking to me and made me feel unwanted. It was like I had the plague of some kind and they all didn't want to catch it. It was a struggle for me to continue attending church there. I didn't want to go to another church because Ronald and I really loved the pastor and loved listening to him bring the Word. Most of all, he was a compassionate, good-hearted person. I wanted so much to give back into the community.

I began to pray about the situation and it was revealed to me that there were a lot of demonic, mean, hateful old spirits in that church that were afraid of change and would block anything new coming into the church if they didn't start it.

I really don't know anyone like that! Do you? Yeah, right!

It almost felt like I belonged to some type of cult or something. I do not do cults or cliques; it wasn't that long ago that I felt like I was in a cult with the kid's father, or in the clique of 'just one mo'.

Section 220

Jesus! What's really going on?

A short time had passed and I stood before the church and announced that I was stepping down from the food pantry or anything else for that matter. I asked that someone else take over managing the ministries that were already in place. I stated that it was never about me, it was about doing God's will to help people that are in need.

I stayed there as a member for another year waiting on the Lord to move me, to take me to a place where I could grow in the Word. I needed to be spirituality fed because being that had taken so much out of me. Somehow, I let it kill my joy, put my fire out and lower my self-esteem. I didn't expect to find such ungodly people like that in a church.

415

I learned a lot during that year. I learned that it's not about what people think or how they feel about you. If the Lord places something on your heart, you shouldn't let anyone stop you in doing God's will. That's a test of your faith and how strong you are rooted in the Lord. I wasn't strong at all and had no one to back me up.

Aunt Dorothy told me that once I understood something or someone, I should move on.

"You will know how to deal with a situation or a person once you have a clear understanding. Do you have an understanding of what just happened?"

"Yes, I do."

"Well, it's time to move on and stop pondering on something that you already have a clear understanding about, and can do nothing about it."

I still had so much other stuff going on in my life to be bothered about that. But, still it hurt so bad, and made me take a different look at people,

I look at life in this way: I had the nerve to turn my nose up at those people on skid row, and then I picked that roach out of my baby's milk. I thought I was so much better than they were because of where I came from, living behind those pretty curtains. Well, listen to this and hear me well...

I think coming into God's house could be a little something like that. We all are there trying to get the same kind of help, regardless of where we come from or what we have done. Everybody has a story to tell, so nobody can look down on you. Why? They are sitting at the same table/pew that you are before the Lord.

Section 221

I had to leave my Brother in Georgia.

When we left for Georgia, my brother Chuckie had just gotten out of prison after doing a 15-year stretch—37 years total of his life—spent behind bars. He was paroled to Georgia because I was there, his only immediate family. Nobody else in our family showed that they cared about him while he was in prison.

Our uncles, aunts and cousins never once came to visit him. He may have gotten five letters from them the entire time he was locked up. They said they didn't have time to visit him or they didn't want to see him in jail. You know, the typical excuses that people give when they do not want to be bothered with you or your situation.

All while he was in prison, I was there for him. I made sure that I sent money, kept a telephone so he could call me and I sent him pictures of my children's birthdays, Thanksgiving, Christmas and other holidays. I tried to make sure he was included in any event that went on. I even sent him pictures of the food spread.

When we had card games going, I took pictures of everything and everybody for him. That's how my brother knew my children and even the grandchildren who were born while he was locked up. If I had not done that, he would not have known any of my children. When Chuckie got out of prison, he had over three thousand pictures and I sent just about all of them.

We went to visit him all the time as a family, just so the kids could see and know their uncle. He was all the family I had. It's always been just me and my little brother.

Once Chuckie was paroled to Georgia, he couldn't come and live with me because at the time we were living in a low-income complex and when an inmate is released from prison, they're not allowed to live in a public housing.

Chuckie was forced to get a job and find his own apartment. Keep in mind, Chuckie had never lived on his own before. Whenever he got out of jail, Mommie was always there to take care of him.

My brother has been out of prison for about six to eight months, close to a year. Well, he was doing well, or at least I thought so.

I told Chuckie we were moving to Alabama because we were blessed with a house shortly after he had arrived in Georgia at the halfway house. I guess he felt a little abandoned because he did not know anyone there. I was really sad about that.

He has his own apartment now and on the weekends he would drive to Alabama to visit with me and go to church every Sunday. He had not ever attended church before, unless he went while he was in prison. I doubt it because every time I mentioned God, he would cut me off.

He just wanted to be close to us, me and my husband. Ronald and Chuckie became good friends. "He's a good brother-in-law, glad you got somebody that care about you."

One night my brother and I were on the phone pretty late. We talked about how he was planning to move to Mobile with us because it was getting hard for him to pay his bills and handle the normal day-to-day expenses.

"Chuckie, it will be alright, but you have to stop going out and buying expensive clothing." He truly got that from Mommie. I would go to Goodwill on a budget; my brother wouldn't dream of it!

We said good night, I love you and went to bed.

Section 222

My brother is back in jail! Do you truly believe in God?

I shut down the computer and began getting ready for bed. The phone

418

rang. What did he forget to tell me? I thought.

"Hello, what you forget, Chuckie?"

"Hello, ma'am, this is College Park Police Department and I'm calling you to let you know that we have your brother in custody.

"Yeah, right... For what?"

"He's being held for six counts of armed robbery, six counts of aggravated assault with a firearm, kidnapping, unlawful assault, battery with a firearm, breaking and entering and a high speed police chase."

"Wait a minute! You said this is who?" as my heart dropped in disbelief. "I don't believe you! I just talked to my brother and he said he was going to bed! Is this a joke?"

"I'm sorry to inform you that this is not a joke. We have your brother down here at the station in College Park."

"My brother's not in jail! What's your phone number so that I can call you back? I don't believe a word you are saying?"

My heart raced as he gave me the phone number. "Oh, my God! Lord, no!" as I hung up the phone.

I dialed the phone number and heard, "College Park Police Department, this is Officer so-in-so. How can I help you?"

I screamed, "God, no! Oh, my God! No, Chuckie! No!"

I was crying like crazy and rushed to the bedroom where Ronald was sleeping. "Ronald! Ronald! Chuckie's in jail!" I fell to my knees handing him the phone so he could talk to the police.

Ronald took the phone. I shouted, "Oh, my dear brother, Lord! Please have mercy on him! Please don't take my brother away from me. Peace be still!"

I was too busy praying to pay attention to what Ronald was saying, but whatever it was, it worked. The next thing I knew, he was handing me the

419

phone so I could talk to Chuckie. I was able to talk and calm myself down once I realized the police were going to let my brother speak to me.

I asked, "Chuckie, what happened? You just told me you were going to bed!"

All Chuckie could say was, "I don't know...I don't know. I love you Debbie, I'm sorry."

I wasn't able to say anything. "They just said I have to get off the phone now. I love you, Sis. Bye-bye."

And he was gone just like that. The next day, Ronald made arrangements to be off from work that night so we could drive to Atlanta to visit my brother in jail. I thought those days were over. I called my brother's parole officer, "Could you please tell me what is going on with my brother?"

"Well, your brother had been indicted and he's facing life in prison without parole."

"No, I don't believe you. My God said that he wasn't going to take my brother away from me, that my brother wasn't going back to prison. But, God..."

Before I could say anything else, "Ma'am, your brother will be spending the rest of his life in prison. He's been indicted and there's nothing your God can do about that! Face it, you have to be realistic!"

I couldn't believe she told me what my God can't do. She clearly didn't know my God! With everything that I had been through in my life, I knew that the God I served could save my brother.

When I finally saw my brother after that long wait, I told him, "This it was out of my hands. There's nothing I can do for you now, Chuckie. I've gone to church and put you before the altar. I have to step back and let God take care of this now. Chuckie, you have to call His name and ask Him for forgiveness!"

"Call whose name?"

"You need to call the name of Jesus! You've got to call on Jesus and ask Him for forgiveness. Let Him know that you believe in Him and that you're really sorry for everything wrong that you've done in your life. You need to ask God to have mercy on your soul."

I asked my brother if he believed that Jesus died on the cross for our sins and that God gave His only begotten Son.

"Debbie, I don't know. Yeah, I believe."

"Chuckie, you have to ask God to forgive you. Let him know that you believe in Him and that you know He will save you. Then He will have mercy on you."

"Debbie, do you believe God will help me?" It had been a long time since I had seen Chuckie cry.

"Yes, Chuckie, I do!" I pleaded with him, trying to make him understand how serious this was, "But, you have to *believe* God will help you. Chuckie, you can't play because you can't fool God! He will know if you're not for real! You have to pray, Chuckie! You have to cry out to the Lord and let him know how sorry you are!"

"Okay, Debbie, I will do it. I'll call on Jesus, and you said that He'll help me!" He wanted desperately to believe me!

"Yeah, Chuckie, but you got to be real! God can see through all mess! He will forgive you for all your sins! I mean all of them!"

I'm a living witness of what God will do! My brother is here in Alabama with me. All charges were dropped and my brother was set free— no additional parole, no probation. He had to finish the last three months of his parole because of the high speed chase.

My God showed up and showed out! He made believers out of the unbelievers! *The Lord may not come when you want him, but he'll always be there on time!*

In court on Chuckie's sentencing day, the judge said, "All charges have been dropped!" I turned to his parole officer, "That's what my God can do!"

What happened to me and my brother happens every day in this world—situations that you could never image happening to your daughter or son. It is about the choices that you make in your life, the foundation that you give your child, and the people, places and things that are before them at a young age.

I praised God right there in the court room, as we walked through the door and never looked back. My brother has a good job as a welder, a trade that he learned while in prison.

Section 223

I sent my son back. What have I done?

My son Jerome came to see me for about a week after several years. He wanted settle down and stop living in that rat race up north. He said he found himself living from pillow to post, only by choice. He said that he didn't want to go back to Milwaukee, but he had legal obligations to take care of—seeing the parole officer and paying restitution. I was so glad to see that he want to be down here with me, but I didn't want him to be on the run.

"Jerome, you have to go back and take care of your obligations. You don't want to be looking over your shoulder all the time."

"Ma, if I go back, I won't make it back."

"Sure you will, son. Don't talk like that."

I saw something come over him. "Okay, Ma, I'll go back."

I had never had life insurance on any of my children and decided to get a policy on Jerome first. Within the first thirty days of that policy, Jerome's restitution—a little over a thousand dollar—was paid by his pastor in Milwaukee. She said that the Lord put it on her heart to pay it for him. Everyday my baby would call me and let me know that he was that much closer to coming back.

"Jerome, when are you coming back?"

"Ma, I coming home. I just want to be here when my baby is born, and right after that I will be on my way."

"Okay, son, but didn't your Pastor pay your restitution for you? So, when is the baby due?'

"In about two weeks. Yeah, she paid it for me. Don't worry, Ma, I'm coming home. I love and talk to you later. Gotta go."

She had the baby a week early, and still he didn't come home. He told me that he had gotten a job and he didn't want to leave without buying some things for the baby.

"Ma, once I get my first check and buy the baby what it needs to come home in and pampers and stuff, I will be on my way."

"Okay, Jerome, okay. Ma loves you and stay out of harm's way."

"All the time, Ma."

"All the time, mama's baby, all the time." We hung up.

Jerome called two days after their birthday to say he was going to call me in the morning or that afternoon after he got off work. He would know if and when he was coming to Mobile. I hadn't heard from him in a several days. He usually called me every morning around seven-thirty. 'Oh, well, he's working.'

Section 224

That day! The day that no mother wants to live through!

423

In the afternoon of May 25, 2007, Tyra called me as she did usually on her way home from school. We would talk until she got home. We were chit-chatting about school and all the things Notorious was into.

"Hey, it's a lot of police and ambulance over here."

"Over where? Where you at?"

"Over here at this McDonald's off of 64th and there go Shawn."

"Do you see your brothers? Do you see Jerome?"

"Wait, Ma, I'll call you back. They trying to flag me down."

"No, Tyra don't you hang this phone up. I'll wait. Tell me, do you see your brothers, if their friends are there."

"Okay, Ma, just let me see what's going on."

I could hear her get out the car and there is a lot of noise—yelling, shouting. I couldn't make it out, then, "Ma, its Jerome! He's been shot!"

"What? Shot?! Who? What? Where is he shot at, Tyra? Is it life-threatening? Is it life- threatening?

I began to pace the floor, praying, "Oh, God, please, protect my baby! Please God protect my baby!"

"I'm his sister, that's my brother! This is our mother on the phone! What happened? Let me by! I'm a nurse! Let me by!"

"What are they saying?! What they say, Tyra?! Where's Tyrone at?! Is your brother there?!"

"Ma, they are doing resuscitation, right now!"

"What?! Like he's died and they're trying to bring my baby back to life?!"

"Yeah, Ma, like they trying to bring him back to life!" I could hear the ambulance siren going off.

"Is that the ambulance that's taking Jerome away now, Tyra?"

"Yeah, Ma, I'm on my way with him. I will call you when I get there. Ma, Jerome was shot in the chest." The phone went dead. She was gone.

"Oh, Jesus, please watch over my baby! Please, Lord, don't take my baby away from me!"

I called my husband, Sister Johnson, my brother, Edna, and Aunt Dorothy. "Please pray for my baby! He's been shot! Jerome's been shot!" I heard the other line click and I clicked over.

"Yes, Tyra! Hello, Tyra!" She was running and I could hear her yelling, "My brother was just brought in here! A gunshot victim! Where is he? What room did they take him to?"

I waited on the other line, waiting to hear what she was going to say next. The phone went dead.

"God, please save my baby! Have mercy Lord! Have mercy on my baby!" was my prayer.

The phone rang again and it was Tyra. "Ma, Jerome is dead! Ma, he's gone! My brother is gone! He's dead!"

"Oh, my God, what have I done?! Oh, my God, what did I do?!" I fell to my knees and I cried so hard, "Jesus, no! Why did you take my baby from me?! No, God! Please, no! Why my baby?!"

I felt like it was my fault, that if I had not told him to go back, this would have never happened! I couldn't understand why God took my baby! "Why my baby?!" I continued to cry out. I remember this as if it happen yesterday, Glory be to God...

The life insurance policy was thirty days old on the day he died.

People from my church came to be with me; the church secretary was the first to come. My pastor and his wife were out of town at the time. My husband came home from work and then the phone started to ring—everyone was calling me. I couldn't talk.

425

I needed answers. I wanted to know why, and what happened. I called Tyra back, or she could have called me. "Who shot him and why?"

Section 224

My God, where do I go from here? There's no pain like it!

"Ma, they say that Jerome went to go get his best friend's brother from work and when he got there, the brother was arguing with someone. The brother went into McDonald's to get his work stuff so Jerome could take him home, and that's when Jerome and the other boy got to arguing. The boy didn't like what Jerome said and he pulled out a gun and shot him as Jerome turned to run the other way."

He ran back into McDonalds, they tell us, patting himself down, saying, "Am I hit? Am I hit?" as the blood came from his mouth. He fell to the floor and the ambulance was called.

He was shot in the aorta vein near the heart and the bullet came out on the other side. He never felt any pain; he didn't even know that he was shot. Tyra told me that all he felt was a sensation of warmth before he died.

"He didn't feel no pain, Tyra?"

"No, Mama, he didn't feel any pain." We both continued to cry.

Someone from the church asked, "Do you have insurance on your son?"

"Oh, my God, I need to call the insurance company, and tell them."

I didn't have any money so my church paid for me and my husband to fly to Milwaukee the next day. Everyone was so nice to me.

I don't remember sleeping that night. I can't describe the sadness and pain. It's a hurt that I wish on no mother, not even the mother of the boy who murdered my son! I prayed a prayer that night for comfort.

"Lord, please hear my cry. Please take this pain away from me. This, I cannot handle. Lord, I feel myself drifting back in a place where I do not

426

want to be. I've overcome a lot with Your grace and mercy. Please take this pain away. My heart hurts so bad and I feel all alone. Lord, my God, please take this pain away. Let me know, Lord, that this too shall pass. Lord, I know that I am not to question You, but I have to ask, why did You take my baby?! Lord, why did You have to let him died? Please take the pain away. This too shall pass."

Losing a mother is nothing, nothing, at all like losing a child.

I had asked the funeral home not do anything to my son until I get there. I told Notorious to make sure they did not touch Jerome until I get there, and I wanted him to be dressed with clothes on. I didn't want to see him with a sheet over his body.

"I got you, Nana. I got one of my outfit that I gonna give him."

"Thank you, Notorious. I see you all when I get there."

The flight was quiet; my husband and I didn't say too much. I just stared out the window, looking into the sky, and all I could say was, "Thank you, Jesus. Thank you, Lord."

I was thanking him for keeping that plane in the air and, hopefully, getting there safely. I had not been on a plane since my mother took us to Disney.

Then, a sense of peace came over me. I could hear, "This too shall pass. This too shall pass."

When we got to the funeral home, everyone was there, including Jerome's twin, my son Tyrone. 'Lord, what must he and sisters be going through?! What pain they must feel in losing their brother?!"

I can't imagine how they felt. I know it would be hard for me if I had lost my brother. I flooded with all these thoughts when I saw them there waiting for me, looking for me to be strong and not break down.

'This too shall pass.' They were looking at me with such sad and hurt expressions on their little faces. My little babies were hurting so bad, and there was nothing I could do to take away that pain. I felt so helpless. They tried to be strong for me by holding back their well of emotions. I embrace them all and we cried for a moment...

"Where is he... Take me to my son. Where is Jerome? Where's your brother?"

"Come this way. He's in here," the funeral home attendant directed.

"Come, Nana. I'll walk with you," Notorious reached for my hand.

"I got you, Mama," said Tyrone. "It's okay."

Everyone gathered around me as I walked toward the room with my husband walking beside me. "Lord, please, Lord," I said to myself, 'please help me, right now, Lord!"

'This too shall pass,' is what I heard. They opened the doors to where my son was lying on the table, waiting for me to come see him. He was stretch out on this table, with a white sheet wrapped around his head and I leaned down to kiss him.

"Be careful of how you touch him. We don't want to leave any imprints," the funeral home attendant instructed as he stood with his hands folded in front of him with white gloves.

"Please, this is my baby, I can't hurt him." I kissed him and stared at him lying there. 'This too shall pass.' I wiped the tears from my eyes.

"I'm okay," I told them, I'm okay." I place my hands on his chest, "Stay out of harm's way, mama baby... Ma loves you, Jerome. Look, who lined up his mustache and goatee?"

"He did that the night before he got killed," Tyra said. "Ma, on the way back from your house, Jerome and I were talking about death and he said that when he died, he wanted this and that," and she gave a little chuckle.

428

"You know how people be saying, 'Nigga you gonna be late for your own funeral'? Well, that's what Jerome said. He didn't want to be waiting on everybody to come in. He wanted them to come and be waiting on him!" They all laughed.

"What, what you say he said?"

She repeated it. I told her, "Well, if that is what he wants, then that is the way that it will be."

Then I turned to the funeral home attendant, "I need for this sheet to come off his head. I want to see his hair." He carefully removed it off his head and I was able to rub my hands over his hair. His hair is so long, black, coarse and so pretty. I ask the mother of his first two children to braid his hair for me.

"Mrs. Bell, I don't know."

"Sure, honey, you can do it. Come braid his hair for the last time. I know how he really felt about you. Come."

Section 225
Jerome said... So shall it be done!

We talked and laughed together, recalling things Jerome used to say. Tyrone recalled, "Jerome said that when he died, it's gonna be a party, and he didn't want nobody crying and falling all out. He wanted to come in on the song 'Party like a Rock Star'!"

"What? 'Party like a Rock Star'? That's a rap song! Is it cursing in that song? Cause we can't do that! Not in church!"

"No, Mama, there's no cursing in it."

"He said that he wanted to be late for his own funeral. Let the people wait on him!" They laughed.

"Well, if that is what he said he wanted, then that's what we will do."

"Ma, you don't have to worry about doing anything. We gonna take care of everything for you."

"Okay, Tyra, it's so much we got to do. Do you have any scissors? I want to cut some of my son's braids to take with me."

As we continued to reflect on Jerome's life, other friends and family came up to offer their stories. His children didn't quite understand, but we were all together, holding each other up in this time of need.

Through the day, I kept hearing 'This too shall pass'. Every time I heard it, a feeling of peace fell over me.

Even now, as I write, I can still hear… 'This too shall pass.'

After we left there, I had so many questions. I just couldn't understand why someone would shoot and kill my son.

"Did Jerome have a gun? Did he hit the boy? Somebody, tell me what happened."

"Ma, what happened is what we told you. That's all they are telling us."

"Twin, have they caught the boy who killed him yet?"

"No, they have not."

"Ma, do you have insurance on Jerome?"

"Yeah, I got it thirty days ago. Thank God."

Section 226

The Home Going Celebration

I never knew how important it is to have insurance. I didn't think that I would need it right now—until this happened. I can't even imagine what we would have done if I had not bought the policy. I didn't even have plane fare to go to my son's body, let alone bury him. I now have insurance on all my children, and working on the grandchildren.

We had one week before the funeral. All my children took part in getting everything ready. I bought Tyrone and Jerome the same suit because Tyrone wanted to be dress alike for the last time. Tyra took the lead in getting the pictures together for the obituary which was filled with messages from them to Jerome.

The children had flyers made with Jerome's picture on it, inviting everyone to his home going celebration. They went out into the community and the places where Jerome hung out.

Ronald made a lot of the phone calls to our family members. Ericka came from Arkansas; she hadn't seen her brother in two years. She really broke down.

Edna was the only singer that I wanted to sing a solo, and Tyrone was able to get their pastor to do the eulogy. I had no idea what church to get, and don't even remember how we got it, but this church was huge. It looked like the perfect church where any bride would want to have her wedding— just beautiful.

The day had arrived and everything was planned. The funeral car came to pick us up. We followed the hearse that carried Jerome's body.

He was about thirty minutes late for his own funeral, and his best friend put Chevy car symbols on his casket. Tyra directed the service, and Tyrone and the girls each read the messages from the obituary. They even had me to read what Jerome told me to put in his obituary… *'This too shall pass'*.

When they brought my son's body to the door, his twin and their friends stood around the casket. They were all wearing a tee-shirt with Jerome's picture on it that one friend had made for everybody. That boy made over one hundred tee shirts within that week.

I could see Tyrone getting ready to lead his brother into the church, but the church music was playing. Tyra held her hand out for him to stop and yelled, "Put the song on!" 'Party like a Rock Star' began to play.

The whole church was standing, clapping and shouting, "Alright!" Of course, some family members and friends were appalled by the song and that we had arranged for Jerome to be brought in.

I remember looking around, in a daze, looking at the people who were there. You would have thought a dignitary or senator had died! There wasn't even standing room; they were turning people around because the church was filled to capacity, so they had to stand outside. I was told later by the funeral home director that the church held a thousand members and we were over the limit! These people came to share in my son's Home Going Celebration, and that it was—a celebration!

This was a home going celebration I had never seen before, all for one of God's angels, my son. After this elderly lady viewed the body, she asked, "Are you his mother?"

"Yes, I am."

"Well, I just wanted to let you know that during the winter, when I was outside shelving my snow, your son came up and asked, "Ma'am, I will do that for you! He finished my drive and walkway for me. I had never seen your son before, but when I saw this flyer at the grocery store, I knew that it was him and I had to come and show my respect to a fine young man."

"Thank you for sharing that with me," as I hugged her.

Another older lady came to me and said, "One time I ran out of gas and it was getting late. I was trying to get home before dark. Your son stopped to help me and when I told him what happened, he went and got some gas for me, put it in my car and he didn't even let me pay him. I never saw that young man again, but when I saw this flyer at the gas station, I knew that it was him, and I had to come. You had a wonderful son. He was a good boy."

"Thank you for sharing that. Thank you."

That meant so much to me to have these elderly women share their encounters with my son. What a blessing.

Before my son Jerome left Mobile, he went to church with me. That day, he joined and gave his life to Christ. My church sent a resolution and beautiful flowers. My daughter read it and I thanked my church family for all that they had done for me.

Lean and depend on God for all our needs; he will be there for you.

Section 227

Lord, help me to forgive.

When it was all over with and I came back home, I wasn't in the best frame of mind. I couldn't understand why the world was still going on as if nothing had happened. The words 'This too Shall Pass' became very faint. I could barely hear it anymore.

"Lord, I know that one day I am going to have to forgive that boy who killed my son because You died on the cross and You forgave me. So, please Lord, help me to have forgiveness in my heart and take away the bitterness, guilt and angry—one day at a time."

I had the picture of my son on my screensaver and every morning I got up and came into the office and talked with him. I began to eat all my meals with him as I talked to the screensaver. I was angry that he was gone, and I didn't know why.

One morning, when I sat down and said, "Good morning, Jerome." I could hear my son tell me, "Ma, stop. You can't keep doing this. You have to stop, I'm okay."

It felt like I was going to have to let him go and I didn't want to do that. He also told me where the boy was that killed him—in Arkansas. I got on the internet and got the fax number for every police station in the entire state of Arkansas. I faxed them a picture of the boy that was wanted for the murder of my son. He was soon caught and is now serving time; he will not be eligible for parole until the year 2065.

Five years later, I still know that I have to forgive the boy that killed my son. The Lord knows my heart and is still working with me.

I tell myself that I am so blessed to have had Jerome for the twenty-five years that the Lord granted him to me. Out of all the mothers in the world, the Lord picked me to be his mother. I am just happy that I was able to be in the presence of one of God's angels for twenty-five years. I will enjoy the time that I have with the rest of my children and grandchildren. So no matter what the situation is, I do know that 'This too shall pass'. This is how I get by now, regarding my son.

Section 228

And finally...

I'm here at the end, but at the beginning of my new life that at one time I thought I would never see. But, God... I made it by the grace and mercy of God, hope, faith, prayers, a sincere heart and a made-up mind. I made it because of my Nana's prayers and the prayers of those who truly loved me. I made it out of a life that had me racing straight to Hell!

I've grown a lot. There were parts of my past life that have taken me years to overcome, but I made it. But, God...

I wanted you to know that it doesn't matter what you've gone through in life or where you are right now in this present moment, there is a brighter day. The sun will shine and you will see a rainbow—you just have to hold on to God's Unchanging Hand, and, please...never look back!

Writing about my life experiences helped me to realize that I had to go through the difficult, lost times to get where I am now and to see where I was going!

During my difficult journey of writing my story, I had to go back to some dark, dark places that were scary and painful. I cried, I got angry and I even laughed at times, but all while I was going back down that path, I realized how truly blessed I was! God has given me favor and power over it all.

People have tried to pull me down, but I came to find out I was my worst enemy—not them. See, sometimes we can blame other people for all the tragedies in our lives, but if we really stop and think about it, we had a choice. Remember that God allows us to make choices of our own free will.

It was a serious battle for me to revisit those dark places, to break the strongholds that Satan had on my soul which were the barriers in my past and could have been barriers to my future.

I had to realize that there will always be temptation in my life. I know that Satan will never stop trying to lure me into his trap of destruction. It's up to me now to do the will of the Lord in order for me to stay on this side of the battlefield.

I have shed many tears and endured many heartaches and pain. I have suffered in this battle of life only to come out standing firm and staying suited up with my Armor of the Lord awaiting the next temptation/battle!

There will always be trials and tribulations in our lives until we die, but God is able. We only have to make up our own minds as to which side of the battlefield we will stand on.

MY CLEANSING LETTERS…..

I would like to apologize to all the people I may have hurt while I was walking the path of destruction.

To my children, I'm so sorry that Mama put you through that life.

I would also like to say to my ex-husband James that I forgive you for all the hurt and pain you caused me. I released it all and I thank you for being part of my strength today; I will continue to pray for you.

I thank my Heavenly Father for life, for the battle of my life and even more for helping me get to this side of the battlefield.

We all need to know that we have choices in our lives. You can stay in the situation that you're in or you can remove yourself from people, places and things.

It is your choice about which way your life is going to continue in this race of we call life.

I've told you my story of how I overcame the trials and tribulations of abuse, alcohol, drugs and the barriers in my past. What's your story?

If I made it, you can too! It's your life; it's your choice. The question is 'Will you make the right decision and make it to the other side of this battlefield?' I will pray that you do. Agape.

Uncle Tom:

I'm writing this letter to you knowing one day you will read my story. Not to support me, but just to see if I had the nerve or gull to write about you. You have shown me how you care for me as a person, a human being, and one of God's children. You played a big part of my childhood and on into my young adult life. Truthfully and honestly, I don't believe you knew how much, nor did you care. As you read about your character in my story, it's the truth and told first hand from best of my knowledge and experiences about the wrath of your physical, verbal and mental abuse.

My Lord looked beyond all my faults and He forgave me for all my sins and casted them in the lake called forgiveness. I've learned in this Christian realm that you must forgive your brothers and sisters in Christ.

Ephesians 4:31-32 tells us: Get rid of all bitterness, rage, anger, harsh words, and slander, as well as all types of malicious behavior. Instead, be kind to each other, tenderhearted, forgiving one another, just as God through Christ has forgiven you.

When you decided to cut all ties from me, my exact words were, as we sat in Nana's kitchen, "We all have skeletons in our closet, and I remember them all, even yours. I wonder does your wife know."

Remember that conversation, right after you told my Auntie never to call me again and to cut all ties with me? See, I wasn't afraid of *pushing* all of my skeletons out of my closet so the whole world could know what the Lord has brought me through.

For all the hearts that my story touches, it will be a reality wakeup call for most, and a blessing for others.

What some people intended as bad for me, God turned it around for the good. Isaiah 54-17 tells us that no weapon that is formed against thee shall prosper.

Still, to this day, you have hardened your heart towards me and have chosen not to allow me to see Nana, my precious grandmother—now 99 years old—even though you see and hear the joy in her voice when she speaks to me on the phone.

You need to know one thing… You didn't win! I got the VICTORY through Jesus Christ! Nana and I will always love each other until death do us part. No one, not even you, can ever take away.

I will continue to pray that despite your mean, hateful ways and your generational demonic curses and spirits that when your judgment day comes, our Lord will soften His heart and show you grace and mercy. I pray I can have a more forgiving heart towards you than what you have shown me.

I have to keep myself before the Lord, when it comes to you. I will always love you in the name of our Lord Jesus the Christ

1 John 4:20 tells us, 'If a man say, I love God, and hateth his brother, he is a liar: for he that loveth not his brother whom he hath seen, how can he love God whom he hath not seen?'

Listen, Uncle Tom, even now I reach my hand out to you. I don't know what higher supreme, as you call it, you serve, but you better believe that every knee shall bow and every tongue shall confess that Jesus Christ is our Lord and Savior.

Grace be with you, mercy, and peace, from God the Father, and from the Lord Jesus Christ, the Son of the Father, in truth and love. (11 John 1:3)

I'm still that unclaimed niece of yours, your sister's child, who the Mighty Jehovah, King of Kings saw fit to cover with His grace and mercy, in spite of all my faults and iniquities! He turned my skeletons into my TESTIMONY that it may give hope to others of what just a little faith can do. God bless you and your family.

438

Dear Mommie:

I love you more today than yesterday. I know that you loved me, and all you wanted was the best for me. I do miss you and wish that you could see that I made it out of that destructive relationship and lifestyle I was in. You would be proud of me now. I know you were a good strong and firm mother, and it will take a lot for me to fill your shoes. I'm so sorry that I was such a disappointment to you. But, I thank God that we were at peace and I had the opportunity to tell you how sorry I was, and how much I loved you, before you left this world.

Mommie, I may not have the love from your brothers and sister, but I have a wonderful, loving, caring and forgiving family that loves me and I love them even more. That curse of unforgiveness that Satan had as a stronghold on your generation has been broken in my family. We have nothing but love for one another and we don't hold on to grudges. Life is too short! Missing and loving you always, your daughter Debbie.

My Mommie

440

My Brother Chuckie

441

My children love me and I love them more!

Dear Sophia:

I've heard and experience many disturbing stories about stepchildren and stepparents who had major difficult in coming together. But, when it comes to you, my dear, it was not case with us. You are the sparkle in my eye, in all aspects. You have shown and given me nothing but the upmost respect and love that any daughter would give to their mom.

I love that fact that you call me Mom, but you introduce me as your stepmom with such a sweet, loving, caring and heartfelt tone in your voice. I feel so honored and proud to have you as my daughter, a part of my life, to share your ups and the downs with me.

My dear Sophia, know that God placed you in my life. I pray that I never let you down and I will continue to make you proud of me. Mom loves you more!

This is Sophia…

Tyra

My oldest daughter Tyra was the baby that I wanted for so many years. Tyra was an A student and had been since the fifth grade. Tyra was involved in activities, on the honor roll and even voted homecoming queen. School had become her outlet from the nightmares and seeing her mother turn into a person she didn't know any more. I'm so proud of her in all her accomplishments.

I've tried to instill in her that she has to believe in herself, set a goal and go for it. That she can be or have whatever she wants in life. I needed her to know that she was better than I was and she can make it in this world—all she had to do was work hard and give it her best.

You must have a dream to stay focus. Dreams can come true. It's all up to you and how badly you want it! The world is yours; get what you want. Put Christ first and all will be added upon to you!

DREAMS REALLY DO COME TRUE... ASK TYRA...

Ericka

My daughter Ericka was just the opposite—she gave me the flux. She was my child that I didn't know how to deal with; she reminded me so much of me, and that was not good. I didn't want to be reminded of all the rebellious ways that I had as a child. She was always running the streets looking for love, and how well did I know what that was like—looking for acceptance, yearning to be needed and loved, trying so hard to fit in with all the wrong people

Yet, she has the biggest heart out of all five of my children. She's so willing to give her last if you are in need. Now, my child is a great God-fearing woman who is faithful to her faith, which makes me so proud.

I love you so much, my dearest Ericka. You had to learn the hard way, just like your mother. I never gave up on you, your child, no matter what! You gave me a run for my money, but I never gave up! I love you more!

449

Patrice

Next in line is Patrice, the sweetest, affectionate and most loving daughter that I have. Yet, she was the quietest and sneakiest, my sweet little baby girl. She stayed under me all the time, never getting in any trouble, playing that hold card of her being the baby girl. She had me wrapped around her baby finger and she knew it. She knew how to play and manipulate me to make sure she never got caught or blamed for doing anything wrong. After all, she was the baby girl.

She learned how to play this game of life by watching her sisters. Tyra did well in school and saw the good rewards that came with it. She saw Ericka seek attention in all the wrong ways and the consequences that followed her behavior. But, most of all, she saw me in all the wrong that I did before them all. Be careful of what you say and do around your children. They may turn out just like you! Remember you reap what you sow!

Tyrone and Jerome

These are my boys, the babies of all my children. I spoiled them rotten and let them run buck wild with really no discipline at all, covering up all their wrong doing. I thought to myself 'I'm ruining their lives. Maybe I should have put them in boot camp.' They always respond when I threatened them with it, "We will get kicked out or run away!" And surely I didn't want them to run away; I saw that in my brother for so many years.

The twins turned out to be quiet, kind, nurturing, good hearted, respectful, protective and somewhat angry and rebellious. But, these are my boys, not yours. How I love them so. Now, you know if I didn't know how to respect myself in front of my daughters, what on earth was my sons seeing of their mother? What type of message did I give them? What have I done?

What type of roll model was I? What type of respect will they have for women and men when they get older? First, their father and then their mother... what a life my children have seen! I know now that the instruction book to bring up a child is God's Holy Word. It starts at home.

I plead the Blood of Jesus over my children, their children and their generations to come to break this generational curse that has been over my family! I break the strongholds and cast them back into the pit of hell from whence they come IN THE NAME OF JESUS!!!

It's too late for me to give my children that Christian foundation. The only thing that I can do now is to live right before them. Give your children that foundation—they will need it. I found out a little too late, but by the grace and mercy of God, they are covered and know Him for themselves. Remember you will reap what you sow!

Jerome

When I got word that my son was murdered, I remember sitting in the airport waiting on my husband to bring me something to drink. I was filled with so many emotions, and unbelief that one of my baby boys was gone.

I cried and said to Jerome, "My dear son, Mama doesn't know what to write in your obituary. This is going to be so hard for me to do." I heard his voice whisper in my ear... "Mama, it's okay. Get a pencil and write this down. This is what my obituary will say: This will be 'A Message from Cruze'...

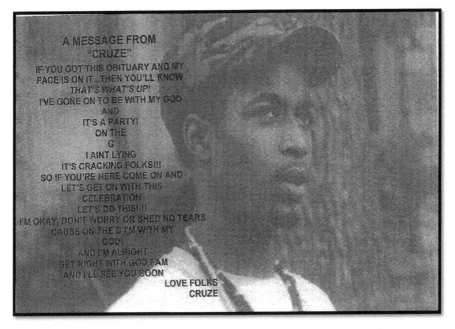

A MESSAGE FROM
"CRUZE"
IF YOU GOT THIS OBITUARY AND MY
FACE IS ON IT...THEN YOU'LL KNOW
THAT'S WHAT'S UP!
I'VE GONE ON TO BE WITH MY GOD
AND
IT'S A PARTY!
ON THE
G
I AINT LYING
IT'S CRACKING FOLKS!!!
SO IF YOU'RE HERE COME ON AND
LET'S GET ON WITH THIS
CELEBRATION
LET'S DO THIS!!!
I'M OKAY, DON'T WORRY OR SHED NO TEARS
CAUSE ON THE G I'M WITH MY
GOD!
AND I'M ALRIGHT
GET RIGHT WITH GOD FAM
AND I'LL SEE YOU SOON
LOVE FOLKS
CRUZE

In this picture, he told me that he saw angels coming down from the sky. Three years later, he was murdered.

455

R.I.P., Jerome.

You my Son will be greatly missed!! It was an Honor to be able to serve you, love and cherish one of God's True Soldiers of his Army, Knowing that you are resting in the Bossism of our Heavenly Father, gives me Peace of Mind..One day, I will be able to embrace you in my arms, and sing Hail to Our King, Oh Heavenly Father, I Thank you for your Son Lord Jesus the Christ.......Ma-Ma, miss & love you Jerome

Some of my grandchildren, less the six not pictured here.

My best friend was there for me...

In my deepest dark hour you were there for me. I will always love you, my friend. I truly miss you with all my heart. One day, when the Lord says the same...we will see each other again. R.I.P., my dear sweet friend, Edna.

To my Nana:

When I spoke with you yesterday, I can tell in your voice that you were so very tired. But, when you heard that it was me, I could tell that it brought joy to your heart and uplifted your spirit.

Well, Nana whenever I speak to you, think of you or even mention your name, love, joy, peace and happiness fill my heart and bring a smile to my face. You have always been the love rock that I had to hold on to. I want to thank you for your prayers, love, kindness, encouragement, patience and for all the times that you told me, "Everything will be alright."

I had to look back over my life to see where I came from. Now, I'm looking ahead to where I'm going and I can truly say you were right, "Everything is alright."

No matter what the circumstances, trails or tribulations that I had or will face in my life, it was and will be your voice and words that I will always hold onto.

When I was put down and my spirits were at its lowest, it was you that built me up. No matter where I was, you have always been there for me—in my heart. I knew that if I could just hear your voice, I could make it through. Hearing your voice has always been like a guardian angel whisper to me. You have always taken me—in my mind—away from the situation that I was in, and brought me peace. Afterwards, and I would tell you whatever happened and you would always laugh out and say, "Ain't that some shit, but yet everything will be alright."

When I was young child, you were the only one that sat me down and taught me the essentials things in life. You know, my personal hygiene, cooking, keeping house and washing clothes, but most of all, how to love. I remember once you told me that if you say you love someone give them your all and be true, but never let the right hand know what the left one is doing, and that is where I fell short.

"Ain't that some shit, but still everything is gonna be alright."

The bond that you and I have no one will ever know or even understand. Nana, you are ninety-nine years old now and it's hard for me to even talk with you, not by choice, but because of your son. If only he really knew how much you love me and how deep our love for one another really is! I know that he hears the joy and laughter when you talk to me, saying to himself 'that must be Debbie she's talking to.' Yet, he still hardens his heart. I'm grateful Nana, for whatever time that I can have to hear that sweet lovely voice of yours.

Even though we both know the situation we are in, we still laugh right over their heads with one another and say, "Ain't that some shit," knowing in our hearts that soon, one day

"Everything will be alright."

Nana, I love you with all my heart. There is no one living on this earth that I love more than you. You said that I was your favorite grandchild and I do know in my heart that there is no other child or grandchild that you have that will ever take my place in your heart. So, until we talk again, let's hold onto and say together as we know, "Ain't that some shit" and "Everything will be alright." I love you, Nana, and you will always be my favorite, just as I am yours.

MY NANA IS 99 YEARS OLD
AND
SHE'S TALKING TO ME.

The Start of a New Beginning

Mr. & Mrs. Oliver (Ronald) and Debra Bell-Vanzant

"Our Wedding Day"

464

"Everything will be alright!"

About the Author…

On April 4, 1958 in Chicago (IL), Debra Denise Dent was born to Charles and Marian Norman Dent. Debra came into this world as a premature two-pound, three-ounce baby girl fighting for her life. Intuitively, she was determined to survive—against all odds.

Her parents separated very early in their marriage, so Debra, her mother and younger brother lived with her maternal grandmother. Her grandmother's unconditional love has been the firm foundation that proved to be a great source of strength during Debra's troubled teen and young adult years. Despite declarations from certain family members that she would never amount to anything in life, Debra says that her life became a living example of God's favor, mercy and grace.

While working for Lens Crafter's in Milwaukee (WI) and later in Mobile (AL), Debra received six Legendary Service pins and countless of acknowledgements for her exemplary customer service. In addition, in 2007, she volunteered to be a Coordinator for the Gift of Sight and provide free vision screenings to low-income families in the local communities. Debra partnered with local churches and organizations such as, The 15th Place/Loaves and Fish , Boys and Girls Club, Salvation Army, The Penelope House, The Lion's Club, Mobile Low-Income Housing , Prichard Head Start Program, Ronald McDonald House, Catholic Social Services and senior citizens homes.

Within three years, with assistance from the doctors and staff at Lens Crafter's, she was able to help over 850 people in the Mobile and Prichard area to receive free eye exams, as well as free eyewear. Because of her passion for helping others, Debra worked with the Bay Area Food Pantry and established the Food Pantry for the needy in Mobile at two local churches in Mobile (AL).

Debra returned to school and achieved the Dean's List, along with other scholastic honors and awards, and graduated with an overall a 3.8 GPA. She earned an associate degree in Occupational Science.

Debra and husband Oliver Bell-Vanzant have ten children. However, one of her twin sons was brutally murdered in 2007. The grief of this tragic experience led to her suffering a stroke months later. Fortunately, she recovered fully. She is a grandmother of 22, all of whom are God's angels to her.

Debra hopes her first book will serve as a beacon to young women (and even young men) as they navigate against those evils that can be avoided. Having made the decision to live a different life, her life soon became worth living, especially for the service of others.

Website: https:///www.createspace.com/3886922
Email Address: bell_debra1@bellsouth.net
Phone: 877-545-9994
P.O. Box 501041
Mobile, Alabama 36605

For assistance, please use or pass on to someone who needs help…

Domestic Violence Hotline

1-800-799-SAFE

(1-800-799-7233)

Alcohol/Drug Abuse Hotline

1-800-662-HELP

(1-800-662-4357)

Homeless/Runaway National Runaway Hotline

1-800-Runaway
1-800-(786-2929)

13516512R00256

Made in the USA
Charleston, SC
15 July 2012